Beyond Walls and (

GEOGRAPHIES OF JUSTICE AND SOCIAL TRANSFORMATION

SERIES EDITORS

Deborah Cowen, University of Toronto
Nik Heynen, University of Georgia
Melissa W. Wright, Pennsylvania State University

ADVISORY BOARD

Sharad Chari, London School of Economics
Bradon Ellem, University of Sydney
Gillian Hart, University of California, Berkeley
Andrew Herod, University of Georgia
Jennifer Hyndman, York University
Larry Knopp, University of Washington, Tacoma
Heidi Nast, DePaul University
Jamie Peck, University of British Columbia
Frances Fox Piven, City University of New York
Laura Pulido, University of Southern California
Paul Routledge, University of Glasgow
Neil Smith, City University of New York
Bobby Wilson, University of Alabama

Beyond Walls and Cages

PRISONS, BORDERS, AND GLOBAL CRISIS

EDITED BY
**JENNA M. LOYD
MATT MITCHELSON
ANDREW BURRIDGE**

THE UNIVERSITY OF GEORGIA PRESS
Athens & London

© 2012 by the University of Georgia Press
Athens, Georgia 30602
www.ugapress.org
All rights reserved
Designed by Walton Harris
Set in 10 /13 Minion Pro
Printed digitally in the United States of America

Library of Congress Cataloging-in-Publication Data

Beyond walls and cages : prisons, borders, and global crisis /
edited by Jenna M. Loyd, Matt Mitchelson, and Andrew Burridge.
    p.   cm. — (Geographies of justice and social
transformation ; 14)
Includes bibliographical references and index.
ISBN 978-0-8203-4411-9 (hbk. : alk. paper) —
ISBN 0-8203-4411-7 (hbk. : alk. paper) —
ISBN 978-0-8203-4412-6 (pbk. : alk. paper) —
ISBN 0-8203-4412-5 (pbk. : alk. paper)
1. Illegal aliens. 2. Detention of persons. 3. Imprisonment.
4. Border security — Government policy. 5. Emigration and
immigration — Government policy. I. Loyd, Jenna M., 1973–
II. Mitchelson, Matt, 1978– III. Burridge, Andrew, 1981–
JV6038.B49 2012
365 — dc23   2012016864

British Library Cataloging-in-Publication Data available

For all the people who have been taking down the walls occupying our freedom dreams, past and present and tomorrow

Contents

Acknowledgments *xi*

Introduction *1*
Borders, Prisons, and Abolitionist Visions
JENNA M. LOYD, MATT MITCHELSON, and ANDREW BURRIDGE

Part I Why Now?
Prisons, Borders, and Global Crisis

Policing Mobility *19*
Maintaining Global Apartheid from South Africa to the United States
JOSEPH NEVINS

Understanding Conquest through a Border Lens *27*
A Comparative Analysis of the Mexico-U.S. and Morocco-Spain Regions
CYNTHIA BEJARANO, MARIA CRISTINA MORALES, and SAID SADDIKI

Race, Capitalist Crisis, and Abolitionist Organizing *42*
An Interview with Ruth Wilson Gilmore, February 2010
JENNA LOYD

Part II Global Crisis, National Struggles
The Work of Policing the Nation around the World

The Texas-Mexico Border Wall and Ndé Memory *57*
Confronting Genocide and State Criminality, beyond the Guise of "Impunity"
MARGO TAMEZ

Prisoners of Passage   74
Immigration Detention in Canada
HARSHA WALIA and PROMA TAGORE

Mapping Remote Detention   91
Dis/location through Isolation
ALISON MOUNTZ

Migration Policy and the Criminalization of Protest   105
OLGA AKSYUTINA

William Bratton in the Other L.A.   115
MICOL SEIGEL

Part III Poverty and Wars at Home
Finding Spaces for Refuge and Change

Building Prisons, Building Poverty   129
Prison Sitings, Dispossession, and Mass Incarceration
ANNE BONDS

Business of Detention   143
RENEE FELTZ and STOKELY BAKSH

Torn Apart   152
Struggling to Stay Together after Deportation
SETH FREED WESSLER and JULIANNE HING

Creating Spaces for Change   163
An Interview with Amy Gottlieb, November 2009
JENNA LOYD

Bajo la Misma Luna   173
(Under the Same Moon)
ELIZABETH VARGAS

Part IV Battleground Arizona
Local Crossroads, National Struggles

Policing Our Border, Policing Our Nation   *181*
An Examination of the Ideological Connections between Border Vigilantism and U.S. National Ideology
JODIE M. LAWSTON and RUBEN R. MURILLO

Resisting the Security-Industrial Complex   *190*
Operation Streamline and the Militarization of the Arizona-Mexico Borderlands
BORDERLANDS AUTONOMIST COLLECTIVE

Detention and Access to Justice   *209*
A Florence Project Case Study
CHRISTOPHER STENKEN

Community, Identity, and Political Struggle   *215*
Challenging Immigrant Prisons in Arizona
ZOE HAMMER

"Live, Love, and Work"   *228*
An Interview with Luis Fernandez, August 2010
JENNA LOYD

Part V Speaking Up! Standing Up!
Local Struggles against Walls and Cages

A Politics for Our Time?   *241*
Organizing against Jails
JOSHUA M. PRICE

"A Prison Is Not a Home"   *253*
Notes from the Campaign to End Immigrant Family Detention
BOB LIBAL, LAUREN MARTIN, and NICOLE PORTER

Fighting for the Vote   266
*The Struggle against Felon and
Immigrant Disenfranchisement*
MONICA W. VARSANYI

¡La Policía, la Migra, la Misma Porquería!   277
Popular Resistance to State Violence
MARIANA VITURRO

Part VI   Ending Border Wars
Building Abolitionist Futures

Mapping Black Bodies for Disease   287
Prisons, Migration, and the Politics of HIV/AIDS
RASHAD SHABAZZ

The War on Drugs Is a War on Relationships   301
*Crossing the Borders of Fear, Silence, and HIV
Vulnerability in the Prison-Created Diaspora*
LAURA McTIGHE

Immigrant Justice from a Trans Perspective   314
An Interview with Gael Guevara, May 2009
JENNA LOYD

Descado en Los Angeles   325
Cycles of Invisible Resistance
IRINA CONTRERAS

Winning the Fight of Our Lives   337
SUBHASH KATEEL

Contributors   347

Index   357

Acknowledgments

The community of supportive, thoughtful, gracious people that sustained the three of us during this project is vast. First, we are grateful to the book's contributors with whom we have been honored to work and from whom we have learned so much. We send tremendous thanks to friends, colleagues, and organizers who have sustained us with their smarts, leadership, generous listening, good humor, and camaraderie over the four years that this project has been in the works. We would like to thank the folks who make the Geographies of Justice and Social Transformation series at the University of Georgia Press run—especially Nik Heynen and Derek Krissoff—for believing in this unique compilation of voices. The book benefited from the thorough readings and suggestions of anonymous reviewers. Finally, thank you to *Left Turn* and *Organizing Upgrade* for giving us permission to reprint Subhash Kateel's articles, to the Southern California Library for permission to reprint Micol Seigel's article, and to Ulyamorsk University Press for permission to reprint Olga Aksyutina's chapter.

Beyond Walls and Cages

Introduction

Borders, Prisons, and Abolitionist Visions

JENNA M. LOYD, MATT MITCHELSON,
AND ANDREW BURRIDGE

> We continue to find that the prison is itself a border. This analysis has come from prisoners, who name the distinction between the "free world" and the space behind the walls of the prison. This is an important interpretation that undoes the illusions of the powerful nation-states on the one hand and the seeming disorganization and chaos of capital's travels on the other. There is a very specific political economy of the prison that brings the intersections of gender and race, colonialism and capitalism, into view.
>
> — ANGELA DAVIS and GINA DENT, "Prison as a Border"

Borders and prisons — walls and cages — are global crises. Walls and cages are fundamental to managing the wealth, social inequalities, and opposition to the harms created by capitalism and the present round of neocolonial dispossession. The work of making and remaking state institutions of citizenship, punishment, and war shapes the human condition at this moment. But what *is* this moment, and what kind of crisis is this?

Global apartheid is one part of the story. It is a condition in which the wealthiest regions of the world erect physical and bureaucratic barriers against the movement of people from poorer regions of the world. Mobility is a fact of the human condition, yet nation-state sovereignty continues to be invoked to deny this freedom and to rationalize the fatalities that these sovereign practices create.[1] *Policing and prison regimes* tell another part of the story, a condition in which the state is built and society is governed through crime legislation. The social sanction afforded to an unchallenged "rule of law" obscures the oppression that is produced through the enforcement of criminal legislation.[2]

Prison and border regimes are the culmination of many histories of struggle over colonialism, the nation-state, and what it means to be human. These histories connect 1492 — a date symbolic of Native genocide, dispossession, and slavery in Africa and the Americas — to 1992, a time when history was said to have stopped because capitalism had won. Yet there is another aspect of this time to be remembered in the Rodney King (1992) and Zapatista (1994) uprisings, which mark a rejection of the celebratory terms of postracial and postcolonial progress. These informed international countercurrents of steady, worldwide opposition to violent occupations, free trade, privatization, and deregulation imposed from above.

Today, people continue to make connections among these struggles across vast distances. In 2009 they were apparent in challenges against military and police violence in Gaza, in Greece, and in Oakland. By 2011 they had accumulated to produce the Arab Spring and the American Fall of occupy/decolonize movements sweeping across cities in the United States and around the world. These are not the only places or times that matter, but connecting the dots between 1492, 1992, and the present draws the boundaries of freedom and humanity that historically have been imposed, inherited, and challenged in world-shattering ways.

This book starts at the prisons, border walls, and detention facilities where brave people are challenging forcible confinement and exclusion in many ways, such as hunger strikes, writing, and building organizations and communication networks to undo the confines of prison walls. This book also starts in the streets, in meeting halls, at kitchen tables, in long-distance phone calls, and in letters exchanged. Were it not for the efforts of loved ones and friends, prisons and detention facilities could become a void where people are forgotten and where collective denial masks the bodily and social harms of systemic dehumanization. And so this book starts in the places where people keep each other together across distances that all too often are widened by economic dislocation and fortified by national boundaries and prison cells. This book was inspired by a lot of hard work to prevent voids in memory and political accountability. It was driven by desires for freedom.

BORDERS, CAGES, AND ABOLITION

Dylan Rodríguez argues that the primary task for liberatory movements today is developing analytical and conceptual tools that work "*against* the assumptive necessity, integrity, and taken-for-grantedness of prisons, policing, and the normalized state violence they reproduce."[3] Because prisons are so thoroughly tied to the nation-state and other institutions of state violence, abolition is a necessarily expansive project that articulates with the "holistic anti-violence agendas" advanced most centrally by women of color.[4] This book helps to develop a key abolitionist tool: the analytic ability to understand how seemingly disconnected institutions of state violence are interconnected and how they produce and police social difference. This capacity is important for practically bridging between social movements that are organizing for a world free of racial, sexual, and gender violence. It also is a tool for developing organizing strategies that don't rely on winning one set of (apparent) privileges through reinforcing someone else's oppression.

Beyond Walls and Cages focuses on the interconnections between contemporary migration and penal policies and illustrates how these are both tied up with war-making. Its goals are twofold. First, the book documents contemporary experiences of and thinking about the pervasive role of state violence in daily life. It seeks to illuminate the concrete and the ideological connections among prisons, migration policing, border fortification, and militarization. In the struggle over war and punishment, specific ideologies of race and security are produced and mobilized to justify the coercive and violent treatment of entire groups of people. The essays collected here challenge existing legitimations of state violence that often rely on the ideology and geographic imagination of foreign wars to protect the domestic peace. They shift the analysis from border and prison regimes' roles *in* war-making to one in which prisons and border fortifications *are* war-making.[5]

Second, we hope this book can be used to help build sturdier bridges between the anti-prison and immigrant justice movements, and we hope it will contribute to the power of these movements to prevent and end state violence. We focus on the intersection between migration and crime policy in order to challenge the idea that borders and prisons create safety, security, and order. Instead, they are being used to naturalize the abandonment of increasing numbers of people who have been placed into categories of "illegal" and "criminal." Focusing on this nexus between the legal production of "alien" and "criminal" humans is politically imperative because it enables us to see the limits of inclusion or representation in an otherwise unchanged legal or political system. It also helps us understand how exclusionary organizing strategies help the state and capital divide us and exploit our vulnerabilities.

Much of this book focuses on the life-and-death effects of U.S. crime, border, and migration policies, and on how people are fighting back. While the United States is not alone in its reliance on prisons and border walls, it continues to be the world's largest purveyor of state violence, both militarily and in the scale of its prison system. The United States is thus an important place of struggle for being able to challenge militarization and oppressive state institutions everywhere.

While migration is often understood as an international issue (concerning who gets to come into a country), and prisons are often thought of as domestic issues (concerning people charged with crimes who are within the boundaries of a country), this powerful ideological distinction hides a shared process of criminalization. The process of outlawing previously legal activities is backed by the militarization of national boundaries and policing practices. This nationalist frame prevents us from seeing the ways in which citizenship, incapacitation, and punishment work together, within and across national boundaries, to legally consign entire groups of people to precarious futures and premature deaths.

STRUCTURE OF THE BOOK

Beyond Walls and Cages is organized into six parts, beginning with worldwide historical and contemporary dynamics and then focusing in on national, state, and local scales of activity and analysis. Part I frames the human crisis of imprisonment, border fortification, and migration restriction on the global scale and within histories of colonialism, imperialism, slavery, and capitalism. This work is continued by the contributors in part II, who focus on the global crisis of the nation-state and on the transnational continuities of nationalism and policing around the world. Together, these parts document the long, troubled history of how walls and cages have been used to create different kinds of nations and states in the past and present.

The remainder of the book traces how these global struggles play out in particular places. Part III focuses on the violent effects of U.S. nation-building and war-making *within* U.S. territory. These invisible domestic wars entrench poverty and divide families and communities. Part IV focuses on the geopolitics of Arizona, a state often singled out for the extremity of its anti-immigrant legislation and border fortification. But copycat legislation enacted in Georgia and Alabama speaks to the danger of the idea that Arizona is unique. Contributors to this part situate twenty-first-century struggles over migration, violence, and race within longer histories of border violence and in relation to the federal policies and practices Arizona shares with the rest of the country.

Part V details the importance of local campaigns in the fight against criminalization and structural violence across the United States. It provides concrete examples of how local struggles over jails, policing, and detention are important to building local political power across social divides. Part VI analyzes the ways in which prison and border regimes perpetuate gender, sexual, and racial violence. It grounds intersectional queer, antiracist, and feminist analyses in abolitionist visions for creating freedom and justice.

Together, parts V and VI carry the analyses of the preceding parts to their logical conclusion. If walls and cages buttress one another, and stem from common capitalist, colonialist, and imperialist projects, then they also require shared solutions. Connecting the dots between these different systems will help in finding collective ways of ending their interlocking harms. Abolitionist principles are explored here, and in the whole book, in practical terms. The contributors offer a set of concrete strategies for change, including organizing around the conditions of a local jail, preventing prison construction, closing detention facilities, and ending mass imprisonment to help prevent the spread of HIV.

This book's unique gathering of contributors includes people who are directly affected by these systems, political organizers, journalists, researchers, teachers, and theorists. These categories are not mutually exclusive; organizers and people who are directly affected are also theorists and researchers documenting their personal and collective histories. The authors convey their narratives, analyses, and desires for social change through poetry, testimonials, research and journalistic essays, and interviews that document the past, present, and future of freedom's movement. This mix of written forms and contributors is important for expressing the power of remembering and sharing our lives and visions for the future.

WHY NOW?: WALLS AND CAGES, CITIZENSHIP AND WAR

Walls and cages share common economic and political histories at the global scale. Liberation movements in colonized places and in imperial centers of the United States and Europe culminated in 1968 in what George Katsiaficas calls a world historical moment.[6] Between the end of World War II and the 1970s, existing relations of racial, gender, and sexual oppression were fundamentally challenged. Demands for better living and working conditions and for self-determination contributed to a global capitalist crisis of profitability and of governance. The subsequent imposition of structural adjustment, "neoliberal" policies, and intensified war-making has aimed to resolve this crisis of profitability in favor of capital and wealth holders.[7]

Without rehearsing the related histories that the contributors to this book trace, what happened next, and what people across the world are contending with now, is how "policing the crisis" became a key way in which relations of domination have been restructured.[8] Stuart Hall and his colleagues examined the increased reliance on law-and-order policing in England in the 1970s, and their analysis remains relevant for the United States and elsewhere today. In England, law-and-order policing was fueled by white nationalism in the form of anti-immigrant racism directed at residents from the UK's former colonies in South Asia and the Caribbean. Restrictionist legislation, such as the 1971 Immigration Act, was an important part of the expanded reliance on state force for governing because it narrowed the legal avenues for "immigrant" people to live and work, and then policed legal statuses that had been newly criminalized.[9] Racialized criminalization and the terror of raids, deportation, and mass expulsion became part of the global condition of what poet Shailja Patel calls "migritude."[10]

BORDER WALLS AND PRISONS SHORE UP CITIZENSHIP

The political point to be drawn from this 1970s story is that criminalization is a tool in a class and racial struggle over the economy and social organization of a particular place. In the contemporary organization of nation-states, much of this has played out in terms of citizenship, or who constitutes "the public" and is rightfully entitled to make political decisions about the current and future organization of social wealth. While the utopian premise of citizenship is universal inclusion and shared decision making, citizenship is always differentiated. It is a state institution and a set of practices that produce and mediate social difference on the basis of race, wealth, gender, and sexuality, among other categories.

Citizenship has not always been attached so firmly to nation-states as it is today, but national citizenship and the nation-state historically were founded through colonization and through creating categories of exclusion. As Ruth Wilson Gilmore and Craig Gilmore write, the prison has been central to nation-state citizenship:

> The connection between the rise of the nation-state and the rise of the prison is located in the contradiction between mobility and immobility: when the conditions attending on a global system that requires constant motion (e.g., capitalism) clash with challenges to maintain order, spatial fixes such as racialization and criminalization temporarily settle things through complicating insider-outsider distinctions with additional, rights-differentiated hierarchical schemes.[11]

Thus, while much of the focus of contemporary struggles over citizenship in the United States and around the world is over the line between citizen and noncitizen, the domestic-foreign divide is not the only (or principal) line of division. Rather, the laws that legitimate the forcible confinement and isolation of some groups of people also draw lines of power between groups of people who will be (or expect to be) entitled to be part of the public, share in the social wealth, and contribute to shaping the common good for present and future generations. These political struggles have been obscured through the apparently apolitical legal categories of the "criminal" and "foreigner."

The process of outlawing previously legal activities is backed by the militarization of national boundaries and policing practices. As contributors to this volume make clear, border militarization projects and prisons go hand in hand as the means of establishing and entrenching colonial dispossession and rule. The steady push toward greater border fortification and policing, particularly since the 1990s, has resulted in a rapid rise in the deaths of migrants attempting to cross spaces such as the deserts of the Mexico-U.S. borderlands and the seas of the Mediterranean between Africa and Europe. For people who are fleeing from varying forms of conflict and oppression, border fortification and the paper walls of restrictive migration and asylum policies add additional layers of violence along their paths to safety.

Mass incarceration, or *mass imprisonment,* refers to the unprecedented growth of the U.S. prison population, the concentrated social and economic effects that it has, and the political economy driving the dramatic emergence of these conditions since the 1970s.[12] The *prison-industrial complex,* or PIC, is the set of institutions, practices, and ideologies responsible for creating and maintaining a condition of mass incarceration. Long-time abolitionist Angela Y. Davis defines the PIC as "an array of relationships linking corporations, government, correctional communities, and media."[13] This array of state and corporate relationships and institutions leads us beyond profit, narrowly conceived, to focus on the public and private project of industrial fear, punishment, and control.

Across the United States in 2009, nearly 2.3 million people were in jails and prisons, and more than twice as many people were under direct state supervision through the parole and probation systems.[14] People of color comprise two-thirds of the people who are imprisoned.[15] As part of this staggering expansion of imprisonment since the early 1980s, the number of women being caged has also jumped, and the majority were unemployed before being imprisoned. Trans and gender-nonconforming people are routinely subjected to police and jail violence. Understanding these trends together illuminates how prisons entrench lines of class, racial, gender, and sexual oppression.[16]

Immigrant detention and deportation stretch the harmful effects of imprisonment and family separation across national borders. At the time of this writing, Immigration and Customs Enforcement is the largest investigative agency of the Department of Homeland Security (DHS) and employs over twenty thousand people.[17] Customs and Border Protection, a separate DHS department, employs nearly twenty-one thousand officers.[18] The federal government relies on a network of some 350 detention facilities and county jails across the country to achieve historic levels of deportation.[19] Nearly four hundred thousand people were deported from October 2010 to September 2011 alone.[20] Nearly one-quarter of the people deported from the United States in the first half of fiscal year 2011 are parents of children who are U.S. citizens.[21]

The U.S. case allows us to trace the ways that crime and migration policies are connected, and how legally expanding and policing the categories of "criminal" and "illegal" are *both* exercises in creating differentiated (second-class) citizenship in a particular nation-state. The struggle over the United States as a nation is a struggle over drawing the lines separating the "good citizens," who have the formal capacity for democratic involvement, family and community responsibilities, and livelihoods, from those who should be ruled. "Being constructed as illegal (and therefore as available for exploitation, abuse, death) entails thoroughgoing containment and incapacitation."[22] Being constructed as criminal does much the same thing, yet the ways in which criminalization and illegalization create shared conditions of "civil death," or exclusion from the social, public, and political spheres, are not always recognized because the exclusion of "criminals" and "foreigners" has been shored up so incessantly for so long.

These conditions clearly are not limited to the United States. Our ambition in this book is thus global in scope: to develop an abolitionist analytic and practice which can connect movements against state violence, and to see the challenging of prisons and border walls as a central dimension in struggles against colonialism, capitalism, white supremacy, and heteropatriarchy within and beyond the United States.

WHAT WOULD IT MEAN TO BE FREE?:
ABOLITIONIST PERSPECTIVES ON ENDING STATE VIOLENCE

People around the world have inherited a crisis of national sovereignty and nation-state citizenship that is evident in states' reliance on forcible confinement, militarized policing, and border fortification. This crisis is the culmination of many challenges to slavery, colonialism, and imperialism, which have rejected elitist understandings of humanity, citizenship, and sovereignty. This history is an accumulation of struggles to define freedom and those who may be free. As part of the historic lineage for this current moment, an abolitionist effort connects the issues of border militarization, mass imprisonment, and immigrant detention and their countervailing forces in order to situate holistic organizing against state violence at the center of struggles for freedom, justice, and a sound ecological future.[23]

This volume develops a key abolitionist tool: the analytic ability to understand how seemingly disconnected institutions of state violence — walls and cages — are interconnected, and how they produce and police social difference. It also provides a tool for developing organizing strategies that don't rely on winning one set of (apparent) privileges through reinforcing someone else's oppression. The contributors make clear the necessity of feminist, queer, and antiracist analyses and strategies in order to challenge multiple relations of oppression simultaneously.[24]

This book advances the imperative of linking abolitionist, no-borders, and anticolonialist perspectives on addressing these crises. We are grateful for a number of important texts that speak to the need for abolition, no-borders, and anticolonial organizing strategies centered around the people who are most vulnerable to interlocking forms of state and social violence.[25] The imperative of freedom now necessarily means finding a way out of the dead end of organizing around exclusions, such as those captured vividly in the common statements "We're not criminals" and "We're innocent; those are the real criminals." Claiming innocence ignores the powerful fact of criminalization as a process of turning people into criminals, and suggests that another set of people are the *real* criminals and thus deserve to be caged. Organizing around innocence does not successfully confront the process of criminalization; it naturalizes it. Failing to recognize criminalization as a political tool naturalizes definitions of violence that underwrite the status quo, and effectively shores up the prison regime.

In the United States, failing to confront criminalization as a political process is particularly dangerous because all too often new immigrant groups' claims to citizenship have been made in opposition to Black citizens, which effectively erases the history and legacy of slavery. Claims of virtuous innocence versus undeserving criminality are doubly pernicious considering the central role that anti-Black conceptions of Black people's inherent violence and criminality have had in restricting Black people's freedom, justifying police violence against them, and fueling mass imprisonment as a generalized institution of surveillance, capture, and discipline.[26]

Happily, there are countercurrents and significant shifts away from this organizing frame. The slogan "No One Is Illegal," inherited from the 1980s and

1990s transnational Sanctuary movement, which worked in solidarity with people seeking refuge from U.S.-funded dirty wars in Central America, challenges the categorical flattening of humanity that the law attempts to accomplish.[27] Likewise, in present-day Arizona, the growing recognition of criminalization as the problem is significant. This is an important departure from the organizing frame of "We're hard workers, not criminals," which seeks inclusion within an unchanged system. Challenging the criminalization of survival, migration, and inhabitance, by contrast, opens up cross-national, inter-ethnic, and interracial avenues to fight against powerful legal tools that dispossess people of their capacities to work, to move freely, and to establish futures for themselves, their families, and their communities.

As migration restrictions grow and punishment expands into our communities and schools, our survival and attempts to build caring, creative, free futures are themselves being criminalized. We hope that walls and cages can be navigated, climbed, and eventually toppled, as more of us do some of the bridging work that this book's questions inspire. In this way, we hope that *Beyond Walls and Cages* contributes to a key abolitionist imperative and practice, a method of analyzing the difference between "reformist reforms," which strengthen the system and its logic of punishment and dispossession, and "nonreformist reforms," or "abolitionist reforms," which shrink the systems of walls and cages so that dreams of freedom can be realized.[28]

A shared abolitionist and no-borders agenda fosters the understanding that freedom of movement and freedom to inhabit are necessarily connected.[29] For Rose Braz, a California-based, anti-prison organizer, "abolition means a world where we do not use prisons, policing, and the larger system of the prison-industrial complex as an 'answer' to what are social, political, and economic problems."[30] While contemporary prison abolition is explicitly rooted in continuing the work of ending slavery in all its forms, this radical vision of freedom also recognizes the non-freedom of forced and restricted mobility. Paul Robeson, the great artist and Black political leader, made this clear: "From the days of chattel slavery until today, the concept of *travel* has been inseparably linked in the minds of our people with the concept of *freedom*."[31] Further, abolition's clear challenge to legalized means of subjection enables a questioning of the use of national citizenship (or other arbitrary exclusionary boundaries) to categorically frame power relations.

There are many stripes of no-borders politics — libertarian, capitalist, liberal, anticolonialist, anarchist.[32] In this book, a no-borders politics opposes and seeks to dismantle the complex array of public and private companies, organizations, and agencies involved in controlling the mobility of people between and within nation-states. No-borders politics is committed to creating places where people can reside without displacement and to being able to move freely. Because mass incarceration is a form of "coercive mobility," prison abolition is a clear extension of radical commitments to the freedom of movement.[33] "Decolonizing" no-borders and abolitionist politics would mean remembering the centrality of imprisonment to colonial rule and broadly developing the theoretical and organizational tools necessary to challenge the colonial and neocolonial relations that drive dispossession and deny self-determination.[34]

As the classic 1970s abolitionist organizing text *Instead of Prisons* and the more recent reader *Abolition Now!* elaborate, building economies and community institutions that foster creativity, care, self-determination, and mutual responsibility are among the abolitionist strategies for building a free, just world.[35] Holistic antiviolence perspectives foster concrete efforts to create accountable, holistic, and just strategies for safety and community well-being.[36] In short, abolition and no-borders frameworks provide visions of the future that can guide current action for making communities that support bodily freedom and fulfilling livelihoods.

The capacity of people's movements to challenge the institutions of state violence and the apparently neutral ideologies of illegal immigration and criminality is one measure of collective dreams of freedom. Fighting against criminalization—understanding the politics of lawmaking and the institutions of enforcement, including the police and the media—is a fundamental part of antiracist, anticapitalist, feminist, and queer struggles. It is the fight for our time and for a freer future. The diverse contributions to this book remind us of some of this history, record some of our present, and offer analyses and ideas for building a different future. How we refuse to comply with unjust laws and organize to fight back, and the "we" these efforts build, are up to us.

Note on Racial/Ethnic Designations: Some of the contributors to this book choose to capitalize "Black" and "Brown" to highlight the political construction of these racial/ethnic terms. Other contributors write the terms "black" and "brown" in lower case. As editors, we have left this decision to the discretion of the authors.

NOTES

1. Sharma, "Global Apartheid and Nation-Statehood"; Nevins, "Thinking Out of Bounds."
2. Rodríguez, "I Would Wish Death on You . . ."
3. Rodríguez, "The Disorientation of the Teaching Act," 9.
4. Sudbury, "Toward a Holistic Anti-Violence Agenda"; Incite!, *Color of Violence*.
5. Davis, *Abolition Democracy*; Gilmore, "Terror Austerity Race Gender Excess Theater"; Gilmore, "Globalisation and U.S. Prison Growth"; Rodríguez, " Terms of Engagement"; James, *Warfare in the American Homeland*.
6. Katsiaficas, *The Imagination of the New Left*.
7. Harvey, *The New Imperialism*.
8. Hall et al., *Policing the Crisis*; Gilmore, "Globalisation and U.S. Prison Growth."
9. Hall et al., *Policing the Crisis*, 289.
10. As the anti-immigrant forces in England were gaining force, the former English colony of Uganda expelled all of its residents of South Asian descent. See Patel, *Migritude*.
11. Gilmore and Gilmore, "Restating the Obvious," 144.
12. Garland, *Mass Imprisonment*; Gilmore, *Golden Gulag*.
13. Davis, *Are Prisons Obsolete?*, 84.
14. Glaze, "Correctional Populations in the United States, 2009."
15. West, "Prison Inmates at Midyear 2009."
16. Ahrens, *The Real Cost of Prisons Comix*; Fosado, "Introduction."
17. U.S. Immigration and Customs Enforcement, "ICE Overview."
18. U.S. Customs and Border Protection, "Securing America's Borders."
19. Detention Watch Network, "About the U.S. Detention and Deportation System."
20. Bennett, "Obama Administration Reports Record Number of Deportations."
21. Applied Research Center, *Shattered Families*.
22. Luibhéid, "Sexuality, Migration, and the Shifting Line," 300.
23. Davis, *Are Prisons Obsolete?*
24. Law, *Resistance behind Bars*; Mogul, Ritchie, and Whitlock, *Queer (In)Justice*; Stanley and Smith, *Captive Genders*.
25. See the references at the end of this and other chapters in this volume.
26. Garland, *Mass Imprisonment*; Chesney-Lind and Mauer, *Invisible Punishment*.
27. Cunningham, *God and Caesar at the Rio Grande*.
28. Gilmore and Gilmore, "Restating the Obvious"; Gordon, *Keeping Good Time*; Kelley, *Freedom Dreams*; Prison Research Education Action Project, *Instead of Prisons*.
29. Bacon, "The Right to Stay Home"; Global Exchange, *The Right to Stay Home*.
30. CR10 Publications Collective, *Abolition Now!*
31. Robeson, *Here I Stand*, 67.
32. Carens, "Aliens and Citizens"; Hayter, "Open Borders"; Wright, "Challenging States of Illegality."
33. Clear et al., "Coercive Mobility and Crime."
34. Lawrence and Dua, "Decolonizing Antiracism"; Sharma and Wright,

"Decolonizing Resistance." See also the *Refuge* special issue "No Borders as Practical Politics," vol. 26, no. 2 (2009).

35. Prison Research Education Action Project, *Instead of Prisons*; CR10 Publications Collective, *Abolition Now!*

36. Sudbury, "Toward a Holistic Anti-Violence Agenda"; Sudbury, *Global Lockdown*; Incite!, *Color of Violence*; Smith, *Conquest*; Smith, "Beyond Restorative Justice."

BIBLIOGRAPHY

Ahrens, Lois, ed. *The Real Cost of Prisons Comix*. Oakland, Calif.: PM Press, 2008.

Applied Research Center. *Shattered Families: The Perilous Intersection of Immigration Enforcement and the Child Welfare System*. Oakland, Calif.: Applied Research Center, 2011. http://arc.org/shatteredfamilies.

Bacon, David. "The Right to Stay Home." *Truthout*, January 11, 2009.

Bennett, Brian. "Obama Administration Reports Record Number of Deportations." *Los Angeles Times*, October 11, 2011. http://articles.latimes.com/2011/oct/18/news/la-pn-deportation-ice-20111018.

Bhattacharjee, Anannya, and Jael Silliman, eds. *Policing the National Body: Race, Gender and Criminalization in the United States*. Boston: South End, 2002.

Bosniak, Linda. "Citizenship Denationalized." *Indiana Journal of Global Legal Studies* 7, no. 2 (2000): 447–509.

Carens, Joseph H. "Aliens and Citizens: The Case for Open Borders." *Review of Politics* 49, no. 2 (1987): 251–73.

Chesney-Lind, Meda, and Marc Mauer, eds. *Invisible Punishment: The Collateral Consequences of Mass Imprisonment*. New York: New Press, 2003.

Clear, Todd R., Dina R. Rose, Elin Waring, and Kristen Scully. "Coercive Mobility and Crime: A Preliminary Examination of Concentrated Incarceration and Social Disorganization." *Justice Quarterly* 20, no. 1 (2003): 33–64.

CR10 Publications Collective, ed. *Abolition Now!: Ten Years of Strategy and Struggle against the Prison Industrial Complex*. Oakland, Calif.: AK Press, 2008.

Cunningham, Hilary. *God and Caesar at the Rio Grande: Sanctuary and the Politics of Religion*. Minneapolis: University of Minnesota Press, 1995.

Davis, Angela Y. *Abolition Democracy: Beyond Empire, Prisons, and Torture*. New York: Seven Stories, 2005.

———. *Are Prisons Obsolete?* New York: Seven Stories, 2003.

———. *Women, Race & Class*. New York: Random House, 1981.

Davis, Angela, and Gina Dent. "Prison as a Border: A Conversation on Gender, Globalization, and Punishment." *Signs* 26, no. 4 (2001): 1235–41.

Detention Watch Network. "About the U.S. Detention and Deportation System." http://www.detentionwatchnetwork.org/aboutdetention.

Fosado, Gisela. "Introduction." *S&F Online* [special issue "Women, Prisons and Change"] 5, no. 3 (2007). http://barnard.edu/sfonline/prison/intro_01.htm.

Garland, David W., ed. *Mass Imprisonment: Social Causes and Consequences*. London: Sage, 2001.
Gilmore, Ruth Wilson. "Globalisation and U.S. Prison Growth: From Military Keynesianism to Post-Keynesian Militarism." *Race & Class* 40, nos. 2–3 (1998): 171–88.
———. *Golden Gulag: Prisons, Surplus, Crisis and Opposition in Globalizing California*. Berkeley: University of California Press, 2007.
———. "Terror Austerity Race Gender Excess Theater." In *Reading Rodney King: Reading Urban Uprising*, edited by Robert Gooding-Williams, 23–37. New York: Routledge, 1993.
Gilmore, Ruth Wilson, and Craig Gilmore. "Restating the Obvious." In *Indefensible Space: The Architecture of the National Insecurity State*, edited by Michael Sorkin, 141–62. New York: Routledge, 2008.
Glaze, Lauren. "Correctional Populations in the United States, 2009." Bureau of Justice Statistics, 2009. http://bjs.ojp.usdoj.gov/index.cfm?ty=pbdetail&iid=2316.
Global Exchange. *The Right to Stay Home: Alternatives to Mass Displacement and Forced Migration in North America*. San Francisco: Global Exchange, 2008.
Gordon, Avery F. *Keeping Good Time: Reflections on Knowledge, Power, and People*. Boulder, Colo.: Paradigm, 2004.
Hall, Stuart, Chas Critcher, Tony Jefferson, John Clarke, and John Roberts. *Policing the Crisis: Mugging, the State, and Law and Order*. New York: Holmes & Meier, 1978.
Harvey, David. *The New Imperialism*. Oxford: Oxford University Press, 2003.
Hayter, Teresa. "Open Borders: The Case against Immigration Controls." *Capital & Class* 75 (2001): 149–56.
Incite! Women of Color Against Violence, ed. *Color of Violence: The Incite! Anthology*. Cambridge, Mass.: South End, 2006.
James, Joy. *Warfare in the American Homeland: Policing and Prison in a Penal Democracy*. Durham, N.C.: Duke University Press, 2007.
Katsiaficas, George. *The Imagination of the New Left: A Global Analysis of 1968*. Boston: South End, 1987.
Kelley, Robin D. G. *Freedom Dreams: The Black Radical Imagination*. Boston: Beacon, 2002.
Law, Victoria. *Resistance behind Bars: The Struggles of Incarcerated Women*. Oakland, Calif.: PM Press, 2009.
Lawrence, Bonita, and Enakshi Dua. "Decolonizing Antiracism." *Social Justice* 32, no. 4 (2005): 120–43.
Luibhéid, Eithne. "Sexuality, Migration, and the Shifting Line between Legal and Illegal Status." *GLQ: A Journal of Lesbian and Gay Studies* 14, nos. 2–3 (2008): 289–315.
Mogul, Joey L., Andrea J. Ritchie, and Kay Whitlock. *Queer (In)Justice: The Criminalization of LGBT People in the United States*. Boston: Beacon, 2011.

Nevins, Joseph. "Thinking Out of Bounds: A Critical Analysis of Academic and Human Rights Writings on Migrant Deaths in the U.S.-Mexico Border Region." *Migraciones Internacionales* 2 (2003): 171–90.

Patel, Shailja. *Migritude*. New York: Kaya, 2010.

Prison Research Education Action Project. *Instead of Prisons*. 1976. Reprint, Oakland, Calif.: Critical Resistance, 2006.

Robeson Paul. *Here I Stand*. 1958. Reprint, Boston: Beacon, 1988.

Rodríguez, Dylan. "The Disorientation of the Teaching Act: Abolition as Pedagogical Position." *Radical Teacher* 88 (2010): 7–19.

———. "'I Would Wish Death on You . . .': Race, Gender, and Immigration in the Globality of the U.S. Prison Regime." *S&F Online* 6, no. 3 (Summer 2008). http://barnard.edu/sfonline/immigration/print_drodriguez.htm.

———. "The Terms of Engagement: Warfare, White Locality, and Abolition." *Critical Sociology* 36, no. 1 (2009): 151–73.

Sentencing Project. "Racial Disparity." [n.d.]. http://www.sentencingproject.org/template/page.cfm?id=122.

Sharma, Nandita. "Global Apartheid and Nation-Statehood: Instituting Border Regimes." In *Nationalism and Global Solidarities: Alternative Projects to Neoliberal Globalisation*, edited by J. Goodman and P. James, 71–90. London: Routledge, 2007.

Sharma, Nandita, and Cynthia Wright. "Decolonizing Resistance: Challenging Colonial States." *Social Justice* 35, no. 3 (2008–9): 120–38.

Smith, Andrea. "Beyond Restorative Justice: Radical Organizing against Violence." In *Restorative Justice and Violence against Women*, edited by James Ptacek, 255–78. Oxford: Oxford University Press, 2010.

———. *Conquest: Sexual Violence and American Indian Genocide*. Cambridge, Mass.: South End, 2005.

Stanley, Eric A., and Nat Smith, eds. *Captive Genders: Trans Embodiment and the Prison Industrial Complex*. Oakland, Calif.: AK Press, 2011.

Sudbury, Julia, ed. *Global Lockdown: Race, Gender, and the Prison-Industrial Complex*. New York: Routledge, 2005.

———. "Toward a Holistic Anti-Violence Agenda: Women of Color as Radical Bridge-Builders." *Social Justice* 30, no. 3 (2003): 134–40.

U.S. Customs and Border Protection, "Securing America's Borders: CBP Fiscal Year 2010 in Review Fact Sheet." http://www.cbp.gov/xp/cgov/newsroom/fact_sheets/cbp_overview/fy2010_factsheet.xml.

U.S. Immigration and Customs Enforcement. "ICE Overview." http://www.ice.gov/about/overview.

West, Heather C. "Prison Inmates at Midyear 2009: Statistical Tables." Bureau of Justice Statistics, 2010. http://bjs.ojp.usdoj.gov/index.cfm?ty=pbdetail&iid=2200.

Wright, Cynthia. "Challenging States of Illegality: From 'Managed Migration' to a Politics of No Borders." *Labour/Le Travail* 62 (2008): 185–98.

Part I

Why Now?

Prisons, Borders, and Global Crisis

The first part of this book analyzes the growth of prisons and migration controls within a context of global crisis. The structural logics of prisons, borders, and capital accumulation have much in common even in seemingly distinct, distant places. The contributors to this part illustrate their theoretical and empirical analyses in a specific geographic context (or contexts). Yet the policing of mobility and the neocolonial project of conquest — in the name of, over, and through nation-states' borders — are visible around the world. Rather than a meta-narration, the contributions to this part can be read as a series of complementary analyses, which resonate across scales from the global to the corporeal.

In the first two chapters that follow, the authors illustrate the global dimension of migration-related violence. We are reminded that an individual's access to resources, political power, and mobility is shaped in large part by the uneven development and division of national territories. Apartheid is neither solely a matter of South African politics, nor has it ended — at least in terms of life and death around the world. The next chapter emphasizes that migrants' material crossing points make manifest political-economic structures, class and gender inequities, agency and resistance. The authors use the concept of border sexual conquest to address the production of vulnerability, manageability, and marginalization for particular people and places in the Mexico-U.S. and Morocco-Spain border regions and beyond.

The concluding chapter of this part continues the analyses of the two preceding chapters and also signals the contributions of authors elsewhere in the book. Through this interview, we are reminded that capital's complicity in the prison-industrial complex is not reducible to prison privatization, and there is a wide range of political-economic motives for the expansion of imprisonment. This analysis of criminalization reminds us that questions of "who crossed the line?" are often far less important than questions of "who drew the line?" — and who has the power to move and reshape the lines in question. The abolitionist analytic pushes for a political praxis that is not premised on — and can move beyond — distinctions and categorizations that yield harm.

Policing Mobility
*Maintaining Global Apartheid from
South Africa to the United States*

JOSEPH NEVINS

In May 2008 anti-immigrant pogroms took place in many of South Africa's main cities. The violence left sixty-two dead — some of them burned alive by mobs — including twenty-one South Africans. Dozens of women were raped, at least a hundred thousand people were displaced, and property worth millions of South African rand was destroyed, looted, or stolen. Coming fourteen years after Nelson Mandela assumed the presidency of the country, which marked the official end of the transition from a national system of formal racial segregation, the violence exposed the enduring nature of apartheid beyond what is normally associated with South Africa. The apartheid that horrifically revealed itself in May 2008 is a global one, embedded in the very fabric of a world order predicated on nation-states.

While the factors that led to the xenophobic terror in South Africa are complex, they are in significant part the result of practices of the South African state, including its creation of a deserving "us" and a threatening, foreign "them."[1] Through its boundary fences and border patrols, its arrests and deportations of unauthorized migrants, and its justifying rhetoric, South African officialdom helped to create the very "problem" that the violent mobs sought to eliminate. As Paul Verryn, a Methodist bishop based in Johannesburg who is critical of South Africa's leadership for not being more welcoming of migrants, asserted at the time of the pogroms, "The locals believe they are doing what the government is doing anyway, getting rid of the 'illegals.'"[2]

South Africa is hardly alone in fomenting cruelty toward migrants. Indeed, it does what all other nation-states do: privilege their nationals over noncitizens and, in doing so, elevate rights granted by states to select individuals over universal human rights. In a context of deep inequality between countries, national territorial divides have profound implications: which side of a boundary one is born on significantly determines the resources to which one has access, the amount of political power on the international stage one has, where one can go and under what conditions, and thus how one lives and dies. Thus, there is an inherent double standard—significant rights for some, fewer for others—a disparity that comes about by accident of birth.

While this privileging manifests in different ways, it draws upon various forms of violence to maintain its underlying inequalities, both within nation-states and between them. Just as in South Africa of old, where the state dictated where the majority of its inhabitants (black South Africans) could live and work, the contemporary regulation of international mobility and residence is inextricably tied to these inequalities. As such they draw upon and reproduce systematic violence and dehumanization.

Across the world, relatively rich and stable nation-states—whose advantages are largely born of imperialism and its associated forms of accumulation and dispossession—are increasingly erecting walls and fences along their perimeters and increasing their boundary and migrant policing units. In doing so, they are growing the number of people they detain for violating laws related to unauthorized entry, residence, and work.

In Malaysia, for example, the government since 2005 has employed a strike force—one that grew out of a civilian militia group that had been created in the 1960s to fight against alleged communists—to hunt down unauthorized migrants. (Most of the migrants come from Indonesia, with many others coming from Bangladesh, Burma/Myanmar, India, Nepal, and Vietnam.) The group's leaders carry arms, and its deputized members have the right to enter homes or search people on the street without a warrant. Called Rela, the force has nearly half a million volunteer members, more than the total number in the country's military and police forces. Their unauthorized migrant arrestees face up to five years in prison and a whipping of up to six strokes. Human rights groups accuse Rela members of violence, extortion, theft, and illegal detention.[3]

In addition to being subject to such overt brutality, the precarious existence of migrants in countries where they are not allowed to be—at least officially—or where they live with less than full citizenship rights facilitates their gross exploitation by capital. For instance, in the United Arab Emirates, where a well-pronounced racial-national hierarchy permeates social relations, an estimated three hundred thousand expatriate workers, most of them unauthorized, perform the most physically difficult work. Bused into wealthy Dubai on a daily basis from outlying camps segregated from the glitzy city, the migrants—from countries such as India, Pakistan, Sri Lanka, Ethiopia, and the Philippines—commonly work very long hours. Their pay is often so little that they are unable to save up sufficient funds to return to their home countries, a situation compounded by the fact that they frequently have to pay off debts to the labor contractors who tricked them into coming with false promises.[4]

While international migrant workers typically receive *some* protection through the legal-social mechanisms of the countries in which they find themselves, these protections are less extensive than those afforded citizen workers. This increases the vulnerability of migrant workers to exploitation and mistreatment by employers.

In theory, workers—unauthorized or not—can organize to defend themselves, but their ability to do so is quite circumscribed, especially if they are "illegal." In the United States, 52 percent of companies where union drives are taking place threaten to call U.S. immigration authorities (a threat that is illegal to make) if the organizing campaign involves unauthorized immigrants.[5] In such situations—given the very poor state of U.S. labor law (especially in the agricultural sector, in which abuse is rife) and its weak enforcement—the right to organize is highly compromised.[6]

The violence, marginalization, and exclusion experienced by migrant workers and their families occur most markedly in the wealthy and privileged countries of the global political economy. Again in the case of the United States—which is just one example among many—in the twenty-first century there has been a huge increase in migrant imprisonment and detention, including of children with their parents; a steep rise in workplace raids; and massive growth of deportations of both legal and unauthorized residents. There has also been a dramatic expansion of boundary enforcement, which means migrants must often literally risk their lives to enter the country clandestinely. The result is frequently death.

These fatalities occur across the globe, but it is the boundaries between the so-called first and third worlds, between the relatively rich and poor, secure and vulnerable, that are deadliest. In the U.S.-Mexico borderlands, the bodies of over five thousand migrants were recovered between 1995 and 2009. Undoubtedly, the true toll is far greater as the figure only includes bodies that are actually found, and relies in part on reporting from U.S. agencies, such as the Border Patrol, which have used very narrow criteria over the years for counting the fatalities of unauthorized crossers.[7] Large numbers of migrants from the Dominican Republic and Haiti have also died—from drowning or shark attacks—while trying to negotiate the waters of the Caribbean to reach the United States. Similarly, along Europe's perimeter many thousands have perished in the twenty-first century (often at sea), trying to clandestinely enter its territory.

"Apartheid" might seem like an inappropriate term to describe the context in which such tragedies unfold, given that there is no legally enshrined racial segregation between the so-called first and third worlds. Moreover, many people of third-world origin have citizenship, or live and work in countries throughout the West. Although national governments regularly discriminate in terms of who they allow to enter, reside, and work—and how and under what conditions—in the territories they oversee, they do so first and foremost on the basis of the would-be immigrant's national citizenship and socioeconomic situation. This is a form of discrimination seen as fully legitimate in international affairs. Nonetheless, if we move beyond the question of the specific motivations that underlie the system of immigration regulation, and instead focus on effects and outcomes, there is little question that immigration enforcement in wealthy countries such as the United States or those of the European Union functions in an apartheid-like manner. Given that they regulate mobility and residence based on, among other factors, geographic origins—one of the foundations of supposed racial distinctions—they inevitably limit the rights and protections afforded to migrants because of an essentialized characteristic over which the migrants have no control. In doing so, state agents (re)produce sociogeographic, nation-state-based distinctions between "us" and "them," "here" and "there," drawing upon and exacerbating global socioeconomic inequalities.

In a similar fashion—by, among other means, creating and maintaining nominally independent black "homelands," or bantustans—apartheid South Africa sought both to limit black mobility and to make certain that there was a sufficient supply of black labor in white-owned enterprises and in nominally white residential areas.[8] All the while, the country denied those workers political rights and made their presence conditional and reversible. The ideal of "apartness" embraced by the champions of apartheid was never fully realized, nor could it have been given the interdependence of white and nonwhite South Africa. Indeed, the production and maintenance of the privilege enjoyed by white South Africans necessitated interaction with nonwhites in a highly exploitative manner (a fact explicitly acknowledged by high-level officials of the apartheid state).[9] Furthermore, resistance by black people and others to legally enshrined segregation also undermined the proclaimed goal of purity.

The fact that there was a gap between the rhetoric and the reality of apartheid South Africa does not mean that its system of formal racial segregation was not significant. The apartheid system ensured unequal access to and unequal influence over the country's sociopolitical and economic resources and processes on the basis of who allegedly belonged and who did not. It thus reflected and reproduced profoundly different life and death experiences for white and nonwhite South Africans as a whole, differential outcomes legitimated on the basis of geographic origin and ancestry.

"Black" and "white"—and other racial categories—are not first and foremost about distinctions of skin color or pigmentation or phenotype. As demonstrated by the historically shifting boundaries of whiteness in the United States, and by the wars in Northern Ireland, the former Yugoslavia, and Rwanda, what are effectively racial distinctions often exist between groups with no discernible physical differences. In this sense, "race" is based on power-imbued differences related to notions of ancestry and geographic origins, and associated ways of seeing and being. Racism reflects and shapes who gets what, who calls the shots. Mobility between countries—who has it and who does not—is one of the most striking worldwide manifestations of these inequalities.

These differences in power on a global scale have unfolded in such a way that "white" and privilege have long been inextricably tied. Our world is one in which the few—the relatively rich and disproportionately white—are generally free to travel and live wherever they would like, and they have the means to access the resources they "need." Meanwhile the many—the relatively poor who are largely people of color—are forced to subsist where there are not enough resources to provide sufficient livelihood. Or, in order to overcome their deprivation and insecurity, they are compelled to risk their lives trying to overcome ever-stronger boundary controls put in place by the countries of privilege that reject them. And if they succeed in reaching the territories to which they are denied, these officially unwelcome migrants must endure all the indignities and hazards associated with being marked as "illegal."

It is widely recognized that limiting mobility within a country is both unjust and harmful to those denied. In Rwanda in the early 1990s, for example, there were all sorts of obstacles to movement and residence within the national territory—obstacles characterized as human rights violations by the U.S. State Department.[10] According to the World Bank, Rwanda's "[r]estrictions on population movements . . . increased poverty by limiting options for the poor and . . . reduced the potential for economic growth." Hence, the bank asserted that "any poverty reducing growth strategy for Rwanda [would] need to start with removing restrictions to free labor movement."[11] In the case of movement between nation-states, however, the injurious implications of limited mobility for people trying to "illegally" cross a border, seeking to live and work within the boundaries of the globe's prosperous territories, do not receive such scrutiny. Nonetheless, it is clear that limited and conditional mobility on the international scale also exacerbates situations of unequal life chances, "limiting options for the poor" and vulnerable by denying access to resources in spaces that provide greater life- and security-enhancing options. At the same time, for those who do succeed in penetrating and residing in national territories without authorization, their illegal status increases their "flexibility" (to borrow a term popular among the champions of neoliberalism) and general vulnerability vis-à-vis myriad forces of depredation — including those of capital and those of the state and its policing agents.

Almost never discussed in establishment circles, these linkages between the denial of mobility and injury are obscured and embedded in the globe's political and economic fabric. The Universal Declaration of Human Rights, for example, embraces "the inherent dignity and . . . the equal and inalienable rights of all members of the human family" and affirms the right of exit from a country. But the document — proclaimed by the United Nations General Assembly as "a common standard of achievement for all peoples and all nations" — does not enshrine a right of entry, except into one's own country. The effect is to deny most people across the globe some of the most basic human rights.

In a world of pervasive poverty, growing inequality, and widespread instability and insecurity, the power to move across national boundaries is tied to the ability to access the resources needed to realize human rights. It is for such a reason that Hannah Arendt spoke of "the right to have rights."[12] If having human rights is part of being a human being, denying someone a "right to have rights" by disallowing them freedom of movement and residence — and thus a whole host of related rights — is to effectively deny their very humanity.

This double standard — full human rights for the globally privileged, far fewer for the rest — is the essence of racism. And given the unjust nature of the global political economy, which embodies this unequal allocation of rights and which national governments enforce, this double standard is also the essence of the nation-state system. It allows for differential treatment based on the assumption that some should have fewer rights because of where they're from.

If such double standards were undoubtedly wrong in apartheid-era South Africa, aren't they equally wrong across the globe today — wherever they take place and whatever the justifications? And if they are equally wrong, does this not require those who profess an antiracist, pro–human rights stance to struggle to abolish nation-state controls over mobility, residence, and work?

Such a struggle does not necessarily seek the abolition of nation-states, just as the struggle to end apartheid in South Africa did not result in that country's disappearance. It does mean, however, that there is a need for a radical redefinition of what the nation-state is because, in its present-day form, control of movement across its territorial boundaries is one of its fundamental attributes. What this redefinition might look like is an open question, but at the very least it should embrace the ideal of all people, regardless of national origins, having a right to work and reside within the boundaries of any nation-state.

Eliminating the restrictions over mobility will not, in and of itself, put an end to all the various disparities that flow from and reproduce these controls, just as the end of apartheid in South Africa did not result in the demise of all of that country's profound inequities. But, again as in South Africa, the end of restrictions on mobility and the creation of formal geopolitical rights for all will create the space to struggle for far greater levels of socioeconomic justice — in this case, across national boundaries. It is for this reason and more that antiracist, pro-migrant advocates and organizers cannot and should not limit their gaze and activism to the terrain bounded by nation-states. A true solidarity beyond borders is essential to put an end to apartheid in its global guise.

NOTES

1. For an overview and analysis of the violence, see Misago et al., *Towards Tolerance, Law, and Dignity*.
2. Quoted in Karimakwenda, "South Africa."
3. Mydans, "Foreign Workers."
4. See Abdul-Ahad, "We Need Slaves to Build Monuments."
5. Brofenbrenner, *Uneasy Terrain*.
6. See, for instance, Anton, "In the Coachella Valley."
7. See, for example, Rubio-Goldsmith et al., *The "Funnel Effect."* See also Jimenez, *Humanitarian Crisis*.
8. For an interesting comparison between apartheid South Africa's and the United States' immigration control regimes, see Burawoy, "The Functions and Reproduction of Migrant Labor."
9. See Bremner, "Border/Skin."
10. Uvin, *Aiding Violence*, 115–16.
11. World Bank, *Rwanda Poverty Reduction and Sustainable Growth*, v–viii, 41.
12. Arendt, *Origins of Totalitarianism*.

BIBLIOGRAPHY

Abdul-Ahad, Ghaith. "We Need Slaves to Build Monuments." *Guardian*, October 8, 2008. http://www.guardian.co.uk/world/2008/oct/08/middleeast.construction.

Anton, Mike. "In the Coachella Valley, Hope Withers on the Vine." *Los Angeles Times*, June 23, 2009. http://www.latimes.com/news/local/la-me-grapes23-2009jun23%2C0%2C6892712.story.

Arendt, Hannah. *The Origins of Totalitarianism*. New York: Meridian, 1951.

Bremner, Lindsay. "Border/Skin." In *Against the Wall: Israel's Barrier to Peace*, edited by Michael Sorkin, 122–37. New York: New Press, 2005.

Brofenbrenner, Kate. *Uneasy Terrain: The Impact of Capital Mobility on Workers, Wages, and Union Organizing*. Report submitted to the U.S. Trade Deficit Review Commission, September 6, 2000. http://digitalcommons.ilr.cornell.edu/reports/1.

Burawoy, Michael. "The Functions and Reproduction of Migrant Labor: Comparative Material from Southern Africa and the United States." *American Journal of Sociology* 81, no. 5 (1976): 1050–87.

Jimenez, Leticia. *Humanitarian Crisis: Migrant Deaths at the U.S.-Mexico Border*, San Diego: American Civil Liberties Union of San Diego and Imperial Counties, October 1, 2009. www.aclu.org/immigrants/gen/41186pub20091001.html.

Karimakwenda, Tererai. "South Africa: Mbeki Blamed after 20 More Die in Xenophobic Attacks." *SW Radio* (London), May 19, 2008. http://allafrica.com/stories/200805191523.html.

Misago, Jean Pierre, Loren B. Landau, and Tamlyn Monson. *Towards Tolerance, Law, and Dignity: Addressing Violence against Foreign Nationals in South Africa*. Johannesburg, South Africa: International Organization for Migration, Regional Office for Southern Africa, February 2009. http://www.wilsoncenter.org/news/docs/Addressing%20Violence%20against%20Foreign%20Nationals_IOM.pdf.

Mydans, Seth. "Foreign Workers Face Campaign of Brutality in Malaysia." *International Herald Tribune*, December 9, 2007.

Rubio-Goldsmith, Raquel M., Melissa McCormick, Daniel Martinez, and Inez Magdalena Duarte. *The "Funnel Effect" and Recovered Bodies of Unauthorized Migrants Processed by the Pima County Office of the Medical Examiner, 1990–2005*. Report submitted to the Pima County Board of Supervisors. Tucson, Ariz.: Binational Migration Institute, University of Arizona, October 2006. http://www.ailf.org/ipc/policybrief/policybrief_020607.pdf.

Uvin, Peter. *Aiding Violence: The Development Enterprise in Rwanda*. West Hartford, Conn.: Kumarian, 1998.

World Bank. *Rwanda Poverty Reduction and Sustainable Growth*. Washington, D.C.: Population and Human Resources Division, South Central and Indian Ocean Department, Africa Region, 1994.

Understanding Conquest through a Border Lens
A Comparative Analysis of the Mexico-U.S. and Morocco-Spain Regions

CYNTHIA BEJARANO, MARIA CRISTINA MORALES, AND SAID SADDIKI

This chapter draws on the experiences of vulnerable populations in the Mexico-U.S. and Morocco-Spain border regions through the concept of *border sexual conquest* (BSC).[1] We have used border sexual conquest in other writings as an apparatus to understand violent phenomena and forms of resistance in vulnerable places (e.g., Mexico-U.S. border). We find the concept's elasticity useful as the basis for a comparative exploration of two transcontinental regions. There are four interlocking components of BSC: (1) political-economic structures that create "disposable" workers; (2) the subjugation of a local place and region due to its exploitable, profitable potential; (3) gender and class inequality; and (4) people's resistance and agency to wrestle with human and regional vulnerability.[2] The subjugation of place is especially relevant since global industries and legal and illegal trade search for the most vulnerable, manageable, and marginalized places and people to exploit.

The examples of such spaces in this chapter are the Mexican-U.S. and Moroccan-Spanish border regions, which are characterized as geopolitically charged, exploitable, and profit-driven. We use BSC as a comparative analytical tool to explore violent phenomena in ostensibly different border regions. We discuss the migration patterns of vulnerable people through these subjugated regions, and the measures used by colonized or colonizing nation-states to stop migration flows and drug trafficking.

Based on our experiences living and working on the Mexico-U.S. border and the Morocco-Spain border, we recognize colonized histories, migratory movements, export processing zones, drug and human trafficking narratives, and border fence enforcement in both places. Both regions have also become increasingly militarized through a variety of strategies and tactics, all coupled with criminal justice systems that are then used to justify "wars" on drugs and immigration. We argue that within the Mexican-U.S. and Moroccan-Spanish border regions, colonialism has resurfaced through neocolonialism; nation-state policies damage vulnerable communities by forcing mass migrations of economic refugees through policed spaces. Using this broad framework, we explore similar phenomena at both borders.

ANALYZING COMPARATIVE TRANSCONTINENTAL CROSSINGS AND FRAGMENTED BORDERS

Mexico and the United States share a highly contested, fortified, and controversial two-thousand-mile border. With the exception of the short territorial boundaries of Ceuta and Melilla and their Moroccan hinterlands, the Spanish-Moroccan border is a maritime border, whether on the Mediterranean or the Moroccan Atlantic coast opposite the Spanish Canary Islands. And it is equally contested. Both borders have marginal status compared to the rest of their respective countries. The U.S.-Mexico border is socially isolated from the rest of the United States, since it neighbors a developing country, has some of the highest levels of poverty in the United States, and is largely populated by people considered to be racial and ethnic minorities.[3]

Ceuta and Melilla are two important enclaves in northern Morocco that have been controlled by Spain since the end of the *reconquista*. Melilla was the first to fall under Spanish rule in 1497, and Ceuta (seized by Portugal in 1415) was transferred to Spain under the Treaty of Lisbon in 1668.[4] Since 1986, with Spain's entry into the European Community (later, the European Union), the two enclaves have been considered EU territories and the frontline of what became known as "Fortress Europe." In 1993, the fencing of the enclaves' perimeters started under the pretext of preventing irregular migration.[5] Today, the Spanish government continues to strengthen and renovate these fences by using new, advanced technologies.

Since the mid-1990s, because of their unique geographical location, the two enclaves — as de facto EU territories in North Africa — are now the desired crossing points for thousands of sub-Saharan African migrants. Irregular migrants prefer this direction because they can reach "European soil" by entering the enclaves even if they are still in Africa, and it is a less costly and less risky route than riding the waves of the Mediterranean or Atlantic seas to an unknown fate. Although stopping and preventing irregular migration and drug trafficking are the principal stated objectives of reinforcing the fences of Ceuta and Melilla, perpetuating the status quo and the Europeanization of the two enclaves remain key long-term goals of Spain's border control policy.

In both the Moroccan-Spanish and Mexican-U.S. border zones, migrants risk their lives in hopes of securing a better future: crossing the Strait of Gibraltar, known as the "moat of Fortress Europe," or traversing the Rio Grande, mountains, and deserts in the U.S. Southwest.[6] Each year, a significant number of irregular migrants die, disappear, or get seriously injured. Since 2002, approximately four thousand people have died trying to cross the strait or other parts of the Mediterranean into Europe.[7] Similarly, human rights advocates along the Mexico-U.S. border have documented approximately five thousand migrant deaths since the 1990s.[8] Migrants in both regions hire smugglers for "safe" passage through borders reinforced by razor-wire fencing, while often danger manifests in the state itself.[9] In 2005 in Ceuta and Melilla, Spanish and Moroccan border police injured or killed several migrants trying to cross. Incidents of violence against migrants and non-migrants, such as the disturbing death of a boy in Juárez, Mexico, who was shot through the international border fence by a U.S. Border Patrol agent, are often reported.[10] Often, state violence in these regions is overlooked and dismissed in the name of national security.

Millions of dollars and euros are spent to keep migrants and economic refugees from Central America, Mexico, North Africa, and sub-Saharan Africa from entering the United States and Spain. Boat smugglers and migrants use *pateras* (small boats) to cross the Strait of Gibraltar, and media coverage from the region calls these migrants "wetbacks," employing the same hateful rhetoric used in the United States.[11] In the United States, before the Border Patrol operation in El Paso, Texas, called Operation Hold the Line (1994), passersby could witness *lancheros* (people who moved migrants on inner tubes across the Rio Grande) crossing laborers or migrants from Juárez into El Paso. In Morocco, especially in the 1980s and 1990s, "in order to pay for the expensive crossing [of the strait; estimated at 700–1,000 U.S. dollars per person], some migrants would carry packages of hashish—which in turn reinforced the popular perception in Spain of a close association between irregular immigration and drug trafficking."[12]

Similar arguments are made about migrants at the Mexico-U.S. border, validating the conflation of drug and irregular immigration enforcement policies and xenophobia.[13] Today, drug trafficking organizations have developed methods of transferring drugs between the two sides of the Mediterranean without using irregular migrants. Furthermore, traffickers not only transfer hashish from Morocco to Europe, but they also smuggle cocaine and hard drugs from Europe to Morocco, using a long and complicated route from Latin America through Africa to Europe. Typically, high-speed powerboats, cargo trucks, cars, and sometimes small planes are used between the two shores of the Mediterranean.

In the United States the dangers of crossing the border escalated with the implementation of the Immigration Reform and Control Act (IRCA) in 1986 and with the rise of border operations.[14] IRCA made it more dangerous and costly to cross the border, and El Paso's Operation Hold the Line changed migration streams from urban areas to more dangerous desert mountainous regions.[15] While it is difficult to determine the number of migration-related deaths, Cornelius documented an increase of 509 percent in the deaths of unauthorized border crossers from 1994 to 2000 in the U.S. Southwest: 499 deaths mostly attributed to hypothermia, dehydration, and sunstroke.[16]

TRANSFERABILITY OF BODIES

Migrants searching for opportunities in an unstable global economy face violence and uncertainty. They are overworked in dangerous industries, discarded when no longer useful, and then forced to relocate elsewhere for employment opportunities. They become *transferable bodies*, displaced and used repeatedly as they travel their migratory route from home to subjugated border region and then are transferred from these areas by smugglers or self-smuggle onto cargo trucks and ships (Morocco-Spain) or cargo freight trains (Mexico-U.S.).[17] If caught, they are held or transferred yet again to deportation centers or back across the border to the subjugated region they launched from.

The southern Mexicans, Central Americans, and sub-Saharan Africans who are deported back to their home countries wait in unfamiliar border zones to cross again. A specific phenomenon has appeared in northern Morocco, where a large number of transient migrants (from Africa and some Asian countries) who fail to enter or do not venture to Europe spend time on Moroccan territory near Ceuta and Melilla. They have created temporary settlements resembling a "third nation" or a "waiting room"; migrants cannot reach their El Dorado, nor can they return to their home countries.[18] Many transient people attempt to transfer once again, or suffer from a paralyzing border stagnation as they wait to be moved by a smuggler or for another chance to cross the border themselves. These border zones are akin to transfer stations where migrants, goods (legal and illegal exports), and services (migrant smuggling and drug trafficking) await the next chance to cross. Border policies have created "trapped refugee communities with residents of similar ethnic, national, and economic backgrounds and circumstances."[19]

If the transfer of bodies successfully occurs, migrants are still often contained in border cities on the other side because of heightened border enforcement and limited access to networks or resources. These processes transform them into better bodies for work and smuggling, and make them vulnerable to border control war rhetoric, further justifying the militarization and policing of borders. This is one way in which neoliberalism and nation-states produce vulnerable bodies at the U.S.-Mexican and Moroccan-Spanish borders.

PROCESSES OF BORDER SEXUAL CONQUEST: INTERLOCKING MULTIPLE FORMS OF SEXUAL AND GENDERED VIOLENCE

The concept of border sexual conquest contends that gender interlocks with neoliberalism and specific regions to reinforce and shape violence. Sexual and gendered violence then embodies gender oppression in subjugated regions where women's statuses as "underdeveloped," "poor," and "brown" translate into exploitable labor.[20] The history of racism and imperialism (slavery and colonialism) illustrates how sexual conquest has permeated the cultures of European and U.S. expansion as a form of eroticized power (i.e., the sexualization and scrutiny of women's bodies).[21] Local interpretations in the Mexican-U.S. and Moroccan-Spanish border regions of women working outside of traditional sociocultural contexts also shape how workers are identified as moral or immoral, as sexually promiscuous, or as unfit single mothers working in sexually charged workplaces.

Despite women's agency — evident in their fights against labor, sexual, patriarchal, and social exploitation — the preferred image of the docile, controllable, subservient female worker is used to justify the control of workers for the sake of the quantity and quality of production. For example, in Morocco, women make up 70 percent of garment industry workers.[22] In Mexico, a country well known for its electronic and garment industries, there are three thousand maquiladoras employing roughly a million workers — a quarter of whom work in Ciudad Juárez, 60 percent of whom are women.[23]

A significant number of women also work in the informal economy. In the Moroccan border province of Tetouan (near Ceuta) and in Nador (near Melilla), the contraband economy provides work for more than forty-five thousand people, 75 percent of whom are women.[24] Although women today are involved in smuggling activities in northern Morocco, they have always participated in social development and in legal forms of work, although their contributions have often been unrecognized.[25] Women also comprise a considerable portion of nonagricultural workers informally employed; they represent an estimated 58 percent of such workers in Latin America and 84 percent in sub-Saharan Africa, where people are migrating north at disquieting rates. In North Africa, less than half (43 percent) of women workers are in the informal sector, which is partly due to social customs that restrict women's mobility.[26]

Neoliberalism, however, has forced women to step out of traditional sociocultural roles and into work outside of the home, making discernible the feminization of labor, poverty, and migration.[27] In Morocco, the significant socioeconomic changes that occurred during the independence period (i.e., since 1956) pushed women to work outside the home in the public sector, and later in both the formal and informal private sectors. In the twenty-first century, the feminization of Moroccan immigration flows (both regular and irregular) to Spain has become a significant concern in a society not yet totally accustomed to women working outside the home, especially in rural areas, where women have been migrating without their families to another country. The most serious problem of this migration is that the vast majority of these women are illiterate and come from very poor families, which heightens their risk for slavery and sexual exploitation by employers and criminal organizations.

As more women are forced across transnational borders for economic survival, their chances increase of victimization by corrupt authorities, kidnappers, and employers, among others. The testimonies of migrants traveling from or through Mexico to the United States include witnessing threats made to women about selling them into forced prostitution, and seeing women raped by kidnappers.[28] These atrocities increase as drug and human trafficking rings grow more ruthless and determined to make a profit by moving "merchandise" across nation-state borders despite government drug interdiction efforts which, ironically, foster more violence.

PLACE SUBJUGATION: SPACE MATTERS TO FORMS OF BORDER SEXUAL CONQUEST

The profits sought by neoliberal capitalism come at the expense of vulnerable places.[29] Neoliberalism heightens the violent sociohistorical realities of places while also shaping the experiences of exploited migrants in the marginal border spaces of nation-states. Indeed, the success of neoliberalism is dependent upon the subjugation of place. Moreover, place is more than the backdrop of social occurrences, but also intersects with oppressive systems of class, race, ethnicity, gender, sexuality,[30] and — in the case of migrants — nationality and citizenship.

Borders become increasingly vulnerable with the increase in militarization, policing, and border fencing. The Mexico-U.S. border is a low-intensity conflict zone where civilians have daily confrontations with armed Border Patrol agents, Immigration and Customs Enforcement, and at times National Guard troops. Border control policing initiatives in the United States have expanded their missions from the apprehension and prevention of entry of irregular immigrants, to drug enforcement and antiterrorism.[31] The Mexican border is also subjected to heavy militarization and policing ostensibly because of drug cartel fighting. Both Mexico and Morocco find themselves, as transit countries, between a rock and a hard place. Since the mid-1990s they have been under pressure by their wealthier neighboring countries to control their territorial boundaries and to stop the flow of migrants entering the United States and Europe. Simultaneously, they have faced a growing demand from national and international human rights groups to provide more protection to irregular migrants crossing or settling in their territory.[32]

According to the Mexican National Population Council, every year approximately 550,000 Mexicans emigrate to the United States; additionally, the Migration National Institute claims that 140,000 Central Americans travel without papers through Mexico annually in efforts to reach the United States.[33] The Comisión Nacional de los Derechos Humanos found that women, adolescents, and older people traveling alone or in small groups through Mexico were more vulnerable than men to ransom and other forms of exploitation. From September 2008 to February 2009, the commission documented 198 cases of migrant kidnappings throughout Mexico; several victims were impacted during every kidnapping attempt, resulting in 9,758 victims. Since most kidnappings go unreported in Mexico for fear of reprisals, the commission estimates that this figure could reach 18,000 migrant victims annually.[34] Part of this violence is attributed to drug traffickers' inability to cross drugs through borders, and thus they have diversified their economic endeavors to also include trafficking in people.

GLOBAL POLICING AND MILITARIZATION: THE FENCING IN AND OUT OF PEOPLE

The global model for policing borders includes barring migrants from access to wealthier nation-states through militarized and technologized strategies of border fencing. Andreas and Nadelmann describe a "transatlantic security community based more on policing alliances against non-state actors than traditional security alliances against state-based military threats. . . . increasingly dense set[s] of transgovernmental policing networks and international agreements [have] been quietly built up and largely overlooked."[35] The militarization of border enforcement—such as the military surveillance and support equipment used by the U.S. Border Patrol—includes ongoing conversations about deploying National Guard troops to the border, a common governmental response during perceived threats despite the Posse Comitatus Act of 1878, which forbids the use of military forces on domestic land.[36] Unequivocally, the Mexico-U.S. border—on both sides—has always been heavily militarized.[37] From 2007 to the present, Mexican president Felipe Calderón has deployed over five thousand troops to fight drug cartels and street violence (kidnappings, carjackings, extortion schemes, robberies, murders) in Juárez, which often exacerbates violence.

The militarization and global policing of border regions subjugate place, and the processes of migration thereby negatively affect vulnerable communities. These billion-dollar economies are easily justified by nation-states, and as one side of drug trafficking or irregular immigration escalates, it is met twofold by nation-state responses. Transcontinental subjugated places begin to eerily resemble each other. The soldiers and the police in one place look like the others, sharing similar uniforms and checkpoints; the differences are the sophistication of their weaponry and the policing technologies employed. What is indisputable though are the parallel treks migrants make through heavily surveilled places en route to the United States or Spain as destination or transit countries.

At the Moroccan-Spanish border, immigration control was a non-issue until the year prior to Spain entering the European Community.[38] Since the adoption in 1985 of the Schengen Agreement, which allows free movement for EU citizens within its member states, the control of external European Community borders is no longer a national matter for each European state independently, but rather a common European problem.[39] Therefore, after joining the European Community in 1986 and the Schengen Agreement zone in 1991, Spain has been obligated, according to its European commitments, to tighten its border. Border control measures include imposing visa restrictions on North Africans in order to reduce the number of migrants coming from Africa; a shared computer system for information exchange; and millions invested in policing apparatus to monitor all forms of contraband.

BORDER ZONES AND THE DRUG TRADE

The Mexican-U.S. and Moroccan-Spanish borders are main transport zones for the drug market. Most discussions about the drug trade focus on how to curb trafficking from less-developed nation-states, while curbing drug use in the United States and Spain is less frequently mentioned. The problem of drug trafficking is framed as poor, violent countries producing dangerous drugs and people. The United States has harnessed cross-border initiatives, influencing the EU and other nations to employ post-9/11 rhetoric for reinforced drug interdiction and policing of people globally, therefore conflating drugs, immigration, and even terrorism. Europe, for instance, is always pressuring Morocco to stop the flow of drugs. In 1992, the late King Hassan II of Morocco declared a "war on drugs and illegal immigration"[40] in an effort to appease the Spanish government. This corresponds with the 1960s–1970s Nixon and later 1980s Reagan administrations' "war on drugs."[41]

This catchall rhetoric obscures the realities of policies that conflate drug trafficking with immigration, terrorism, and national security, while effacing the real impact on the marginalized populations victimized by neoliberalism. Thus, the "war on drugs" directs attention toward the "enemies" — drug producers, traffickers, and Others — and away from "us," the societies consuming the drugs. The war-on-drugs rhetoric is also used for justifying the mass incarceration of nonviolent drug offenders, who comprise most of the prison population in the United States, affecting millions of poor, disenfranchised people of color. This caging approach through three-strikes laws and other comprehensive federal guidelines have given rise to the penal state.[42] Corva argues that the "illiberal" militarization and transnationalization of the war on drugs in other countries is a pinnacle feature of global policing and the taming and controlling of unruly nation-states. *Illiberal governance* refers to the legitimation and application of coercive power by liberal nation-states to subjects whose actions are represented as disrupting the security required for the operation of free choice for the society in question — be it national or global. Two significant illiberal ways of governing are the application of military apparatus (the strategy of warfare) and the application of the criminal justice apparatus (the strategy of policing citizens).[43]

Police checkpoints dot the borders as agents attempt to stop hashish and cannabis coming from the Rif mountainous region of northern Morocco, or drugs and undocumented people in the U.S. Southwest's deserts. The drug trafficking industry continues to grow by leaps and bounds while vulnerable communities struggling to survive in these places become more reliant on drugs for their livelihoods.[44] Violence associated with drugs and other forms of street-level violence escalate with further militarization responses; from 2008 to early May 2011, over eight thousand people (including many innocent bystanders) were killed in Juárez, Mexico. Indeed, Juárez is now one of the most violent cities in the world because of its place in what Campbell calls the "drug war zone."[45] As nation-states build greater global powers and economies under the rubric of security, policing, and fighting drug trafficking, communities must learn to resist and protect themselves from those who prey on them as well as from those charged to protect them.

WHERE CONQUEST MEETS RESISTANCE

The final dimension of border sexual conquest concerns individual and collective resistance to the exploitation of people and place.[46] At the Mexico-U.S. border, youth are resisting: protesting the murders in Juárez and severe border control initiatives through cross-border activism. These mobilizations also have responded to the feminicides in Juárez, which received attention from the 2009 Inter-American Court of Human Rights.[47] Cross-border youth have ignited grassroots activism through Peace and Justice without Borders, a grassroots organization started by students and professors who held a demonstration at the border fence between Juárez, Mexico, and Sunland Park, New Mexico, United States, to denounce the violence and militarization in Juárez.[48] Moroccan youth, referred to as the "new rebels of globalization," resist differently by "show[ing] the ruptures in the socio-economic conditions of the[ir] countries of origin and the paradoxes in the policies, external and internal of European states."[49] For their survival, youth learn through networks where Moroccan enclaves exist throughout Europe.

Through necessity, vulnerable communities employ strategies to resist and defy the restraints of nation-states throughout border regions. Despite significant levels of human and civil rights violations at both borders, the most defiantly brave act of resistance by vulnerable people is to continue to migrate across borders and to resist human rights abuses. Ironically, the billions in pesos and dirhams received as remittances by Mexico and Morocco keep those countries from acute economic and social crises; Spain, the EU, and the United States are also heavily reliant on this cash flow, since their global economies are built on the backs of migrants, who generate billions in dollars and euros.

CONCLUSION

In this chapter we have used the concept of border sexual conquest as a tool to analyze the Mexican-U.S. and Moroccan-Spanish borders. In line with the components of border sexual conquest, both places suffer from sexual and gendered violence that results from an interlocking of the subjugation of place, neoliberal political and economic exploitation, and gender and class inequality, yet this violence is confronted by the resistance of community members. While border sexual conquest has been used to explain the feminicides and economic violence against women on both sides of the Mexico-U.S. border, here we have applied it to violence confronted by migrants at both borders.

One of the forms in which violence surfaces is through the transferability of bodies. Foucault notes that "in our societies, the systems of punishment are to be situated in a certain 'political economy' of the body: even if they do not make use of violent or bloody punishment, even when they use 'lenient' methods involving confinement or correction, it is always the body that is at issue — the body and its forces, their utility and their docility, their distribution and their submission."[50] The notion of the transferability of bodies illustrates Foucault's political economy of the body where those displaced by neoliberalism migrate in search of better economic opportunities but find themselves in border zones consumed by drug and human trafficking and the militarization of policing bodies and fences. Border crises such as these continue to escalate at alarming rates, and the end result devastates marginalized regions and vulnerable communities that are increasingly exposed, neglected, and exploited.

The components of border sexual conquest help to illuminate the transferability of bodies and migrant-related deaths. First, the subjugation of place occurs at both the Mexican-U.S. and Moroccan-Spanish borders via the militarization of tactics of border control, the paralyzing border stagnation where migrants cannot return home nor reach their destinations, and the war on drugs. Second, gendered violence is evident in the pushing of women toward a stagnant informal economy where the difficulty in surviving encourages migration. Third, despite the intimidation of migrant and border-related violence, this violence is confronted by community members at both places. Thus, while efforts to "conquer" these borders and their people are ongoing, they are met with strong opposition.

NOTES

1. Morales and Bejarano, "Transnational Sexual and Gendered Violence."
2. Ibid.
3. Ibid.
4. Saddiki, "Ceuta and Melilla Fences."
5. We use the phrase "irregular migration" as a neutral term consistent with contemporary international official documents, which avoid using "illegal migration" because of its negative connotation and its association with criminality. See, for example, Resolution no. 3449 of the U.N. General Assembly, entitled Measures to Ensure the Human Rights and Dignity of All Migrant Workers, adopted on December 9, 1975; the International Convention on the Protection of the Rights of All Migrant Workers and Members of Their Families, adopted by the General Assembly on December 18, 1990; and Resolution no. 1509 of the Parliamentary Assembly of the Council of Europe (June 27, 2006), entitled Human Rights of Irregular Immigrants. U.S.-based terms like "unauthorized border crosser" attempt to humanize migrants' crossing borders for survival. We acknowledge the difficulty in finding terms that accurately depict the humanitarian crisis represented in these movements. Undeniably, terms like "irregular," "undocumented," and "illegal" fall short of portraying with dignity the plight of the migrant. See Rubio-Goldsmith et al., *The "Funnel Effect."*
6. Driessen, "At the Edge of Europe."
7. No Border Network, "Meanwhile at the Borders."
8. Coalición de Derechos Humanos, "Arizona Recovered Remains."
9. Border fencing systems adopted by the U.S. and Spanish governments include — in addition to materials like corrugated steel, razor barbed wire, and cement barriers — advanced technologies like infrared cameras, optic and acoustic sensors, watchtowers, satellites, and radar systems. While the U.S. border fence at San Diego juts into the Pacific Ocean, coasts controlled by Spain on the Atlantic Ocean and the Mediterranean Sea are not physically fenced; instead, they are controlled by an electronic system called the "virtual fence."
10. News reports stated that a Border Patrol agent shot and killed Sergio Adrian Hernandez Güereca, fifteen, after he allegedly threw rocks at the agent near the Paso del Norte Bridge along the U.S.-Mexico border. Ybarra, "Boy Shot and Killed by Border Patrol Agent."
11. Driessen, "At the Edge of Europe."
12. Hibbs, "Immigration Policy and the Quotidian Hassles of Being."
13. Cornelius, "Death at the Border."
14. Massey, Durand, and Malone, *Beyond Smoke and Mirrors*; Dunn, *The Militarization of the U.S.-Mexico Border.*
15. Heyman, Morales, and Núñez, "Engaging with the Immigrant Human Rights Movement"; Bejarano, "Senseless Deaths and Holding the Line"; Massey, Durand, and Malone, *Beyond Smoke and Mirrors.*
16. Cornelius, "Death at the Border," 669.

17. Bejarano and Morales, "Analyzing Conquest through a Border Lens."
18. Saddiki, "Ceuta and Melilla Fences," 14.
19. Núñez and Heyman, "Entrapment Processes and Immigrant Communities."
20. Morales and Bejarano, "Transnational Sexual and Gendered Violence."
21. Bhattacharyya, Gabriel, and Small, *Race and Power*.
22. Henderson and Jeydel, *Participation and Protest*.
23. Wright, *Disposable Women and Other Myths*.
24. Chouvey, "Morocco's Smuggling Rackets."
25. Boraki, "Les Contrebandières."
26. International Labour Organization, *Women and Men in the Informal Economy*.
27. Morales and Bejarano, "Transnational Sexual and Gendered Violence."
28. Comisión Nacional de los Derechos Humanos, "Special Report."
29. Morales and Bejarano, "Transnational Sexual and Gendered Violence."
30. Ibid.
31. Dunn, *The Militarization of the U.S.-Mexico Border*; Andreas and Nadelmann, *Policing the Globe*.
32. Saddiki, "Ceuta and Melilla Fences," 14.
33. Comisión Nacional de los Derechos Humanos, "Special Report."
34. Ibid.
35. Andreas and Nadelmann, *Policing the Globe*, 190.
36. Corva, "Neoliberal Globalization and the War on Drugs."
37. Dunn, *The Militarization of the U.S.-Mexico Border*.
38. Andreas, *Border Games*.
39. Saddiki, "Ceuta and Melilla Fences," 10.
40. Beck and De Mas, "The Strait of Gibraltar," 120.
41. Massey, Durand, and Malone, *Beyond Smoke and Mirrors*.
42. Corva, "Neoliberal Globalization and the War on Drugs," 180.
43. Ibid., 177.
44. Empez, Jiménez, and Vacchiano, "Independent Migrant Children across the Mediterranean."
45. Campbell, *Drug War Zone*.
46. Morales and Bejarano, "Transnational Sexual and Gendered Violence."
47. Ibid.; Frontera NorteSur, "The New Wave of Cross-Border Activism."
48. Frontera NorteSur, "The New Wave of Cross-Border Activism."
49. Empez, Jiménez, and Vacchiano, "Independent Migrant Children across the Mediterranean," 12.
50. Foucault, *Discipline and Punish*, 84.

BIBLIOGRAPHY

Andreas, Peter. *Border Games: Policing the U.S.-Mexico Divide*. Ithaca, N.Y.: Cornell University Press, 2001.

Andreas, Peter, and Ethan Nadelmann. *Policing the Globe: Criminalization and Crime Control in International Relations*. New York: Oxford University Press, 2006.

Beck, J. Mansvelt, and Paolo De Mas. "The Strait of Gibraltar: Europe's Rio Grande?" In *Geography, Environment and Development in the Mediterranean*, edited by Russell King, P. De Mas, and J. M. Beck, 117–36. Brighton, England: Sussex Academic, 2001.

Bejarano, Cynthia. "Senseless Deaths and Holding the Line." *Criminology and Public Policy* 6, no. 2 (2007): 267–74.

Bejarano, Cynthia, and M. Morales. "Analyzing Conquest through a Border Lens: Vulnerable Communities at the Mexico-U.S. and Moroccan-Spanish Border Regions." *Edicions Bellaterra* (First Quarter/Winter 2011): 117–30.

Bhattacharyya, G., J. Gabriel, and S. Small. *Race and Power: Global Racism in the Twenty-First Century*. London: Routledge, 2002.

Boraki, Chemseddoha. "Les Contrebandières: Woman as Smuggler." *Women: A Cultural Review* 12, no. 2 (2001): 176–91.

Campbell, Howard. *Drug War Zone: Frontline Dispatches from the Streets of El Paso and Juárez*. Austin: University of Texas Press, 2009.

Carabaza, Enrique, and Máximo de Santos. *Melilla y Ceuta: Las Últimas Colonias*. Madrid: Talasa, 1992.

Chouvey, Pierre-Arnaud. "Morocco's Smuggling Rackets: Hashish, People and Contraband." *Jane's Intelligence Review* 17, no. 12 (November 2005): 40–43.

Coalición de Derechos Humanos. "Arizona Recovered Remains." 2007. http://www.derechoshumanosaz.net/index.php?option=com_content&task=view&id=20&Itemid=34.

Comisión Nacional de los Derechos Humanos. "Special Report of the Human Rights National Commission about the Kidnapping of Migrants." 2009. www.cndh.org.mx.

Cornelius, Wayne A. "Death at the Border: Efficacy and Unintended Consequences of U.S. Immigration Control Policy 1993–2000." *Population and Development Review* 27, no. 4 (December 2001): 661–89.

Corva, Dominic. "Neoliberal Globalization and the War on Drugs: Transnationalizing Illiberal Governance in the Americas." *Political Geography* 27 (2008): 176–93.

Driessen, Henk. "At the Edge of Europe: Crossing and Marking the Mediterranean Divide." In *Borders, Nations, and States: Frontiers of Sovereignty in the New Europe*, edited by L. O'Dowd and T. M. Wilson, 179–98. Brookfield, Vt.: Avebury, 1996.

Dunn, Timothy J. *The Militarization of the U.S.-Mexico Border 1978–1992: Low-Intensity Conflict Doctrine Comes Home*. Austin, Tex.: Center for Mexican American Studies Books, 1996.

Empez, N., M. Jiménez, and F. Vacchiano. "Independent Migrant Children across the Mediterranean: The Case of Moroccan Minors in Spain and Italy." Unpublished manuscript in possession of authors, 2009.

Foucault, Michel. *Discipline and Punish: The Birth of the Prison*. Translated by Alan Sheridan. New York: Vintage, 1979.

Frontera NorteSur. "The New Wave of Cross-Border Activism." Las Cruces: New Mexico State University, January 20, 2011. http://www.nmsu.edu/~frontera/hmrt.html.

Henderson, Sarah L., and Alana S. Jeydel. *Participation and Protest: Women and Politics in a Global World*. New York: Oxford University Press, 2007.

Heyman, Josiah, M. Cristina Morales, and Guillermina G. Núñez. "Engaging with the Immigrant Human Rights Movement in a Besieged Border Region: What Do Applied Social Scientists Bring to the Policy Process?" In *Anthropology and Immigration*, edited by A. Unterberger, 13–29. Arlington, Va.: American Anthropological Association, 2009.

Hibbs, Cynthia R. "Immigration Policy and the Quotidian Hassles of Being: Foreign Workers in Madrid and San Diego." MA thesis, University of California, San Diego, 1994.

International Labour Organization. *Women and Men in the Informal Economy: A Statistical Picture*. Geneva: ILO, 2002.

Massey, Douglas S., Jorge Durand, and Nolan J. Malone. *Beyond Smoke and Mirrors: Mexican Immigration in an Era of Economic Integration*. New York: Sage Foundation, 2002.

Morales, Maria C., and Cynthia Bejarano. "Transnational Sexual and Gendered Violence: An Application of Border Sexual Conquest at a Mexico-US Border." *Global Networks* 9, no. 3 (2009): 420–39.

No Border Network. "Meanwhile at the Borders." [n.d.]. http://www.noborder.org/dead.php.

Núñez, Guillermina G., and Josiah Heyman. "Entrapment Processes and Immigrant Communities in a Time of Heightened Border Vigilance." *Human Organization* 66, no. 4 (2007): 354–65.

Rubio-Goldsmith, R., M. M. McCormick, D. Martinez, and I. M. Duarte. *The "Funnel Effect" and Recovered Bodies of Unauthorized Migrants Processed by the Pima County Office of the Medical Examiner, 1990–2005*. Tucson, Ariz.: Binational Migration Institute, Mexican American Studies and Research Center, 2006.

Saddiki, Said. "Ceuta and Melilla Fences: A[n] EU Multidimensional Border?" Paper presented at the annual conference of the Canadian Political Science Association, Montreal, June 1–3, 2010. http://www.cpsa-acsp.ca/papers-2010/Saddiki.pdf.

Wright, Melissa W. *Disposable Women and Other Myths of Global Capitalism*. New York: Routledge, 2006.

Ybarra, Maggie. "Boy Shot and Killed by Border Patrol Agent Will Be Buried Thursday." *El Paso Times*, June 9, 2010. http://www.elpasotimes.com/ci_15259824.

Race, Capitalist Crisis, and Abolitionist Organizing
An Interview with Ruth Wilson Gilmore
FEBRUARY 2010

JENNA LOYD

JENNA LOYD (JL): It's great to be talking with you, Ruthie. Can you tell us how you got involved in anti-prison work?

RUTH WILSON GILMORE (RWG): I started working on anti-prison organizing about twenty years ago. It was never not on my agenda, but it became the focus of a good deal of my work when I realized that people who were trying to organize themselves around all different kinds of issues kept running up against the criminal justice system, which then seemed to become a focal point for people who were trying to achieve other goals, whether the goals were adequate education for children, health care, immigrant rights, you name it. People kept running up against the criminal justice system and what seemed to be a wholly new relationship with prisons and policing and jails.

I don't think once upon a time prisons and jails were used judiciously and then just got out of control recently. That is *not* what I think. But what I do know is that the use of prisons and jails as all-purpose solutions for all different kinds of social, political, and economic problems and challenges *is* different than what it was in the past. This is to say that the practices perfected in the past on the working class, people of color, and people without certain kinds of documentation have reached a new level of industrialized efficiency, and we see all different kinds of people being sucked into that kind of machinery at an incredibly fantastic rate. What has happened over the last twenty years is that different kinds of people have found themselves confronted with suddenly having to prove or assert innocence or non-guilt in the face of criminalizing machinery, including legislation and the ideologically produced representation of all different kinds of people as already criminals.

In recent years, one way that people have joined the struggle against the all-purpose use of prisons to solve social problems has been to try to assert that certain kinds of people are actually innocent. So they will say, for example, that long-distance migrants who are not documented to work are not really criminals because they didn't do anything, they just showed up to work. Or they will say, "Oh, look. People who are in prison or who are in jail because they are addicted to certain kinds of substances are not really guilty of any crimes. They're really innocent and should be released."

In my view, while saving anyone is a good thing to do, to try to assert innocence as a key anti-prison political activity is to turn a blind eye to the system and how it works. The way the system works is to move the line of what counts as criminal to encompass and engulf more and more people into the territory of prison eligibility, if you will. So the problem, then, is not to figure out how to determine or prove the innocence of certain individuals or certain classes of people, but to attack the general system through which criminalization proceeds.

JL: It seems like there's a gap between this analysis of criminalization as a political process and a widespread explanation for prison expansion, which puts the blame on private prison corporations as the major culprits. Could you talk about how you think about the prison-industrial complex (PIC), and how this term can help us understand the dynamics of both criminalization and privatization?

RWG: The first thing I want to say is that over the last thirty years, . . . the prison and jail capacity of the United States has swelled to such a point that one in a hundred adult residents in the United States is in a jail, in a cell, even as we speak. *Right now, one out of a hundred.* As this has happened, the percentage, or fraction, of cells that are operated or managed by private entities has stayed about the same. It's less than 10 percent of all capacity. Now, since absolute capacity has expanded, obviously the number of cages that are privately managed on behalf of public entities has expanded as well.

A lot of people imagine that it is private prison operators that lobby for the draconian laws that keep people locked up so they can make more money. While there is no doubt in my mind that there are places in which such private prison operators do lobby for certain kinds of laws, the fact of the matter is they're parasites — and this is not to excuse them, they're totally nasty — coming in the wake of an entire criminalization project rather than being the people who make it happen. They're not the ones who make it happen.

What *do* they make happen? One of the things that has happened, especially in the area of immigrant detention, is that investment bankers — and this is separate from Corrections Corporation of America or Wackenhut or any other private prison entities — will persuade communities, especially communities in southern borderlands areas and especially in South Texas, that if they agree to build or expand their jail in their county that eventually the U.S. Marshals Service or Immigration and Customs Enforcement will put detained immigrants in them.

There are jails that have been developed that are "privately managed," but what makes them private is that they're not managed by the entity — the U.S. Marshals or ICE — that is authorized by law to take people into custody. Some of these "private prisons" are actually managed by private prison management companies, like Wackenhut and CCA. Others are managed by counties and cities; they're called private, but they're not actually private in the sense that you and I understand the term private. They are contracted with the entity that has jurisdiction to hold people against their will.

The second thing I want to say is that if we collectively could bring a halt to the private management of all cells tomorrow, including the management contracted with city and county officials, not a single person would get out of prison or jail. That would only end a certain kind of management activity. And the rooting out of Corrections Corporation of America or Wackenhut or the city of Shafter [California] from managing these facilities would not change the laws and regulations under which the people who are in the cages are held in the cages at all. So it doesn't end the problem; it just shifts it back to the public sphere.

So that's a way of leading into a mini-rant on the prison-industrial complex. Rather famously, in 1995, Mike Davis published an article in the *Nation* magazine in which he more or less coined the phrase "prison-industrial complex." It was modeled on the phrase used by Jim Austin, who's a criminologist, the "corrections-industrial complex." What both of these guys were trying to think through was whether or not the ways in which the courts and prisons and industry and the state operate in tandem, or complexly together, could be understood through the lens of the military-industrial complex. It wasn't, in my view, a cute phrase just to be cute. But what happened, in my view, is that people took up the phrase and they thought that all that . . . Austin, Mike Davis, and by extension Critical Resistance, which picked up Mike Davis's phrase, meant was: "Are private corporations calling the shots?"

If we go back to Dwight Eisenhower (or his writer), who coined the phrase "military-industrial complex," we can think about what he meant. Who all are included in that complex? What makes the "complex" complex? How is it not simply that weapons manufacturers were telling the United States Congress what to do and when to go to war? The latter is not exactly what Eisenhower was worried about when he warned against the military-industrial complex. Rather, Eisenhower — who revered war and who loved capitalism — was worried that this dyadic relationship between the Pentagon, on the one hand, which had become incredibly insulated and powerful by the end of the 1950s, and the military-industrial providers and beneficiaries, on the other hand, were going to set the stage and determine the path of *all* industrial development in the United States. That's what he was worried about. He wasn't worried about whether they were going to decide when the next war was, but rather that all of our industrial development would be shaped by the needs of perfecting the capacity to make war.

It's a slightly different emphasis, which is important for thinking about the prison-industrial complex because the complex evoked by the term "military-industrial complex" did not only include the elected and appointed officials in the Pentagon and in Washington, or the heads of corporations like McDonnell Douglas and General Electric, but also the places with military bases, all of the people who work for the military, the boosters who wanted more military installations in their communities in order to produce jobs, and the intellectuals in universities and think tanks who made plans about who should be appropriate targets for war, or the most efficient way[s] to kill the most people.

All of that is the military-industrial complex, which means to me that all of that is the prison-industrial complex. It's not only the private entrepreneurs or firms that make a profit, although they're important, but it's also the ways in which an entire path has been created around how to deal with certain problems. An entire development path has been created through the assumption that there is a perpetual enemy who must always be fought, but who can never be conquered. And that's where international militarization and domestic militarization meet — at this notion that there is the production of an enemy around which we organize everything, *everything*, not simply profit.

That said, when we think about the profit motive in prison expansion, in thinking in a detailed way through the notion of a *complex*, we are compelled to think about: What are all the ways in which people, firms, and entities — including law enforcement — are sweeping off from the top, as it were, the value that is circulating in the form of expenditures in policing, courts, and prisons? This means everyone who works in the courts. This means everyone who works in the prisons. This means every vendor who sells anything to the prisons. This means all of those outrageous costs that are heaped on top of ordinary costs for telephones, and so forth. But it also means what's happening in public education, not only the dollar trade-off, but the assumption that there is a place awaiting everyone who doesn't make it in the teach-to-the-test educational system in K-12, and for many the place is in some cage. *All of that.* It's an entire way of life that we're looking at when we think about the prison-industrial complex. And that is a lot to say to somebody who gets their interest fired up by the phrase "PIC," who thinks that the problem is private prisons or slave labor. You can't say it fast!

JL: Who has been targeted by criminalization, and how does this fit with the recent history of class and capitalism?

RWG: When I describe who all are in prison, the phrase that I always use is "modestly educated women and men in the prime of their lives." That phrase enables me — in fact, compels me — to think about: How do women and men *become* modestly educated? How is it that people in the prime of their lives who otherwise would be making, moving, growing, and caring for things instead are in cages? What has happened to the making, moving, growing, and caring for things that has changed through the participation of modestly educated women and men in those economic sectors? What did the activities and organizing of such folks become in capitalist terms? (And that's not always the same everywhere.) What is it about the regions that these folks come from that has changed, since once upon a time, without question, there was absorption into a certain labor market niche — often, but not always, a low-wage labor force — that is now unquestionably impossible?

Each of these questions enables a certain thinking about: How are these folks organized or not organized? What are potential, already existing organizations or institutions through which organizing on behalf of, or in favor of, people sucked into prison might happen? What is working against them in an organized way? And, finally, are there new organizations that can come into being? I'm a firm believer in founding new organizations, not for the organizations to become the center of our attention such that what we do is tend the organization (which is where I think a lot of people in the voluntary sector have unwittingly arrived). Rather, new organizations make for new combinations and new possibilities. I totally agree with Paulo Freire and Myles Horton that organizations are the substance of social movements.

JL: How do you explain the paradox that so many modestly educated folks are being shoved out of the labor market, while other people, many of whom are migrating across national boundaries, are finding low-paid work? And on top of it, there's been an expansion of immigrant detention.

RWG: At least part of what's happened was that when the ideological and material conditions for the intense expansion of prisons took place, union busting was at the top of all agendas connected with how to revive capitalism in the Golden State after the difficult decade of the seventies. This was a period marked by a very long economic recession, by the United States being run out of Vietnam by the triumph of the Vietnamese People's Army, by the United States going off the gold standard, and by the beginning of the shift in who set prices for oil, and what they called the "oil shock." All of that economic ferment on a global scale was met not exclusively, but in a widespread way, in the United States by a very strong focus on getting rid of unions or at least weakening them.

So we see, starting in the late seventies and early eighties, outsourcing and multiple-tier contracts for union workers who entered a firm at different times. We see the busting of the unions, which was really profound. Firms wanted to employ people who were the least organized and most difficult to organize, so that having successfully clamped down on (and, in some cases, almost obliterated) the capacity of unions, the firms wouldn't have to go through that again.

Rather than imagining that workers line up outside a factory every day and that Brown workers without documents were hired before the Black workers with documents, this was actually much more structural and was much more systemically put into effect. For example, here in Los Angeles, janitors had organized from the 1930s forward. A lot of them organized during World War II under the CIO [Congress of Industrial Organizations], and then continued to organize post–World War II. The janitorial services became eventually a niche dominated by Black men. (My grandfather was a Black man who was a janitor who organized on the East Coast, and my father was a machinist and janitor who did the same.) Black men fought and fought and fought to secure their jobs, wages, and benefits such that in 1980 janitors who were organized in Los Angeles County were making *good* money. They were making $10 an hour, which in 1980 was a lot of money — I was making $5 at the time. This meant a lot of things. It meant that they could pay for their houses, their little houses in South Central, they could let their children go to college. They didn't have to pay for it because it was free. They could allow their children to leave the household and not contribute to the household income because they had fought so hard.

It was right at the moment of success that failure kicked in systemically. Firms decided to lay off all their janitors and outsource janitorial services. They didn't hire new janitors who were undocumented people from Central America. They laid off all their janitors and then they hired Joe's Janitorial Contracting Firm to bring in new janitors. The contracting firms went and found people who were not already organized, who didn't have the local knowledge base, the local community networks, and so on that those former janitors had developed in order to organize. And they hired those whom they imagined were the least organizable people — immigrants not documented to work, women rather than men (in many cases, although not exclusively) — and those are the people who succeeded the other janitors. And they succeeded them at less than half the hourly wages. What seems to be a conflict between group one and group two, and in some ways might actually play out to be a conflict, was actually a calculated decision made on the part of firms to reduce the cost of business. And, of course, the employers were wrong about the people they hired, as I'll discuss in a minute.

Now imagine that we're looking at a Los Angeles County graph of race and gender in relation to jobs and employment, over time. You will see that as the best-waged jobs for Black men disappeared, the number of Black men going to prison shot up. Then we move across in time a little bit, and we see that as the well-waged jobs for Chicanos start to disappear, we see the number of Chicanos going to prison shoots up. And every time we see a certain labor market niche shrink, there's a sudden, secular rise — it's not just a spike; it goes up, and it keeps going up — in the number of people from that demographic category going to prison. When it comes to the question of long-distance migrants who are undocumented, we see again, as certain kinds of reorganizations in the economic landscape happen, there's a rise in the percentage of people going to prison who are undocumented.

Thinking about these issues in this way gives us some insights into the various ways to connect the need to (re)organize low-wage workers as part of the struggle against the expansion of prisons as all-purpose solutions to social problems. One meeting I went to in the nineties in which people who were organizing Justice for Janitors — the very immigrants whom firms thought were not organizable — presented what they had been doing at a meeting that included representatives of the first Sandinista government in Nicaragua. When they finished their presentation, the Sandinista representative said, "That's really great, but what happened to the people who used to have these jobs? Are you organizing with them, too?" And that was exactly the right question. Not, "Should the long-distance migrants be organizing?" Of course they should. "And should they be organizing back along the migration trail so that people who might be coming from Central America or Mexico would understand that when you get there, you've got to join the union, so as not to be exploited?" But the question was, "What about the people who are right down the street? Why are you not organizing with them as well? Because if you're not, there's something wrong with this project."

JL: How do you understand the connections between slavery and prison?

RWG: I spend a lot of time trying to think about how to take the concept of slavery, which people respond to for good reasons, and open it up to a contemporary understanding of what is going on. Thinking through Orlando Patterson, and thinking through the constituent features of slavery as being secondarily or tertiarily about uncompensated labor, and more about the construction and consolidation of a certain kind of enemy status is important.[1] What makes the enemy is what makes the enemy different from everybody else. So, while that difference might be conceived of or understood as race, which is to say "undifferentiated difference," Orlando Patterson's thinking can help us ask: What is it about people who have been criminalized that keeps them permanently, rather than temporarily (during an unfortunate period in their lives), in this enemy status?

The way that Patterson puts it in describing enemies, and the distinction between those who become enslaved who are from within the polity and those who become enslaved as a result of war with an external force, is: "One fell because they were enemy. The other became the enemy because they had fallen." How can we think about this nexus between those who are "the enemy," that is, those who immigrate to the United States without authorization, and those who become the enemy because, although legally in the United States, they are criminalized?

Both groups being criminalized come to share certain features, and those constitutive elements of slavery have to do with alienation from their families and communities, and violent domination, which is to say, they are held against their will and made to do certain things that they otherwise wouldn't do. It's coercive, not consensual, force. And the third is general dishonor; who you are and what you are does not change because this singular category of criminal, which has been ascribed to you, becomes *the* category that defines everything about you in terms of the social order in which this coercion takes place. This doesn't mean that people who have been criminalized or enslaved themselves become this one thing to themselves; Du Bois's concept of double-consciousness takes care of that analytical error for us.²

That said, if we start to think about all of the people who are caught up in this category as blending into a new category of person—a new category, thinking through the processes of racialization—then one of the things that we might be able to do is to echo what a former white supremacist, who is a prisoner, said in the wake of an uprising in which white supremacist prisoners organized with Black supremacist prisoners and Brown supremacist prisoners: "Well, maybe what we are is the prison race." This is endlessly interesting for me to think about and to try to get people to connect to.

JL: How do you think about organizing different groups of people together?

RWG: When I think about organizing, I ask myself: What would people actually do? Because organizing is constrained by recognition, and recognition is not only a matter of whether some people recognize other people who might become part of an organization as in some way similar to themselves, but also the recognition that this is something we *can* do. We *can* fight this, or we *can* protest that, or we *can* reorganize, whatever it is. As we all like to say, "You have to start where people are at." But as Stuart Hall reminds us, where people are at is more complicated than perhaps it might seem at first blush.

For example, people organize against three strikes. What can happen that opens up that organizing focus to the multiple dimensions of the all-purpose use of prisons, even if the fight in the short term is to reform a law, which would still stand as a law? How can such organizing open up people to the consciousness of the *impossibility* for such a reform to be durable as long as that kind of law can also endure? How, in other words, might organizing around a reform issue do significant work in building political consciousness?

I worked for many years with Families to Amend California's Three Strikes (FACTS), and I was around when it started. Another organization, Mothers Reclaiming Our Children, brought FACTS into being. The MROC constantly asked itself: "What can we do, what can we do, what can we do?" And the women from Mothers Reclaiming Our Children decided to kick off FACTS because three strikes seemed the most blatant example of the whole set of laws and practices that was sweeping people into prison at a dizzying rate.

What we talked about at first was getting rid of that whole law because people completely understood what that law was really doing, which was taking modestly educated women and men in the prime of their lives, documented or not, and putting them into prisons for the rest of their lives. Everyone understood that, and having debated the perceived extent and purpose of the law, everyone understood that it was happening to all different kinds of people, but the high-profile way in which it was happening at the time to Black people made the struggle against the law understandable, acceptable, and justifiable to a whole political community, including Black people. The group developed a keen recognition of how anti-Black racism was doing the work of justifying mass incarceration and life terms and so on.

As FACTS transitioned from an idea for an organization into an organization for itself, people in the organization decided they would fight for an amendment, which would not completely blow up the law, but they were trying constantly to open up the law and make it vulnerable. What struck me was that there were people in that organization who were fighting for an amendment even though their loved ones in prison would not get out were the amendment to pass. That blew me away. These people were fighting just as hard as people whose loved ones would get out if the amendment were passed.

That's an example to me of people coming to the consciousness of how the complex works and therefore the complexity of arrangements that people would have to get themselves into to fight it out. People — and these are people who are themselves modestly educated women and men in the prime of their lives, or elderly people — fighting for this amendment were fighting in a sense for a "non-reformist reform," as André Gorz would have it, even though they knew that they ran the risk of just consolidating the rest of the law. They knew that, but were willing to take that risk. That's an example of people who might not call themselves abolitionists having an abolitionist agenda.

Another example is the Central California Environmental Justice Network, which is composed mostly of EJ communities in the vast San Joaquin Valley struggling around issues of air quality and water quality. When we in the California Prison Moratorium Project (CPMP) went to the conference that led to the formation of the organization, we asked for some time to be on their agenda to explain why we thought that prisons fit the criteria by which the network was organizing itself, and therefore that CPMP would like to be part of any organizations that came out of the conference. They gave us twenty minutes to make our pitch, and at the end of twenty minutes everyone was convinced. They didn't have to think hard about it. People in urban areas of CPMP or [in] Critical Resistance said, "They gotta be crazy!" We went out to rural California, and they said, "Oh, yeah. We see what you're saying." So we could talk about both the ways in which prisons are cities, and therefore their environmental footprint is huge, and we could talk about how part of the life-threatening conditions for people in rural California has to do with the ramping up of policing and criminalization there. Everyone saw that. It wasn't rocket science, just a little harder.

Therefore, the California Prison Moratorium Project, which doesn't have the word "abolition" in its mission statement, could join forces with grassroots environmental justice organizations in the Central Valley in order to fight against prison expansion. And to fight against prison expansion, we would, by joining forces, also have to fight on behalf of clean water and adequate schools, and against pesticide drift, toxic incinerators, all of that stuff. This raised anti-prison organizing in that region to a true abolitionist agenda, which is fighting for the right of people who work in the Central Valley to have good health and secure working conditions and not be subject to toxicity, in spite of the fact that so many of the workers in the valley are not documented workers.

JL: This brings us to the specific connections that you see between abolitionist organizing and migrant justice organizing.

RWG: Abolitionists should be thinking about what kinds of social practices and political and economic configurations make it possible for us to know that we finally ended the capacity for some of us to designate others of us as enemies in the way that Orlando Patterson so eloquently describes slavery as social death. In other words, if abolitionists are, first and foremost, committed to the possibility of full and rich lives for everybody, then that would mean that all kinds of distinctions and categorizations that divide us — innocent/guilty; documented/not; Black, white, Brown; citizen/not-citizen — would have to yield in favor of other things, like the right to water, the right to air, the right to the countryside, the right to the city, whatever these rights are. Of course, then, we have to ask ourselves: What is the substance of rights? What is a right anyway? Is it a thing, or is it a practice? If a right is a practice rather than a thing, then that requires that these little instances of social organization in which people work on behalf of themselves and others with a purpose in mind, rather than a short-term interest that can be met through a little bit of lawmaking or other haggling, changes the entire landscape of how we live.

To me, abolition is utopian in the sense that it's looking forward to a world in which prisons are not necessary because not only are the political-economic motives behind mass incarceration gone, but also the instances in which people might harm each other are minimized because the causes for that harm (setting aside, for the moment, psychopaths) are minimized as well. In that sense, I think the greatest abolitionist organization that exists in the United States today, with all due respect to my beloved brothers and sisters in Critical Resistance, is the Harm Reduction Coalition. That's an abolitionist organization no matter what the people who do that work think of the word "abolition."

And that's where I'm at today. If we're not organizing between the very groups who imagine they have some "structural antagonism," we're never going to win. As a result, to go back to something I was saying earlier, the extent to which people try to differentiate between those who are convicted of crimes and sent to prison, those who are guilty, compared to people who aren't documented to work, but only showed up to work as noncriminals is a *big* mistake. One, if the law has been set that crossing the border is a criminal act, you are a criminal. Two, that's not the issue. The issue is: Let's get everybody who's been criminalized together and figure out how we can undo this state of affairs.

JL: So ending the possibility of defining other people as enemies comes back to not just an analogy with the military-industrial complex, but the PIC's connections with the MIC.

RWG: Yes, exactly. Industrialized punishment and industrialized killing are following the same trajectories. The motives, the organizational strategies, in the United States, the fiscal and bureaucratic capacities, are all modeled on each other. The great irony is that, as Greg Hooks so brilliantly showed, the whole structure, the fiscal and bureaucratic capacities and the organization of the Pentagon coming out of World War II were modeled on the fiscal and bureaucratic structures that were designed, and never fully operationalized, for social and economic and cultural programs in response to the Great Depression.[3] They were formations organized for capitalism to save capitalism from capitalism, and were sucked into the War Department and then emerged as the Pentagon and the warfare state. And then sucked into prisons and policing, and emerged as the carceral state. Our job is to look at how capitalism saves capitalism from capitalism and figure out other directions—which does not mean help in saving capitalism from saving capitalism from capitalism, but to say, "Okay, there's something vulnerable here, obviously, because look at what changed. Let's get busy."

NOTES

1. Patterson, *Slavery and Social Death*.
2. Du Bois, *The Souls of Black Folk*.
3. Hooks, *Forging the Military-Industrial Complex*.

BIBLIOGRAPHY

Du Bois, W. E. B. *The Souls of Black Folk*. 1903. Reprint, New York: St. Martin's, 1997.
Hooks, Gregory M. *Forging the Military-Industrial Complex: World War II's Battle of the Potomac*. Champaign: University of Illinois Press, 1991.
Patterson, Orlando. *Slavery and Social Death: A Comparative Study*. Cambridge, Mass.: Harvard University Press, 1985.

Part II

Global Crisis, National Struggles
The Work of Policing the Nation around the World

This part focuses on how border enforcement, imprisonment, and criminalization are fundamental to nation-state-building projects around the world. The contributors analyze these processes in a number of different places, but also draw attention to the ways in which policing technologies and practices are shared among states internationally. This part of the book is explicitly concerned with the role of nationalism and state sovereignty in forging exclusionary and discriminatory migration and citizenship policies.

The specific case studies and regional foci on Australia and the Pacific, the European Union and northern Africa, and the Americas provide a comparative lens to see the continuities among different projects of nation-state building and colonial conquest. While such policing aims to protect the myth or ideology of a coherent, singular, and territorially bounded national citizenry, the authors articulate the many ways in which states' sovereignty exceeds their territorial boundaries through offshore interdiction, detention, and international policing efforts.

To justify violent exclusion and regulation, nation-states frequently invoke the unique or exceptional circumstances they face. However, such nationalist claims belie the transnational continuities that this part of the book makes clear. Such continuities become especially clear in the manner in which nation-states continually draw upon the rhetoric of terrorism as justification for increased spending on border security. As the "war on terror" and the "war on drugs" continue across the globe, nation-states' individual and collective fortification and securitization of borders create a system of global apartheid. This system furthers global inequalities and the conditions for still more "exceptional" responses.

The authors show how such efforts fail to create security for communities that are targeted and disrupted through immigration and drug raids, communities whose lands are occupied and partitioned, or for people migrating in search of work or safety. They highlight the various roles that activists, grassroots organizations, and researchers play in challenging these deadly practices of isolation and suppression. They also place challenging settler colonialism and the nation-state at the center of social justice struggles.

The Texas-Mexico Border Wall and Ndé Memory

Confronting Genocide and State Criminality, beyond the Guise of "Impunity"

MARGO TAMEZ

> The imagination of genocide begins with a body count. Numbers are crucial in determining whether or not a group was killed "in whole or in part" to justify the term genocide. Yet this visceral reaction is only the beginning. . . . genocide does not end when the killing stops, but . . . it may echo in efforts at social mourning, repair, and reconciliation. Finally, genocide does not occur in a vacuum, but is embedded in an ambivalent international community that is quick to condemn mass killings but slow to mobilize into action.
> — ANTONIUS C. G. M. ROBBEN, "Epilogue: The Imagination of Genocide"

INTRODUCTION: SHI NDÉ — I AM OF/FROM THE PEOPLE

Ha'shi? Shi Kónitsąąhįį dáʼáášį gokíyaa, gòłgàʼ Gònìcéi. I am Ndé from there, our homeland, along the Big Water, also known as the Rio Bravo/Rio Grande. I was born from Gochish (Lightning People), Gònìcéindé (Big Water People), Suma Ndé (Red Mud Painted People), Cúelcahén (Tall Grass People), and Cìšįįhííndé (Black Rock People). In this chapter, I use "Ndé Lipan Apache" and "Lipan Apache" interchangeably. Since the mid- to late eighteenth century, Ndé have interrelated in kinship, marriage, reciprocity, ceremony, governance, cosmology, justice, and land-based knowledge systems with Tlaxcaltecas, Nahuas, Coahuilas, Kickapoo, Jumano Apaches, and Mescalero Apaches. Interexchange and alliance building through inclusive kinship relations — rural to urban — are persistent features of Ndé forms of cultural resilience and adaptation, responses to ongoing threats to indigenous worldviews and rights.

I situate the Texas-Mexico border wall within Ndé oral history and narratives of genocide, colonization, carceral containment systems, and land-based struggles as an act of reclaiming the Ndé homeland, Kónitsąąhįį gokíyaa. This chapter challenges the state's normative sovereignty and the uncritical acceptance of zones of impunity, such as the U.S. "constitution-free zone" identified by the American Civil Liberties Union.[1]

It is time for a radical rethinking of indigenous anticolonial movements along and traversing U.S. borders as a key nexus where indigenous revolutionary consciousness, resistances to state violence, and reclamations of indigenous rights are reshaping the governance of lands, territories, and communities. On and across the Texas-Mexico border, Ndé people's memories of genocide point to sites where indigenous knowledge challenges Texas, the United States, and the Texas-Mexico border wall as constructions of "the state of exception, and the state of siege."[2]

Situating the border wall within the Ndé genocide and social memory of the prison offers a counterhistory of indigenous narrative memory locked up in bodies, photographs, earth, and containment. This witnessing shatters the normative conception of European American history as predetermined, compartmentalized periods where indigenous peoples in the Texas-Mexico border region are merely shadows, dehumanized and dismembered figures.

I build upon Achille Mbembe's analysis of necropolitics, and indigenize it to Ndé constructions of history wherein the wall is an architecture of necropower. Necropolitics creates a "new form of sovereignty [which] is no longer the body as such, but the dead body of the 'civilian.'"[3] Necropower — wielded by the United States, Texas, corporations, and a group of elite local actors — accumulates, consolidates, and reinscribes colonial and patriarchal power both horizontally and vertically, through exploitation, bribery, manipulation, coercion, blacklisting, and threats of extreme exclusion.

I will focus on the narratives and analyses of indigenous peoples in resistance to death, what Mbembe refers to as "war machines," where "severing power imagines itself and is deployed in the interest of maximum destruction of persons and the creation of deathscapes, new and unique forms of social existence in which vast populations are subjected to conditions of life conferring upon them the status of living dead."[4] The border wall is one of these war machines.

Indigenous confrontations with settler colonialism defy the official public memory, which normalizes the Texas deathscape, the killing fields, the prisons, the internment camps, the mega-ranches, monoculture cotton and citrus fields, and oilfields. Ndé views, within enclosed and supervised spaces, continually narrate against forgetting the truth of what was witnessed, that "colonial occupation itself was a matter of seizing, delimiting, and asserting control over a physical geographical area — of writing on the ground a new set of social and spatial relations."[5]

The Ndé extended kin — who ground resistance to the border wall in a community-based, antistate alliance — bear indigenous witness in defense of a worldview connected to responsibilities and accountability. This framework demands from them a confrontation against capitalist and patriarchal normality, atrocity, gender violence, and settlers' ritual coloniality. Ndé are actors in a resurging revolutionary consciousness across the region; Ndé popular constructions (denouncements, posters, artwork, song, poetry, film) demonstrate the resilience and persistence of more than four centuries of forging alliances with Tlaxcaltecas, Nahuas, Coahuilas, Purepechas, Mescaleros, Jumanos, Kickapoos, and urban Xicanos — *all* Mexico border region indigenous peoples in extended kinships impacted by the wall. Drawing from the taproots of this history, Ndé have galvanized a multiplural indigenous reality, challenging identities imposed by state and oligarchic wardens upon indigenous peoples: "Mexicans," "Latinos," "illegals," "foreigners."

Privileging the testimonies of elders, women, and chiefly peoples, I illustrate the importance of Ndé's inherent relationship to a homeland not bounded by borders, nor based in biological "Native" authenticity, ethnicity, or race. Rather, it is bound up in a worldview of kinship, remembrance, and the recovery of mother tongues, first foods and water governance, and gender complementarity in self-governance. Demanding an interrogation of state criminality relative to the border wall has been at the front of indigenous women's call for shared participation in decision making, critical ethics, and revitalizing indigenous protocols and principles based in respect and regard for elders and indigenous knowledge systems. As witnessed in the creation of women-led lawsuits against the government, indigenous women's concepts of self-governance — founded in reclaiming and recovering matrilineal, matrilocal, and matrifocal knowledge systems — critique the patriarchal violence aligned with coloniality. Ndé elders', women's, extended families' and chiefly peoples' knowledge systems, in conversation with each other, have historically been a resource shaping indigenous peoples' analyses and interrogations of genocide and state crimes.

Since 2006, I have been working alongside Ndé people in the recovery of memories, stories, and documents for the express purpose of supporting self-determination and rights recovery. Here, I provide remembered

FIGURE 1. Eloisa García Tamez (Gochish ndédeeshch'ił Ndé, Lightning Clan), El Calaboz Ranchería, 2009. Photo by Jeff Gaines Wilson.

and recovered Ndé clan and kinship knowledges from Kónitsąąhįį dá'áásį gokíyaa — the Ndé customary territory encompassing over 6.5 million acres in the Texas-Mexico binational region. These are fragments from a much larger project by, with, for, and alongside indigenous peoples, involving mapping and digitizing Ndé experiences prior to and after genocide and state criminality.[6]

From the Ndé methods approach, the U.S. border wall and its attendant capitalist, development, and destructive intent are situated within Ndé memory and story.[7] This perspective centers indigenous agency prior to and enduring *beyond* the wall. I borrow Patrick Wolfe's statement on settler colonialism, which is useful for understanding the European American occupation of indigenous time, place, and space. Thus, decolonizing the construct of European American history is understanding the indigenous viewpoint: "invasion is structure not an event."[8]

For generations, indigenous decolonialist challenges and defenses were enacted through ritualized remembering, memorializing, and returning. Reclaiming indigeneity as a positive — as a struggle to protect indigenous self-governance in a multi-gender value system and within a constellation of gendered worldviews of Kónitsąąhįį dá'áásį gokíyaa — is central to rethinking

FIGURE 2. Elizabeth García (Nahua-Mexica), El Calaboz Ranchería, 2009. Photo from the collection of Eloisa García Tamez.

indigenous peoples' genocidal trauma, and its reoccurrences. Recovering is inevitably interwoven with remembering and reenvisioning ourselves as the landowners of our customary lands, and with breaking the chains of anthropological objectification. It is within the indigenous conception of temporal, spiritual, psychic, and physical continuums of endurance and adaptation that confrontations, refusal, dissidence, and resistance to replacement and elimination get enacted.

WAR RESPATIALIZED, CONTAINMENT REMEMBERED, AND AMERICANIZATION AS DEATHSCAPE

To experience the community lands in the current period is to be subjected to peering through the narrow gaps between heavy, thick, steel bars. Eloisa García Tamez and elders, women, youth, and workers from Brownsville, El Calaboz, El Ranchito, La Encantada, La Paloma, Las Milpas, Los Indios, and Las Rusias — a whole kinship and ecological knowledge system — are experiencing life radically reduced, as people are prevented access to movement on their own lands, cemeteries, cornfields, and the pathways between residences. Concerted efforts to challenge the impunity of U.S. deathscapes and U.S. sovereign immunity in one of the poorest counties in the United States, Cameron County, rather than being addressed through "aid," are instead answered with war:

> i.e.: a technology-saturated "roof" of militarized airspace,
> is a resistance against the enclosure, surrounded
> by satellites, space debris plummeting to Earth
> zapped
> by NASA Space Engineers in Florida
> night Sky is no longer shell in blue-black corn mosaic,
> but steel-colored ceiling
> spotted with stadium lights positioned arbitrarily,
> where Border Patrol agents stalk indigenous women
> refusing sentence in shadows of wall
> aiming cell phones at agents
> government purchased soldiers of war
> and the colonized perform ritual control
> community wardens,
> harvested for payroll and benefits,
> under cover uniform surveilling an Elder rebel refuser
> infrared radar, watch towers, drones, and cyber fusion centers
> pieces of colonizer's status,
> mimicking master's crackdowns, spearheading individual roles
>   in his "Virtual Border Neighborhood Watch Program,"
> "border radio interoperability,"
> "Texas Data Exchange" programs,
> yanked to the Elder's scent by "K-9 units."[9]

"This is an occupation" and "We're in the open-air prison now" were two frequently repeated statements made by Ndé elders, women, youth, and men after October 20, 2009, when the United States condemned community lands with armed force. Elders had refused the government's taking of the lands through other methods. From their views, sovereignty, steel, concrete, transnational corporations, the rhetoric of "terrorism" and "aliens," U.S. Army Corps bulldozers, low-wage labor, and dispossession all symbolized the history of American white supremacy, brutality, and expropriation in the region. The wall currently bifurcates community lands. This leaves elders, women, men, children, and workers cut off from family-held and individually held lands, which have a complex legal history bound up in Spanish crown title ("land grants"), treaties (also known as "constructive mechanisms"), and Aboriginal title (indigenous proprietary title predating and still existing *beneath* European American fee

FIGURE 3. The border wall in the middle of residential and subsistence pasture areas, El Calaboz Ranchería, Cameron County, Texas, 2011. Photo by Margo Tamez.

simple and scrip). From indigenous views, crown title, Aboriginal title, and treaties are not extinguishable by the United States.[10]

"Americanizing" Texas was contingent upon the death, or violent removal, or subjugation of surviving indigenous peoples. Texas deathscapes were birthed through the giveaway of so-called free lands through a "head right" system, "allowing anyone residing in the state prior to March 1, 1836, to receive 4,605 acres free."[11] This was only one of numerous illegal measures in the Anglicization of Texas, and it has been followed by many waves of destruction. Between 1845 and 1860, roughly six hundred thousand people had settled in Texas and were growing cotton. This came about through heavily militarized zones containing indigenous resistance, "cleansings," and the establishment of U.S. military bases across Texas.

In 1938, Ndé captive of war Augustina Zuazua challenged the American anthropologist Harry Hoijer. She deflected his attempts to enclose her narrative histories within the prison camp of the American military anthropological gaze. She would not be corralled into his notebook, in which he chronicled the "tribes" of the U.S. Southwest and peoples of "the past": "ni'ąą sháhanát'ahí biyaayá kónitsąą gokíyaa kįgołgah. 'akaa konitsąą gokiyaaná. 'áshį nóóshch'eshį naagókáh (Over there the east to it the Lipan their country [was] Many Houses. Right there the Lipan [was] their country, it is said. And to this way they went across)."[12] Confronting Hoijer with a more profound reality—"konitsąą gokiyaaná"—this Ndé elder simultaneously challenged Americans as fraud "sovereigns."

Indigenous memory structures perceptions of enclosure and taking. Ndé survivors of killing fields remember the 1873 Remolino massacre; the subsequent abduction of Ndé massacre-survivor children by U.S. Army employees and their internment in U.S. industrial boarding schools; and the erasure of Ndé children's and massacre survivors' indigenous cultural and political identity by Mexico, Texas, and the United States at the beginning of the twentieth century. Ndé remember the 1873–1930 forced separation of Ndé peoples into Mexico, California, New Mexico, and Texas; the 1903 death marches from Mexico to New Mexico; the subsequent escapes, diasporas, seclusions, isolations, starvations, and undergrounding of identity; the 1915–1916 Cameron County killing fields; the 1916 "blueprint" by South Texas oligarchic, white, ranching elites to construct concentration camps in Cameron County; and the 1919 executions of indigenous rebel leaders in El Ranchito and El Calaboz. And they remember the 1938 El Caraboz women's rebel movement against the state's and corporations' land and water grabs; the 1954 El Calaboz antisegregation rebel movement; and the backlash by elites, who continue to target lands and peoples along the Texas-Mexico border with low-intensity conflict measures into the post-NAFTA terrorizing present.[13]

In 2009, many witnesses along the last seventy miles of the border wall saw firsthand how the United States cleared and excavated the earth through their residential places. The bulldozing destroyed mature biodiversity in a riparian zone known worldwide as one of the last diverse regions in the hemisphere. Digging eight to ten feet into the earth, the government filled deep trenches with cement, making a footer for the wall. Thousands of cubic feet of earth were dumped to the side. It was only a matter of time before the ancestral presence surfaced: shards and other objects accumulated from intense human activity over generations (undoubtedly deemed "trash," "waste," "dirt," or perhaps even "nothing" by the U.S. bulldozer operators). These occupied spaces, these walls, penetrate women's and elders' intimate living spaces, culturally significant sacred lands, and traditional subsistence areas.[14]

These clearances offer an eerie, troubling view of Ndé-settler and Ndé-state relationships, past and present. After many years of drought, the rains of June 2011 exposed objects emerging out of the large, eroding heaps created by the

FIGURE 4. Materials rescued from earthen heaps, El Caboz Ranchería, 2011. Photo by Margo Tamez.

wall construction. On close study, I soon realized that these artifact fragments belonged to our ancestor generations, who lived here and experienced a bare existence, persecution, excessive discrimination, and killing fields in the 1875–1919 period (documented extensively in my dissertation). Well aware that my every move by the wall was under constant surveillance by drive-by U.S. agents and by agents flying above me in helicopters and drones, I gathered what I could. I shared this information with elders, our traditional medicine people, and our community legal partners.

I struggle to articulate what confronts the Ndé elders and community members at this moment. We see what faces us inside the many heaps of earth along the wall in the lower Rio Grande valley. What will the fragments of daily life of our ancestors who suffered during former U.S. occupations say? We are confronted by the narrative continuum which will not be silenced. Chief Daniel Castro Romero Jr. stated, "When this happened, before, the Anglos came in many waves, and the ancestors had to leave our northern homeland, rather than face harm and destruction by white settlers and the armies. We are here because they protected the women, elders, and children. It wasn't just the U.S. Army, but many branches of armies, like roving gangs, professional killers,

Rangers, and killers that some people just hired privately . . . [who were] wanting the lands cleared."[15]

IMPUNITY AND TYRANNICAL GOVERNANCE

The material, structural, and legal containments and enclosures which maintain indigenous peoples like the Ndé in a political limbo in Texas and along the Texas-Mexico border region can be seen in Ndé confrontations of the so-called impunity of state sovereignty. The guise of impunity is a tactical move to avoid discovery, evidence, unmasking. State criminality and the fiction of legal impunity mask a troubling concept — sovereign immunity. Denise Gilman, a legal scholar who spearheaded the University of Texas School of Law's human rights investigation into the Texas-Mexico border wall, has challenged sovereign immunity as a legal "bluff," or, put another way, a fiction. Gilman argues:

> International human rights law seeks to protect individuals against abuse by governments. The United States system, through the operation of broad sovereign immunity doctrines, instead protects the government against individuals who lay claim to redress for abuses they have suffered. . . . while it is theoretically possible to overcome governmental immunity to many cases by suing individual officials, qualified immunity also constitutes a major impediment for victims seeking to obtain a remedy for violations of their rights. The gap between right and remedy is real and severe.[16]

Indeed, this "gap" has had serious consequences for those historically constructed as racialized Others ("Apaches," "Mexicans," "illegals," border wall "refusers"). For example, Esequiel Hernández was a Jumano-Apache youth, labeled "Mexican," "Hispanic," and "ethnic Mexican," who was murdered upriver from El Caloboz in May 1997. Hernández's death is often considered a sign of the modern U.S. militarization of the U.S.-Mexico border. Esequiel, a teenage goat herder, was murdered by a U.S. Marine under the direct orders of Joint Task Force 6, which authorized an operation in Esequiel's home village. The reality of snipers burrowed near the intimate living spaces of families, in a remote West Texas border community, and that the U.S. Border Patrol was aware of this operation, was a flashpoint for movement among people who were familiar with U.S. methods in Nicaragua, El Salvador, Honduras, and Guatemala. The naturalization of low-intensity conflict and militarization in a remote community on the Texas border became a subject of great debate, concern, and activism among many people. But, after years of struggling to open up new inquiries, community voices have been muted by government rhetoric about sovereign immunity and by the palpable fear of community members whose lives are at risk for challenging the state and exposing a conspiracy. There has been a monetary payoff to the loved ones of the deceased. Case closed.[17]

Esequiel Hernández's death is also part of a longer history of killing fields. The massacre of Remolino, which occurred on the Texas-Mexico border, is forever etched in the social memory of Ndé and related indigenous peoples with whom they share a territory — and with whom they share historical trauma and experiences of U.S. and Texas criminality. On May 18, 1873, U.S. colonel Ranald S. Mackenzie led four hundred soldiers to destroy Lipan Apache peoples in the customary land near Remolino, Coahuila, Mexico. The exact number of survivors is still unknown due to the level of undergrounding which occurred to protect the ones who escaped. Today, in the process of recovering indigenous community histories in the shadow of the border wall, it is being revealed that many Lipans dispersed to South Texas, Coahuila, and Tamaulipas, while many were driven into hiding and absorbed as "Mexican American" laborers. Some were captured and taken into U.S. prisons and internment camps ("reservations"). Some captured children were separated from their parents and contracted out to U.S. white families for domestic labor, while others were forced into the Carlisle Indian Industrial School.[18]

In 1915–1919, in Cameron County on the Texas-Mexico border, it is conservatively estimated that over five thousand people were destroyed (dismembered, mutilated, lynched, burned, shot, hacked, dragged) in waves of white violence directed against indigenous peoples and rebel leaders. The boom days of industrial agriculture, including cotton and citrus farming, ushered in industrial-scale removals and the overthrow of the indigenous primary governing institution — the extended family.[19]

In 1919 at La Encantada and El Calaboz on the Texas-Mexico border, a group of Anglo males entered the rancherías, located the men in traditional jacals (huts, wikiups), and murdered them. This was a massacre of all-male victims by all-male killers. The executed men were all family heads, brothers, and cousins of the Esparza (de Moctezuma) family, from a large extended kinship network of rancherías in crown land grants on both sides of the Rio Grande. One survivor, Nicolás Villarreal Esparza, escaped with a bullet wound to his leg. However, he was later found hanging from a tree.

REIMAGINING TEXAS: CRITICAL INDIGENOUS GENOCIDE

Customary Ndé lands have been bifurcated by what Chief Daniel Castro Romero Jr. refers to as "a line of death," evoking the still grim reality that for

FIGURE 5. El Calaboz Gathering on Knowledge, Lands, Territories, and Human Rights, June 24–26, 2011. Elder Richard Gonzalez (right), Chief Daniel Castro Romero Jr. (left), and soundman Gino DiStefano (center) discuss impacts of the border wall on Ndé peoples. Photo by Erik Tamez Hrabovsky.

Ndé, the Texas border was established through and by the structures and institutions of race and ethnicity, and Ndé have been persecuted by Mexico, Texas, and the United States.[20] According to Eloisa García Tamez, her father, José Emilio Cavazos García, described the border as "a *political* line, *not* a cultural line." Following in his footsteps, Tamez learned to challenge the line and confront those who demanded that she assimilate to the regulations and management of the state's fictive histories of the "Native."[21]

One lesson of the border wall — which indigenous rights defenders are learning daily — is that American genocide returns, comes back for more, and forces indigenous peoples along the border to live a bare existence. Our elders are forced to witness the desecration of our sacred grounds, the memory of our ancestors, and our culture, and to deal with the brutal process involved in being forced to exhume fragments from the current genocide (the wall) and the heaps of earth where a whole new confrontation is beginning.

I have been struck by my discovery of these excavation heaps and their contents, the ongoing disregard for elder rights defenders, and the troubling adaptations to the wall in the Texas-Mexico region. I am against forgetting. Yet, I am confronted by silences among some people *along the wall*. Exhuming the loss of their everyday intimate physical spaces, silence spreads like illness; people adapt to the treadmill; outrage is repressed.

The aim of this chapter has been to enact indigenous rights by speaking with, for, and alongside indigenous peoples against what Mbembe calls the "permanent spatial arrangement that remains continually outside the normal state law."[22] The Ndé prison camp, the internment configuration normalized, was firmly challenged between 2007 and 2009 by Eloisa García Tamez et al. But why was she the *only* indigenous person along the entire U.S.-Mexico border to take up formal legal actions of defiance against the United States? This question, relative to Native American co-optation along the wall, deserves sustained engagement. Ndé challenges to the state's use of sovereignty to dispossess and to contain engage in what Speed and Reyes call "a more direct confrontation with the logic of the State, and a more direct engagement with the law as an aspect of it, [which] is not only desirable, but necessary."[23] Ndé resilience and revolutionary consciousness, before and after the border wall, demand new analytical tools engaging indigenous peoples' self-determination and autonomy movements.

In this chapter, I focused on three interlocking concepts: indigenized situating of the border wall within Ndé oral history, genocide and criminality in settler South Texas, and normalization of carceral containment in South Texas's industrial-scape. Elevated here as protest and as a denouncement against the state, the "generalized instrumentalization of human existence and the material destruction of human bodies and populations" are occurring in Texas as a legacy, where the wall works to "uphol[d] the work of death" in the lives of indigenous peoples along the Texas-Mexico border.[24] The Ndé community's demands, as articulated by the elders, are these: the dismantling of the wall, the return of all lands, an official apology from the Obama government, and a truth commission to call for the trial of George W. Bush and Michael Chertoff for mass human rights violations.[25]

The prison complex of South Texas, open-air containment warehouses designed in parallel with the extermination of Ndé and the industrialization of cattle production and slaughter, was always designed for the industrialization of death on a mass scale. Refuting Ndé defiance against the wall, based in indigeneity and our inherent rights to land and territories, the state masks the fictive basis of its claim to sovereignty — the doctrine of "discovery," the

European legal rationale giving Europeans so-called rights to steal lands from indigenous peoples. The wall, as a carceral architecture of containment, produces slow deaths and deaths nationalized as nothing more than taking life from nonsubjects. However, Ndé and related peoples in the impacted communities have been existing in a space beyond, where genocide and bureaucracy are performed by wage-earning functionaries and high-paid technocrats in Washington, D.C., Austin, and Mexico City, deploying decisions by cell phones. This has no currency, no legitimacy, in indigenous collective consensus building, and is a denial that the indigenous Other on the Texas-Mexico border is recuperating memory, reclaiming a community social memory, and counternarrating the carceral worldview.[26]

A product of force, the wall has catalyzed the excavation and eruption of repressed memories, artifacts, and the flashpoints of killing fields and carceral systems incising indigenous peoples' shadowy existence in Texas for two centuries. I propose an ongoing engagement with Texas indigenous killing fields, and the creation of transformative legal genealogies and cartographies of indigenous memory. These will reveal the rupture points where we must confront how, by whom, and from whom lands were taken, most recently by U.S. DHS agents between August 2007 and October 2009. We are confronted by the suffering of deeply harmed and managed peoples still residing in and defending marginalized colonias, ranchitos, rancherías, and barrios along the Texas-Mexico border.

Ndé memory ruptures the projects of the deathscape and the prison. To the Ndé, working in alliances to confront the violent cartographies unfolding along the wall links Texas to the hemisphere and to global resistances. National discourses targeting indigenous and multiply raced and minoritized peoples as foreign Others have engendered a solidarity movement of counter-occupations foregrounding peace and consensus to address indigenous peoples' principles and protocols in the new, emerging Indigecas in the Americas. A direct confrontation of the state's brutality and negation of indigenous peoples on the Texas-Mexico border will make this the birthplace for transformative redress and restitution in Kónitsąąhįį gokíyaa, Lipan country.

NOTES

Special thanks to Eloisa García Tamez and Chief Daniel Castro Romero Jr. for interviews, oral history transmission, photographs, genealogies, letters, court records, land studies, historical, anthropological, and archaeological cultural analyses, and critical reflections. A special thanks to the readers who offered invaluable feedback. The author acknowledges and bears responsibility for any errors or omissions.

1. American Civil Liberties Union, "Are You Living in a Constitution Free Zone?"
2. Mbembe, "Necropolitics," 16.
3. Hoeller and Mbembe, "Interview with Achille Mbembe."
4. Ibid.
5. Mbembe, "Necropolitics," 25.
6. See Tamez, "Nádasi'né' nde."
7. Due to limitations of space, it is not possible to provide here the full relevant history, context, and policy analysis of the U.S. border wall and its impacts on indigenous peoples. For analysis related to the Texas-Mexico border wall, see Gilman et al., "Obstructing Human Rights"; Gilman, "Seeking Breaches in the Wall"; Miller, "How Property Rights Are Affected by the Texas-Mexico Border Fence"; Sancho, "Environmental Concerns Created by Current United States Border Policy"; Eagle Woman, "The Eagle and the Condor of the Western Hemisphere."
8. Wolfe, *Settler Colonialism and the Transformation of Anthropology*, 163.
9. Tamez, "Decolonize U.S. Brdr Prznz: #4."
10. On Aboriginal title, see Langton, "Ancient Jurisdictions."
11. Anderson, *Conquest of Texas*, 213.
12. Hoijer, "History and Customs of the Lipan, as told by Augustina Zuazua," 25. Augustina Zuazua, a Gònìcéindé, or "Lipan" woman, was a U.S. war prisoner, who along with "nineteen Lipan Apaches" was forcibly removed from Mexico to a U.S. internment camp ("reservation") in 1903 or 1905. See also Webster, "Lipan Apache Placenames of Augustina Zuazua."
13. Eloisa García Tamez and Daniel Castro Romero Jr., interviews with author. See also Tamez, "Nádasi'né' nde," 507.
14. Tamez, "Report."
15. Daniel Castro Romero Jr., interview with author, December 15, 2008.
16. Gilman, "Calling the United States' Bluff," 5.
17. See Nevins, "Death as a Way of Life"; Serafino, "Congressional Research Service Report 98-767"; WikiLeaks, document release, October 25, 2011.
18. Daniel Castro Romero Jr., oral history, June 25, 2011, El Caloboz Ranchería.
19. See Tamez, "Nádasi'né' nde."
20. Daniel Castro Romero Jr., interview with author, June 26, 2011.
21. José Emilio Cavazos García, oral history spoken to Eloisa García Tamez; transmitted to the author in history lessons.
22. Mbembe, "Necropolitics."
23. Speed and Reyes, "In Our Own Defense."
24. Mbembe, "Necropolitics," 14.
25. Tamez, "Mandate."
26. Ibid., 23.

BIBLIOGRAPHY

American Civil Liberties Union. "Are You Living in a Constitution Free Zone?" Last modified December 15, 2006. http://www.aclu.org/national-security_technology-and-liberty/are-you-living-constitution-free-zone.

Anderson, Gary Clayton. *The Conquest of Texas: Ethnic Cleansing in the Promised Land, 1820–1875*. Norman: University of Oklahoma Press, 2005.

Eagle Woman, Angelique. "The Eagle and the Condor of the Western Hemisphere.: Application of International Indigenous Principles to Halt the United States Border Wall." *Idaho Law Review* 45, no. 3 (2009): 1–18.

Gilman, Denise. "Calling the United States' Bluff: How Sovereign Immunity Undermines the United States' Claim to an Effective Domestic Human Rights System." Bepress Legal series, paper no. 1528 (2006).

———. "Seeking Breaches in the Wall: An International Human Rights Law Challenge to the Texas-Mexico Border Wall." *Texas International Law Journal* 46 (2011): 257–93.

Gilman, Denise, et al. "Obstructing Human Rights: The Texas-Mexico Border Wall." Working Group Briefing Papers on Human Rights Impact, University of Texas, School of Law. Last modified June 2008. http://www.utexas.edu/law/centers/humanrights/borderwall/analysis/briefing-papers.html.

Hoeller, Christian, and Achille Mbembe. "Interview with Achille Mbembe." [n.d.]. http://www.utexas.edu/conferences/africa/ads/1528.html.

Hoijer, Harry. "The History and Customs of the Lipan, as Told by Augustina Zuazua." *Linguistics* 161, no. 7 (1975): 5–37.

Langton, Marcia. "Ancient Jurisdictions: Aboriginal Polities and Sovereignty." Keynote address at the Indigenous Governance Conference, Canberra, Australia, April 3–5, 2002.

Mbembe, Achille. "Necropolitics." *Public Culture* 15, no. 1 (2003): 11–40.

Miller, Nicole. "How Property Rights Are Affected by the Texas-Mexico Border Fence: A Failure Due to Insufficient Procedure." *Texas International Law Journal* 45 (2010): 631–54.

Nevins, Joseph. "Death as a Way of Life: Ezequial [sic] Hernández Jr. and the Making of the U.S.-Mexico Borderlands." *Znet*, July 26, 2008. http://www.zcommunications.org/death-as-a-way-of-life-esequial-hern-ndez-jr-and-the-making-of-the-u-s-mexico-borderlands-by-joseph-nevins.

Robben, Antonius C. G. M. "Epilogue: The Imagination of Genocide." In *Genocide: Truth, Memory, and Representation*, edited by Alexander Laban Hinton and Kevin Lewis O'Neill, 317–32. Durham, N.C.: Duke University Press, 2009.

Sancho, Andrea C. "Environmental Concerns Created by Current United States Border Policy: Challenging the Extreme Waiver Authority Granted to the Secretary of the Department of Homeland Security under the Real ID Act of 2005." *Southeastern Environmental Law Journal* 16 (2008): 421–56.

Serafino, Nina M. "Congressional Research Service Report 98-767, U.S. Military Participation in Southwest Border Drug Control: Questions and Answers." Washington, D.C.: Foreign Affairs and National Defense Division, September 14, 1998.

Speed, Shannon, and Alvaro Reyes. "In Our Own Defense: Rights and Resistance in Chiapas." *Political and Legal Anthropology Review* 5, no. 1 (2002): 60–89.

Tamez, Margo. "Decolonize U.S. Brdr Prznz: #4." From *Indigenous Brdr Narratives after the Wall, Indigifem,* October 26, 2011. http://indigifem.blogspot.com/2011/10/decolonize-us-brdr-prznz-4-series-from.html.

———. "Nádasi'né' nde' isdzáné begoz'aahi' shimaa shini' gokal Gowa goshjaa ha'ána'idiłí texas-nakaiyé godesdzog" [Returning Lipan Apache Women's Laws, Lands, and Strength in El Caláboz Ranchería, Texas-Mexico Border]. PhD diss., Washington State University, 2010.

———."Report: Ndé Principles & Protocols from El Caláboz Ranchería after the Wall: Indigenous Peoples, Knowledge, Land, Territories & Human Rights." (Forthcoming).

Tamez, Margo, ed. "Mandate from the El Caláboz Summer 2011 Gathering on Indigenous Peoples, Knowledge, Lands, Territories and Human Rights, June 24–26, 2011." (Forthcoming.)

Webster, Anthony K. "Lipan Apache Placenames of Augustina Zuazua: Some Structural and Discursive Features." *Names* 55, no. 2 (2007): 103–22.

WikiLeaks. Document release, October 25, 2011. http://stuff.mit.edu/afs/sipb/contrib/wikileaks-crs/wikileaks-crs-reports/98-767.pdf.

Wolfe, Patrick. *Settler Colonialism and the Transformation of Anthropology: The Politics and Poetics of an Ethnographic Event.* London: Cassell, 1999.

Prisoners of Passage
Immigration Detention in Canada

HARSHA WALIA AND PROMA TAGORE

> Beyond the fences, the cages, these walls, beyond these gates, alarms and cameras, there is no place that I am seeking anymore. I no longer believe there is a humanitarian Canada, immoral laws may be legal but the slaves will rebel. Everyone is caged, whether here or there, whether now or later. Today me, maybe tomorrow someone else. Revolutionaries, historians, mothers, humans, all queue jumpers. As if we were all born by waiting in some line.
> — DETAINEE

The myth of Canadian benevolence, the ideology of Canadian peacekeeping, and the veneer of Canadian multiculturalism have served to cast Canada as a liberal counterpoint to aggressive U.S. immigration enforcement tactics. However, the lack of sensationalized stories about workplace raids, massive roundups, or overflowing detention centers does not point to a humane migration policy in Canada. Rather, Canadian migration policy is a perfected system of social control, containment, and expulsion. The extolled multiculturalism of the Canadian government's handpicked diaspora exists parallel to what Peter Nyers has termed the "deport-spora."[1] In fact, during talks for the Security and Prosperity Partnership agreement, the United States specifically pointed to Canada's skilled worker program and temporary guest worker program as possible models for U.S. immigration policy.

Although attention to national borders has figured prominently in the post-9/11 world, Canadian border policies have always reflected a distrust of racialized migrants. The denigration of refugee claimants; anxieties about undocumented migrants; and efforts to fortify the border against so-called crime, security breaches, and fraud have been prominent features of Canadian border control policies for decades. The assertion of absolute state sovereignty is nowhere more apparent than within the immigrant detention regime. Unlike traditional prisons, detention centers have never pretended to serve any purpose other than the forcible confinement and control of migrants to ensure deportation. Migrant detainees are thus prisoners of passage, criminalized for the mere act of migration and confined by zones of exclusion demarcated by border crossings.

The granting or withholding of citizenship rights becomes the way for the state to determine and regulate who is part of the national community. As Nandita Sharma observes, "[T]heir categorization positions them within Canadian space in particular, always hierarchically-organized, ways."[2] In this sense, the constant imagining of Canadian identity is far more than a legal exercise; it is ultimately linked to the deliberate actions of imperial nation-building that deny human self-determination to colonized peoples both within and beyond the nation's borders.

OVERVIEW OF IMMIGRATION DETENTION

Most immigration detention in Canada is administrative detention, also known as "detention for convenience." Detention centers are formally known as "holding centers," where "noncriminal noncitizens" are held for suspected violations of immigration laws, primarily for overstaying their visas, that is, being undocumented. In Canada, most undocumented migrants are failed refugee claimants who did not appear for their deportation date, rendering them "non-status" in the eyes of the state: "illegal aliens." Most incarcerations are for short periods of time since speedy deportation is preferred; lengthy detentions are a constant reminder of the transgressions of migrants.

Detention also takes place to ensure the deportation of migrants deemed "likely not to appear for removal" in the *future*. Regulations in the 2001 Immigration and Refugee Protection Act (IRPA) now allow for arrests without warrants and detention even when deportation is not imminent. This creates a serious catch-22 for refugee claimants in particular. When they express fears of deportation, the state considers them flight risks, and they then become subject to detention. The IRPA has also increased the powers of detention based on identity, which allows officers to detain any foreign national if "unsatisfied" with the person's identity at any point in the refugee claim process. The expansion of detention on the basis of identity is of particular concern because those seeking asylum are often forced to leave their countries without proper identification documents because it is their very identity which puts them at risk.

Canada is currently embroiled in a debate about further expanding the powers of detention through the introduction of Bill C-49. The bill subjects asylum seekers, including children, suspected of using a smuggler to mandatory detention for at least the first year after their arrival. The proposed bill also would deny these asylum seekers the right to appeal a negative refugee decision, and they would be prohibited from obtaining permanent residency and from sponsoring family members for a five-year probationary period. Bill C-49 is modeled after Australia's internationally condemned policies of mandatory detention. On the notorious Christmas Island off Australia's shores, where detainees can be held for years, there were at least two suicides in 2010.

There are three principal holding centers in Canada — in Toronto, Vancouver, and Laval. Laval's facility in Quebec is formally known as the Immigration Prevention Centre and is located in a refurbished prison facility. Despite the deliberate use of innocuous terminology, such as "holding center," the conditions of detention are similar to imprisonment, although far less regulated to afford detainees minimal protections. Detainees are held in secure facilities with surveillance cameras, guards, and metal detectors. The holding centers are equipped with segregation units and solitary confinement for detainees deemed "uncooperative." Long-term confinement of those labeled uncooperative is often the result of detainees refusing to sign the papers necessary to secure travel documents for their deportation. Thus, refusing to be complicit in one's own deportation results in further punishment. Prohibitive rules abound, including limited access to telephones, regulations on personal belongings, restrictions on mobility, and a curfew for visiting hours. Shackles, handcuffs, and leg irons are standard protocol for transportation, serving not only to subjugate and humiliate migrants but also to cast them as deviant, reinforcing their so-called illegality.[3]

Citizenship and Immigration Canada statistics reveal that on any given day in the twenty-first century, an average of 550–650 people are being detained for immigration purposes across the country. However, given a high turnover rate due to rapid deportations, this estimate does not provide the full picture: annually, around 11,000–12,000 people are detained for time periods ranging from forty-eight hours to eighteen months. There are approximately 20 minors detained at any given time, although authorities maintain that they only detain adults and that children are "guests" who are in the company of their parents. In 2011 Canada experienced national hysteria about "illegals" with the arrival of two boats of Tamil refugees. The MV *Sun Sea* arrived at the end of 2010 with 492 Tamil refugees, who made the three-month journey from Sri Lanka to the shores of the west coast only to be forced upon their arrival into three detention centers across the lower mainland. Up to one year later, over half of the detainees, including mothers and children, remained behind bars.

With a growing detainee population since 9/11, an increasing number of migrants are being held in provincial prisons; in 2011 the number of migrants in prisons exceeded the number in holding centers. The "tough-on-illegals" spin is linked to the "tough-on-crime" approach. While regurgitating sound bites about financial austerity and cutbacks, the federal Conservative government has increased the prison budget by 50 percent, paralleled only by the ballooning military budget. Despite falling crime rates, over $400 million has been allocated for at least twenty new prisons. It is only logical, then, that the government will fill these prisons through the creation of a growing prison population — made up particularly of indigenous people, sex workers, homeless people, street-involved youth, and migrants of color — all of whom are already over-surveilled and over-incarcerated. One Fujianese woman, a migrant incarcerated in the Burnaby Correctional Centre for Women in 1999, expressed her despair and outrage through a hunger strike and the following song:

> Since I've been locked in prison,
> My life has never been peaceful.
> I was taken from here to there,
> I do not know what crime I have committed,
> Days passed, nights passed, my tears never stop.
> May I ask the Immigration Board and the judge
> When you will release me?
> I have suffered on the ship
> And risked my life to come
> Is this my fate to be in prison
> I do not understand why
> Judge, oh judge, please give me my freedom.[4]

THREAT CONTAINMENT

In *Securing Borders: Detention and Deportation in Canada*, Anna Pratt writes, "Detention and deportation are the two most extreme and bodily sanctions of this immigration penalty, which constitutes and enforces borders, polices non-citizens, identifies those deemed dangerous, diseased, deceitful, or destitute, and refuses them entry or casts them out. As such, detention and deportation and the borders they sustain are also key technologies in the continuous processes that make up citizens and govern populations."[5]

Canadian nationalism has consistently emphasized the country as a contained entity threatened by outside forces. The illusion of the nation as a place of safety and security is reified through state bureaucracies, such as the military, federal intelligence, and immigration departments, which produce the sense that "the enemy" is outside the realm of "us." Catherine Dauvergne has written, "One reason why the concept of 'national interest' is so vital to immigration law is because of the role this law plays in constituting the nation."[6] Although different eras have been dominated by different perceptions of threats, they have always been externalized as third world imports. For example, within days of the attack on Pearl Harbor in 1941, Japanese people living in North America were seen as enemy aliens, even if they were citizens. A federal minister of parliament announced, "Let our slogan be for British Columbia: no Japs from the Rockies to the seas." Upon the enactment of the War Measures Act in 1942, the state interned about twenty-two thousand Japanese people, 75 percent of whom were Canadians.

From Pearl Harbor to fighting the war on drugs and the war on terrorism, the ability to designate and attack non-European citizens — including Japanese Canadians and Arab Canadians — reveals the racially segregated configuration of the Canadian nation, despite the shallow rhetoric of multiculturalism. In the current climate, the vilification of Muslim Canadians depends on the reductionist image of Osama bin Laden to personify all Arabs and Muslims. (By comparison, the 1995 Oklahoma City bombing was considered to be the act of one lone man and did not result in the state-sanctioned profiling, incarceration, and stigmatization of all young white males in any western settler state.) All of this is based on and reinforces the normalization of "Canadian" as white. As Prime Minister Mackenzie King declared in 1947, "The people of Canada do not wish, as a result of mass immigration, to make any fundamental alteration in the character of our population."[7] This statement is symptomatic of not only historic, but current-day sentiments to maintain Canada's white supremacist purity. Therefore, undesirable migrants are those who are racialized, in addition to those who are poor, queer, disabled, or socialist.

While certain government policies facilitate the entry of those deemed worthy, the coercive practices of state sovereignty expel others. The protection of "deserving" immigrants and refugees is contingent upon the identification and exclusion of those labeled as security threats, criminals, or system abusers. The state's ability to control people's movements reveals a system of apartheid where migrants are consistently constructed as problems to be managed and contained. A term like "immigrant" does not actually reflect anyone's legal status; rather, it is a euphemism for racialized migrants from the third world — even if they are citizens whose families have resided for generations on Turtle Island. Similarly, the category of "illegal" does not conjure up images of Americans who illegally overstay their tourist visas or Australian students illegally working without permits. Rather, the term plays on existing social hierarchies based on race and class. In popular consciousness, the word "illegal" is associated with poor, brown migrants without any actual knowledge of any so-called illegal act being committed.

This construction of illegality is similar to the construction of criminality that justifies the incarceration of poor, racialized, and indigenous women and men in the prison system. People do not think of specific criminal acts (especially corporate crime) as much as they conceive of the imaginary criminal class that commits them. Within capitalism, this criminal class is defined by racialized and class-based lifestyles: welfare bums, drug dealers, and thugs. In this way, members of marginalized communities exist as "criminals" even before any crime is committed. Similarly, poor migrants of color are eternally cast as outsiders, their presence is erased, and their mere existence within Canada is viewed as an act of trespass and an infringement of a colonially imposed border. As Nandita Sharma argues, "Categories of legality and illegality are . . . deeply ideological. They help to conceal the fact that both those represented as foreigners and those seen as Canadian work within the same labour market and live within the same society."[8]

The victim of the crime of migration is supposedly the Canadian state through the assault on its borders. The invocation of the state as a victim is related to two flawed presumptions. First, it facilitates fundamentalist defenses of the state as a self-contained entity in need of protection. Second, it positions Canada specifically as a country whose benevolence and laudable values of peacekeeping and diversity is under attack. But the reality is that Canadian nationhood is based on the genocide of indigenous people. On the global stage, while the United States is perceived as the sole imperialist power, Canada has lent its support to occupations in Vietnam, East Timor, Afghanistan, Haiti, Palestine, and Iraq. Canadian corporations, particularly mining firms, are among the most aggressive foreign investors in Asia, Latin America, and the Caribbean, and are responsible for environmental destruction, human and labor rights violations, and the forced displacement of communities. Regimes of border imperialism are deployed against those whose very recourse to migration results from capitalist ravages and military occupations in the Global South. McKenzie Wark reminds us that "migration is globalisation from below,"[5] while Sunera Thobani offers the challenge, "What makes it alright for us to buy a T-shirt on the streets of Vancouver for $3, which was made in China, then stand up all outraged as Canadian citizens when the woman who made that T-shirt tries to come here and live with us on a basis of equality?"[10]

Just as prison "reform" has tended to strengthen the prison system, immigration and detention reform based on false divisions between those who are deserving and those who are undeserving strengthens the nationalistic processes of who is entitled to free movement. As many movements like No Borders and No One Is Illegal have reiterated, the categorization of legitimate versus illegitimate migrants merely strengthens the power of the state to construct categories that control people's right to self-determination. This makes it even more critical to challenge immigrant rights movements that are organized on nationalistic or assimilationist lines, which remain based on state-sanctioned rights and citizenship discourses. As Bakan writes, "Citizenship plays a role in accessing a wide range of rights, but as importantly in creating and reproducing inequality among individuals and groups in the context of contemporary globalization."[11] Instead of making declarations about whether others can migrate simply by virtue of the fact that we have already migrated or have inherited the privilege of citizenship by birth, No One Is Illegal is building a grassroots movement where all humans are supported to live a life of well-being and dignity.

WAR ON TERROR DETENTIONS

While detentions and deportations are a fundamental feature of historic immigration policy, the post-9/11 climate has further entrenched the crime-security nexus. The expanding security apparatus is less about protecting people than about protecting racist and colonialist border interests and creating a culture of fear in the context of the war on terrorism. As one detainee has written, "I would rather die than stay here forever, and I have tried to commit suicide many times. The purpose of this is to destroy people, and I have been destroyed. I am hopeless because our voices are not heard from the depths of the detention center. If I die, please remember that there was a human here whose beliefs, dignity, and humanity were abused. Do not believe their lies, I have not been charged with any crime. Please remember that there are hundreds of detainees suffering the same misfortune."

As noted above, the IRPA has broadened the circumstances in which detention can occur, and the proclaimed benefits of the new regime are to "provide enhanced protection of Canadian society." This furthers the presumed links between migrants and terrorism, despite Citizenship and Immigration Canada's own records showing that at any given time only five to seven immigrant detainees have been confronted with serious terrorism allegations (a number of which are often politically motivated and the result of the criminalization of groups such as the Popular Front for the Liberation of Palestine, Hezbollah, the Liberation Tigers of Tamil Eelam, etc.). Just as false assumptions are persistent about prisoners and violent crime, contrary to popular belief the majority of detentions are not based on real or even purported grounds of terrorism. Nonetheless, the threat of terrorism has created a sense of detention's inevitability with clipped "better safe than sorry" policy responses. This is not unlike the emotive response to crime and the legitimacy given to the growing prison-industrial complex.

Upgraded security measures in the post-9/11 climate have led to an increase in racial profiling, the invasion of privacy rights through extensive surveillance and lengthy interrogations, and heightened rates of incarceration. Canada has implemented a wide array of new sanctions in the areas of criminal law, immigration law, tax law, employment, intelligence services, and airport security, while the current Conservative government plans on spending an additional $1.4 billion on border security and policing.

One such measure is the use of security certificates which, while embedded within immigration law for a long time, have come to have new meaning. Under the 2001 IRPA, a security certificate can be issued to a permanent resident or foreign national who is deemed "inadmissible on grounds of security," and on this basis the person "shall be detained without the issue of a warrant." Detainees may be held and imprisoned indefinitely without any charges ever being laid against them, and they face possible deportation or torture, all on the basis of secret evidence that is never revealed to them. In 2006, the $3.5 million Kingston Immigration Holding Centre, dubbed Guantanamo North and run by the Canadian Border Services Agency, was opened especially for security certificate detainees. Even though security certificates were deemed unconstitutional in 2007, the Canadian government reintroduced them a year later, and they continue to be used. Given the ongoing complicity of the government on the issue, security certificates must be seen as nothing other than the state's continued effort to criminalize, terrorize, and subject particular individuals and whole communities (particularly Arab, Muslim, and South Asian) to torture, imprisonment, surveillance, punishment, persecution, and intimidation on the basis of race, ethnicity, and alleged religious and political affiliations.

Critically, security certificates only apply to refugees and permanent residents and thus constitute a form of double punishment for noncitizens whom the state has the power to imprison *and* deport under its immigration laws. Noncitizens face the same double punishment — the ability of the state to imprison and deport — if they are convicted of a criminal offense. Steve Cohen describes this measure as "double racism" and as "an exercise in imperial arrogance" intended to "ship the offending conduct overseas."[12] Double punishment laws reveal the apartheid nature of immigration policy, where citizens do not face the same consequences as noncitizens. The following excerpt of a poem by security certificate detainee Adil Charkaoui (translated from French) provides an important perspective:

> What is a security certificate?
> A security certificate,
> It's the right to be treated outside the law
> It's two-speed justice
> It's precedent for secret trials . . .
> It's contact visits with no contact
> It's the glass that separates you from loved ones,
> It's deadlock, solitude; it's breathing corruption . . .
> It's the guilt of being born elsewhere . . .
> It's human folly clothed as wisdom.
> It's me today, maybe you tomorrow!

SECURING CHEAP LABOR AND ENSURING CORPORATE PROFITS

While Canada detains and deports an increasing number of "undesirables," it is not in the interest of the state to deport all non-status migrants nor to close down the border to all migrants. Rather, as David McNally observes, "It [the state] simply wants this labour on its own terms: frightened, oppressed, and vulnerable."[13] The political purpose of tightened security and immigration measures, especially the constant threat of incarceration, is to demobilize racialized populations and to increase their collective vulnerability.

Capitalism's drive to maximize profit intrinsically involves a constant search for cheaper labor and the need to perfect the mechanisms for controlling workers. Despite its rhetoric, capitalism does not aim to eliminate national borders; the nation-state is the political pillar that allows for the expansion of capitalism. The state creates the legal framework that guarantees the ownership of private property and provides support for disciplining the workforce, while maintaining an economic infrastructure for capital flows. The borders of the modern nation-state increase competition as governments try to offer cheaper workforces to attract investments. The ability of multinational corporations to transcend national boundaries results in the need for state-facilitated temporary exploitations of labor to attract investments. As Harold Troper has noted, the denial of legal citizenship to workers allows states to accumulate domestic capital by the "in-gathering of off-shore labour" in order to compete in the global market.[14] Thus, Canadian border controls and immigration policies legalize pools of undocumented labor and temporary workers for the benefit of capital interests.

Canada and its economy are built on the theft of indigenous lands; the exploitation of labor, especially slave, migrant, and reproductive labor; and the global appropriation of natural resources. In the twenty-first century, Canada has been able to pursue economic growth through instituting distinctions between citizen and noncitizen workers, especially through the use of temporary worker programs. Such programs are models of transient servitude where employers maintain control of both labor *and* the laborer (figuratively and literally, since workers are virtually held captive by employers or contractors who seize their identification documents). Migrant worker programs allow for capital interests to access cheap labor, which exists under precarious conditions, the most severe of which is the condition of being deportable. As Stasiulis and Bakan observe, "[T]he First World state's ability to deny Third World migrants access to naturalization becomes a legal and internationally sanctioned means of discrimination by withholding many basic human rights, and increasing oppression based on race and gender."[15] These programs are structured to facilitate zones of internal and domesticated detention, confinement, and exploitation.

Under the Seasonal Agricultural Worker Program (SAWP), approximately eighteen thousand migrant farmworkers from the Caribbean and Mexico arrive in Canada every year to work the fields, orchards, and greenhouses, typically for periods of three to ten months. Workers are separated from their families and perform rigorous labor that few (white) Canadians choose to do; the low wages of migrant workers contribute to the profits of the multimillion-dollar agricultural industry. Documented abuses in the SAWP include wages lower than those of their Canadian counterparts and long hours of work — in some cases up to sixteen hours a day — without overtime or vacation pay. Many workers are required to work with pesticides without proper training or safety equipment. Some employers retain workers' passports, health cards, social insurance cards, and work permits, limiting their options and their mobility. Furthermore, workers have been sent home for filing complaints, and a negative report from an employer at the end of a season can result in their suspension from the program for future seasons. Finally, for SAWP workers, there is no option of permanent residency regardless of how many years — and even generations — they toil in the fields.

The system of border policing and immigrant detention works in tandem with the expansion of the pools of undocumented and temporary labor. While subsidizing economic production through precarious labor conditions and the denial of basic rights and services, temporary guest worker programs also maintain the sanctity of racialized national identities by legalizing the "foreignness" of these workers.[16] This is a critical move in the dehumanization cycle necessary to create a hierarchical order based on race. That hierarchy is then legitimized through the processes of citizenship, justifying the deplorable working conditions and state securitization processes that disproportionately target migrant women. In her book *Global Lockdown*, Julia Sudbury describes the explosion of women's imprisonment as a "crisis of working women of colour and indigenous women globally,"[17] linking the increasing mass imprisonment of women to the criminalization of migration, increased border security, and the ongoing colonization of women's bodies.

Under the Live-In Caregiver Program (LCP), migrant women — predominantly Filipinas — enter Canada as temporary workers. These women are required to work for twenty-four months within a window of thirty-six months in order to qualify for permanent residency. During this period, the women must work only in the home of the employer whose name appears on the work permit. Although the program calls for a maximum of forty-nine hours of work per week, the live-in aspect of these jobs allows employers to call on the caregivers at any time. This exposes the women to labor rights violations and gross abuse, including unpaid or excessive work hours, additional job responsibilities, the forced confiscation of travel documents, gross violations of privacy, and sexual harassment and sexual assault. As one domestic worker remarked, "We know that, under the LCP, we are like modern slaves who have to wait for at least two years to get our freedom." In addition to the supply of cheap labor provided by migrant women under the LCP, the program serves other functions in the capitalist economy. By facilitating the supply of domestic labor for middle-class and rich women through the LCP, the state and market are absolved from the responsibility of creating a universal childcare program.

According to Stasiulis and Bakan, "Multilateral state discussions now take as their priority the curbing of unwanted migration — as illegals, asylum seekers, designated 'criminals' or 'terrorists,' and so on — while selectively promoting the circulation of desired human capital."[18] In Canada and the United States, this has been made possible through the declaration "Beyond the Border: A Shared Vision for Perimeter Security and Economic Competitiveness," under which a series of initiatives has been implemented since 2002. A central feature of this declaration is to ensure the increased mobility of capital and of people

FIGURE 6. *No Borders* by Tania Willard, an artist and designer from the Secwepemc (Shuswap) nation in the interior of British Columbia. "I have been working with narrative and story throughout my work in the arts, media, and advocacy to share our people's stories, history, and experiences. I believe we all have a story to share, the stories of this land, our cultures, and our experiences." From No One Is Illegal: People's History of Kanada Poster Project, 2007.

who represent capital, through measures such as biometric pre-clearance programs; the expansion of temporary foreign worker programs; and the development of trilateral policy frameworks to enhance the free movement of goods, capital, and electronic commerce. Simultaneously, in the post-9/11 climate and its accompanying construction of a constant imminent threat, the border security apparatus has been fortified through the joint "Smart Border Declaration," a thirty-point plan which includes coordinated border surveillance technologies; increased arming of border guards; increased tracking of foreign nationals; and speedier deportations. These two initiatives intensify the practices of both state selection and state expulsion.

ABOLITION OF PRISON AND DETENTION COMPLEXES

The images reproduced in this chapter are part of the People's History of Kanada Poster Project, a collaborative effort between No One Is Illegal (Vancouver) and grassroots artists. These original art pieces explore moments of repression and resistance in Canadian history. The artists working on this project come

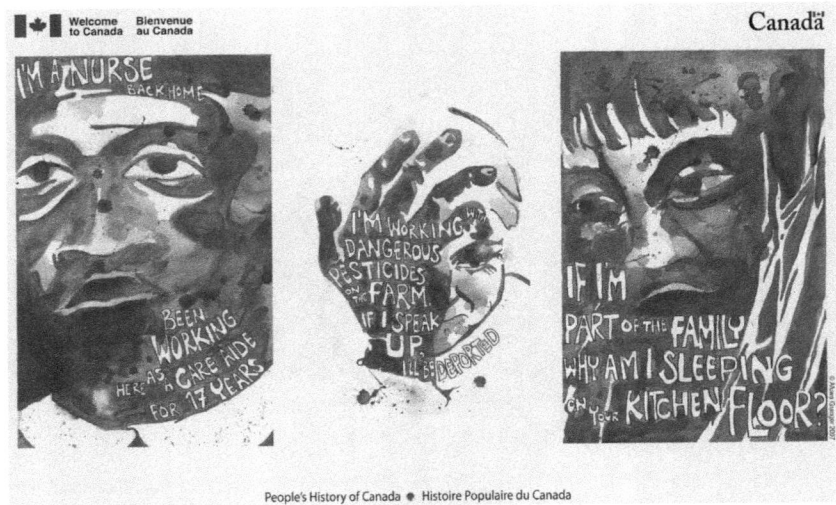

FIGURE 7. *Welcome to Canada* by Afuwa Granger. Granger knows firsthand what structural adjustment policies do to a small South American country. Her work articulates both this consciousness and the cultural inheritance of centuries of disruption. The primary images and voices in her poster on foreign/migrant worker programs are those of women she has met, who have told their stories to her. From No One Is Illegal: People's History of Kanada Poster Project, 2007.

from a diversity of communities and almost all carry their own stories and direct experiences of colonization and displacement.

Canada's regime of detention and deportation can be seen as part of a larger and growing prison-industrial complex, where at least one-quarter of Canada's prison population is made up of immigrants and refugees who are being held for deportation without any criminal charges. Disciplinary regimes, such as those in prisons, detention centers, and factories, work to instill obedience by encouraging the internalization of methods of control. The detention of migrants and non-status people, along with mass arrests that target not just single individuals but entire communities, are part of the larger system of a colonizing police state, where, to borrow the words of Angela Davis, "regardless of who has or has not committed crimes, punishment, in brief, can be seen more as a consequence of racialized surveillance."[19] Indeed, prison abolitionists have long pointed to the colonialist roots of the North American prison system. The disproportionate number of poor people and people of color who are imprisoned is evidence of the racism and classism that underlies the prison system. The

FIGURE 8. *Abolish Security Certificates* by Annie Banks, a youth worker and printmaker in Victoria, B.C., who has been living, working, learning, and printmaking in her community for sixteen years. Coming from a white/European background, Banks aspires to be an ally to groups facing and fighting oppression. She currently works with schools and youth groups, facilitating antihomophobia workshops and creativity-based programs. She is involved with No One Is Illegal (Victoria) and seeks to follow in the footsteps of the many revolutionary printmakers, activists, and individuals who inspire her. From No One Is Illegal: People's History of Kanada Poster Project, 2007.

FIGURE 9. *No One Is Illegal* by Harjap Grewal.

stereotyping of racialized people in the public and through the media is at the same time used to validate the belief that practices of punishment are "fair" or "just" responses of the law to particular groups of people. As one detainee at the Immigration Prevention Centre in Laval said in an interview:

> What is freedom? In a country that claims no torture, or execution, where hidden racism and the hypocrisy of disguised torture work to silence through psychological pressure, and where immigrants are treated as imported goods . . . it is a freedom stained with injustice. What unforgivable offence have immigrants committed to be so mistreated and humiliated? Is this a life of immigration or humiliation?

Prisons and detention centers disappear human beings whose only crime in most cases is to be brown or black, to be a noncitizen, to defy colonially defined border controls, or to seek self-determination. In 2005, No One Is Illegal

(Vancouver) presented a submission to the UN Working Group on Arbitrary Detention, concluding:

> Given that the detention and deportation of non-citizens is so readily accepted and unquestioned in society as the legitimate exercise of state sovereignty, we aim to make visible the material conditions and tangible practices of the detention and deportation of "undeserving" and "undesirable" non-citizens, who are essentially being criminalized for the mere act of migration. Rather, we aim for a world where freedom of movement and human mobility is guaranteed and the social control of migrants through the detention and deportation regime is abolished.[20]

NOTES

1. Nyers, "Abject Cosmopolitanism."
2. Sharma, *Home Economics*.
3. Pratt, *Securing Borders*.
4. Courtesy of Direct Action against Refugee Exploitation.
5. Ibid., 1.
6. Quoted in Walia, "Colonialism, Capitalism and the Making of the Apartheid System of Migration in Canada."
7. See http://faculty.marianopolis.edu/c.belanger/quebechistory/readings/MackenzieKingonImmigration.html.
8 Quoted ibid.
9. Wark, "Globalization from Below."
10. Quoted in Walia, "Colonialism, Capitalism and the Making of the Apartheid System of Migration in Canada."
11. Stasiulis and Bakan, *Negotiating Citizenship*.
12. Cohen, *No One Is Illegal*, 263.
13. McNally, *Another World Is Possible*, 190.
14. Troper, "Commentary."
15. Stasiulis and Bakan, *Negotiating Citizenship*, 14.
16. Sharma, *Home Economics*.
17. Sudbury, *Global Lockdown*.
18. Stasiulis and Bakan, *Negotiating Citizenship*, 28.
19. Davis, *Abolition Democracy*, 40.
20. The full statement is at http://users.resist.ca/noii-van.resist.ca/submissions_to_un.html.

BIBLIOGRAPHY

Cohen, S., ed. *No One Is Illegal: Asylum and Immigration Control, Past and Present.* Staffordshire, England: Trentham, 2003.

Davis, A. *Abolition Democracy: Beyond Empire, Prisons, and Torture.* New York: Seven Stories, 2005.

McNally, D. *Another World Is Possible: Globalization and Anti-Capitalism.* Winnipeg: Arbeiter Ring, 2006.

Nyers, P. "Abject Cosmopolitanism: The Politics of Protection in the Anti-Deportation Movement." *Third World Quarterly* 24, no. 6 (2003): 1069–93.

Pratt, A. *Securing Borders: Detention and Deportation in Canada.* Vancouver: University of British Columbia Press, 2006.

Sharma, N. *Home Economics: Nationalism and the Making of "Migrant Workers" in Canada.* Toronto: University of Toronto Press, 2006.

Stasiulis, D. K., and A. B Bakan. *Negotiating Citizenship: Migrant Women in Canada and the Global System.* Hampshire, England: Macmillan, 2003.

Sudbury, J., ed. *Global Lockdown: Race, Gender, and the Prison-Industrial Complex.* London: Routledge, 2005.

Troper, H. "Commentary." In *Controlling Immigration: A Global Perspective*, edited by W. Cornelius, P. Martin, and J. Hollifield, 136–38. Stanford, Calif.: Stanford University Press, 2004.

Walia, H. "Colonialism, Capitalism and the Making of the Apartheid System of Migration in Canada." Znet, March 2006. http://www.zmag.org/znet/viewArticle/4297.

Wark, M. "Globalization from Below: Migration, Sovereignty, Communication." Paper presented at the Nation/States Conference, University of Adelaide, December 13–16, 2001. http://subsol.c3.hu/subsol_2/contributors2/warktext3.html.

Mapping Remote Detention
Dis/location through Isolation

ALISON MOUNTZ

THE POWER OF ISOLATION

Detention is a punitive measure that relies on geographical isolation. The stories of what happens to migrants who are detained in remote locations speak of the power of isolation. Detention often removes migrant workers from the places where they were living and working prior to their arrest. Once spatially entrapped within national systems of detention, detainees are funneled quickly to the ever more remote locations where detention happens. As a result they find themselves far from family members, friends, coworkers, resources, and potential advocates.

While remote detention sites may appear ad hoc, they must be viewed together to show how geographies of exclusion operate beyond local and regional scales, and actually connect national contexts with global trends. This chapter reviews a range of ways in which this isolation occurs and calls attention to the ways that states have entered into the intimacies of the daily lives of migrant workers on a security continuum. Nation-states operate across borders to capture migrants through arrest, detention, and — for some — deportation. In so doing, states extend the field of security, linking internal and external security measures and "converging on the figure of the migrant, as the key point inside a continuum of threats."[1] Sometimes, detainees move through this continuum rapidly, and other times they are in a painstakingly prolonged limbo, languishing behind bars in remote locales.

This chapter also discusses efforts by activists to locate detainees and to map detention in Europe, the United States, and Australia. Campaigns designed to counter the isolation of detention create opposing cartographies: the desire of states, on the one hand, to conceal, and the projects of activists — detainees and former detainees among them — to reveal. These efforts offer political potential because locating and mapping can reconnect migrants to families, communities, and networks of advocates.

GEOGRAPHIES OF EXCLUSION: MAPPING PATTERNS OF ISOLATION

Obviously, detention isolates individuals. But beyond this fact, the *manner* and *location* in which people are isolated matter. Authorities and policymakers rehearse a wide array of strategies to explain the detention of immigrants, asylum seekers, and noncitizens.[2] Some call detention "suppression" or "disruption," signaling an effort to curb human-smuggling industries. Still others use the term "deterrence," which is the idea that detention will discourage future migration when word gets out that detention is among the punishments migrants will suffer for crossing borders without papers. But few will readily discuss the ways that enforcement practices pull (im)migrant workers into detention via increased policing in the intimate and mundane spaces of daily life, such as homes, workplaces, shops, and churches. Detention is one stage of a series of state security strategies that are increasingly dispersed and pervasive.

Here I discuss six of the many ways in which detention isolates individuals, populations, and communities: through dispersal, separation, concealment, control, death, and the creation and creative use of islands.

First, *dispersal* is a form of isolation that occurs in many countries.[3] In Ireland, asylum seekers are detained in facilities in deindustrialized, poor, urban areas.[4] In Australia, under former Prime Minister John Howard, most asylum seekers were held indiscriminately in remote locations in the outback or on the sparsely populated northern coast. Additional Australian detention centers are located offshore, on remote isolated locations such as Christmas Island (Australian territory) and Nauru (a small, independent island state). Whether onshore or offshore, these locations remove detainees from their communities and from the infrastructure for advocacy — interpreters, legal representation, and advocacy groups — more commonly located in large cities such as Sydney or Melbourne.

In the United States, dispersal and dislocation take different forms. Whereas fewer than 50 percent of detainees are held in federal detention facilities that only hold persons with foreign citizenship, many others are incarcerated in remote rural county jails that are not dedicated to migrant detention. Not only are migrants often detained in locations that are distant from where they lived and worked, but they are moved quickly among detention centers.[5] At the time of this writing, about half of detainees are quickly funneled south in the United

States.[6] Arrests are high in dense urban areas in the Northeast and on the West Coast, but large detention facilities are being built more quickly in the South.

This dispersal, in the form of moving people through the system to remote sites, makes the initial location of and communication with detainees difficult and obscures the statistical accounting of the numbers of foreigners being held by authorities at any given time. People are moved quickly, overnight, without warning to detainees, families, or lawyers. Not only is it difficult for their families to find them, but networks of advocacy must be restored or created anew. While legal advocates have fought to reduce these transfers of detainees among centers because they inhibit and complicate legal representation, the practice continues.

In Syracuse, the small, Rust Belt city in upstate New York where I lived for eight years, the U.S. Border Patrol heavily polices the Regional Transportation Center, the local bus and train station where Amtrak, Greyhound, and Trailways operate.[7] Because the station falls within a hundred miles of the U.S. border with Canada, it has been designated a "port of entry" where people are questioned as though they are entering the country. In choosing whom they question, federal authorities rely on racial profiling, routinely approaching people of color and people with accents in the station and on trains and buses in order to ask them for identification. There have been hundreds of arrests of persons who were picked up on either the bus or train, in the process of boarding, or in the small station. Because they are often en route from Chicago to Boston or from New York City to Buffalo, when people disappear in Syracuse, family and friends have a difficult time locating their loved ones. This dislocation is exacerbated by the rapid transfer of detainees from the Public Security Building in Syracuse to county jails in Cayuga, Onondaga, Oneida, Oswego, and Wayne counties or to the large federal detention facility for men in the small town of Batavia, over a hundred miles west of Syracuse, near Buffalo.[8]

The local Task Force on Detention at the Workers' Center of Central New York formed in 2007 in response to raids upstate, where what are called "collateral arrests" were taking place: the arrest of those present in a home or workplace where another person might have been the target of an enforcement operation. The very nature of these local raids reflected the ways that enforcement authorities capitalize on the vulnerability of undocumented workers by isolating them. They surround work sites, homes, churches, and local stores in their raids, and those under siege are often not aware of their rights to refuse search or entry. Activists in Syracuse, Rochester, Buffalo, and the much smaller rural towns in between — such as Sodus, where the harshest enforcement campaigns unfolded — referred to this as a "campaign of fear and intimidation."[9] It was challenging for the group to respond to enforcement strategies because they happened in small communities and targeted people who were at risk if they spoke out because of their precarious legal status. A class action lawsuit, for example, requires extensive documentation of systematic violations of rights, which is challenging to gather in a landscape of fear where the intimate spaces of home, the community spaces of church, and mundane spaces such as grocery stores, buses, and health clinics are targeted for enforcement.

Second, dispersal leads to *separation* from family and community networks, often by sudden disappearance. In countries such as Australia and the United States, where rapid transfers carry detainees across the country to other facilities, families affected by detention may spend weeks and months looking for relatives arrested in workplace raids or on public transit. Much of the work to support detainees has been the labor of location: families and organizations try to locate loved ones who have disappeared into the system. Beyond disorientation and dislocation, raids, arrests, and detentions of individuals have serious effects for households. While the individual is detained, families often lose a source of financial support for the household. Advocates in Syracuse witnessed this form of isolation time and again. At work-site raids, for example, often the person providing the main income for a household was arrested. The detainees' separation from home leaves their families without money to buy food or clothing or pay rent. Detention thus disrupts not only the life of the individual, but the family, social, economic, and community networks maintained prior to arrest.

Third, the process of locating detainees proves difficult because of state practices of *concealing* identities. This is even more onerous for family members searching for people from locations outside the country. For example, remittances sent to Ecuador from the United States have decreased and deportations back to Ecuador have grown because of increased enforcement in the United States. Casa del Migrante is a government-funded organization in Ecuador dedicated to supporting migrants and their families. When family or friends contact the organization, employees and volunteers embark on an intricate process of locating the detained person in the United States by calling county jails, federal facilities, and workers inside the detention system.[10] The process is so complicated that when Nancy Hiemstra volunteered with this organization, she created a sixteen-page guide detailing how to find people in the U.S. detention system.[11]

Government methods of suppressing identities differ across national contexts. In Australia and the United States, only named detainees can be visited or telephoned. In the United States, an "alien number," or "A number," is assigned to every detainee from the time of detention to release or eventual deportation. All visits, information, telephone calls (which are centralized), and mail are dependent on this A number, making the number the key to identification and location. Yet this number is neither publicly available nor readily released by detention center staff.

In Syracuse, the task force worked to build alliances with workers and visitation ministries at local jails to help get these numbers. Often, however, by the time a volunteer learned the identification of a detainee, she had been transferred to another facility. Across Australia, activists pursued similar strategies by befriending local guards and prison clergy in order to reveal names and make first contact. They then would find out the names of other detainees through detainee networks of friends.

In response to the concealing of identities, activist nuns in Australia and the United States are often sent into jails because they are the least likely to be searched or challenged by guards and can hide identity documents in their clothing in order to assist migrants and asylum seekers with legal cases. Sisters in Chicago who were denied access to an ICE staging facility held weekly prayer vigils outside (since they were not allowed inside the facility) for over three years. When they threatened civil disobedience to block an entrance to the facility, they were granted permission to board the buses carrying detainees to longer-term facilities.[12]

Dispersal fosters concealment: migrants are hidden from view in multiple ways, not only locked behind bars, but omitted from or hidden within records and statistics. Hidden identities isolate detainees because without known identities, they cannot be accounted for in statistics, and they cannot be visited or helped.

A fourth form of isolation involves the *control* of information. Authorities have the power to control information moving in two directions: information about detainees released to the public (including their families); and information provided to detainees about their rights, resources for legal representation, and other details about their cases. This control of information further isolates detainees, who sometimes do not even know where they are detained, much less when they may have a chance to see a lawyer or a judge or be released. Whereas detainees are often denied information, authorities exercise their right to information connected to detainees by reading their mail and monitoring telephone calls and visits.

One former detainee from Palestine whom I interviewed in Sydney, Australia, in 2006 had been held for several years, first in Port Hedland and then in the Villawood Immigration Detention Centre on the outskirts of Sydney.[13] At Villawood, on the edge of Australia's largest city, he had more contact with the outside world. Prior to that, in Port Hedland, he was more isolated on the coast of northern Australia and had access to little information. He described what it was like to not know even the most basic world news until months later: "Six months they kept us in small buildings. Twenty-four inside. Just we have one hour [outdoors] in the morning. One hour in the morning we get outside, and then back inside. . . . Six months inside there not knowing anything about what is happening in the world. After six months, I heard the news that George W. Bush was elected president six months ago."[14]

Additional micro-geographies of information control take place within and immediately surrounding detention centers. In Australia, newly arrived asylum seekers are commonly held separately from those who have been detained for longer periods of time and have learned how to make asylum claims and contact lawyers. In the United States, detainees held in mainstream facilities frequently do not even know where they are located, and they find themselves without the resources to contact friends, family, or lawyers, or to make telephone calls at all.

Whereas a lack of knowledge about world affairs makes detainees feel isolated and forgotten by the world, the control of information about their case status and detention and deportation processes inhibits the resolution of their detention, prolongs uncertainty, and restricts access to outside support, including legal representation.

Fifth, medical neglect (which sometimes leads to *death*) in detention facilities is common and has been well documented by activists, researchers, former detainees, and journalists. There have been many deaths of migrants held in detention facilities in Australia, the United States, Canada, and elsewhere. One notorious case in the United States involved a thirty-four-year-old computer engineer, Hiu Lui Ng, who died while detained in a Rhode Island facility in 2007. The autopsy showed Ng to be riddled with cancer and suffering from a broken spine. For months he was refused a wheelchair and denied visits for medical appointments.[15] His is one of many deaths that have occurred in U.S. facilities[16]; this particular death resulted in the removal of all migrant detainees from the facility.

Other times, death is self-inflicted: suicide as protest, suicide in despair when there seems no way out and no safe way home. Suicides have taken place commonly in countries where asylum seekers are held in detention for long periods of time, including in Canada and in greater numbers in Australia and the United States. Suicide in detention centers happens not only quietly among those facing extreme isolation, but in highly publicized episodes staged to call attention to poor treatment. At the infamous Woomera facility in the Australian outback, several detainees sewed their lips shut in protest, while others killed themselves on the barbed-wire fences that enclosed them.[17]

Along the security continuum, deaths also happen long before migrants become detainees. Several researchers have documented the relationship between intensified border enforcement and more harrowing risk taking on the part of human smugglers and their clients.[18] Intensified border enforcement measures have translated into increased deaths among those desperate to cross borders.[19] No More Deaths counted 206 fatalities along the Mexico-U.S. border in Arizona between October 2008 and October 2009.[20] African migrants traveling the Sahara Desert in Libya en route to the Mediterranean pass clusters of bodies, the skeletons of those who died of hunger and dehydration. Bodies have washed ashore regularly onto the coast of Morocco and Spain's Canary Islands. Combined with the deaths that happen in detention centers, these deaths en route paint perhaps the most powerful evidence of the geographical isolation experienced by migrants globally.

Sixth, *islands* are used as spatial control strategies. "Gitmos across America," an editorial published by the *New York Times* on June 27, 2007, references yet another geographic strategy used to isolate detainees: the construction of detention centers on islands.[21] The title of the editorial also signals the important relationship between detention offshore and detention onshore. The Bush administration placed people labeled as "foreign enemy combatants" in Guantanamo precisely because of the legal ambiguity surrounding the geography of this location. The Obama administration has not removed many detainees from Guantanamo. Where this has happened, former detainees have not been freed, but have been sent to other islands willing to accept them, including Palau and Bermuda.

There are many islands where asylum seekers have been detained in spatial and legal limbo for years; U.S. offshore detentions occur not only in Cuba, but on Guam, its westernmost territory. Australia specialized in remote island locations under Prime Minister John Howard's "Pacific solution": asylum seekers' access to the asylum process and any legal representation was restricted due to their detention offshore on Australian territory (e.g., Christmas Island) and not-Australian territory (e.g., Nauru, Indonesian islands). Australian detention is contracted out to third parties, such as the International Organization for Migration, or to third states, such as Indonesia and Nauru. A degree of geographical and legal ambiguity accompanies the many disparate locations of detention, particularly those offshore.

Geography is used to deny access to rights. The growth of detention centers on islands, which are often distant from the mainland, is a global trend that reflects the characteristics and patterns of isolation outlined above. The harms of isolation are exacerbated by remote physical geography. Islands offer extreme forms of dispersal, keeping potential asylum seekers at a distance from sovereign territory where they could make an asylum claim. It is easier for authorities to control information entering and exiting island detention facilities, and the infrastructure there to support asylum claims and other migrant services is often thin. On Guam, for example, where many migrants work on visas and many others make asylum claims on a regular basis, there are no migrant advocacy organizations and no immigration judges posted on the island to hear claims. On islands, migrants and entire detention facilities can be better hidden from the view of publics, journalists, and human rights monitors. This was the case on Lampedusa, an Italian island close to Tunisia, where human rights monitors were denied entry for several years.[22] When the EU Commissioner for Human Rights finally gained entry to tour the facility, it was rumored that authorities deported detainees en masse and cleaned up the night before to provide the appearance of better conditions.[23]

Those held internally within sovereign territory also find themselves isolated in legal and geographical limbo, but detainees on islands are even more isolated. They are difficult to locate, and it is challenging for them to learn information about their cases or to access legal representation.

RADICAL MAPPINGS AND OTHER PROJECTS TO LOCATE AND REVEAL

I would like to highlight a few of the growing number of activist groups that have been working to counter these various forms of isolation. By mapping detainee locations and providing statistical information of the numbers in detention, activists locate and call attention to those who have been dislocated and silenced. In Australia, a tightly networked coalition movement took off in the late 1990s and early 2000s in response to the extreme isolation experienced by asylum seekers held in remote detention facilities. Similarly, in the United States, the Detention Watch Network (DWN) is a national coalition that formed in 1997 to respond to the substantial growth in detention after restrictive immigration legislation was implemented in 1996. The DWN became a member-driven organization in 2005 with eighty-four organizational members (and many more individual members) across the country. The network has launched an interactive mapping project, which uses a combination of geographic information systems and community participation to map detention sites across the country. Network members and members of the public are invited to add information to the map when they discover additional sites of detention.[24] A group that has undertaken mapping at a global scale is the Global Detention Project.[25] Like the DWN, the Global Detention Project created a dynamic interface where developments in detention can be readily updated. In addition to maps, the site provides detailed information on detention policies and statistics in as many countries as possible.

Some of the challenges these groups face involve the transitional and sometimes fleeting nature of detention and the concealment of detainees. In the EU, for example, there are over 200 sites where detention takes place, some near or within airports, some very small. There are additional detentions happening along and beyond EU borders, but they are not all known or documented. In the United States, there are over 350 sites where migrants are detained. Australia has attempted to conceal some of its offshore detentions in other countries, particularly Indonesia.[26]

Mapping projects often are bound by national borders. Maps may not include offshore detentions undertaken by the country where the maps are made. In other words, detention offshore is so remote from large population centers and seats of political power that its locations cannot even be mapped. Both the DWN and the Global Detention Project struggle to map those more interstitial sites along borders and on islands where sovereign jurisdiction grows more ambiguous, including sites on the outer edges of the EU where detention has increased.

Where states remove detainees from urban loci of support, advocates respond by forming groups in more rural locations to visit, support, and connect detainees to local communities and national networks. One such group in Australia was Rural Australians for Refugees. This group successfully visited detainees, hosted those who were released, and convinced rural small towns to become "welcoming centers" for refugees.[27] Similar groups have organized visitation programs in urban and rural locations across the United States, notably in New York, New Jersey, Arizona, and Georgia.[28] Networks of former detainees also organize visits to friends still being held in detention. These networks and visits are easier when detainees are not transferred to remote sites.

Detainees themselves exercise resistance by working together to counter isolation, befriending each other and the friendlier guards to share information, and working with legal counsel and local visitors who smuggle in documents, cameras, and other tools to build legal cases. They also provide support in the form of connection to sources of support on the outside when things are looking bleak. Former detainees work to stop their friends from sliding deeper into depression and despair as they languish on the inside. I had the opportunity to accompany one such group in Sydney, Australia, in 2006. We brought a picnic that included halal meat (which detainees did not receive at the center), chocolate, new underwear, cigarettes, mobile phones, and calling cards. Because the former detainees knew the guards working there, they had more freedom in carrying these items into the detention center.

Alongside mapping, additional technologies have been utilized to transcend national borders and the vast geographical distances that isolate both advocates and detainees. Email lists have proven highly effective when detainees are moved suddenly from one location to another, because advocates located thousands of miles apart are able to inform each other when someone disappears and then reappears in another facility. Australians undertook letter-writing and telephoning campaigns to communicate with those far away, who were either unable or not allowed to visit islands such as Nauru.[29]

Central to all of these efforts — mapping, visits, letter writing, advocacy, and resistance — are the simple and not-so-simple projects of identification and location. Mapping detention centers in North America and Europe is a crucial project of representation: figuring out who is detained, and where, and how that information can be publicized to garner public attention, to advocate, to change policies and practices, and to support detainees in the immediate challenges they face, survival key among them. These strategies have been designed to fight the modes of isolation discussed earlier.

While states conceal, these maps reveal, and the revelations are ripe with political potential for national lobbying efforts and more localized resistance on the ground. Locating detainees offers political possibilities for reconnection: bringing migrants back into families and communities, and into contact with networks of advocates and legal avenues to emancipation. Mapping patterns of detention and isolation also may prove to be a crucial step in holding states accountable for their policies: documenting and publicizing detention practices with the hope of eventually changing them.

WHERE DOES MAPPING LEAVE US?

In January 2010, Nina Bernstein published an article in the *New York Times* detailing the ways that immigration authorities had hidden immigrant deaths in detention facilities across the United States. Figure 10 is a map of the locations of these deaths, which demonstrate all five modes of isolation discussed

Mapping Remote Detention • 101

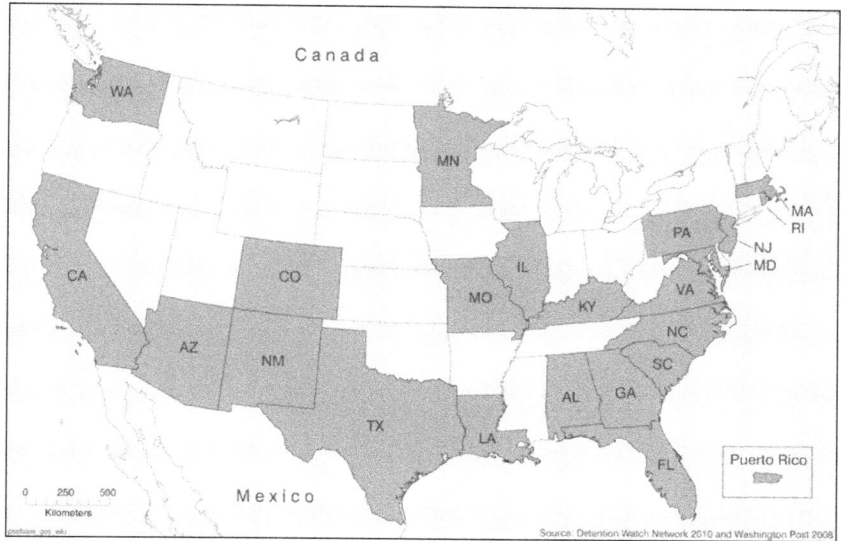

FIGURE 10. States where men and women died in ICE custody between October 2003 and November 2010. Map by Pam Schaus.

here. Those who died were dispersed across the country in a range of facilities, separated from family and community. State authorities concealed their identities and controlled information about their deaths, treating detainees as though they lived and died on islands, isolated from other detainees, families, journalists, and basic protections of their human rights. This documentation gave rise to statements by the Detention Watch Network and other groups calling attention to neglect and abuse on the part of authorities.

The intimate, localized forms of isolation are shared globally. Detention facilities are built strategically in proximity to borders, as projects with the promise of providing jobs to local communities, and in places where they are less likely to be opposed. Using geography, law, and psychology, states hide, isolate, and dehumanize detainees, manipulating their location to deny access to information and rights. As a result, dehumanization through incarceration has intensified. As important as it is to highlight the ways in which detention isolates, it is equally important to contextualize detention as one piece of the broader strategies of immigration enforcement that isolate migrants and communities. But, there is hope for social justice in the remarkable, creative, and broadly based coalitions that have formed in response to these strategies, countering isolation with revelation.

Maps have colonial histories linked to the control of space, but they can also be tools of liberation in the most elemental sense of the term. To be identified and located is to exist. Having an A number and a released name means that one can be visited, receive mail, and be accounted for in the most basic of ways. To be located, even as a dot on the map or as a participant in map making where detention is hidden, is to call out the secrets barely whispered by state authorities. Once revealed, this information offers political potential if it is taken up, publicized, and used as a catalyst for change.

NOTES

1. Bigo, "When Two Become One," 174.
2. People without citizenship who are held in detention fall into a broad array of legal categories. Some are asylum seekers asking for protection; some are undocumented migrants, who are often picked up for working without valid work papers; and still others may have been arrested on criminal charges but find themselves funneled into national detention and deportation regimes. Unless referring to a specific population, I use "migrant" as an inclusive term signifying those without citizenship in the country where they are detained.
3. See, for example, Bloch and Schuster, "At the Extremes of Exclusion."
4. Conlon, "The Nation as Embodied Practice."
5. Human Rights Watch, "Locked Up Far Away."
6. Schriro, "Immigration Detention Overview and Recommendations."
7. See Kim and Loyd, "Is Riding the Bus a Ticket to Jail?"
8. Because Batavia is a men's facility, women are usually placed in detention among "mainstream" populations in county jails across western New York.
9. In Sodus, a small town near Rochester, the Border Patrol has arrested migrant workers on their way to church services. They also have surrounded the trailer homes of migrant workers in local apple orchards; adults and children were then roused from bed and arrested in early morning raids. For more information, see http://detentiontaskforce.org/en/node/13.
10. Hiemstra, "The View from Ecuador."
11. Hiemstra, "Como Buscar Ecuatorianos Detenidos en Estados Unidos."
12. Personal communication, September 2009.
13. Interview, Sydney, March 2006.
14. Ibid.

15. Bernstein, "Detention Center Facing Inquiries."
16. Bernstein, "Officials Hid Truth of Immigration Deaths in Jails."
17. See Perera, "What Is a Camp . . . ?"
18. See, for example, Koser, "Asylum Policies, Trafficking and Vulnerability"; Nadig, "Human Smuggling, National Security, and Refugee Protection"; Andreas, *A Tale of Two Borders*.
19. See, for example, Nevins and Aizeki, *Dying to Live*.
20. Where possible, No More Deaths keeps various counts of deaths along the U.S.-Mexico border; see http://www.nomoredeaths.org/index.php/Information/deaths.html. These are contested figures and only reflect the bodies found.
21. Mountz, *Seeking Asylum*.
22. See Andrijasevic, *How to Balance Rights and Responsibilities*.
23. Interview, Rome, May 2006.
24. Detention Watch Network map, http://www.detentionwatchnetwork.org/dwnmap.
25. See http://www.globaldetentionproject.org.
26. Marr, "The Indian Ocean Solution."
27. Coombs, "Mobilising Rural Australia"; interview, Mudgee, Australia, March 2006.
28. These groups reported on their campaigns at the annual meeting of the Detention Watch Network in Washington, D.C., in September 2009.
29. Burnside, *From Nothing to Zero*.

BIBLIOGRAPHY

Andreas, P. *A Tale of Two Borders: The U.S.-Mexico and U.S.-Canada Lines after 9/11*. San Diego: Center for Comparative Immigration Studies, University of California, 2003.

Andrijasevic, R. *How to Balance Rights and Responsibilities on Asylum at the EU's Southern Border of Italy and Libya*. 2006. http://www.compas.ox.ac.uk/publications/Working%20papers/Rutvica%20Andrijasevic%20WP0627.pdf.

Bernstein, N. "Detention Center Facing Inquiries Will Get No More Immigrant Detainees." *New York Times*, December 6, 2008.

———. "Officials Hid Truth of Immigration Deaths in Jails." *New York Times*, January 9, 2010.

Bigo, D. "When Two Become One: Internal and External Securitizations in Europe." In *International Relations Theory and the Politics of European Integration*, edited by M. Kelstrup and M. Williams, 171–204. London: Routledge, 2000.

Bloch, A., and L. Schuster. "At the Extremes of Exclusion: Deportation, Detention and Dispersal." *Ethnic and Racial Studies* 28, no. 3 (2005): 491–512.

Burnside, J. *From Nothing to Zero: Letters from Refugees in Australia's Detention Centres*. Melbourne: Lonely Planet, 2003.

Conlon, D. "The Nation as Embodied Practice: Women, Migration and the Social Production of Nationhood in Ireland." Doctoral diss., City University of New York, 2007.

Coombs, A. "Mobilising Rural Australia." *Griffith Review* 3 (Autumn 2004): 96–106.

Hiemstra, N. "Como Buscar Ecuatorianos Detenidos en Estados Unidos." Unpublished manuscript, in possession of author. Department of Geography, Syracuse University, 2009.

———. "The View from Ecuador: Security, Insecurity, and Chaotic Geographies of U.S. Migrant Detention and Deportation." Doctoral diss., Syracuse University, 2011.

Human Rights Watch. "Locked Up Far Away: The Transfer of Immigrants to Remote Detention Centers in the United States." December 2, 2009. http://www.hrw.org/en/reports/2009/12/02/locked-far-away.

Kim, C., and J. Loyd. "Is Riding the Bus a Ticket to Jail?" *Colorlines*, July–August 2008. http://www.colorlines.com/article.php?ID=304.

Koser, K. "Asylum Policies, Trafficking and Vulnerability." *International Migration* 38 (2000): 91–111.

Marr, D. "The Indian Ocean Solution." *The Monthly*, 2009. http://www.the monthly.com.au/print/1040.

Mountz, A. *Seeking Asylum: Human Smuggling and Bureaucracy at the Border*. Minneapolis: University of Minnesota Press, 2010.

Nadig, A. "Human Smuggling, National Security, and Refugee Protection." *Journal of Refugee Studies* 15, no. 1 (2002): 1–25.

Nevins, J., and M. Aizeki. *Dying to Live: A Story of U.S. Immigration in an Age of Global Apartheid*. San Francisco: City Lights Open Media, 2008.

Perera, S. "What Is a Camp . . . ?" *Borderlands e-Journal* 1, no. 1 (2002): 1–10. http://www.borderlandsejournal.adelaide.edu.au/vol1no1_2002/perera_camp.html.

Schriro, D. "Immigration Detention Overview and Recommendations." *Homeland Security: Immigration and Customs Enforcement*, October 6, 2009. http:/documents.nytimes.com/immigration-detention-overview-and-recommendations#p=1.

Sudbury, J., ed. *Global Lockdown: Race, Gender, and the Prison-Industrial Complex*. New York: Routledge, 2005.

Migration Policy and the Criminalization of Protest

OLGA AKSYUTINA

"REFUGEES MUST FLEE AGAIN!" OR, THE *POTENTIAL* OF AN OFFENSE IS PUNISHABLE

On November 8, 2006, I was present at an action of the Dutch Stray Insurgent Clown Army (Clolonel). Four activists dressed as clowns and calling themselves Rita's Clowns Promotion Team handed out leaflets near the Vredenburg conference center in Utrecht. They were there to "agitate" for the conservative-liberal party of Rita Verdonk, the minister for immigration and integration (2003–2007), who was speaking at an event organized by the Institute for Multicultural Development's Forum, a think tank promoting multiculturalism, which is understood by most as forced integration.

For many people in the Netherlands, Verdonk, a former prison director, became the face of growing racism in Dutch society and the main executor of a policy of migrants' dehumanization. On her initiative, new discriminatory laws were created and new restrictions introduced. Russian journalist Boris Al'ter in "Multicultural Jihad" characterized Rita Verdonk's policy of integration as follows:

> Under her, the very name of this agency became a joke: there is nothing about integration of foreigners in Holland. The opposition assumes that it should be renamed into the "Ministry of Protection from Aliens." . . . In January, madam Verdonk was even called to testify in front of the European Council because her subordinates seized children of rejected [asylum] seekers, directly at schools, and in handcuffs, as if they were dangerous criminals, took them away to deportation camps.[1]

This was not the first time that Rita's Promotion Team came out to the streets to "support" the minister. Altogether there were five such actions carried out in Utrecht, Rotterdam, Amsterdam, and Haarlem during the 2006 election year. Their mock campaign urged passersby to vote for the minister's party, VVD (People's Party for Freedom and Democracy), which activists renamed the People's Party for Aliens' Deportation. Their slogans — "More and more refugees should be declared illegal after many years of procedures," "Let's go! Speak only Dutch in the streets!," "Refugees must flee again," "More children into cells!" — referred to actual proposals of the minister with some exaggeration to show the inhumanity of her policies.

The activists used carnivalesque tactics to show the cruelty and racism of Dutch migration policy. The clowns communicated with passersby, smiled, scattered confetti and paper streamers, chanting: "Support our minister of deportation!" For the most part, people reacted positively, understanding the clowns' bitter humor. But just as Minister Verdonk arrived, the police without warning attacked the clowns. The police aggressively pushed them about fifty meters back, threw their painted faces against a wall, and handcuffed them.

The activists were taken to the police station, confused about what was happening and which laws they might have broken. After speaking with the police, the activists assumed that they were being accused of breaking the recently enacted Compulsory Identification Law. Yet, no charges were brought against them, and five hours later all the detainees were released. Six months later one of the participants in the action — the only one who was identified — had to appear in court. She was found guilty of refusal to follow a police officer's order and disturbance of the public peace. She was sentenced to a penalty of 250 euros or five days in prison.

This was not a random attack on freedom of assembly and freedom of speech but must be situated in the context of the so-called war on terrorism. The criminalization of protest and immigration frequently occurs under the guise of fighting "terrorism" and "extremism." It is accompanied by a rigorous assault on the practices and the very paradigm of human rights, which has been aggressively displaced by the paradigm of "safety." The events of 9/11 have provided an opportunity to solidify an image of "the enemy" — the Muslim, the migrant — and dissidents in general. This has created certain categories of people who are excluded from the realm of civil and human rights, and migrants and protesters have become suspect number one. Today, protesting against governmental policy or corporate activities can easily turn you into a "criminal," "extremist," or "terrorist."

In this chapter, I will analyze how the struggle against state racism is turned into "extremism," or, more precisely, how the Dutch state criminalizes protest against migration policy.[2] I focus my attention on the Netherlands, a country whose image used to be one of the most tolerant in the world. Today, however, the Dutch state has some of the harshest anti-immigrant policies in Europe. The level of racism in the society has grown swiftly, expressed in both the rise of everyday xenophobia and the increase in the popularity of far right parties.

STATE RACISM AND DUTCH IMMIGRATION AND ASYLUM POLICIES

Since World War II, the content of racism has shifted from discredited categories of "biological" difference to rely on "cultural" differences and "ethnicity." However, this shift has not changed how racism functions to legitimize inequality and discrimination. The state's nationalist discourse plays an important role in sustaining racist beliefs in society. It creates a moral context for the emergence of anti-immigrant legislation and the implementation of repressive racist practices, including the imprisonment of migrants, deportations, and so on. The demonization of migrants constitutes an important component for the formation of racist societies. It justifies policies which make immigration to "rich" countries nearly impossible and serves to maintain a system of international inequality which critics call "global apartheid."

From the moment of its introduction in 1849, immigration legislation in the Netherlands has been intended for the exclusion of refugees. At the beginning of the 1990s, a new stage of exclusion began: illegalization. It promoted the formation of a new form of racism in which some people do not have a right to be a part of society because they are "illegals."

The Netherlands announced officially that it was opening deportation centers and prisons for rejected asylum seekers and undocumented migrants in 2003. Deportation prisons are a contemporary form of concentration camp where civilians are contained. In order to imprison people without any charges, trials, or sentences, a legal basis was necessary. In the Netherlands this legal basis for the deprivation of freedom of undocumented migrants and rejected asylum seekers was created by the Aliens Act (Vreemdelingenwet 2000), which came into effect on April 1, 2001.

People who do not have the documents demanded by authorities have been outlawed, and can be legally deprived of their freedom for periods of up to one and a half years (according to the EU Directive 2008/115/EC). Longer terms have been common, and people can be detained repeatedly. Moreover, they are imprisoned without an investigation or trial. British immigration lawyer Steven Cohen highlights the exceptionality of immigration legislation: "Under all other laws it is the act that is illegal, but under immigration law it is the person who is illegal. Those subject to immigration control are dehumanised, are reduced to non-persons, are nobodies."[3]

The increasing imprisonment of migrants has spread throughout Europe since the mid-1990s as a consequence of migrants' dehumanization. An association of lawyers who fight for migrants' rights in the Netherlands demanded that detainees in detention centers not be treated worse than prisoners in regular Dutch prisons. Indeed, detention centers are situated outside the general framework of the Dutch law. Because they are not officially recognized as prisons, they are exempt from policies regulating the institutions that confine Dutch citizens. In practice, even when a judge decides that a person should be released, the IND (the Dutch Immigration and Naturalization Service, an agency of the Ministry of Justice, responsible for deportations) regularly keeps people in detention for months despite the legal decision.

Because of the inhumane treatment, the horrors that people often endured in their countries of origin, and the constant threat of being returned against their will, some prisoners in deportation centers attempt suicide. Authorities respond by locking them up for one to two weeks in solitary confinement. Authorities also cruelly suppress the regular hunger strikes. Complaints are often answered with aggression and beatings by the guards, and for even the smallest offense, detainees are put in solitary confinement.

These anti-immigrant policies have earned the Netherlands a spot on the blacklists of Amnesty International, Human Rights Watch, and other international human rights organizations. In a 2008 report, Amnesty International wrote, "Irregular migrants are detained under more restrictive conditions than ordinary remand prisoners or sentenced prisoners subjected to the same penitentiary rules and regulations. . . . As such, immigration detention has effectively become a tool of *deterrence* and *punishment*."[4]

For the immigration officials of the Dutch state (as for the European Union as a whole), it does not matter why refugees arrive. Participants in the collective Autonoom Centrum write:

> The detention and deportation of refugees and migrants from the Netherlands is a "breech-block" policy that aims to regulate migration. This means that the number of refugees is reduced to an "acceptable" level, regardless of the motives of their arrival. In the regulation of migration the situation beyond the (European) borders is hardly taken into consideration. A solution to the *causes* of "forced" migration is not being pursued.[5]

For this purpose, the Dublin Convention was adopted in 1990 (in September 2003, it was replaced by the Dublin II regulation), and readmission treaties between the European Union and other states were signed.[6] All of these efforts aim to preserve the inequality between the rich countries and their (former) colonies. Since legitimization of inequality is the main function of racism, we can say that state racism lies at the basis of the Dutch and EU migration policy.

The situation was further aggravated by the crumbling of Western European "welfare states" in the 1990s and 2000s after the reforms brought by neoliberal globalization. New labor, housing, and other codes and laws were adopted in many countries, which deprived people of social welfare and many other entitlements. Neoliberal policy reforms have led to an explosion of inequality between the poor and the rich within "the West" itself. In this situation, the redirection of public discontent toward "aliens," "strangers," and "newcomers" made sense for the authorities because, as Vladimir Malakhov explains: "it is better to channel anger of the lower classes into a safe 'ethnic' channel than to let it be concentrated on the ruling class."[7] Consequently, there has been a significant shift of the political center to the right in the majority of European states. The Netherlands has not been an exception to this process; during the November 2006 elections the three parties fighting over which would exclude and deport the most got 31 of 150 seats in the House of Representatives. In 2010 the most vocally xenophobic parties (VVD and PVV) got 55 seats, or one-third. This characterizes the current state of Dutch society. In the twenty-first century, xenophobia has grown swiftly. This is in many respects exactly the predictable outcome of state racism, which plays on such moods.

PROTEST AS "EXTREMISM"

How does the criminalization of protest against migration policy occur? State-produced discourses are one of the most important tools for forming the image of "the enemy." In essence, the state possesses the monopoly on the production of official meanings. The secret service is the main agency for classifying security threats and defining phenomena dangerous to the state. According to the Dutch General Intelligence and Security Service (AIVD), it "investigates people and organizations which, by virtue of their aims and methods, give rise to a reasonable suspicion that they pose a serious danger to the democratic legal order."[8]

In its annual reports, AIVD used to categorize protest activities under the heading "Politically Motivated Violent Activism," but in 2005 the category "Political Extremism" was created instead. "Opposition to Government Immigration and Asylum Policy" was classified within the category "Left-

Wing Extremism." While AIVD had used the word "extremism" at least since 2005, it was defined for the first time in 2009 in the report "The Flames of Resistance: Growing Opposition to Dutch Immigration and Asylum Policy" as a "phenomenon whereby, in their struggle for particular rights, individuals or groups deliberately overstep the bounds of the law to commit illegal, sometimes violent, acts" (13). Defined this way, "extremism" contains a wide range of protest tactics, including blockades and other acts of civil disobedience. The practices covered by this definition make it clear that its aim is to include the activities of particular groups the authorities are seeking to criminalize.

In 2006 AIVD reported: "the minister for immigration and integration was systematically, [while] on campaign for the elections, verbally abused by one or two obstinate individuals."[9] While the report did not explicitly name Rita's Promotion Team, its actions were specifically implied. The courts also tried to portray the group's activities as threatening to the immigration minister. A state prosecutor "stated in court that Verdonk was many times stalked by *this* group, and, therefore, the group was dangerous, because they didn't respect her freedom."[10] When, on the grounds of "rhetorical" criminalization, damning verdicts are delivered, protest is turned into crime at the juridical level, and protesters are put behind bars.

Here I would like to consider some other examples of the criminalization of protests against anti-immigrant policy in the Netherlands. In October 2005, these protests took the form of a "banner war." Information about the unbearable conditions in deportation prisons came to the surface after a fire in the deportation prison at Schiphol airport, where eleven people died. Some guards aimed their guns at prisoners who were trying to help others get away from the fire. Minister Verdonk's response was especially outrageous: she stated that the guards behaved "adequately." Following the fire, many people hung banners from their houses to show their indignation about the events. One on an Amsterdam squat read: "Verdonk, still no blood on your hands?" The riot police attacked and raided the squat. The banner was torn down without explanation, and people who were in the house were beaten and detained, again without any charges.

Then activists hung out another banner: "Eleven burned alive. Thanks, Rita." Other Amsterdam squats followed their lead. Soon, banners spread over the whole country. Squatters, activists, and people who did not typically voice their opinion through public statements felt a need to express their views and hang banners or posters such as "Agency Rita: Arrest, deportation, cremation." The state responded with even greater repression. But as banners were torn down by the police, more of them were hung, and stickers, postcards, and stencils appeared.

The AIVD report characterized the banner war as follows: "The fire at Schiphol-East caused a series of fierce protests across the country. Everywhere banners showing offensive texts were seen. Because the banners were removed by the police, the activists turned against local policymakers rather than against the minister herself."[11] This cynicism illustrates the real aim of the repression: indeed, the content of the protest was moved from state immigration policy to the problem of state repression.

The most striking repression of protest is locking up activists (regardless of citizenship) in *deportation* prisons. Here the criminalization of migrants and protesters converges through the repressive state practices used against both "undesirable elements." For confinement to a deportation prison, the assumption that someone is a foreigner is not enough (though the police often take it as such). Under the Aliens Act, substantive evidence is necessary to prove that someone is on Dutch territory "without proper documents." In practice, even this absurd formulation is not satisfied: activists who refuse to identify themselves can spend months in detention centers under the accusation that they are "illegal migrants." (For many activists, this practice of non-identification is important because it expresses practical solidarity with people "without papers" and serves as a challenge to the institution of citizenship which separates "Dutch" and "foreigner.")

This type of repression serves as frightening intimidation: activists know about the hell of deportation prisons, and when faced with a threat of being locked up in one for an uncertain period, some might give in and identify themselves. Thus, processes of the illegalization of "unwanted Others" are extended, and the suspicion of being "illegal" is enough to deprive anybody of rights and freedom.

A final significant example of the criminalization of protest against immigration policy is the case of the working group Stop Deportations. The group was created to draw public attention to the problem of the illegalization of migrants and to challenge deportation prisons. From June 2006 till December 2007, its members carried out monthly lock-on blockade actions of deportation prisons, detention centers, and the construction sites of these institutions. (In lock-on actions, activists connect their hands together inside a metal tube in order to frustrate those trying to remove them.) In 2008 the group switched its tactics to noisy demonstrations at detention centers and more symbolic performance actions (like die-ins) directed at the state agencies and companies responsible for the planning, construction, and maintenance of detention centers.

Stop Deportations has become an object of intense interest to the Dutch security service. Within a year of its formation, it was placed in AIVD's annual report in the section "Left-Wing Extremism" under the subsection "Resistance against Asylum Policy." In its 2009 special report on opposition to immigration and asylum policy, AIVD accused Stop Deportations of "nocturnal attacks on property," though there had not been a trial or even an arraignment. The vague formulations ("quite plausible," "in all likelihood," and "at least some of these activities") of the report[12] nonetheless have far-reaching consequences. Defining as "extremism" any kind of protest which does not strictly follow the law blends together different protest tactics and narrows the space for the expression of dissent. Official discourses discredit and delegitimize protest, and the label "extremist" is an important part of this.

CONCLUSION

State discourses that transmit racism as official ideology help to create conditions for discriminatory and exclusionary laws and practices. Moreover, they officially justify repression. When migrants are outlawed — by the very naming "illegals" — the state also renders protests against these policies as "criminal activities."

The repression of protest against migration policy is a logical outcome of the institution of citizenship, which is built on a policy of exclusion. From its very appearance the concept of citizen served as a tool of exclusion, including from human rights because these are theoretically for citizens only. Protesting against state policy can put one into a similar vulnerable position as that of a noncitizen. When one is labeled and treated as extremist, one can lose the rights of a citizen. Thus, the very privilege of being a citizen depends not only on how well one follows the national laws, but also on whether one questions the status quo or stays passive toward the state acting in our names. In contemporary Western "democracies," when authorities try to reduce protest to voting (as Tony Blair put it, "If you have got something to say, say it democratically. Come out and vote"),[13] a person protesting in the streets is presented as a threat to security.

Within the new paradigm of security, repression toward migrants and protesters and the formation of new legislation are springboards for the creation of more repressive societies, as the measures (including emergency legislation) taken against these categories gradually become part of everyday life for the entire society. Protesters and, especially, migrants are used by authorities as a testing area for the development of technologies and strategies of control and suppression, while the fear of "terrorism" makes it possible to introduce any measures "for the provision of safety."

"Extremism" has been used by Western "democracies" as a tool for the criminalization of politically unwanted people. It serves for the production of the Other as an enemy. It demonizes those who do not support the status quo, who do not fit the state hegemonic ideology, who fall out of the mainstream culture: "illegal" immigrants, "militant" activists, "delinquent" teenagers. Will you be next?

NOTES

I dedicate this chapter to those who fight against the borders and for the freedom of movement. I offer hearty gratitude to Roelof Pieters for his help and inspiration in the writing of this chapter, as well as to all the people who read, commented, and corrected it, especially the editors of the journal *De Fabel van de illegaal/Doorbraak*, Eric Krebbers and Harry Westerink. I am very thankful to Meredith Gill and R. Konstantin Rechitsky for their proofreading. This chapter is based on research undertaken with support of the INTAS foundation (05-109-5185). It originally appeared in somewhat different form in Russian as "Protestors' Extremism: The Criminalization of Dissent against the Dutch Immigration Policy," in *Not Final Analysis: Xenophobic Attitudes among Young People*, edited by E. Omelchenko and E. Lukyanova, 159–92 (Ulyanovsk: Ulyanovsk University Press, 2009).

1. Al'ter, "Mul'tikul'turnyj dzhihad." All translations from Russian are by the author.

2. Here, *criminalization* is understood as "the institutionalised process through which certain acts and behaviours are labelled as 'crimes' and 'outlawed.' . . . Further, however, it is a political, economic and ideological process through which individuals and identifiable groups are selectively policed and disciplined" (Chadwick and Scraton, "Criminalisation," 68–69).

3. Cohen, "No One Is Illegal," 190.

4. Amnesty International, "The Detention of Irregular Migrants and Asylum-Seekers," 13, 51; emphases added.

5. Autonoom Centrum, *Over de Grens*. English translation from http://www.autonoomcentrum.nl/overdegrens/9/index_en.html; emphasis added.

6. The Dublin Convention (which first came into force on September 1, 1997) determines which state is responsible for examining applications for asylum lodged in one of the member states of the European Communities. The main point of Dublin II is that those fleeing persecution should apply for asylum in the first EU country in which they arrive.

7. Malakhov, "Natsiostroitel'stvo i ego proraby," 25.

8. General Intelligence and Security Service, "The Flames of Resistance," 13.
9. General Intelligence and Security Service, *Annual Report*, 2006, 50.
10. Interview by the author with clown Elfie Tinkel, Clolonel, July 8, 2007.
11. General Intelligence and Security Service, *Annual Report*, 2006, 31.
12. General Intelligence and Security Service, "The Flames of Resistance," 8.
13. Quoted in Hopkins et al., "Peace in Paris, Skirmishes on the Streets of London," 1.

BIBLIOGRAPHY

Al'ter, Boris. "Mul'tikul'turnyj dzhihad." March 15, 2006. http://www.rosbalt.ru/2006 /03/15/246831.html.
Amnesty International. "The Detention of Irregular Migrants and Asylum-Seekers, EUR 35/002/2008." June 27, 2008. http://www.amnesty.org/en/library/info /eur35/002/2008/en.
Autonoom Centrum. *Over de Grens: Verwijdering vluchtelingen en migranten uit Nederland*. Amsterdam: Autonoom Centrum, 2004.
Chadwick, Kathryn, and Phil Scraton. "Criminalisation." In *Sage Dictionary of Criminology*, edited by Eugene McLaughlin and John Muncie, 68–69. London: Sage, 2001.
Cohen, Steven. "No One Is Illegal: Manifesto of the No One Is Illegal Group (UK), 6 September 2003." In *No One Is Illegal: Asylum and Immigration Control, Past and Present*, edited by Steven Cohen, 190. Staffordshire, England: Trentham, 2003.
General Intelligence and Security Service. *Annual Report*, 2005. http://www.aivd.nl /contents/pages/81211/aivd_annual_2005.pdf.
———. *Annual Report*, 2006. https://www.aivd.nl/publish/ pages/1205/20070872jv2006_en.pdf.
———. "The Flames of Resistance: Growing Opposition to Dutch Immigration and Asylum Policy." 2009. https://www.aivd.nl/publish/pages/1349 /theflamesofresistance.pdf.
Hopkins, N., P. Kelso, J. Wilson, and J. Vasagar. "Peace in Paris, Skirmishes on the Streets of London." *Guardian*, May 2, 2002, 1.
Malakhov, Vladimir. "Natsiostroitel'stvo i ego proraby." In *Ponaehali tut . . . Ocherki o natsionalizme, rasizme i kul'turnom pljuralizme*, edited by Vladimir Malakhov, 25. Moscow: Novoe Literaturnoe Obozrenie, 2007.

William Bratton in the Other L.A.

MICOL SEIGEL

Most Los Angelenos know that William Bratton headed up police departments elsewhere before he came to L.A. They know he was chief in New York. They may even know he was chief in Boston first. Fewer are aware of Bratton's ventures abroad, despite their impressive scope. Bratton has literally been around the world, offering consulting services to police departments on demand. He tries not to publicize his travels during his chieftaincies for fear of criticism that he is distracting himself from the places he ought to be protecting, and he doesn't trumpet the work performed during his moments of private-sector employment either. Perhaps that is because those projects haven't exactly been an unmitigated success. All the more reason to consider them, then, particularly for those of us interested in policing, state repression, and the relationship between the United States and the rest of the world. As a historian of the Americas I am deeply curious about those phenomena, and I am drawn to examine Bratton's travels, particularly to Latin America — the "other L.A." As a social critic I am concerned with what I have discovered so far. This chapter shares some of my preliminary research in the hope of provoking productive conversations on policing in and beyond Los Angeles.

Let me begin by providing a few of my hunches about the history of U.S. "assistance" to Latin American policing before I narrate what I know of Bratton's movement through its landscape. Over the last half century, the United States has provided extensive support for foreign policing in Latin America. Because policing is supposedly "civil," this assistance has come under less scrutiny and provoked less protest than the military aid Cold Warriors provided overtly and covertly to the region. There is now no question of the United States' involvement in Argentina's post-Perón "dirty war" between 1976 and 1983; in the "generals' coup" in Brazil in 1964 and its brutal 1968 constriction; and in Pinochet's rise to power in Chile in 1973; and that those interventions (and others) were only the ABC of a whole alphabet of U.S.-assisted regime changes in postwar Latin America.

The role played by U.S. police assistance in buttressing these authoritarian regimes is less noticed but no less clear. Martha Huggins, for example, has documented the history of the extensive support the United States has provided for foreign policing in the region, from the police instructors who traveled to the Panama Canal zone in 1946 to teach in the Latin American Ground School (precursor of the School of the Americas), to the constabulary forces of Eisenhower's Overseas Internal Security Program (active in twenty countries within a year of its 1957 launch), to the State Department staff of the International Narcotics Control program who took their posts in 1961, to the police trainers of the Office of Public Safety, the soon-to-be-notorious AID program established by JFK in 1962. These programs' close collaborations with Latin American military governments militarized and politicized the process of policing, tying it even more closely to state interests in maintaining power and suppressing dissent.[1]

Certainly there are many reasons to remember this history and consider its contemporary manifestations. It unquestionably continues to shape everyday life in Latin America, and it affects those of us in the United States for whom Latin America means family in this or recent generations, and the inhabitants of Los Angeles, that great Latino metropolis, who share space and co-create culture with Latin American immigrants and their descendants. Yet how can it not also equally shade and constrain patterns of experience in the United States, even for people who do not identify as Latino? How could these chickens, too, not come home to roost? That the history of U.S. police assistance to Latin America has shaped policing and incarceration practices *in the United States* is my hunch, the spark for my research, and the reason I want to contribute to this forum.

A tighter focus on the details of U.S.–Latin America collaboration in Cold War policing feeds this hunch. Individual North Americans involved in policing Latin America have sometimes returned to criminal justice work in the United States. Did they bring their observations and experiences home? Consider Nelson Rockefeller, who governed New York state after far-reaching experience in Latin America, including years holding the post of coordinator of inter-American affairs. While governor of New York, Rockefeller led a 1969 presidential mission to Latin America for Nixon and came to deeply anticommunist conclusions, just two short years before Attica inmates rioted on his watch.[2] Did Rockefeller draw on his encounter with exported counterinsurgency tactics in deciding how to respond at Attica? Later, as he crafted the 1973 drug sentencing laws that bear his name (objects of the Drop the Rock campaign), did he reflect on his familiarity with the policing of narcotics trafficking in Cold War Latin America?

The career trajectories of more numerous, less well-known vehicles of U.S. police assistance abroad may be even more enlightening. FBI Special Intelligence Service agent Rolf Larson, for example, spent five years in Brazil and a shorter stint in Bolivia in the 1940s and 1950s. Upon his return, Larson was assigned to carry out anticommunist work in Arizona, "fortified," as Huggins points out, "by a wealth of counterespionage intelligence-gathering skills further developed and tested abroad."[3] What did Larson and other North Americans involved in policing Latin America learn there? Did they apply those lessons back on the domestic front?

What about Bratton, then? What did he learn in Latin America? How do his policing tactics in Los Angeles reflect his travels there? How does his policing incorporate the assumptions woven into state disciplinary tactics by the long history of U.S. police assistance to Latin America? These are the questions I hope my research will eventually answer. I cannot answer them yet. What I can do here is set out the trajectory of Bratton's Latin American travels in the years between his New York and Los Angeles employments, reflect upon them, and invite your reflections.

To draw this map, I went first to the source: Bratton's funding. Follow the money. The Manhattan Institute, the well-endowed foundation for which Bratton is a poster boy of sorts, suggested that I speak with Bill Andrews, a Bratton associate on the MI payroll who worked on Bratton's Latin American projects in the interim between chieftaincies in New York and Los Angeles. I interviewed Andrews three times by phone in January and February 2006. Eventually I interviewed Bratton himself in person in his downtown office in July 2006, with videographer Ashley Hunt recording. Perhaps unsurprisingly, Bratton added virtually nothing to my understanding of the relevance of his travels. His smooth facade provides little entrée, though that in itself is impressive and instructive. Andrews was a far more revealing interview subject.

To those interviews, I added newspaper articles from the mainstream press, promotional materials from both Bratton and the Manhattan Institute, web-based accounts, and materials from the Southern California Library, whose wonderful social movement archives and clippings files were invaluable in ferreting out salient connections. Triangulating those sources, I have pieced together a rough view of Bratton's work in Latin America. Here is what I know of this story so far.[4]

In April 1996, William Bratton resigned as chief of police of the city of New York. Apparently, then-mayor Rudolph Giuliani had begun to resent Bratton's media-grabbing style, or so the story goes among Bratton partisans.[5] Bratton was hired to preside over a private security company, First Security Consulting, but he quit to take on another presidency, this time of a car insurance anti-fraud company, Carco.[6] During this time he also began to work as a motivational speaker, playing a range of venues that included the FBI National Academy.[7] Soon, he moved on to his eponymous consulting firm, the Bratton Group, which is affiliated with the Manhattan Institute.

The MI is a conservative think tank founded in New York in 1978. It supports fellows and field projects in NYC and worldwide. The MI's pet issues are school vouchers and policing; in all endeavors it seeks greater "economic choice and individual responsibility." It is absurdly wealthy and correspondingly generous, particularly with "information." As its website touts, "We don't sell information. We give it away for free." In its work to shape police policy, the institute has organized itself around its senior fellow George Kelling's "broken windows" theory (fix small ills to prevent big crimes), publicized in a famous 1982 *Atlantic Monthly* article.[8] Bratton is a deep believer in and practitioner of "broken windows" policing.

To sell these tactics and the institute's school-reform agenda to our neighbors to the south, the MI launched in 2002 the Inter-American Policy Exchange, an initiative "working to share ideas for urban renewal with leaders in Latin America," according to its president's introduction.[9] Beyond the projects detailed here that it has supported through Bratton, the MI contracts with government officials in Honduras, Argentina, Mexico, and Chile, and the list surely continues.[10] In 2002, when the Bratton Group designed security plans for Barnard College and Brown University, campus news services reported the hiring of an "international security consulting firm," a scope surely enabled by its relation to the MI.[11]

The forming of the Bratton Group via the MI had come on the heels of visible prison crises in a handful of Latin American countries, which were heavily reported in the U.S. media in 1996 and early 1997.[12] In the summer of 1997, Bratton launched his first project in Latin America, beginning in Fortaleza, Brazil, where he helped establish "model precincts" and other favored strategies, remaining under contract until early 2000. His other relatively long-term work was in Caracas from late 2000 (a formal contract began in the spring of 2001) through 2002.[13] He had brief experimental forays into Buenos Aires in 1998, Cordoba in February and April 2000, Guayaquil in January 2002, and

Lima that May. Cordoba remained a pending project for some time, but the others did not pan out.

The Fortaleza project began in June or July 1997, when Bratton and John Timoney, a former Bratton collaborator in New York and at the time police chief of Miami, spent about a week looking into possibilities in that northeastern Brazilian city. They fulfilled two contracts, each several months long, traveling to Fortaleza for short periods several times during the life of each contract. On the first trip the firm pitched its model-precinct strategy, U.S.-type systems in a few select neighborhoods (rather than, say, citywide technical training). On the second visit, the principals chose a site: the Conjunto Ceará, a stretch of a dozen working-class and poor neighborhoods on the western side of the city, mostly service-poor favelas but also including one (in Andrews's count) "developed neighborhood," where city services had penetrated. They set up the precinct in February 1998. The centerpiece of Bratton's vaunted strategy, a sophisticated reporting system, immediately began gathering statistics. For the second model precinct, the group chose the neighborhood of Aliota. In marked contrast to the Conjunto Ceará, Aliota is an affluent, mixed residential and commercial neighborhood in which high-end commercial activities have relocated from the original city center, leaving *el centro* mostly to lower-end businesses and shabby buildings. That precinct went up in September 1998, followed soon after by a third in *el centro* around January 1999.

At the end of 1999, after fulfilling both contracts, Fortaleza's city officials declined to retain the Bratton Group. In speculating about the reasons they were not contracted again, Andrews offered an illustrative critique of the structure of the police system in Brazil. Police power rests with the federal state there, so it cannot be reformed at the municipal level. Working city by city, Andrews thought, would have been a simpler task. This is an odd critique, however, given that the Bratton Group *was* working in a single city; I therefore think it is a red herring. Andrews also pointed to the difficulty of working in a system divided between military and civil police. In Fortaleza, he explained, civil police work is mostly investigative and legal; it is the civil police who create "inquiries," the legal documents required for trial. Military police make the arrests; civil police process them. Civil police are all *delegados* (law school graduates) and protective of their prerogatives. Most resources go to their work, which is to say, most resources are expended on the part of the process *after* the arrest. As Andrews put it, this means resources are over-allocated to crimes that are already "solved." For Andrews, an arrest is a solution.

The explanation for Bratton's firing, Andrews was implying with this critique, may lie in the Bratton Group's attempt to reroute power from civil to military police, a move that would surely have been richly resented by the former. What is suggestive to me in Andrews's explanation is the palpable disdain he expresses for the civil police, who emerge as pompous bureaucrats in his portrayal. Andrews, like Bratton, clearly prefers arrest-focused policing without the "burden" of legal process. This is telling, since the civil-military distinction is usually a sign of an attempt to safeguard human rights, and in Brazil's case probably codifies compelling protests against violently oppressive police activity, perhaps during one of Brazil's several eras of military dictatorship (all amply supported by the United States).

With the Fortaleza contract ongoing, the Bratton Group moved to expand its circle of influence. The group explored the possibility of a Buenos Aires project near the end of 1998 when mayoral candidate Gustavo Beliz invited them to visit. Andrews described Beliz as a "leftie," who nonetheless had a "relationship with" the Manhattan Institute. Beliz lost the mayoral race in May 2000 to Anibal Ibarra, and so the contract was off. When Nestor Kirchner became Argentina's president in 2003, Beliz briefly became his public safety officer, but he was fired in July 2004 — not serving long enough to move forward with his Bratton collaboration, I guess.[14]

Just as the Fortaleza project was petering out in September 2000, Bratton flew to Caracas on what Andrews described as a sort of VIP tour. The team sent the city a plan in December, and started work on that basis in early 2001. Following the same model in Caracas they had used in Fortaleza, they assessed, produced a report, and then established model precincts in a poor neighborhood, in this case Katia, one of Caracas's five municipalities, situated on the west side of the city. Andrews told me they intended to branch out to an east-side neighborhood, but their contract ended in December 2001, and it was not renewed. They continued to travel to Caracas in 2002, making one last visit in September, but the people with whom they had been working were no longer in power and the new city leadership "put the brakes on," Andrews explained.

This timing is interesting. Hugo Chávez became president of Venezuela in January 1999. He quickly set about crafting a new constitution, and then, following its directives, called for new elections to "relegitimize" the government. He won reelection and in August 2000 was sworn in.[15] A month later Bratton touched down. Did the Manhattan Institute's overtures to its contacts there or Caracans' response to them coordinate or simply coincide with Chávez's political trajectory? Bratton's host in Caracas was Alfredo Peña, then the new mayor, who told the *New York Times* in April 2001 that "visits to New York had made him eager to have Mr. Bratton."[16] Who invited Peña to New York? Might the MI have paid his way?

Remember also that Chávez was the target of an attempted coup in April 2002. The placements of Bratton's contacts in that coup are startling. Besides Mayor Peña, Bratton's team also worked with Ivan Simonovis, who in September 2000 was the newly appointed public safety secretary (he also liked to call himself the commissioner of police); Simonovis's number two, Edgar Barrientes, chief of security; Lazaro Forero, who replaced Barrientes (Simonovis decided Barrientes was undermining him, Andrews speculated); deputy public secretary Luis Carrasquel; and the Caracas Metropolitan Police commander, Henry Vivas. After the coup, Peña fled to Florida, and Simonovis, Forero, and Vivas landed in jail, where they remain. Simonovis was arrested in an airport trying to leave for the United States, Vivas and Forero after seeking asylum in El Salvador at the Salvadoran embassy.[17]

Vivas and Forero were accused of ordering police to fire at pro-Chávez demonstrators on the day of the coup. They were accused by four police officers, according to a pro-Chávez website, Hands Off Venezuela, which reports the bewildered court testimony of one of the four: "I do not know why Superintendents Vivas, Iván Simonovis and Forero did not give the order to break up the march." According to Hands Off Venezuela, state prosecutor Danilo Anderson charged Vivas and Forero with participation in the coup in November 2004 — and was assassinated two weeks later.

Andrews expressed real regret at not being able to continue the Caracas project. He really thought they had potential there. In the fall of 2002, he maintained, there was a noticeable decline in the murder rate in Katia, which he attributed to the investigations his group had carried out and trained others to continue. Still, in Andrews's critique-by-proxy of Chávez (I mean, his repeated mentions of Chávez friends who turned against him), little hints about other aspects of the Bratton-trained police emerge. Chávez began to swipe at the Metropolitan Police, Andrews noted. For what? I wondered. In what Andrews described as a "very unfortunate incident," an MP shot the son of interior minister Luis Miquilena. Pretty soon, "Bratton Go Home" graffiti began to appear.

I think Andrews mentioned the graffiti because he suspected I would see it. He was right. I quickly came across a photograph of precisely that, in a booklet archived at the Southern California Library. The October 22nd Coalition, a radical anti–police brutality group, produced the booklet when Bratton was new to the LAPD; it is one of many protests launched by Los Angeles social movements against Bratton's hiring. Interestingly, the bilingual graffiti implicates Bratton along with his host; it reads "Peña traidor [traitor]; Bratton Go Home." In another discordant note, the booklet's caption connects the rejection of Bratton to the 2001 shooting of Miquilena's grandson (not son; either the booklet or Andrews is wrong).[18] What, I wonder, was the link?

Clearly, there are many research leads to be pursued in this part of the story, which is ongoing. Bratton's hand is probably still in the mix, though he appears to have no active projects in Latin America just now. That may reflect a response to public outcry: when Bratton resumed his public service by accepting the chieftaincy of the LAPD, there was audible muttering about his extensive travels. On the occasion of a trip to Israel in December 2002, Police Commission president Rick Caruso defended Bratton. Caruso encouraged city leadership to "go around the world to learn about a multitude of issues. There's a lot to learn from the Israelis," he explained. "That's no different from people coming here to learn from the LAPD."[19]

Caruso's suggestion that Bratton went to learn rather than teach is telling. Andrews never suggested that Bratton had picked up anything of use in his Latin American projects. This is one of the areas I had hoped to explore in my conversation with Bratton. I had crafted carefully stepwise questions designed to reveal whether he thought he would learn from Latin America; whether he thinks now that he learned from Latin America; and whether he actually did learn from his experiences there — the most important as well as the most unequivocal question. Bratton refused them all. When pushed to consider what he might have gleaned, he offered only the blandest, most politic homage to Latinos' family values. He had realized how important *familia* is to people there and therefore in L.A. Cue the violins.

In 1997, when Bratton was a free agent, the New York *Daily News* reported that he was "introducing New York's COMSTAT crime-fighting computer program to Birmingham, Ala., and Brazil."[20] This is a telling alignment. Juxtaposing these two places reinforces their deeply etched racial and colonial codings. The policies implemented within the United States that disproportionately affect internally colonized, racially disfranchised groups echo in the practices exported to control the subjects of U.S. empire, the mostly brown and black people in situations of neocolonialism, economic colonialism, or the outright colonialism of the post–Cold War world. There is no longer (if there ever was) any originary moment in this cycle of comparative logic, whose agents cite the behavior of one to justify the policing of the other. Bratton's work in New York propelled him to Brazil, and then to Venezuela; his "success" as an international security consultant helped to secure him a job in L.A. Even before that, practices developed in the Latino metropolis of L.A. and in the black urban ghettos there and in northern California's East Bay — namely, anti-gang initiatives such as the database system — laid the ground on which Bratton would build in New York. Then in L.A. he closed another circle by collaborating with ICE and other forces working to continue the militarization of the border. Since leaving L.A., he continues to offer his services for hire, including working in London in August 2011 during that city's anti–police brutality riots. What next?

NOTES

This chapter was originally written in 2007 and has been only lightly updated.
1. Huggins, *Political Policing*.
2. Rockefeller, *The Rockefeller Report on the Americas*.
3. Huggins, *Political Policing*, 66.
4. Except where otherwise noted, the material is from the Andrews interviews.
5. Bratton, *Turnaround*.
6. Bratton, "Blood, Sweat, & Databases," 56; Ravo, "Fraud Investigator Hires Bratton."
7. Bratton, *Turnaround*, 309.
8. Kelling and Wilson, "Broken Windows."
9. Mone, "President's Welcome."
10. Hayden, "Ending the War in Los Angeles"; DePalma, "The Americas Court." Interestingly, DePalma also mentions a security consulting firm with no MI ties, the Giuliani Group.
11. "Brown Commissions Bratton Group to Lead Campus Security Study"; "New Master Plan Development to Include Campus Safety Review."
12. "Latin America's Inhumane Prisons"; "Dismal Dungeons"; Aquila Lawrence, "In Latin America, Revolting Jail Life"; "Latin America's Prisons"; Sims, "Human Remains Found in Prison Oven after Riot"; Sims, "Prison Riots in Sixth Day in Argentina."
13. Rother, "A Veteran Cop on a Tough New Beat," dates Bratton's start date as a consultant for the Caracas Metropolitan Police to April 2001. Lifsher reports it earlier in "If He Can Fight Crime There, He'll Fight It . . . Anywhere."
14. Rother, "Police Corruption Plagues Argentines and President."
15. "Venezuela's Chavez Sworn in Saturday."
16. Rother, "A Veteran Cop on a Tough New Beat."
17. "Balance Sobre las Investigaciones de los Sucesos de Abril de 2002."
18. October 22nd Coalition, "Decoding William J. Bratton, New LAPD Chief."
19. Blankstein, "Chief to Meet with Israeli Police, Political Leaders."
20. Rush and Molloy, "Bratton Says Maple Remains True-Blue Friend."

BIBLIOGRAPHY

Aquila Lawrence, David. "In Latin America, Revolting Jail Life." *Christian Science Monitor*, April 14, 1997, 6.

"Balance Sobre las Investigaciones de los Sucesos de Abril de 2002." *Infovenezuela*. http://infovenezuela.org/democracy/attachments-spanish/T5%20ST01%20N4%20Balance%20de%20Investigaciones_%20Pte%20Llaguno.pdf.

Blankstein, Andrew. "Chief to Meet with Israeli Police, Political Leaders." *Los Angeles Times*, December 10, 2002.

Bratton, William. "Blood, Sweat, & Databases." *Forbes*, December 2, 1997, 56.

———. *Turnaround: How America's Top Cop Reversed the Crime Epidemic*. New York: Random House, 1998.

"Brown Commissions Bratton Group to Lead Campus Security Study." Brown University News Service. Last modified March 11, 2002. www.brown.edu/Administration/News_Bureau/2001-02/01-097.html.

DePalma, Anthony. "The Americas Court: A Group That Changed New York." *New York Times*, November 11, 2002. Accessed from www.manhattan-institute.org/html/_nyt-the-americas.htm.

"Dismal Dungeons: Cruel Latin American Prisons Hold Many without Trial." *Houston Chronicle*, January 11, 1997, 34.

Hayden, Tom. "Ending the War in Los Angeles." Public letter sent via e-mail, December 5, 2002. Southern California Library clippings file.

Huggins, Martha K. *Political Policing: The United States and Latin America*. Durham, N.C.: Duke University Press, 1998.

Kelling, George L., and James Q. Wilson. "Broken Windows: The Police and Neighborhood Safety." *Atlantic Monthly*, March 1982. http://www.theatlantic.com/doc/prem/198203/broken-windows.

"Latin America's Inhumane Prisons." *New York Times*, January 5, 1997.

"Latin America's Prisons: Cries Rise Out of the Pit." *Los Angeles Times*, September 20, 1997, B7.

Lifsher, Marc. "If He Can Fight Crime There, He'll Fight It . . . Anywhere. Bratton, of New York Cleanup, Works in South America." *Wall Street Journal*, March 8, 2001. Accessed from www.manhattan-institute.org/html/_wsj-if_he_can_fight.htm.

Mone, Lawrence. "President's Welcome." *Manhattan Institute*. http://www.manhattan-institute.org/html/iape.htm.

"New Master Plan Development to Include Campus Safety Review." *Barnard News Center*, October 14, 2002. www.barnard.edu/newnews/news101402b.html.

October 22nd Coalition. "Decoding William J. Bratton, New LAPD Chief." October 22nd Coalition, n.d. [2002?]. Southern California Library.

Ravo, Nick. "Fraud Investigator Hires Bratton." *New York Times*, November 24, 1997, B3.

Rockefeller, Nelson A. *The Rockefeller Report on the Americas: The Official Report of a Presidential Mission for the Western Hemisphere*. Chicago: Quadrangle, 1969.

Rother, Larry. "Police Corruption Plagues Argentines and President." *New York Times*, August 4, 2004.

———. "A Veteran Cop on a Tough New Beat." *New York Times*, April 21, 2001, A4.

Rush, George, and Joanna Molloy. "Bratton Says Maple Remains True-Blue Friend." *Daily News*, August 22, 1997, 14.

Sims, Calvin. "Human Remains Found in Prison Oven after Riot." *New York Times*, April 10, 1996, A5.

———. "Prison Riots in Sixth Day in Argentina: Severe Overcrowding Blamed for Violence." *New York Times*, April 5, 1996, A10.

"Venezuela's Chavez Sworn In Saturday Despite Claims of Vote Fraud." *CNN.com*, August 20, 2000. http://archives.cnn.com/2000/WORLD/americas/08/19/venezuela.chavez.01/index.html.

Part III

Poverty and Wars at Home
Finding Spaces for Refuge and Change

This part shifts our focus from the transnational lens of the previous two sections, where state migration and criminal justice policies are premised on waging wars against outsiders and criminal insiders to create safety. In this part we focus on the economic and political crises of poverty and war-making on the U.S. "home front." Previous chapters identified nationalist definitions of violence that depict the nation as threatened by outsiders or by "criminals" internally. The chapters in this part show how policing, imprisonment, and deportation projects make some families and communities *less* secure and entrench poverty and economic inequality.

Whereas part VI focuses on the ways prison and migration regimes build social borders of race, gender, and sexuality, here we trace the effects that forms of intranational violence have on the domestic spaces of homes and communities. The idea of border and prison walls as barriers hides the ways in which mass imprisonment and deportation divide *and* tie families and communities. Prison and border walls seek to delimit social relationships through forcible confinement and isolation. Indeed, these chapters show the painful distance created by and through physical and political boundaries. These divisions separate parents and children, partners, friends, and neighbors from each other, and as part V shows, they also foster political and economic disenfranchisement.

In the abstract, arrest, imprisonment, and removal are single moments. However, as these authors make clear, imprisonment and deportation are longer *processes*, which neither begin nor end at a boundary. Mass incarceration links prison towns to places where people who have been imprisoned were living (and where most will return), and to places where their families and communities reside. Walls do not end social relationships. They do, though, create barriers to and stretch personal and social relationships across vast distances,

distances often lengthened by deportation across national boundaries. The contributors draw attention to the important role of material and immaterial spaces for maintaining families. They also point to the need to develop spaces for sharing stories about the harms created by these systems as fundamental aspects of organizing for social justice.

Building Prisons, Building Poverty

Prison Sitings, Dispossession, and Mass Incarceration

ANNE BONDS

> [T]he prison is not some building "over there" but a set of relationships that undermine rather than stabilize everyday lives everywhere.
> — RUTH WILSON GILMORE, *Golden Gulag*

A troubling paradox characterizes the current political and economic landscape in the United States: poverty, inequality, and homelessness have all but disappeared from the contemporary political agenda except in ideological campaigns that advocate individual responsibility and the market as the solution to impoverishment and inequality. Yet poverty persists across all places, and inequalities across gender, race/ethnicity, and class have significantly deepened. Increasing numbers of the poor and people of color are incarcerated; between 1970 and 2003 the U.S. prison system grew sevenfold; and the United States now has the largest prison system in the world.[1] Currently over 7 million people — overwhelmingly people of color and the poor — are under some sort of correctional supervision, including those incarcerated, on probation, or on parole.[2] Many in the United States view prisons as peripheral institutions, separating the criminal few from the mainstream majority. Yet the impacts of mass incarceration extend far beyond the walls of the American prison to encompass whole families, neighborhoods, and communities.[3] What do prisons have to do with the deepening of poverty and inequality?

A particularly compelling picture of the interconnected dynamics of mass incarceration and its power to transform communities — urban and rural alike — emerges when we examine where prisoners are locked up and the politics surrounding how those prisons get built. Prison sitings themselves are the outcome of powerful spatial and social relationships, highlighted by the processes funneling prisoners from metropolitan spaces to nonmetropolitan prisons. Following decades of increasingly punitive crime policies and "get tough" sentencing reforms that have worked to create abhorrently bloated prisons across the country, corrections has become a growth industry and prison development has become a prominent component of economic growth initiatives in rural communities.[4] In fact, some rural communities are actively recruiting prisons in order to stimulate local economic growth. Illustrating the popularity of such economic development agendas, 350 rural prisons have been sited since the 1980s.[5] Even more striking, an average of 25 new rural prisons opened each year during the decade of the 1990s, meaning that a new prison opened in rural America every fifteen days.[6]

This expansion of prisons into rural communities is commonly framed as an issue of economic development, a perspective that is generally devoid of any discussion of the undeniable fact that more prisons necessitate the continued mass incarceration of people of color and the poor. Therefore, the siting of correctional institutions in impoverished rural communities depends upon and reinforces the continued impoverishment, policing, and incarceration of urban communities of color. The entrepreneurial communities vying for prisons, however, often have much in common with the urban places from which the vast majority of prisoners are drawn.[7] Depressed rural communities have been dispossessed by similar sorts of processes, (re)producing disinvestment, unemployment, and entrenched poverty across urban and rural spaces. But prisons do not solve poverty in either place. As governments endeavor to finance their growing prison systems and as communities offer up investments, tax breaks, and cheap land as incentives for prisons, limited resources are further directed away from public welfare and social investments in urban and rural places alike.

This chapter explores the contradictions of rural prison development in communities experiencing deep poverty. My analysis draws from in-depth research in three rural communities in the states of Washington, Oregon, and Montana that successfully recruited prisons. I focus specifically on Carson, a community in Ridge County, Montana.[8] First, I introduce the paradox of prison expansion in the United States alongside the retrenchment of social welfare and increased levels of poverty and racialized and classed inequality. I then discuss how these dynamics are playing out in the rural American Northwest. I conclude by discussing how the processes fueling prison growth and the entrenchment of poverty span and connect urban and rural places. Rather than highlighting the dissimilarities between prison-hosting towns and their urban counterparts, underscoring the linkages between dispossession and disinvestment across these places opens up the possibility for a more critical dialogue about the consequences of mass incarceration for rural *and* urban communities. Identifying how large-scale processes are dismantling poor communities in both rural and urban areas powerfully demonstrates that few benefit from prison expansion.

PRISONS, POVERTY, AND RURAL PRISON DEVELOPMENT

Increased poverty and inequality seems to contradict the U.S. economic boom and historically low levels of unemployment of the 1990s and the early part of the 2000s. In fact, the expanding gap between the rich and the poor has reached an unprecedented high over the past three decades, and this expansion corresponds with the period of rural prison building considered in this chapter. Workers' median weekly earnings, adjusted for inflation, have *declined* and now remain far below their 1973 peak. This wage decline has disproportionately impacted those at the bottom of the economy, as increasing numbers of full-time, low-wage workers remain unable to secure wages high enough to keep themselves and their families out of poverty.[9] In 2003, the number of the working poor had reached 7.4 million, and half of all poor full-time workers had no health insurance for the entire year.[10] By 2009, the Census Bureau found, 58.9 percent of the 8.8 million families living below the poverty line had at least one household member who was working.

During the 1970s and 1980s, federal spending on social welfare and cash assistance programs for the poor dramatically declined. Most decisively, in 1996, politicians from both political parties came together to create legislation that slashed funding for welfare programs and mandated a new block-grant system. This legislation eliminated entitlement to services by repealing the Aid to Families with Dependent Children program originally created by the Social Security Act of 1935. Thus, the Personal Responsibility and Work Opportunity Reconciliation Act concluded sixty years of welfare as a nationally funded entitlement, and states and local communities assumed the primary responsibility of social welfare policy and distribution. Those most dispossessed through welfare reform now encounter increasing levels of surveillance, fewer support programs, and shortened periods of eligibility. Service provision has been further complicated by the enforcement of strict work and time limitations and expanding amounts of red tape and paperwork resulting from new funding structures and increased levels of scrutiny.[11] As a result, the number of people receiving cash assistance has decreased significantly. Between 1999 and 2002 the share of all welfare recipients who had left the welfare rolls but were not employed, did not have an employed partner, or were not receiving any sort of income assistance rose from 10 to 14 percent.[12]

People of color are disproportionately poor, and poor people of color continue to be most impacted by the restructuring of economies over the past three decades. Communities ravaged by deindustrialization, unemployment, and the expansion of low-wage labor markets have been further devastated by the financial withdrawal of the state. Economic and social polarization, compounded by the dismantling of welfare, has created a host of problems that the state has, at least in part, elected to resolve through incarceration.

At the same time that programs supporting the poor were eradicated, police state strategies permeated urban communities, criminalizing the poor and communities of color. Reflecting a sharp turn in the ostensibly rehabilitative history of punishment, in the 1970s incarceration became a vehicle for punishment, deterrence, and incapacitation. Since the 1980s, state and federal governments have passed more punitive crime legislation, which has fueled a remarkable growth in imprisonment rates and prison overcrowding. This shift was crystallized in "tough on crime" policies that were designed to send more people to prison and keep them there longer.

By the 1980s and 1990s, state lawmakers and politicians vowed to be even tougher on crime than their predecessors, ruling out the possibility for plea bargaining for some offenses and imposing mandatory minimum sentencing as well as "three strikes" statutes, which require life sentences for third felony convictions and, in some cases, the abolition of parole. The federal government's War on Poverty was officially replaced first by a war on crime and then by a war on drugs as stringent sentences were attached to narcotics and other drug offenses. Between 1980 and 1996, the rate of drug arrests rose by 250 percent, although rates of drug use were not increasing.[13] This increase was driven by a sharp rise in the arrests of young men of color for drug offenses, resulting in swelling prison populations and more than doubling the share of people in state prisons for drug convictions.[14]

These policies help us to understand why so many people of color are behind bars. Mandatory minimum sentencing for drug offenses and three-strikes laws have resulted in a dramatic increase in people of color in prison. African American men make up more than 40 percent of the prison population, though they comprise just 12 percent of the general population; nearly one in three black men will spend some time in prison.[15] Latinos and Native Americans are also grossly overrepresented in prisons, and immigrants make up a fast growing segment of those imprisoned in the United States.

The twin processes of welfare retrenchment and mass incarceration in the context of punitive public policy are underscored by massive investments in policing, corrections, and detention and the profound disinvestment in the poor at federal, state, and local scales. These shifts have aided corrections in becoming one of the fastest growing industries and one of the most rapidly increasing portions of state budgets. The increasingly punitive character of both the welfare and penal systems in the United States underpins a shift from what Wacquant calls the "social welfare management" of poverty to its treatment through incarceration.[16] He argues that the crime control apparatus functions as a powerful mechanism to manage social divisions and rising insecurity resulting from economic deregulation and the retrenchment of social welfare. Social and economic disparities are shored up both by "tough on crime" attitudes and sentencing and by restrictive welfare policies. In this context, as Gilmore writes in *Golden Gulag*, prisons operate as a "geographical solution" for absorbing surplus land, labor, and capital (26). They are a mechanism that manages the growing number of poor and the unemployed and masks joblessness, thereby artificially suppressing the U.S. unemployment rate.[17] Taken together, the "reform" of welfare and poverty policy, the criminalization of poverty, and the expansion of the prison-industrial complex clearly demonstrate that rather than diminishing in power or withdrawing from the lives of the poor, the state has instead extended and redefined its role through surveillance, regulation, and incarceration.

Some argue that the sharpening of racial and class inequality leads to expanding incarceration rates and that declining opportunities for the most marginalized populations lead to growing levels of crime. Yet a closer examination of crime rates and increases in incarceration contradicts this commonplace assumption: mass incarceration has occurred even as violent crime rates have declined. That is, mounting levels of crime cannot explain the expansion of the prison system in the United States. Western finds that the largest growth in crime rates actually predates the explosion in the prison population, clearly highlighting the disjuncture between crime and incarceration.[18] Rather, the racialized and classed nature of the criminal justice apparatus has worked to extend state intervention into every aspect of the lives of the poor; criminalize people of color; pathologize communities, families, and individuals; and legitimate state violence.[19] The contemporary trend in mass incarceration is, therefore, more about race and poverty than it is about crime, disorder, and delinquency.[20]

This raises a number of points about the problems that accompany prison growth, not least of which is the unequal treatment of people of color and economically marginalized populations within the criminal justice system. Prisons have not eradicated crime nor reduced recidivism, yet the system continues to endure and grow. Bolstered by punitive law-and-order policies promoting prisons as the solution to all social problems, crime-fighting investments target the poor, further diverting funds from already emaciated public welfare programs. Given these failing outcomes and the devastating impacts of the prison system on dispossessed communities, it's hard to believe that any community would want a prison to be located in their town. But a prison is just what is wanted by many rural towns whose agricultural and industrial economies have been decimated by the North American Free Trade Agreement (NAFTA).

Since the 1980s, the majority of new prison construction has occurred in rural communities. Why is this the case? What happened to the not-in-my-backyard sentiments often associated with prison sitings? Rural towns experiencing job loss and high unemployment see prisons as a vehicle for community economic development. Looking for perceived benefits, such as job growth and increased tax revenue, communities employ a variety of recruiting techniques — often competing with one another in their offers of donated land, infrastructure, and property and tax breaks — to secure state and federal prisons. Struggling rural communities also associate prisons with multiplier effects, or the expansion of related industries and business establishments as an outcome of their placement. These include construction, housing, hotels, gas stations, and restaurants intended to accommodate increasing numbers of workers, visitors, and new residents. In addition to the growth of employment opportunities, communities expect sizable revenues from property and sales taxes. Furthermore, rural town leaders are keen to benefit from federal grant programs and community development funds, which are allocated based on census data on population and poverty, numbers to which prison populations heavily contribute. Powerfully illustrating the entrepreneurial nature of contemporary corrections, some communities completely bypass state authority and contract directly with private correctional firms in their prison development strategies.[21]

This rural preference for prison sitings is related to a range of well-documented elements: the desire for industrial recruitment in economically depressed communities and the seeming benefits of prison sitings; the abundance of surplus labor and cheap land in rural areas; the perception that rural communities will show less resistance to the placement of a correctional facility; and the remoteness of rural places, which provides a geographical advantage when seeking to place contained populations and "undesirable" facilities out of the view of mainstream society.

The local officials with whom I spoke repeatedly argued that expanded levels of employment, new business opportunities, and revenues generated from property and sales taxes outweigh the negative aspects of "being a prison town." However, research on the long-term impacts of rural prisons contradicts such boosterism. Studies demonstrate that prison development generally fails to bring the positive benefits they are alleged to produce. Hooks and colleagues' statistical analysis of the impact of prisons on economic growth in counties across the nation found that not only do prisons fail to bring employment growth, tax revenue, and other multiplier effects, they actually *impede* economic growth in the places where they are located.[22] Similarly, research demonstrates that towns in rural New York hosting state and federal prisons saw little growth in employment opportunities, in part because positions were filled with outside candidates commuting from surrounding areas.[23]

PRISONS AND POVERTY IN THE AMERICAN NORTHWEST

With its world-renowned environmental amenities, booming regional economy, and prominent multinational corporations, such as Microsoft, Amazon, Starbucks, and Weyerhaeuser, the American Northwest[24] is not often considered to be a distressed region with persistent poverty or deep inequality. This region is more often associated with the rise of the "new economy" based in information and computer technologies, high-end service sector expansion, and entrepreneurship. However, alongside the expansion of the region's high-end service sector and computer- and technology-driven industries, deep pockets of racialized poverty exist, particularly in rural areas.[25]

The challenges brought about by national welfare policy shifts and prison expansion are evident in rural localities of the American Northwest. Although the numbers of prisons and incarcerated individuals in the region are smaller on the whole than in other parts of the country, the states in this area are engaged in immense prison expansion projects. In fact, the rate of expansion occurring in these states is quite startling relative to population sizes and crime rates, both of which are well below the national averages. One report locates all but one of the states with the projected highest rate of prison growth in the American West.[26] Idaho, for instance, has the second fastest rate of prison growth in the nation, falling just behind Texas.[27] The state of Oregon's prison population has more than doubled since 1994,[28] Washington has approved new prison construction, and Montana is expanding its privately managed state prison facility to relieve state prison overcrowding.

Even as prison growth has surged and some sectors of the economy have boomed, poverty and inequality have deepened. The region contains strikingly high levels of poverty, with poverty rates approaching 30 percent in some rural counties.[29] Rural communities of all races exhibit higher poverty rates than those in urban areas in the region. County poverty rates by race reveal that 107 of 150 counties in the rural Northwest are above the national white nonmetropolitan poverty rate (10.4 percent). Equally remarkable, 71 of these counties are above the Latino poverty rate of 27 percent as immigration to the region continues to boom.[30] Furthermore, the rural poor, particularly Native Americans and Latinos, constitute the fastest growing segments of the prison population in the region. The decline of historically dominant extractive industries, together with economic downturns and budget shortfalls, has contributed to the shrinking of social policy funds. These threaten to further intensify hardship, particularly in rural communities, which depend on public services even more than cities do.[31]

In Montana, the volatile nature of ranching has been compounded by increased flows of wheat and beef from Canada under NAFTA, which have increased competition and driven down prices for local ranchers.[32] Resonating with this broader state trend, Ridge County is experiencing the shrinking of extractive and agricultural establishments. At one time, the area had a more robust economic base built upon agricultural and oil and gas production; however, the decline of both of these sectors since the 1980s has sharpened poverty and joblessness in the county.

Ridge County is a place whose history has been shaped by the colonization of its indigenous peoples, struggles over land and resources, racial inequality, and persistent poverty. Located in southeastern Montana, this county is the site of the often mythologized Battle of the Little Big Horn, also known as "Custer's Last Stand," and nearly two-thirds of the county is designated tribal land. The town of Carson, where I did my research, sits just on the border of a reservation, and a growing portion of the tribal community lives in the town. Despite its small population of just over three thousand, inequality in Carson is conspicuous. Like other reservation counties, the area has some of the most historically entrenched levels of poverty in the state and, indeed, in the nation. The county's 2005 poverty rate stood at 29 percent, more than double the national poverty rate of 12.4 percent and the state rate of 14 percent.[33]

The county was the potential site for two private corrections facilities in the 1990s. With its large areas of now unproductive land, the area apparently became an attractive place for private correctional firms looking to minimize operating costs. In the 1980s, the community was nearly selected as the location for a new state prison to be managed by the Corrections Corporation of America (CCA). However, county commissioners, representing their largely tribal constituency, prohibited the prison siting from moving forward on county land just outside of Carson. Then, city — not county — officials were approached by another private corrections corporation with a feasibility study highlighting the appropriateness of Carson for a correctional facility. Ultimately, city leaders, together with a private local economic development corporation and a Texas-based corrections corporation called CiviGenics, expedited efforts to build a 464-bed detention center, despite having no secured inmate contracts with the state of Montana.

With construction complete and employees in place, the facility was scheduled to open in August 2007. Yet, in a stunning turn of events, the detention center continues to sit empty as the city struggles to obtain inmate contracts and struggles with a $27 million bond that went into default shortly after the facility was to be opened. Although the community and the private firm had tentative assurance that the Department of Corrections would need the space, this agreement collapsed after the election of a new governor in 2005. Attempting to address this lack of inmates, the private correctional company sought out-of-state contracts, particularly with the state of Wyoming. However, the Montana attorney general ruled that the facility cannot legally house out-of-state inmates. Since then, city officials have made offers to host ever more politically marginalized populations. In 2009, the city council drew international media coverage when it unanimously passed a resolution offering to house 240 detainees from the Guantanamo Bay detention center after President Barack Obama's executive order to close the facility. But senators from that state have strongly opposed such an idea. For example, Senator Max Baucus stated, "I understand the need for jobs, but we're not going to bring al-Qaeda to Big Sky Country. No way, not on my watch."[34]

During my visits to Carson in 2005 and 2006, city leaders expressed nothing but optimism about the prison siting, repeatedly highlighting the number of expected jobs associated with the facility and dodging questions about who would actually fill those jobs. County leaders, however, were much more critical. One commissioner best highlighted this sentiment and, in many ways, seemed to anticipate the ill-fated consequences of the facility: "But once [the prison's] here, it's here. It's not going anywhere and so even if we don't like it, it's not going to go away. And so what will that mean in our community? And while the city realizes the benefits of the taxes, the outside community may suffer the consequences of their [city leaders'] greed" (personal interview, 2006).

As the city grapples with the ruinous outcomes of its prison development efforts, the barbed-wire-surrounded facility sits empty, literally in the middle of town. Meanwhile, the county's poverty rate continues to soar, unemployment rates climb, and service providers struggle to offer much-needed provisions to the community's most poor. While the city, now saddled with debt that it cannot pay, continues to seek inmates through a series of increasingly desperate efforts, those ultimately left "suffer[ing] the consequences of their greed" are the community members most in need.

CONCLUSION: DISPOSSESSION AND MASS INCARCERATION

The monumental trend in mass incarceration that has generated the rural prison boom has failed to increase public safety. Rather, this dynamic has severed neighborhoods and families by relocating prisoners far from their homes and communities. This process has been especially costly for the economic and social well-being of urban communities of color. Yet the consequences do not end there. Depressed rural communities have recruited prisons to solve deep poverty, stagnating economies, high unemployment, and decades of disinvestment, deindustrialization, and agricultural decline. But the processes that have promoted markets, economic growth, and the disinvestment in public services have come at the expense of marginalized rural and urban communities alike. The dynamics that have hollowed out urban cores, while not identical, cannot be considered as separate from the dynamics that have produced rural decline. These policies are framed to the public in ways that represent correctional facilities as vehicles for industrial investment, well-paid jobs, and economic growth. But decisions to site rural prisons more often than not fall into the hands of a few corporate and political leaders. As in the case of Carson, prison development agendas are pushed through by a host of powerful interests: influential private corrections corporations, local development corporations, and community elites whose political careers become entangled with prison development agendas. Even in the face of local opposition — in the case of Carson, challenges from some tribal leaders and county commissioners who successfully prevented the siting of one private prison — powerful discourses about the alleged benefits of prisons often eclipse the many negative outcomes that accompany prison sitings. These discourses further obscure and overshadow critical discussions about the implications of prisons and mass incarceration for rural and urban areas.

As depressed rural communities struggle to retain financial solvency and provide services in the context of neoliberal restructuring and the retrenchment of social and economic supports, they recruit prisons, which not only depend on the continued incarceration of others who have been dispossessed (particularly, urban people of color), but also require further disinvestment in social welfare. The irony of rural prison sitings in the context of deep poverty is that prison development redirects social spending away from important public services and sustains continued social exclusion (not to mention expanding rates of incarceration). States have diminished resources for social welfare and have rolled back provisions at the same time that they have rolled out increasingly punitive measures that further restrict, monitor, and criminalize the poor. This situation emphasizes the connections between the 7 million people managed by the prison-industrial complex and the 6 million who have been removed from the welfare rolls since 1996.

Imprisonment has become the mechanism for dealing with the social problems that burden the most marginalized members of our society, rather than dealing with the structural issues creating poverty and dispossession. Other contributors to this book demonstrate that immigrant detention is becoming yet another growth industry as migrants, constructed as criminals and terrorists, are increasingly arrested, detained, and deported through workplaces raids, day labor policing, and border militarization. This boom in immigrant detention is yet another reminder that the consequences of mass imprisonment stretch well beyond the walls of the prison and, indeed, across borders. This system is unjust, unsustainable, and unproductive. Furthermore, examples like Carson demonstrate the profoundly negative impacts of prison development strategies and disrupt the idea that communities can grow their local economies by putting people in cages.

What kinds of options exist for rural leaders seeking to build living-wage communities rather than recruiting dubious investments like prisons? Ultimately, rural communities must decide what kind of world they want to live in: one in which community leaders pander to lock up ever more politically marginalized populations, or one in which the poor are supported, not scapegoated? To promote stable economies with solid futures, communities need to focus on socially just economic development that connects, rather than divides, towns. Instead of viewing prisons as simply industrial investments, rural community leaders first need to acknowledge how the mechanisms producing poverty in rural places are connected to the dynamics fueling prison growth and dispossession in urban places. Considering how disinvestment and misinvestment connect places, rather than separate them, is a powerful way to open up critical conversations about mass incarceration and to build solidarity in prison abolition movements.

The impacts of mass incarceration are concentrated among those most marginalized, and the gross overrepresentation of people of color and the poor in prisons reinforces and sharpens lines of social disadvantage. The expansive and interconnected nature of this institution palpably highlights the social meanings and economic consequences of incarceration. How have prisons become so naturalized? At what cost — to families, communities, and states — will this trend continue? Perhaps this is the best phrase: "it's time to stop building walls between us and start building bridges."[35]

NOTES

1. Garland, *Culture of Control*.
2. Western, *Punishment and Inequality in America*.
3. Mauer and Chesney-Lind, *Invisible Punishment*.
4. Bonds, "Discipline and Devolution"; Huling, "Building a Prison Economy in Rural America."
5. Beale, "Cellular Rural Development"; Huling, "Building a Prison Economy in Rural America."
6. Beale, "Cellular Rural Development"; Huling, "Building a Prison Economy in Rural America."
7. Bonds, "The Politics of Poverty, Prisons, and Neoliberal Restructuring"; Gilmore, *Golden Gulag*.
8. I have changed the name of this community for confidentiality.
9. Goode and Maskovsky, *The New Poverty Studies*.
10. Teller-Elsberg et al., *Field Guide to the U.S. Economy*, 22–23.
11. Schram, Welfare Discipline; Bonds, "The Politics of Poverty, Prisons, and Neoliberal Restructuring."
12. Teller-Elsberg et al., *Field Guide to the U.S. Economy*, 99.
13. Western, *Punishment and Inequality in America*, 58.
14. Ibid.
15. Pager, *Marked*.
16. Wacquant, "Deadly Symbiosis," 98.
17. Western and Beckett, "How Unregulated Is the U.S. Labor Market?"
18. Western, *Punishment and Inequality in America*, 48.
19. Davis, "Race, Gender and Prison History"; Gilmore, *Golden Gulag*; Wacquant, "Deadly Symbiosis"; Western, *Punishment and Inequality in America*.
20. Davis, "Race, Gender and Prison History"; Gilmore, *Golden Gulag*; Wacquant, "Deadly Symbiosis"; Western, *Punishment and Inequality in America*.
21. Bonds, "The Politics of Poverty, Prisons, and Neoliberal Restructuring."

22. Hooks et al., "The Prison Industry."
23. King et al., *Big Prisons, Small Towns*.
24. The American Northwest is defined here as Washington, Oregon, Montana, and Idaho.
25. Lawson et al., "Building Economies from the Bottom Up."
26. Pew Charitable Trusts, "Public Safety, Public Spending."
27. Jacobson, *Downsizing Prisons*.
28. Goldsmith, "Budget Crisis Could Curtail Oregon's Prison Boom."
29. U.S. Census Bureau, "Summary File 3."
30. Kandel and Cromartie, *New Patterns of Hispanic Settlement in Rural America*.
31. McGranahan, "How People Make a Living in Rural America."
32. Gallaher, "Farmers Warned to Be Aware of Stress and Economic Turmoil."
33. U.S. Census Bureau, "Summary File 3."
34. Dawson, "The Montana Town That Wanted to Be Gitmo."
35. Sklar, *Chaos or Community?*, 176.

BIBLIOGRAPHY

Beale, C. "Cellular Rural Development: New Prisons in Rural and Small Town Areas in the 1990s." Presented at the annual meeting of the Rural Sociology Society, Albuquerque, N.M., August 18, 2001.

Bonds, A. "Discipline and Devolution: Constructions of Poverty, Race, and Criminality in the Politics of Rural Prison Development." *Antipode* 41, no. 3 (2009): 416-38.

———. "The Politics of Poverty, Prisons, and Neoliberal Restructuring in the Rural American Northwest." Unpublished diss., University of Washington, 2008.

Davis, A. Y. "Race, Gender and Prison History: From the Convict Lease System to the Supermax Prison." In *Prison Masculinities*, edited by D. Sabo, T. A. Kupers, and W. London, 34-45. Philadelphia: Temple University Press, 2001.

Dawson, Pat. "The Montana Town That Wanted to Be Gitmo." *Time* (May 3, 2009). http://www.time.com/time/nation/article/0,8599,1894373,00.html.

Gallaher, S. "Farmers Warned to Be Aware of Stress and Economic Turmoil." *Associated Press State and Local Wire*. Helena, Mont., December 18, 1998.

Garland, D. *The Culture of Control: Crime and Social Order in Contemporary Society*. Chicago: University of Chicago Press, 2001.

Gilmore, R. W. *Golden Gulag: Prisons, Surplus, Crisis, and Opposition in Globalizing California*. Berkeley: University of California Press, 2007.

Goldsmith, S. "Budget Crisis Could Curtail Oregon's Prison Boom." *Oregonian* (May 26, 2009): A1-A4.

Goode J., and J. Maskovsky, eds. *The New Poverty Studies: The Ethnography of Power, Politics, and Impoverished People in the United States*. New York: New York University Press, 2001.

Hooks, G., C. Mosher, T. Rotolo, and L. Labao. "The Prison Industry: Carceral Expansion and Employment in U.S. Counties." *Social Science Quarterly* 85, no. 1 (2004): 37–57.

Huling, T. "Building a Prison Economy in Rural America." In *Invisible Punishment: The Collateral Consequences of Mass Imprisonment*, edited by M. Mauer and. M. Chesney-Lind, 197–213. New York: New Press, 2002.

Jacobson, M. *Downsizing Prisons: How to Reduce Crime and End Mass Incarceration.* New York: New York University Press, 2005.

Kandel, W., and J. Cromartie. *New Patterns of Hispanic Settlement in Rural America.* Washington, D.C.: USDA Economic Research Service, 2004.

King, R. S., M. Mauer, and T. Huling. *Big Prisons, Small Towns: Prison in Rural America.* Washington, D.C.: Sentencing Project, 2003.

Lawson, V., L. Jarosz, and A. Bonds. "Building Economies from the Bottom Up: (Mis) Representations of Poverty in the Rural American Northwest." *Social and Cultural Geography* 9, no. 7 (2008): 737–53.

Mauer, M., and M. Chesney-Lind. *Invisible Punishment: The Collateral Consequences of Mass Imprisonment.* New York: New Press, 2002.

McGranahan, D. A. "How People Make a Living in Rural America." In *Challenges for Rural America in the Twenty-First Century*, edited by D. L. Brown and Louis E. Swanson, 135–51. University Park: Pennsylvania State University Press, 2003.

Pager, D. *Marked: Race, Crime, and Finding Work in an Era of Mass Incarceration.* Chicago: University of Chicago Press, 2007.

Pager, D., and A. Tickell. "Neoliberalizing Space." *Antipode* 34 (2002): 380–404.

Pew Charitable Trusts. "Public Safety, Public Spending: Forecasting America's Prison Population 2007–2011." 2007. http://www.pewtrusts.org/our_work_ektid29967.aspx?category=74.

Schram, S. F. *Welfare Discipline: Discourse, Governance, and Globalization.* Philadelphia: Temple University Press, 2006.

Sklar, H. *Chaos or Community?: Seeking Solutions, Not Scapegoats for Bad Economics.* Boston: South End, 1995.

Teller-Elsberg, J., N. Folbre, J. Heintz, and the Center for Popular Economics. *Field Guide to the U.S. Economy: A Compact and Irreverent Guide to Economic Life in America.* New York: New Press, 2006.

U.S. Census Bureau. "Summary File 3." *American FactFinder, Bureau of the Census*, 2000. http://factfinder.census.gov.

Wacquant, L. "Deadly Symbiosis: When Ghetto and Prison Meet and Mesh." *Punishment and Society* 3, no. 1 (2001): 95–133.

Western, B. *Punishment and Inequality in America.* New York: Sage Foundation, 2006.

Western, B., and K. Beckett. "How Unregulated Is the U.S. Labor Market?: The Penal System as a Labor Market Institution." *American Journal of Sociology* 104, no. 4 (1999): 1030–60.

Business of Detention

RENEE FELTZ AND STOKELY BAKSH

Immigrant rights advocates cheered when the Obama administration announced in August 2009 that it would stop holding immigrant children inside a former medium-security prison run by the nation's largest private prison company. But by then, immigrant detention contracts with the federal government had become a key part of Corrections Corporation of America's expansion plan. The company's executives seem unfazed by the development, noting that immigrant women would continue to be held at the facility. "In some respects there may not have been much of a change," Damon Hininger, CCA's president and chief operating officer, told investors in a conference call following the announcement.[1]

CCA's confidence level corresponds with the amount of money it has spent to convince lawmakers and their constituents that undocumented immigrants are criminals who need to be locked up, and that private detention centers are the fastest and cheapest way to solve the "immigration dilemma." Immigrant detention — which has increased more than 75 percent since 2005 — provides close to half of CCA's business. The company expects detention, which has tripled in the twenty-first century, to provide a "recession-proof" business.

CCA maximizes its profits from immigrant detention contracts by scrimping on the already minimal services it is required to provide. Unlike prison contracts, immigrant detention contracts only require housing, food, and medical services, not rehabilitation or education services. The resulting conditions inside CCA's facilities make them key to ICE's mandate to ensure the departure of 12 million "removable aliens" from the United States.

Sergia Santibanez's experience provides a window onto this mutually beneficial arrangement. In a business park on the outskirts of Houston aptly named Export Plaza, CCA runs a complex of concrete buildings surrounded by razor wire that comprises the nation's first private immigrant detention center. Like thousands of migrants each year, Santibanez was held there until she agreed to leave the country. "When you first get there, they tell you you're nobody," said Santibanez, who spent sixteen months at CCA's Houston Processing Center. She still breaks into tears when she recalls the experience.

In 2005, this mother of three U.S.-born children was giving several people a ride outside of Austin, where she had been living as a legal resident since arriving in the United States from Mexico in the 1980s. She got into an accident, and when the police came, she was arrested and eventually convicted for transporting undocumented immigrants, an aggravated felony that revoked her legal status. She served four months in a federal prison before ending up at CCA's Houston Processing Center while an immigration judge decided whether she should be deported. "There, it was worse," Santibanez said. "They told you that you had to put up with it because we came to them, not them to us, and so we didn't have a right to anything."

When she was in federal prison, Santibanez was able to visit with her children in a large room with other families. Her daughter, Luisanna, thought the detention center would be more open to visitors, given that people there had not been convicted of crimes but were awaiting civil immigration proceedings. "It was the exact opposite," recalled Luisanna. "We were separated by a plexiglass window. There's this little space where we all tried to talk to my mom over the phone."

Santibanez spent eighteen months fighting her deportation in order to be able to stay in the country with her children. "As the months went by, she kept looking more depressed," her daughter said. "The color of her skin started fading as she tried to survive prison life." In August 2007, Santibanez agreed to be deported. "My lawyer had all kinds of reasons to keep fighting," she said when contacted by phone in Mexico. "He asked me, 'Are you sure you want that?' And in the end, I was fed up and I signed."

Santibanez is one of a quarter million undocumented migrants who are deported each year after they are held in an immigrant detention center. Her detention was part of a crackdown on immigrants that began in 2004 when the Bush administration stepped up enforcement of laws already on the books since the Illegal Immigration Reform and Immigrant Responsibility Act of 1996. When the crackdown began, the increase in arrests outpaced the amount of space available for detainees. As a result, the government followed a policy referred to by its detractors as "catch and release." This fueled criticisms against then DHS secretary Tom Ridge for releasing undocumented migrants into the community while they awaited deportation hearings.

By 2006, the government shifted to a catch-and-return policy as part of its Secure Border Initiative under Ridge's successor, Michael Chertoff. The new initiative focused on substantially expanding the nation's detention capacity so that immigrants with pending status hearings would be detained until they went before a judge, instead of being released into the community. The demand for more space helped to secure CCA's place as the leading private prison company, surpassing competitors such as the Geo Group and Cornell Companies. The space available for detaining immigrants grew from 19,500 beds in FY 2006 to 27,500 in FY 2007. As of 2009, ICE had the capacity to detain about 32,000 immigrants on an average day. "We're here to take care of the product they deliver to us," said Michael Davis, who doubles as the chaplain and spokesman for CCA's Houston Processing Center, where Sergia Santibanez was held. "Until they're deported we take care of the detainees the best we can."[2]

The company has had its eye on privatizing the entire immigrant detention system for some time. In 2004, it proposed taking over all federal detention operations. "It was a huge potential market for them," said Ronald Jones, who helped prepare CCA's proposal as the head of the company's Research and Analysis Department.[3] He claims ICE never responded to the proposal. In its 2010 budget request, ICE proposed a plan to completely privatize the detention system, including a general provision which would allow ICE to sell its eight federally owned detention centers to private operators. The provision was included in the Senate version of the 2010 appropriations bill.

For CCA, the math is simple. More demand for immigrant detention space plus more government funding equals more business for Corrections Corporation of America. Every year since 2003, the company has made record profits. For example, CCA generated extremely high revenue in 2006, when ICE increased its detention beds from 19,500 to 27,500, and the company won contracts to provide about half of these new beds. "We've never seen the wind at our back like it is today," CCA's president and chief executive officer, John D. Ferguson, said in a May 3, 2006, conference call with investors after discussing $1.3 billion in revenue.[4]

Investors recognized that CCA's inventory of prison space meant the company was best suited to meet a flood of demand from the crackdown under Bush. Over the next few years, CCA's stock price more than doubled. In 2004, the company's stock had traded at a low of $12.15 and by March 2008 investor confidence had lifted the price to $26.86. "Certainly, the forces of supply and demand are working in the company's favor," observed Bank of America analyst T. C. Robillard, who had a "buy" rating on CCA stock in February 2007.[5]

Each new program to increase immigration enforcement has been a business opportunity for CCA. Amid high demand, CCA has been able to charge as much as $95 per detainee per day in some facilities, although the amount varies widely. Five of the company's lucrative contracts to imprison immigrants have no end date. Several of its other contracts contain "take or pay" clauses that guarantee a certain amount of revenue regardless of occupancy rates, as well as periodic rate increases. The company's contracts are renewed at a rate of almost 95 percent.

The broader discussion of how cages are used to confine immigrants and transform them into profitable "products" must be informed by how companies such as CCA drive federal policy on the evolving issue of immigrant detention. Money enables rhetoric and shapes the direction of policy in Washington, D.C., and one of the major companies throwing around vast amounts of lobbying dollars is CCA. Forty percent of its revenue comes from federal contracts. The company backs key politicians who support immigration crackdowns and has intensified its lobbying in order to influence those still on the fence.

When Republicans and Democrats failed to agree on comprehensive immigration reform, CCA backed lawmakers who found common ground on the issue of funding detention. The rest of its political giving goes directly to lawmakers who determine detention funding through their positions on appropriations committees in the House and Senate. In 2008, the committees approved a $2.3 billion budget for ICE detention and deportation of undocumented immigrants, including funds for an additional 4,870 new beds. More than half the senators backed by CCA's PAC are on appropriations committees, and four of them are on the Committee on Homeland Security. In the House, CCA's political action committee gave $5,000 to Hal Rogers (R-Ky.), who sits on the Subcommittee on Homeland Security Appropriations. Another $2,500 went to fellow committee member John Carter (R-Tex.), who is also on the Committee on Homeland Security. Carter's district is where CCA's T. Don Hutto detention center is located. He is a major advocate for "a system of 100 percent catch and return." Republican members of the House Immigration Reform Caucus reaped CCA's support for backing the Secure America through Verification and Enforcement Act. The act increases funding for detention and calls for expediting "the removal of illegal aliens by expanding detention capacity."

To influence lawmakers who do not receive direct donations, CCA spends millions each year on lobbyists who focus on immigration and national security. During the creation of the Department of Homeland Security, CCA's CEO, John D. Ferguson, was the vice president of the industry lobbying group the Association of Private Correctional and Treatment Organizations, which works to "educate key elected officials about our membership and the whole spectrum of vital public services we provide." The group created a privatization caucus in 2002 to push its federal legislative agenda, and in 2003 it met with more than fifty congressional members and their staffs.

One of CCA's key lobbyists was Philip J. Perry, son-in-law of former vice president Dick Cheney, before he was appointed general counsel for DHS in 2005. The next year CCA reported its highest revenue to date. As the immigration debate continued in 2007, CCA spent $3.25 million lobbying members of Congress to approve funding that would ultimately lead to increased spending on immigration detention capacity.

To complete the seamless connections between CCA and its federal funders, the company has hired former government officials to coordinate its federal relations. Among them is CCA's senior vice president Mike Quinlan, who is credited with helping to secure the company's credibility among federal clients; he came to the company after a twenty-two-year career in public sector corrections that included a stint as the director of the federal Bureau of Prisons from 1987 to 1992. "The collective corrections experience of CCA's operations and management team, much of it gained during distinguished careers in federal or state corrections systems, is one of the most impressive in the country," notes Quinlan on the company's website.

In 2004, after nearly twenty-five years with the Immigration and Naturalization Service, Kim Porter joined CCA as senior director of federal customer relations. Porter's primary responsibility is to manage CCA's relationship with ICE. Anthony Odom came on board to manage CCA's relations with the U.S. Marshals Service, which detains immigrants mostly along the Mexican border, after he retired in 2004 from a thirty-two-year career with that agency. CCA's general counsel, Gustavus Puryear IV, made headlines in 2008 when President Bush nominated him for a federal judgeship in the Middle District of Tennessee, where CCA is headquartered. Puryear testified during a Senate hearing that he would recuse himself from cases involving the company, but ultimately his appointment was rejected.

In order to maximize the opportunity for profits offered by federal contracts, CCA operates many of its detention centers at full capacity, sometimes more. In 2006, the CCA-run San Diego Correctional Facility was so crowded that three immigrant detainees lived in cells designed for two. So where did the third person sleep? "They would put what they called a boat, a plastic unit, on the floor in the only floor space available in the room — beneath the toilet," explained Tom Jawetz, an attorney with the American Civil Liberties Union's National Prison Project.[6] By the time Jawetz filed suit to stop the overcrowding, CCA was housing the overflow population in the facility's dayrooms. His lawsuit prompted ICE to move some of the detainees to other detention centers. It also prompted CCA to propose constructing a new facility nearby that would hold four times more detainees. Rather than being penalized for overcrowding, CCA won the new contract.

CCA also provides substandard medical care. At the San Diego facility, conditions were so bad that DHS's Division of Immigration Health Services (now known as the ICE Health Service Corps) was forced to take over. "The DHS concluded [that] CCA's provision of medical care was deficient and that CCA was attempting to increase its profits by decreasing the medical services to detainees," said Jawetz. But even with DHS involved, detainees still need to request medical services through CCA staff. Detainees have charged that staff members often deny medical care in order both to reduce costs and to coerce detainees into voluntary deportation.

Similar problems were cited in a March 2007 Department of Justice audit of CCA's Webb County Detention Center, a facility near Laredo, Texas, that holds six hundred U.S. Marshals Service detainees for an average stay of 150 days. Most of the detainees are undocumented immigrants awaiting deportation hearings. Among other things, the audit criticized CCA's failure to provide or arrange for health care even in potentially life-threatening cases. The audit showed CCA had only nine health care staff in the facility even though its contract said it could employ fourteen. Despite this, the audit determined that the Webb County Detention Center was in "acceptable" compliance with federal standards.

CCA conducts its own internal audits on the state of its facilities. However, in an interview for this chapter in February 2008, Ronald T. Jones, a former CCA senior quality assurance manager, alleged he was asked to make violent incidents like riots or attacks on detainees by guards appear to be less serious than they were. These "cooked" audits, which could have led to the contracts' nonrenewal, were provided to CCA's customers, including ICE and the U.S. Marshals Service. The original reports remained in-house, Jones said.

When outside audits were completed at congressional request — such as a 2005 Alien Detention Standards audit by the U.S. Government Accountability Office that included three of CCA's twenty-three detention facilities — problems with telephone access were pervasive. Telephone access is crucial for detainees to lodge complaints with the Office of Inspector General about their conditions, to reach legal counsel, and to contact their friends and families. At CCA's Elizabeth Detention Center in New Jersey, the list of consulate numbers was six years old. When auditors called thirty of the consulate numbers on the posted listings, they found nine were incorrect. "Insufficient internal controls and weaknesses in ICE's compliance review process" resulted in ICE's failure to identify the telephone problems, reported the Government Accountability Office.[7]

Investigations and reports have continued to expose problems of mistreatment, violence, overcrowding, and legal access, and these have led to congressional hearings. In August 2009, the Obama administration put forth plans to overhaul the detention complex that included the creation of an Office of Oversight and an Office of Detention Policy and Planning, and the addition of twenty-three ICE detention managers. But progress toward addressing the transparency concerns of the detention system has been slow, due in part to resistance from CCA and its corporate counterparts.

As conditions in detention centers garner more attention, the programs that drive immigrants into these cages are casting a wider net that ensures they remain full. Consider the case of Maria del Carmen Garcia-Martinez.

When Garcia-Martinez emerged in 2008 from an Immigration and Customs Enforcement holding cell in Maricopa County, Arizona, her arm had been broken and her hand was covered in blue ink. She had been booked for forgery at a Phoenix jail, where six officers twisted her arm after she resisted putting her fingerprint on what she thought was a form that would deport her to Mexico. Garcia-Martinez speaks only Spanish, the form was in English, and she believed that after nineteen years in the United States she had a good case for staying in the country, despite her lack of documentation. Her forgery charge stemmed from a California driver's license she showed to an officer who asked for identification while telling her not to post yard-sale signs on city property. But the license wasn't a forgery; it was just expired. The charges were dropped.

The case of Maria del Carmen Garcia-Martinez occurred under President Bush, but is perhaps even more likely under the Obama administration. Garcia-Martinez's experience of being harassed and detained on a flimsy pretext has been common under ICE's 287(g) program, which has maintained the program's funding to train local law enforcement to help federal immigration authorities apprehend "criminal aliens."

Civil rights advocates note that the bulk of the counties signed up to participate in the 287(g) program are in southern states with rapidly growing Latino populations. "The program gets mediated by a history of racism and nativist hostility," says Deborah Weissman, a law professor at the University of North Carolina at Chapel Hill.[8] One study recounts how Alamance County sheriff Terry Johnson told the *Raleigh News and Observer* that he applied to participate in the 287(g) program because Mexican "values are a lot different — their morals — than what we have here." He linked the county's growing Latino population with a rise in crime rates.⁹ Never mind that Latinos make up 10 percent of the population in Alamance County and account for about 12 percent of its criminal cases. About 70 percent of immigrants detained in Alamance County through 287(g) are guilty only of traffic offenses.

The Obama administration has responded to criticism of the 287(g) program by touting Secure Communities, an initiative that supporters say will be more focused in its pursuit of undocumented immigrants with felony records. Lawmakers argue that the Secure Communities program shifts the responsibility for immigration enforcement back to federal officials. The program relies on police in jails like the one where Garcia-Martinez was processed to enter fingerprints into a joint Department of Homeland Security and FBI database monitored by ICE. Federal officials then decide whether to take "appropriate action" and issue a detainer on an immigrant before he or she is released. The program began in Texas in late 2008 and by March 2012 was in place in 2,385 law enforcement jurisdictions in forty-six states and territories. This was 75 percent of capacity; the program was set to reach full implementation by 2013.

There is growing concern among immigrants' rights activists that this new program has begun to veer off course just like 287(g). Secure Communities has a mandate to identify and detain immigrant "level 1 offenders" who have committed felonies such as robbery or murder, as well as those with drug convictions. But in April 2009 the program's executive director, David Venturella, told Representative David Price's Appropriations Subcommittee on Homeland Security that even if ICE decides to allow immigrants identified in the database to be released after serving their sentences, they could later be detained or deported "at any time." He said that since the program was introduced, it has "resulted in the identification of over 12,000 criminal aliens," of which 862 were identified as dangerous criminals. According to ICE's website, in its first three months the database yielded a match for 5,707 undocumented immigrants with criminal records. Of these, "124 were violent or narcotic offenders."¹⁰ Yet ICE detained 955 of those identified, which suggests it is also using the program to target lower-level offenders.

With more detainees comes the need for more detention, and the Obama administration continues to rely on companies such as CCA to provide this service. In early 2009, CCA won a contract with the Bureau of Prisons to operate a 4,000-bed facility that will primarily hold "criminal aliens." In the first half of that year, the company received four new federal contracts: two with ICE, one with the Bureau of Prisons, and one with the U.S. Marshals Service to detain immigrants along the border.

While outrage over the conditions inside detention centers has led to congressional hearings and the appointment of a detention and removal "special adviser" at ICE, this should not be allowed to serve as an opportunity to expand the detention industry under the guise of reforming it. Nor should this distract from reforms that decrease people's vulnerability to detention. So far, ICE has responded to public outrage by planning to shift the roughly 70 percent of its population detained in local jails into larger detention centers such as those run by CCA.

Understanding the detention business and the profit motive that drives it can inform the movement to put a halt to this continued reliance on cages to solve the "immigration dilemma." Advocates for alternatives to detention must oppose the increasing emphasis on "criminal aliens" with programs that have been shown to bleed over into targeting the entire population of undocumented migrants. The characterization of women such as Sergia Santibanez and Maria del Carmen Garcia-Martinez as criminals enables such "reform." As long as undocumented migrants are portrayed as criminals, their detention will be palatable for the public.

NOTES

1. CCA conference call, August 6, 2009.
2. http://www.businessofdetention.com/?p=74; for video of this interview, see http://blip.tv/detention/houston-processing-center-830293.
3. http://www.time.com/time/nation/article/0,8599,1722065,00.html.
4. http://ir.correctionscorp.com/phoenix.zhtml?c=117983&p=irol-newsArticle&ID=1335468&highlight=.
5. http://www.businessweek.com/investor/content/jun2006/pi20060602_072092.htm.
6. http://www.businessofdetention.com/?p=66.
7. See GAO report GAO-07-875: "Alien Detention Standards: Telephone Access Problems Were Pervasive at Detention Facilities; Other Deficiencies Did Not Show a Pattern of Noncompliance" (June 6, 2007). http://www.gao.gov/htext/d07875.html.
8. Quoted in Renee Feltz, "Detention Retention," *American Prospect* (June 2, 2009). http://prospect.org/article/detention-retention.
9. Quoted in Kristen Collins, "Sheriffs Help Feds Deport Illegal Aliens," *Raleigh News and Observer*, April 22, 2007.
10. http://www.dhs.gov/ynews/testimony/testimony_1239800126329.shtm.

Torn Apart
Struggling to Stay Together after Deportation

SETH FREED WESSLER AND JULIANNE HING

It was shortly after five on the morning of June 2, 2004, when Calvin James woke up, put on his bathrobe, and headed outside to put the trash bins on the street for pickup. As the super of his building in Jersey City, New Jersey, James liked taking the trash out early in the morning before the humidity settled in. Besides, the forty-five-year-old had to be at the first of his two bike messenger jobs in New York City by 7:00 a.m. He had left his girlfriend, Kathy McArdle, asleep in their bed. In the next room was their six-year-old son, Josh.

As he walked outside, James spotted a black SUV across the road. He thought nothing of it and continued his work. But as he pulled the last trash bin to the curb, four people dressed in black clothing marked with the letters ICE got out of the vehicle. They bolted toward James, demanded he confirm his name, handcuffed him, and pulled him into the back of the SUV, where other officers were sitting in silence.

Inside, McArdle was startled awake by the sound of banging, followed by yelling. Immigration and Customs Enforcement officers were pounding on her front door and screaming, "Federal agents, federal agents! We have Calvin James! We want pants, shirts, socks, and shoes, right now!" McArdle pulled on some clothes and rushed to the front of the apartment. As she opened the door, four officers charged into the hallway. Immediately, her eyes fell to the guns in their holsters. The officers took James's clothes and shoes and left as quickly as they had arrived.

After spending four months in immigration detention, first in New Jersey and then in Louisiana, James was put on a charter flight and deported to Jamaica, a place he had not set foot in since he was twelve years old.

On a balmy summer night, Calvin James stepped off the plane in Kingston. In the dark, he could not make out any of the landmarks he remembered from growing up there before he emigrated to the United States as a young boy. Weeks later, he'd recognize his old school buildings and back alley playgrounds on those Kingston streets. But that first night, he recognized nothing. He had never expected to return to Jamaica that way. Upon their arrival, James and the other deportees were taken to the central police station for questioning.

It is standard policy for Jamaican police to detain and question deportees immediately. In practice, this means that the police ask the same questions several thousand times every year — "Do you have family you will be contacting? What address will you be staying at? What are your local relatives' names?" Like most deportees, James knew of distant relatives in the country, but he had no phone numbers or addresses for them. He gave what answers he could to the police and was released into the streets of the notoriously dangerous Kingston.

"I landed in Spanish Town in, like, a battle zone," James recalled. "And that's where they leave you. A foreigner don't make it past a night on those streets."

Even though he was born in Jamaica, James considered himself a foreigner. He had not been back since leaving for the United States when he was twelve. He had long considered New York his home. After all, it was where Josh and Kathy were. He spoke very American English, having lost much of his Jamaican patois. Now, he was forty-five years old and exiled to Kingston. "When I first arrived in Jamaica, I could think about nothing else but, basically, survival," James said. And every day he missed his family in New Jersey.

For years in the United States, prisons have been filling up. When inmates are released back to their communities, they face a range of challenges, including racial profiling by police and discrimination against people with criminal records. Despite the U.S. Constitution's prohibition on double jeopardy — being tried twice for the same crime — incarceration is just the beginning of a barrage of legal and informal punishments that follow.

For immigrants who enter the criminal justice system, double punishment is a formal part of their legal landscape. While it has been true to some extent since the early part of the twentieth century that immigrants convicted of some crimes could face the possibility of deportation after completing their sentences, the passage of the Illegal Immigration Reform and Immigrant Responsibility Act in 1996 changed this possibility into an airtight conclusion. Before 1996, immigrants convicted of crimes served their time in prison and then could petition a judge to let them stay in the United States. In most cases, judges held the power to weigh the many factors in people's cases, including how long they had been in the country, if they had partners and children, if they were committed to turning their lives around. The system led to the deportation of tens of thousands of people each year, but, for many, legal relief was available. But in 1996, immigration courts were suddenly stripped of the power to consider a person's full situation. It no longer mattered that someone had children or had been in the United States almost all their lives as legal permanent residents. For immigrants found guilty of a crime, deportation became the mandatory result of their conviction.

Now, anyone who is not a citizen can be deported even if convicted of a relatively minor misdemeanor and even if this conviction happened many years ago. By broadening the number of crimes that trigger mandatory deportation — called "aggravated felonies" in immigration nomenclature — the 1996 laws have pushed hundreds of thousands of immigrants who have already served time in prison into detention and deportation. These people are very often legal permanent residents, people who migrated with their families as children and were raised, educated, and socialized in the United States. They have owned businesses, bought homes, and started families of their own in the United States. They are, save for a piece of paper, Americans.

After their criminal cases have ended, immigrants are subject to the civil procedures of immigration courts, which are administrative bodies. Dana Leigh Marks, a federal immigration judge and president of the National Association of Immigration Judges, described the civil nature of the courts in an interview with the authors: "We are basically doing death penalty cases in a traffic court setting."

In 2008, almost 360,000 people were deported from the United States, about 100,000 as a result of some non-immigration-related criminal conviction. This is about three times the number of people deported as a result of criminal conviction before 1996. Eighty percent of criminal deportations were for nonviolent crimes.

In 2004, the year James was deported from the United States, Jamaica received 4,118 deportees from various countries, an all-time high. That year, 1,845 were deported from the United States alone, according to numbers provided by the Jamaica Ministry of National Security. The rest came from mainly the United Kingdom and Canada. The majority of these people were deported as a result of drug convictions. Communities of color, especially Black people in the United States, are targeted by law enforcement for drug enforcement despite the fact that rates of drug use are equal across racial groups. The result is that people of color are disproportionately incarcerated for drugs, and Black immigrants face deportation on criminal grounds at rates far higher than other immigrants.

Deportees are separated from their families and lose forever their chance to rebuild their lives in the United States. Indeed, several long-time U.S. residents who were deported to Jamaica and interviewed for this chapter described the experience as a "life sentence," a "death sentence," a process akin to "ripping up a flower from its roots and letting the buds fall where they will." Many people deported from the United States to Jamaica, including Calvin James, describe an experience that's defined by the struggle to make basic ends meet, and by a forced social isolation and the desperate longing for family left behind in the United States.

Already out of place, a harsh stigma follows deportees wherever they go in Jamaica. Knowledge of a person's deportee status can cut off job opportunities and close doors to housing. The Jamaican public, which looks down on deportees, is unsympathetic. "You were supposed to go abroad and send home remittances, but now you come back here a worthless deportee," said Bernard Headley, a professor of criminology at the University of the West Indies, summarizing the popular sentiment during an interview with the authors. According to Headley, 85 percent of people deported to Jamaica had only one conviction. And yet deportees as a class are blamed for much of Jamaica's preexisting crime problems.

"It is a perception that has no evidential basis at all," argued Nancy Anderson, the director of the Independent Jamaica Council for Human Rights. "You have to try and fight it, but it's a prejudice people have. The word 'deportee' is a bad word. Even used cars that break down on the road, you say, 'It's a deportee.'"

A connection between deportees and Jamaican crime remains undocumented, yet it functions as more than cultural myth. The *Jamaica Gleaner*, the country's daily paper, reports infractions committed by deportees with enthusiastic furor on its front pages. And politicians who are hard-pressed to respond to public pressure over violent crime in Jamaica have taken to blaming the deportees. "Jamaica has the highest rates of murder and violent crime in the world. And we also have a constant flow of deported persons back to Jamaica," said Peter Phillips, Jamaica's former minister of national security, in an interview. The connection between deportees and violent crime in Jamaica was implied rather than stated directly. He pointed to a purported increase in types of crime that, he said, had not originated in Jamaica, including identity theft and kidnapping. "The removal of persons from a more to less secure environment leaves the potential for recidivism or the possibility of people becoming a burden on society," Phillips said. Noting that Jamaica will always accept its citizens, he continued: "It is an illusion to think that having removed the person, you remove the problem."

Headley called such political scapegoating on the part of government officials "irresponsible," but he also laid blame on changes in U.S. immigration law that created a whole class of deportable crimes. "Check forging had not been considered a felony before [1996], but it was now made a felony," he said. "It's criminalization. It's creating criminals out of whole cloth. Class A misdemeanors are now felonies? And it's a felony because what we really want to do is extricate people."

In large part because of stigmatization, deported people arrive in Jamaica with few work options. When deportees apply for jobs, they risk having their convictions exposed with background checks, which almost always disqualifies them for the job. Often, the only option available to them in Jamaica, as in the United States, is low-wage work. As it is, there are few jobs to be had in the small island country, and trade work requires job-specific certification by a local Caribbean body, which takes years of study and testing, according to Wendel Abel, a professor of psychiatry at the University of the West Indies in Mona who has worked with deported people. Deportees become ineligible for jobs that might provide some stability. Many are forced into the secondary economy to scrape together a living as street vendors or handymen.

James was able to get work relatively quickly, though. He found a job as a night security guard at a restaurant in Montego Bay and picked up another job as a driver transporting inventory for a wholesaler on the western side of the island. He does pickups and deliveries around the island, not unlike his days in New York, where he worked as a bike messenger. James's initial idea was to make enough to save and send for his partner and their son. But working sixteen hours a day on Jamaican wages — with take-home pay averaging $75 a week — does not yield nearly as much as his family would need to make the move.

"Most deportees are men in their early forties; we do have men in their fifties and sixties," said Marleen Brown, a coordinator with FURI Jamaica (Family Unification and Resettlement Initiative), a resettlement group that works to connect deportees with family, jobs, and housing. According to Brown, most left Jamaica as children. She provides newly arrived deportees with advice to ease their adjustment. "You have to unlearn to relearn. Let go of your past," Brown said she tells them. "You have to work with what you have, as limited as it is." It is hard-won wisdom; Brown was herself deported in 2006. Since then, her oldest son graduated from West Point, and her younger son graduated from high school. She missed both ceremonies.

According to Abel, "Deportees arrive, and they are homeless, effectively stateless, and without family." This trauma of being cast out is compounded by high rates of mental illness among deported people, according to Abel and others. Because those who end up in U.S. prisons and jails suffer disproportionately from mental disabilities, those deported as a result of a criminal conviction are likely to be dealing with these challenges. On top of this, the trauma of deportation — being torn from home and sent somewhere largely unknown — affects everyone's mental well-being. "I would say all the deportees come back here with adjustment disorder," said Myo Oo, a psychiatrist in Jamaica who works in the mental health system. "You don't know what to eat; you don't know where to sleep. I could almost say 100 percent of deportees deal with depression and anxiety."

Further, deported people are culturally disconnected from Jamaica after twenty or thirty years abroad. "For deportees, the social integration and adjustment process alone is a big problem," said Oo. "Deportees feel marginalized, because nobody is here for them. Often, everyone in their family is abroad." Christopher Bryan, who makes a living selling cigarettes and orange juice from the front yard of his Kingston home since he was deported nine years ago, talked only about his daughter, Jamilah. He hasn't seen her in ten years. She lives in Cleveland, Ohio, with her mother, and Bryan speaks with her when he can. He said his daughter dreams of becoming a doctor. "I just want to be a father for my daughter, and I think she deserves it," said Bryan in a plaintive, measured tone. "She's my only child, and she deserves it, and she wants to be a doctor, and I can't do it from here because of the economy. But maybe if I can get back there, I can do something for the betterment of my child."

Calvin James migrated to Queens, New York, when he was twelve, following his mother, Ena Edmond. Edmond had left Jamaica six years earlier, moving first to Chicago and then to New York, where she found work cleaning hotels — a job she held for thirty years, working overtime to raise her four children.

Edmond says her son was a shy boy who kept to himself. But after several years in Queens, James started getting beat up by a classmate. "I was this strange kid from another country, and he just felt like he wanted to make me his target," said James. "I thought, 'Why am I going to go to class to get tortured?'" At seventeen, James dropped out of high school.

To make some money, James and his older brother tried fixing electronics. In Jamaica, to earn some pocket change, they had taught themselves to fix TVs and radios, but fixing neighbors' broken stuff did not bring in enough cash in the United States. The brothers began selling marijuana in city parks. In 1992, after years of mostly avoiding the attention of police, James was arrested and spent eighteen months in jail for possession and dealing large quantities of marijuana. "I always told them not to get into drugs. . . . I wanted them to go to school," said Ena Edmond. "I don't know what happened. When you're poor, you try your best, but you don't have the money to help. . . . I wish I had made Calvin a citizen, but I didn't know I had to."

James was released from prison in 1994 and brought to an immigration center in Manhattan, where he was told that as an immigrant who had committed a crime, he was at risk of deportation. His mother bailed him out, and James began a process of petitioning for relief from deportation — still a possibility before the 1996 law. His case was adjourned several times because he was unable to find documents proving his place of birth. But in late 1996, James stopped showing up for his hearings, knowing that if he did go, he would be detained and deported. The new immigration law had left him with no grounds for relief. Several months after the passage of the immigration bill, an order of deportation was issued for James without his being present and without legal counsel. For a time after his deportation order was issued, he said, "I lived with my head down."

He got a job as a bike messenger in the city and hoped he could put his conviction and his deportation order behind him. Several months after the court ordered James to be deported, he met Kathy McArdle. They dated, and their relationship quickly became serious. Almost two years later, their son, Josh, was born. They both worked, but James wanted to move his family into "a nicer place in New York." He went back to dealing drugs, hoping to get enough money to do that. James was caught and did another stint in jail, this time in New Jersey. The New Jersey jail had no agreement with immigration authorities to enforce immigration laws or to hand over noncitizen inmates to immigration agents. James was released and returned home to McArdle and Josh, thinking himself lucky to avoid deportation.

James was hired again as a bike messenger for two different companies and worked from 7:00 a.m. until 3:00 p.m., allowing him to pick up six-year-old Josh from school. James also joined a cycling club in Central Park and started riding competitively. "He took [Josh] to all his grocery shopping, all his errands," remembers McArdle. "Wherever he went, Josh was with him." James bought his son a bike, and they'd go to the park together and ride around. In the evenings, James would cook dinner. Josh, now eleven, with a round face and a head of sandy, shoulder-length hair, remembers those days: "I miss his cooking. I really liked his rice that he used to make. It had coconut milk in it."

James said he stopped selling drugs before he was deported. "I did not want my son to grow up like that, with a father in and out of the house. And for the first time, I was doing really, really well." According to Neil Tannenbaum, the boss at Bellair Expediting, where James worked in the mornings, "There was nobody who rode like him. He got more done in less time than anyone else." Tannenbaum says that the company was planning to make James the manager of the whole team of messengers when he suddenly stopped coming to work. Bellair found out weeks later that James had been deported when McArdle came to collect his last checks. "If he were here today, Calvin would definitely have a job here."

James would probably have been able to continue living under the radar had it not been for the Bush administration's policy changes after September 11. Before September 11, many migrants were able to continue living their lives, working and supporting their families, even after an order of deportation. But the political climate that bound immigration and national security concerns tightly together changed this.

In 2003, the Department of Homeland Security initiated a program to conduct home raids to round up, detain, and deport immigrants like James who had outstanding deportation orders. In 2004, they came for him. James was taken to New Jersey, where he was locked up for three weeks in an immigration detention center. One day, McArdle and Josh went to visit him there, but found that he'd been moved to a federal prison in Louisiana, where he spent three months waiting before he was put on a chartered plane — locals call it "Deportee Airways" — and deported.

Dan Kanstroom, a professor of law at Boston College, says that the United States is in many ways unique in its treatment of deportation as a totally civil sanction as opposed to a criminal punishment. "In many situations in Europe," said Kanstroom in an interview with the authors, "deportation after a person has served their sentence would be considered double jeopardy." And, he says, "EU law holds that the state must consider the crime and the effect of deportation on families and children." Yet the United States continues to deport parents with criminal convictions without considering the impact on their families. Stories from people around the country expose a harsh reality for families, who continue to be separated. Stripped of a major source of income and burdened with the financial strains of legal fees or of remitting money to their deported relatives, families are falling into poverty and losing homes to foreclosure.

Yvonne Johnson, a Jamaican American woman in her sixties, has been thrust into economic turmoil by the deportation of her son. Christopher Johnson, who is forty, was deported after spending over half his life in prison or juvenile detention; suffering from bipolar disorder and schizophrenia, he has almost no memory of a Jamaican childhood. He now sleeps in a temporary shelter for deportees in Kingston. In an attempt to keep her son from becoming homeless and losing access to mental health services in Kingston, Yvonne Johnson has gone into debt wiring him money. She is now struggling to keep her house from sliding into foreclosure.

In the United States, many families of deported people find themselves corralled into other government institutions like foster care, welfare, and public housing.

Kathy McArdle was evicted from her Jersey City apartment three years after James was deported, after losing her job. She and her son spent time on friends' couches and eventually ended up in a shelter in New Jersey. They now live in a different shelter in Harlem — a converted apartment building where they have their own unit. But if McArdle can't find a job and move out of the shelter soon, the city will move her to a less-private shelter where she and Josh will have to share a room with other families. McArdle said that her welfare case manager raised the possibility of involving the New York City Administration for Children's Services in their case. She is afraid that the worker was suggesting Josh could be removed from her custody if she has to move into another shelter. Having already lost her long-time partner, McArdle is adamant about not losing her son to the state as well. "I'm not going to put ourselves at risk of being separated again," she says.

In 2006, before McArdle was forced onto welfare, she and Josh visited James in Montego Bay for several weeks. They went swimming at the beach, James cooked the coconut rice and chicken his son loves so much, and his parents embarrassed Josh with their open affection around town. But visiting is not how a family stays strong together.

Today, James lives in a two-room apartment in the mountains just outside of Montego Bay. His home sits near a steep drop into a valley below. All around, the brilliant green of Jamaica's famed forests stuns the eye, but inside, his dark, cramped apartment is filled with mismatched furniture and cycling paraphernalia. James spends most of his days by himself. Like many other deportees, his is a solitary existence, marked by the never-ending shifts at work and the long bike rides he takes for exercise. Often, usually at night, James is struck by pangs of loneliness. "When I feel that way, I get on the phone. Kathy, she knows, because I'll get on the phone, and we'll be on the phone for hours." They talk about their days, their worries, their son. Like any other family.

James is adamant that he won't lose touch with Josh and McArdle. Photos of Josh, all smiles and curly hair jutting out of a hat, rest on a credenza in James's apartment that also holds his small television set. James and his family speak on the phone every day, and he stays up-to-date about Josh's school projects and skateboarding adventures. He also steps in to scold Josh when his mother says he's stepped out of line.

It's been many years since James was deported, and the days still stretch on endlessly. "It's kind of heartbreaking. Right now, the period that we're going through, away from each other, I mark every day and week," said James. "I think to myself, like, 'This is time that I have to make up when we do get back together.'"

The Obama administration continues to buttress immigration enforcement practices. In place of a comprehensive reform of the country's immigration system, the Department of Homeland Security has expanded local enforcement programs like 287(g) and Secure Communities, a program that promises to put immigration checks in all local jails.

Obama's enforcement tactics, taken from priorities and built on legal structures established during the Clinton administration, have exacerbated the most damaging effects of the Illegal Immigration Reform and Immigrant Responsibility Act. In the first three quarters of 2009, deportations had already surpassed Bush-era levels. According to a report commissioned by the Department of Homeland Security by Dora B. Schriro, a former adviser to DHS who is now the corrections commissioner in New York City, 60 percent of the 380,000 people who were placed in immigration custody that year were sent there by state and local police and jails. Two-thirds of those picked up by local police under 287(g) had committed no crime. Families of color are hit the hardest because the criminal justice system targets Black and Brown communities, profiling, arresting, and locking up far more people of color than whites as a proportion of the total population.

In Jamaica and in the United States, families are organizing for more fair policies while they support each other after deportation's blow. In New York, McArdle is an active member of Families for Freedom, a network of families who have faced the trauma of deportation. Families for Freedom is organizing around the Child Citizen Protection Act, a simple solution to avoid the devastating collateral effects of deportation. Advocates are hopeful the Child Citizen Protection Act, proposed by Congressman José Serrano of New York, might curb the number of families who deal with the trauma of forced separation. The bill would give immigration judges more discretion to consider the effect a parent's removal from the country would have on a U.S.-citizen child before ordering deportation. "While the bill is not reform," said Manisha Vaze, an organizer with Families for Freedom, "it's definitely a first step to just immigration reform. Because it looks at the immigration system from the eyes of families."

Until there is comprehensive immigration reform, though, immigration policies that were passed in the name of national security will continue to scatter thousands of families across the world.

Creating Spaces for Change
An Interview with Amy Gottlieb
NOVEMBER 2009

JENNA LOYD

JENNA LOYD (JL): I wonder if you can give the readers a bit of background about your work in migrant justice and the kinds of organizing you are doing with the American Friends Service Committee.

AMY GOTTLIEB (AG): Sure. I am an attorney; I have been since 1996. I graduated from Rutgers Law in Newark, and my first job after law school was as a staff attorney at the AFSC in Newark, where I am currently the director.

The AFSC has long been known for its work on prison and criminal justice issues. In recent years we have changed the name of the local program to Healing Justice, in recognition of our focus on healing, rather than punishment. The American Friends Service Committee, both nationally and locally, has had a long-standing commitment to the rights of prisoners, but also to abolishing prisons. We envision a criminal legal system where the focus is on healing and transformative responses to crime or bad acts in communities, rather than on increasing prosecution and incarceration. These perspectives on healing have helped inform my own sense of how to link the criminal justice work to immigrant rights work.

When I started working here, the immigration laws dramatically changed and began to require mandatory detention for certain people who had committed crimes — even if they were lawful residents in this country. They were subject to mandatory detention, along with asylum seekers coming into the United States to seek protection from persecution. Simply being a part of the immigrant rights movement for a long time, and beginning to recognize the absolute absurdity of having a mandatory detention policy — the government refusing to look individually at each case — that was the beginning of my real focus on the criminalization of migrants, particularly related to immigration status.

In the immigration context, which involves so-called civil detention, the U.S. government can jail people who are undocumented, people who are permanent residents if they have committed a crime, people who are asylum seekers, people who have prior deportation orders, and basically can do that at will. In building a response to that, my work has been very much informed by the AFSC positions on healing and transformative justice, and realizing that deportation and immigration detention are as misguided as the over-focus on prosecution and incarceration in the criminal legal system.

All of this takes place in Newark, New Jersey, which has an exceptionally high crime rate. It is a predominantly African American city, although approximately 25 percent of the population is foreign-born, so it's also a very high immigrant population. The communities tend to be pretty separate, the immigrant communities and the African American communities, yet both are facing similar levels of crime and community issues in terms of access to resources, access to education, access to health care, access to services that might create secure communities.

There were three murders in one day in 2007 when three young African American college students were killed in a schoolyard in Newark, and the people who were arrested for that were undocumented immigrants. The outcry about the murders became in large part an outcry against immigrants, with many voices claiming that if we had a more stringent immigration policy the murders would not have happened. That led to what I felt was a real need, particularly in the immigrant rights movement, for us to take a hard look at how we were talking about the issues related to crime and migration.

The violence continues to increase here, and so I keep pushing myself to think about: How do we talk about these issues? What are the common links, what are the common areas that criminalized migrant communities and criminalized African American communities are facing? How can we build movements that help to resolve those common issues instead of create more divisiveness?

JL: You've mentioned the idea of "healing justice." What does that concept mean, and how does it inform how you organize and do policy work?

AG: "Healing justice" is a term that helps to refocus the way we think about crime and harm in this country. It encompasses both healing from harm and the transformation of harm to wholeness. Its focus is achieving fundamental balance and fairness in response to harm and rejecting violence, dominance, and exploitation.

The principles of healing and transformative justice are responsibility, mutuality, and love. In practice, it means:

- being able to care for yourself, your family, and all your relations
- taking responsibility
- repairing "harm" at all levels — personal, community, governmental, and international
- having the power, right, and mechanisms of self-determination
- being able to lead your life "in a good way"
- having the power and mechanisms to hold community and governmental entities to these same principles and actions when they cause harm

We are cautious in how we do any organizing work. Our approach tends to focus on building leadership (or building leaders, or facilitating leadership) through a deeper political analysis. We shy away from anything that is a top-down "this is how the world should be" organizing model, and instead provide opportunities for people to come together, look at hard questions, do an analysis of how current policies impact communities, and develop alternative solutions to harm in communities.

Through that analysis, we are able to help build awareness of the negative outcomes of current policies. In healing justice, we can have a conversation with people about the issue of hate crimes, for example. The AFSC doesn't support hate crimes legislation because it tends to increase penalties for crimes that are labeled hate crimes, rather than address underlying causes. Given that we challenge the penalty system as it currently stands, we cannot support anything that expands or gives more power to that system.

As part of our organizing work, we want to help raise awareness that there are other ways to think about justice, and other possibilities for change. So in that sense, the policy work informs some of our organizing work, and a lot of it is pushing people to have hard conversations. It doesn't always work. A lot of people don't want to go there, but as much as we can, we try to open up a space for a much deeper political analysis.

JL: That seems like really hard, long-term work. When you talk about long-term change, what do you mean?

AG: I was on a conference call the other day, and someone from the Center for Media Justice said that there are studies that show it takes seven to ten years to really change the framing of an issue. We are talking really long term; we are saying that our work is about fundamentally changing attitudes, about changing the perspectives on crime, punishment, and justice. And that means you are fighting. You are up against not only long-held principles and beliefs that people have, but you are also fighting a media machine that really controls how people think about things, not just how people talk about things, but how people *think* about things.

We have a big battle on our hands, but we see our organizing work as going beyond the base building we have been doing with immigrant groups to working with broader communities, including faith-based and other advocacy groups, as well as the general public, to engage in these conversations. It's about opening up that space and getting people to think about things a little bit differently. We are not putting campaign target goals on this stuff; it's a much different kind of process. I guess you could say we work toward a fundamental change of attitudes simultaneously with other shorter-term organizing work, which might allow us a little victory here and there, or, if not a victory, at least some concrete outcome.

JL: To what extent does this long-term perspective inform your shorter-term policy or campaign work? And on the policy side of things, what sort of "comprehensive immigration reform" would you actually advocate?

AG: That's tricky. We did actually write a policy paper that for the first time goes into more depth about what we would want, "A New Path toward Humane Immigration Reform."[1] We know that there are certain compromises we cannot make, such as supporting a legalization program that ends up with more arrests, detentions, or deportations, or a program that continues to tear apart families where one member is deported because of a criminal background. But we do offer clear recommendations based on human rights principles that include legalization for undocumented individuals, restoration of due process, ensuring worker rights, and ending the immigration detention system. At the same time, we also have the political pragmatism to know that the world we envision is not going to be proposed in Congress. We are also up against big, mainstream organizations that are very, very well funded and that are currently guiding the language and the debate.

Our approach has been to be sure that people truly understand what is being presented by Congress through deep consultations with communities that are directly impacted by the proposed policies. And we are sharing what we think immigration policy can really be, even if it may not seem politically viable at the moment. We do organizing work around immigration policy by making sure that people know exactly what the proposals are, and what the direct consequences of a bill would be. We do an analysis of what has been the impact so far, based on the current law and using individual experiences, people's own stories — everybody has a story about how the current law impacts their family — then take it a step further and say, "Okay, how would the new proposal fix or not fix that?" And we give people the opportunity to do the analysis.

At the same time, organizationally, we do have certain principles. We want to be sure that we are properly evaluating what the actual implications of proposals might be, and make sure we can speak to that from a Quaker perspective. If there are [plans for] twenty thousand more detention beds, then we are going to come out against that. If there is language that pushes for more border fencing, we are going to be against that. And we are going to be against that at the same time as we are doing consultations with communities to see what their responses are.

JL: How do Quaker values and principles inform AFSC's organizing?

AG: In a couple of ways. One is that as a Quaker organization, we all agree that everybody who works here, even if not a Quaker, upholds the Quaker principles that the organization was founded on. That includes principles of peace, equality, . . . respect for all individuals, simplicity, and community. Within that, a lot of our work becomes learning to facilitate conversations, hearing all perspectives, finding ways to incorporate all perspectives, while at the same time holding true to the positions AFSC has taken as an organization based on Quaker principles.

In the immigration context, our policy principles are informed by many years of Quaker experience accompanying immigrants through different types of struggles, whether it was helping people who were released from refugee camps in World War II, supporting interned Japanese here in the U.S., providing sanctuary for Central Americans in the eighties, or helping detainees try to get legal status *now*. That history of accompanying migrants has informed what we believe should be humane immigration policy.

JL: Do you see prisons and immigrant detention, or migration policy . . . in general, as "peace" issues? Do you think about anti-prison or immigrant justice organizing in terms of antiviolence work?

AG: Definitely. I think we see all of our work in some way or other as peace work. People are not able to live peaceful and sustainable lives if their lives are interrupted by the violence of incarceration, separation of their families, loss of income due to the deportation of a breadwinner, or the many other ways that families can be impacted by our immigration and criminal systems. We don't always talk about it that way, but I think that it underlies, or undergirds, the work in a lot of different areas.

This is especially true in the healing justice work — we have seen so many examples of how people's lives are shattered through the incarceration of a loved one. The social consequences of incarceration go far beyond the impact on one individual family to touch the lives of all community members. Poverty rates, access to education and health care, and other social indicators are directly affected by incarceration. It is absolutely a peace issue.

The parallel is happening in the immigration context now: lives are shattered because of mandatory sentencing, or mandatory incarceration, or mandatory deportation. That imposes violence on people's lives because of the forced lack of liberty or forced separation.

JL: From a healing justice perspective, how do you try to broaden the conversation on migration and penal policy?

AG: I think it kind of comes down to how people are willing to engage in a conversation about harm. AFSC has looked at redefining or changing the use of the word "crime." Using "harm" rather than "crime" means looking deeper: Where's the harm? Who suffers when a bad act is committed, and how do you identify the stakeholders? A victim or survivor of a crime is harmed, as well as the family and community in which the act takes place. At the same time, the person who commits a bad act may have been harmed in the past, and may be harmed by the type of punishment imposed. That person's family and community are impacted as well, especially where incarceration and possible deportation are the punishments.

In the immigration context, how do you engage in a conversation about why we are punishing people when we are not able to identify any harm? There is harm in the *consequences* when somebody is arrested or detained or deported, but where is the harm when somebody migrates? Or where is the harm when somebody is a lawful permanent resident and has committed a crime, but has already served their time and has already been determined by the criminal justice system to be eligible for release, yet our immigration system decides they need to be deported?

Part of the work is, how do you have that conversation with people when there are such strong, angry attitudes about crime, and also about migrants? There are people who believe their lives have been harmed by migrants, and you want to hear answers to "How are you harmed?" Unfortunately, responses tend to be racist or fear-driven, like "Those people come to my community," "They're in the street," "They speak another language." They say this in much harsher words than I just said, but this demonstrates a fear of the Other.

How do you reach a point where we are able to come together on that, and say, "Okay, look, if we want to heal, what is it that we are healing from? What do we need to heal from in the migration context?" People who migrate need to heal from the damage and violence that are inflicted on their communities by bad trade agreements, for example, or privatization of basic services that has made it impossible for them to live a decent life or to access education. Basic human rights are being denied for many reasons, not only because of trade agreements, and they are forced to migrate in search of freedom and safety and security, so why are we not putting our efforts toward fixing that harm, as opposed to this imagined harm that migrants bring to the United States?

JL: In the economic crisis we're living through, these harms seem to be deepening, but our capacities to deal with them seem to be scattered and intermittent. How do you link the big picture with the day-to-day? How do you bring your own analysis of this big picture to long-term organizing that emphasizes people strengthening and acting on their own?

AG: On one level you have the opportunity and responsibility to educate, and that's a huge part of the organizing work, but you also have this opportunity and responsibility to ask the questions, and to help people figure out or work through other ways to think about crime and migration, and other ways to find a solution. If somebody were to say, "There's harm to the United States because we have 12 million undocumented people, and they are working off the books," or "They are driving down wages," or "They are taking jobs away from U.S. citizens," one, we try to look at the truth of those statements. And if they are true, how do you work through to find a solution that doesn't just create more harm?

Where's the peaceful, open response to the accusation that immigrants are driving down wages? One possibility is to say that we should protect worker rights across the board. Let's not target and arrest one group of people who, in fact, face high rates of exploitation in the workplace. There is an incredible quote in the *New York Times* from Texas congressman Lamar Smith about Immigration and Customs Enforcement increasing its focus on finding employers who hire undocumented immigrants. The ICE program is premised on the assumption that the way to stop undocumented migration is by stopping companies from hiring undocumented workers. Lamar Smith, who is quoted as a "leading Republican on immigration policy," criticized the Obama administration's approach because they are not doing work-site enforcement actions or raids, like under Bush, and now they are just checking records. This is what he said: "The most effective means we have of making these jobs available to American citizens and legal immigrants is U.S. Immigration and Customs Enforcement worksite enforcement actions.... Each time ICE detains and deports an illegal immigrant worker, ICE creates a job for an American worker."[2]

Not only is it unclear that jobs *are* created for U.S. workers through ICE actions, this belief disregards entirely the very real impact and consequences of the actions. We see over and over and over again the devastating impact of raids, arrests, and deportations on individuals, families, communities, and ultimately on the workforce. It's a much broader set of consequences, but nobody wants to talk about it. Again, the system is creating more harm with the policies that we are using.

JL: Is this principle of harm reduction how you think about the really tough question of distinguishing between reforms that strengthen the system and reforms that don't? For example, there are not codified standards for immigrant detention, people are dying, and there is pervasive arbitrariness. How do you simultaneously try to care for the people who are inside, while at the same time not want immigrant detention to exist?

AG: That's a huge problem. We struggle with that everyday. I don't think we have found a solution except that we try to be really careful in our conversations about maintaining a position that we think detention is wrong. Detention is not the way to go; we want to end detention.

At the same time, we are very much aware of the political reality, and we are working both on ending detention on the larger scale, but also on finding ways to at least change it at the moment until it's ended, or something like that! We do have a really difficult time with that, constantly, and it's our biggest struggle, particularly as a Quaker organization. People look to us often within the mainstream immigrant rights movement to kind of set a baseline, like "How far are you willing to go? What's your standard on this?" And if we end up being the compromisers, then we are nowhere. So we don't want to do that, but at the same time we don't want to be left out of the room.

JL: Maybe that's precisely the issue: the struggle over defining that line is part of what abolitionist practice is, or what healing justice practice is. Even having the end of detention on the agenda in the first place gives the possibility of discerning something different. That is part of grappling with the question of what justice means, and how are harms accounted for. It seems you are suggesting that there is a broader way of defining what harms are such that accountability for individual acts must be placed in a broader context of structural violence.

AG: That conversation about structural violence, I believe, needs to be a part of the broader organizing strategy in order to really get at the root causes. If you are only focusing on individual acts, you don't get to the root causes and you never create change. It's not an easy conversation to have anywhere, even internally within AFSC.

JL: When you talk about making little inroads, how do these steps chip away at structural violence, or contribute to sustained organizing?

AG: I think that there is a political moment right now to work with ICE; they have discretion. There are two things going on. One is that they are saying they are just the officers, they are the local implementers of the law, they are just following the law, and they have no discretion. Well, that's not true. They do have discretion and they can exercise discretion. And we have seen a few examples recently of where they have chosen to exercise discretion and actually have released people from jail, and have made a difference in people's lives in a positive way.

Where we have no inroads, and where I feel like we are really stuck, is that they are not going to bend on finding humanitarian reasons to protect somebody who might have had a prior bad act in their life, who has a prior criminal history. Those folks are the ones who are totally going to get put out to pasture. And that's an urgent organizing issue that I think we need to be really strong on really soon. If we are only saying "these policies are bad because of how they are affecting migrants," versus "these policies are overall bad because people of color are disproportionately caught up and their lives are destroyed in the system because of how the policies are implemented," we are alienating ourselves and not respecting so much of the work that has been done around the unjust criminal system.

We've failed pretty seriously in immigrant rights organizing because so many people are willing to accept a predominant message of "people who have committed crimes — or people who are charged with a crime, or people who have been convicted of a crime — are bad, and those people need to be locked up and put away. And if they are immigrants, they need to be deported." That fundamental message hasn't been challenged in many places beyond the prison abolition movement. Where do you see this stuff except in very alternative publications? To get that message out, not only the message, to get that *reality* out in the mainstream is a huge burden, but I think this is a real conflict in the immigrant rights movement.

I have been in this a long time, and it is a little bit shocking that I am not totally burnt out and defeated, after having pretty much zero policy wins, and in fact losing on most fronts. At some point I think that some people just get tired of being oppressed. There are political moments when things happen, and I feel like creating those open spaces for conversations is where that does happen. I guess I still have this little bit of optimism in me and I need to hold onto that. As much as we are building more jails, and people are making way too much money off the backs of poor people and immigrants, there are also so many new people coming out against it, that I feel inspired and good about that.

NOTES

1. American Friends Service Committee, "A New Path toward Humane Immigration Reform." http://afsc.org/document/new-path.
2. Quoted in Neil Lewis, "Immigration Officials to Audit 1,000 More Companies," *New York Times*, November 19, 2009.

Bajo la Misma Luna
(Under the Same Moon)

ELIZABETH VARGAS

My last memory of my dad is him sitting across from me in an orange suit in handcuffs with his head to the floor because he was too embarrassed to even look at me. We talked but I couldn't hug him or touch him. There were two large tables in between us where we had to put our hands because if the guard saw you put your hands under the table they would kick you out.

My dad was in jail after I had to call the police on him when he hit my mom. But right now the only thing that was running through my mind was the faded memory of when I was a child and I had eaten a bad McNugget from McDonald's. My dad told me not to eat it but I had to prove him wrong and when I ate it I found out that he was right, I shouldn't have eaten that McNugget. Because of that nugget I had such a bad stomachache and all I can remember is my dad grabbing me up and just hugging me, wiping the tears from my eyes because I was his little girl and making everything better. Then I realized that it was my turn to help him out and wipe the tears from his eyes, but I couldn't because there was this big man standing there in between us. That man with his revolver was the only thing stopping me from jumping on top of the table to run and hug my dad. A month later my dad would be deported to Nicaragua, separating our family forever. This wasn't how I pictured things turning out when I called the police that night.

When I was little my dad was awesome. He taught me and my sisters and brothers to ride bikes. Saturdays was our special day with our dad and we would always do something fun. He would drive us up a mountain with all the bikes and then ride down playing hide and seek along the way. He took us rock climbing on Bernal Hill. He taught us to respect others but also that we need respect. Especially the girls. He wouldn't let anyone, even his friends who were guys, speak to us disrespectfully.

But as I got older my dad began drinking more and more. He had started drinking when he was only thirteen. He came from a family of twelve kids in Nicaragua and he had to leave school after second grade to work selling fruit. His dad would send him out with money to buy fruit and sell it for double, and if he didn't sell enough he would get beat when he got home. My grandfather was a really bad alcoholic and my dad still has scars from my grandpa hitting him.

As time went on, my father started repeating those patterns. He started drinking more and he wouldn't come home for weeks and would ignore us when he did. When we tried to get him to go out with us as a family he wouldn't come. I think he felt guilty and embarrassed. He would say, "I'm just a drunken old man, why would you want me around?" On my eleventh birthday, my older half brother died, and his death really affected my dad.

My dad got locked up the first time when I was eight. He came home really drunk, screaming and threatening my mom. My grandma, my mom's mom, lived with us, and when she heard him she called the cops. Then when I was twelve years old he got arrested again but this time it was for domestic violence against us, his children. My dad had always hit us with a belt to punish us, but it got to where it was for nothing. And he always acted jealous around my mom. One day he couldn't find the phone because he'd been using it the night before drunk and didn't remember where it was. But he said, "Your mom must have been using the phone to talk to her boyfriend. You should have been watching her instead of letting her do that." Then he whupped us for that. Finally my mom decided it was abuse and she called the police. But she was also the one who went to pay $1,600 to bail him out.

As my dad's drinking and threats of violence escalated, my mom would sometimes say, "I'm praying he doesn't come home tonight." I would tell her, "Mom, it's way too much," but she would say, "How am I going to support you if we leave?" By that time there were five kids — my brothers Tony and Dennis, my little sisters Sara and Esther, and me. My mom was a low-paid secretary with the school district so we depended on my dad for money.

But one day we were at Serramonte Mall, about to buy smoothies, when my older brother Tony called and said, "Elizabeth, make sure Mom doesn't come home because Dad's threatening to kill her." I called back and my grandmother answered. She held the phone so we could hear everything my dad was saying. He was threatening to kill my grandmother and calling her a "ho." My mom just sank down in the middle of the mall with her head in her hands. Even though my brother had warned us not to, we went straight home because we were worried about my grandma. Luckily when we got home my dad had passed out. My older brother and I sneaked around, got clothes and all that we needed for my brothers and sisters for two or three weeks. We felt like spies. Then, while my dad was still sleeping, we secretly left the house.

We were gone for a week or two. We sought help with the church — the pastors gave us a place to stay and provided us with everything. We were running away from Dad, so my mom said don't go to school because he'll look for us there. I was the only one of us kids who had a cell phone and my dad kept calling it. My mom told me not to pick up. But eventually my dad called from an unknown number. He was crying and apologizing, "I'm never going to do this again." I started crying and said, "My mom told me not to talk to you." I hung up. When I went to meet my mom I told her to give my dad a second chance but she said no. But then he showed up at our church on Friday night and talked to my brother Tony. He kept calling and kept promising my mom that he had changed until he convinced us all. He swore to us: no more drinking. For a couple of weeks he was different until he came home drunk one day and then it was just back to the same thing.

But on January 17, 2009, something changed. That day my mom and siblings and I had been rearranging the house, in preparation for my grandma coming home from the hospital after knee surgery. So we were so tired that night, and not even done yet. Dad came home and got mad at my mom, saying, "Where's my food? I was working all day and you can't even do this?" She hadn't made dinner because she'd been too busy moving furniture, but she told him, "I'll go buy you some food." But when she came back and served him the food, he was still arguing with her. My sister Esther, who was five, heard them and ran upstairs to where the rest of us were. My brother Dennis was out, but Tony and I were upstairs and Sara was taking a shower. Esther covered her face and started crying. She said, "My dad is saying this and this to my mom." I grabbed Esther and told Tony and we ran downstairs. Sara came out of the shower, with just a towel, saying, "What's going on?"

My mom opened the door and ran out of the room, with a hand on her neck and holding herself, my dad running right after her. Tony stood between my mom and dad, shouting, "Hold up, did you just hit my mom?" That's when I realized what happened. I grabbed Esther and Sara and my mom, then took out my cell phone and dialed 911. My dad looked like he was about to explode and kill us. I ran outside, pulling my mother and sisters with me.

My mom could barely walk and talk. She had bruises on her face, neck, and body from where my dad had hit her. She sat down and I asked her frantically, "Are you okay?" I thought she was going to die. "I can't believe he hit me," she said. When Tony came outside, she screamed, "Go get Tony," afraid my dad would come after him. There we stood, my two younger sisters and my older brother and my mom, outside on the corner of the block, feeling the strong breeze hit our faces. Times like that are when you really get to understand why, when you go to the pier of San Francisco you see all these T-shirts with San Francisco logos like "The Windy City." Sara was shivering, her bathrobe dripping water and her skin turning purple. Esther was just looking up at my mom without a clue what was happening, tears running down her cheeks. And then me, the oldest sister just there trying to not bust a tear and if it did fall just turning my face to wipe it off the corner of my eye. I remember the feeling of the back of my head turning so hot, as if someone had put my head down against the floor and slowly put more and more pressure on it until it felt like it was about to explode. Waiting there for the cops to come, and finally when they came knowing that it was going to have to be up to me and Tony to explain to the cops what was going on because my mom wasn't in the condition to talk.

When the cops came, I started walking over to talk to them as they were heading inside the house. But my mom was yelling, "Don't leave me." I asked a woman cop to please take care of my mom and sisters. She hugged my mom and sisters, and stayed with them while Tony and I talked to the other police. I really appreciated that. Even though I was just a random sixteen-year-old, she listened to me.

But then things got bad. I decided to go get some clothes for Sara, and as I turned around to walk back to the house I heard Esther yell behind me that she didn't want me to leave her. So I grabbed her and as we were heading into the house the cops were taking my dad out of the house and putting handcuffs on him. As my dad saw me walking in with Esther, he started to cry. So then Esther started to scream, "Papa, te quiero." My dad threw himself on his knees, crying and yelling out, "Perdoname, hija." I guess the police thought he was resisting arrest, so they started beating my dad with their batons right in front of my little sister. Just imagine what went through my seven-year-old sister's head just looking at my dad getting beat by the guys that are supposed to be helping us.

Once the police had taken my dad away, we went back inside and my mom lay down. The cops wanted her taken to the hospital but my mom refused. So they took pictures of where she was hit and made us kids go upstairs and talk to them. They wanted names and information from all of us. When one big, bald, buff officer walked up, Esther started screaming and holding onto me because she had just seen him beat the crap out of my dad. His voice was demanding, and I tried to answer for Esther because she was too scared, but he said no, she has to tell us herself. I had to calm her down in Spanish before she could even talk. To this day, she is terrified of police.

When all the police officers left we felt so alone. When I called 911 the first thing I was thinking of was the immediate safety of my family. But I had really been hoping the cops would give us some resources and reassurance. I know it might not be their job, but I was hoping they would show us that we were safe, hoping they'd say, "Okay, the counselor's on the way." I was hoping for some type of emotional support for us and for my mom and my grandma. I was hoping for someone to talk to my mom about what she could do financially, let her know there's help out there and you don't have to depend on this guy. And I was hoping for safety for my dad — I felt like he was going crazy and needed someone to counsel him, maybe someone Nicaraguense, who would understand what he'd been through and could talk to him.

Instead, my dad was sent to immigration. Although he was a resident and was in process to get his papers, they told him because of his incarceration he had messed up his chances. He was sent back to Nicaragua a month after his arrest. This pretty much killed any chance of communication with my father. I've seen this happen to a lot of families, where they are completely separated because of immigration law. I wish immigration would understand what it means when a family member is suddenly taken out of your life. Even though things got so bad with my dad, I didn't want to lose my relationship with him. It costs us $5 just for a half-hour phone call to Nicaragua and visiting would cost like $700. Meanwhile we are under so much financial stress because he's gone.

My oldest brother Tony and I have taken over a lot of the parental duties, earning money and making sure my younger siblings are safe and go to school. Sometimes I think it's funny that people think children with incarcerated parents are more likely to get in trouble, because my situation has made me have to be much more mature and responsible than I would be otherwise. The church has really given us a lot of support. The pastor offered to find me and Tony jobs and even drive us to them if we needed. My brother has two jobs from that — really good jobs. The first night that things got bad, the pastor's wife came over and went straight to my room, hugged us, holding Esther, reassuring her, and waiting for her to fall asleep. When my mom left my dad, she said, "You made the right decision, and no matter what we'll be here for you." The church helped us with money, housing, and food. They're still helping us, bringing us big sacks of rice, beans, and potatoes. They have been so supportive to us and to my mom and grandma. They kept our struggles a secret when we didn't want anyone to know. When we went to church, no one looked at us different.

We were lucky that we had that connection to the church, but imagine a family who didn't. When a family member gets arrested this way, the remaining parent and children really need support. I hope police and the justice system can be aware of what happens in a family, both in the moment when someone gets arrested and afterward. I really appreciate the work that the cops do for us. I just want them to see things from our point of view.

Part IV

Battleground Arizona
Local Crossroads, National Struggles

The contributions in this part focus on struggles over nation, race, and citizenship in the state of Arizona. The media attention paid to Arizona in 2010, following the passage of SB1070 — whose stated mission is "attrition through enforcement" — consistently treated the conflict in this state as exceptional and as new. These contributors remind us that contemporary struggles over who can reside in this territory, and under what conditions, are tied up with longer histories of colonialism, border making, and economic displacement.

Indeed, by drawing out the many past and present forms of resistance to detention, border militarization, and prison expansion in Arizona, the contributors highlight the protracted nature of many of these struggles. People involved in Arizona politics — as residents and allies — recognize that their fights will not be won overnight, but instead will continue to require deeply engaged commitments to end racial policies that undermine entire communities. The chapters in this part highlight concrete abolitionist, no-borders strategies to develop connections and solidarity across racial, gender, and class lines.

At the time of this writing, copycat laws implemented in Georgia and Alabama are in the spotlight. Learning from the situation in Arizona presents an opportunity for communities across the United States and elsewhere to challenge the ways in which the criminalization of migrants is being used to resolve conflicts over wrenching economic dislocation, the role of the state in providing social services, and who may be part of shaping the future.

Policing Our Border, Policing Our Nation

An Examination of the Ideological Connections between Border Vigilantism and U.S. National Ideology

JODIE M. LAWSTON AND RUBEN R. MURILLO

In February 2009 Maricopa County's notorious sheriff, Joe Arpaio, staged a chain-gang-style parade of two hundred undocumented people down the streets of Phoenix.[1] Pictures of the parade disseminated in the media featured mostly Latino men — shackled at the feet and hands and clothed in old-fashioned black-and-white-striped prison uniforms — flanked by an array of burly, shotgun-wielding officers dressed in commando garb. The spectacularly punitive and martial images were orchestrated to convey the message that Sheriff Joe is willing and able to go above and beyond the status quo of twenty-first-century law enforcement; apparently, present law does not treat immigrants and incarcerated people harshly enough.

While some may dismiss Arpaio's antics as aberrant or as a publicity stunt, it is important to situate his tactics in the broader anti-immigrant context and a longer U.S. history of chain gangs, lynchings, and posses, all of which are inherently racist. Mainstream understandings of white supremacy usually focus on extremists like the Ku Klux Klan or other blatant hate groups. There is more to it than that, though. We define *white supremacy* as "the real material, institutional, and structural forces that have been deployed to facilitate the accumulation of political, social, and economic power specifically for whites." Such forces include slave labor, legalized segregation, Federal Housing Administration (FHA) redlining, miscegenation laws, unequal distribution of educational resources, and numerous other forms of racialized inclusion and exclusion. The law and its apparatuses—the police, court, and penal systems—historically have been deployed to establish and then perpetuate white supremacy. For example, the 1790 congressional act which legislated that only whites could naturalize as U.S. citizens established a telling precursor to present immigration law. Given this social and political function of the law, it is not surprising that present-day vigilante groups turn to discourses of legality to target racialized immigrants.

In many ways, Arpaio's parade mirrors the tactics, motives, and logic of present-day anti-immigrant vigilante groups like the Minuteman Project, Ranch Rescue, American Border Patrol, and the Civil Homeland Defense Corps. The tactics of Arpaio and such vigilante groups—who also dress in military-style attire and sometimes wield guns[2]—both rely on creating a spectacle as they roam along the border or search ranches for undocumented migrants.[3] Interestingly, the word "vigilante" has a highly visual dimension, as it derives from the Latin, meaning "watchful"; however, there is no evidence that vigilante tactics reduce undocumented immigration into the United States. Likewise, increased militarization of the U.S.-Mexico border has failed to reduce unauthorized immigration.[4] The motives for their activities, then, must lie elsewhere. In this chapter we locate the motives of the aggressive and punitive nature of both vigilante groups and Sheriff Arpaio within a history of racial domination. We show that both Arpaio and vigilante groups are logical extensions of a white supremacist national formation. Treating them as anything but extensions of white supremacy legitimizes U.S. migration policy, which is inhumane, exploitative, and deadly.

Following the logics of racial domination, one motive of Arpaio and vigilante groups is to intimidate and instill fear in migrants and Latino/as, who, even when U.S. citizens, are racially profiled.[5] However, Arpaio and vigilante groups insist repeatedly that they only aim to enforce the law. Jim Gilchrist—who founded the Minuteman Project in 2004—explains on his website that he "is only one of millions of twenty-first century minutemen/women/children who want the United States to remain governed by the 'rule of law' and who want proactive enforcement of our national security protections and our immigration legal code."[6] Chris Simcox—founder of the Civil Homeland Defense Corps in Arizona in 2002 and, later, the Minuteman Civil Defense Corps—claims he is merely working to protect national security and American sovereignty;[7] his mission is "to secure United States borders and coastal boundaries against unlawful and unauthorized entry of all individuals, contraband, and foreign military."[8] Finally, Arpaio claims that he is only enforcing the laws of Arizona and "serving the public."[9] In a 2008 interview, the sheriff defended his demeaning and humiliating treatment of undocumented immigrants: "We do know there's [sic] many illegals in [Maricopa] county, that have already been designated criminals. Just by coming here they are criminals. Everybody forgets that. Illegal means that you've done something wrong, you're illegal. But that goes by the wayside, nobody talks about that."[10]

The anti-immigrant and "illegal immigration" crowds have been so successful at criminalizing immigrants that Arpaio's comments reflect the national discourse that immigrants are indeed "criminals." In fact, immigration law falls under administrative law, *not* criminal law. Entry without inspection, which is what most undocumented migrants are charged with, is an administrative violation; it is neither a misdemeanor nor a felony, and does not carry a jail or prison sentence. The use of the language "criminal" and "lawbreakers" effectively justifies the bellicose posturing of anti-immigrant discourses and practices.

The paradox of Arpaio's and vigilante groups' claims to uphold the law and national security is that they themselves push the envelope in terms of following the law. Arpaio is currently under investigation by the Department of Justice for allegations of discrimination and unconstitutional searches and seizures,[11] while vigilante organizations function similarly to paramilitary groups in that they act as law enforcement even though they are not. Moreover, "vigilante groups have been responsible for cases of 'immigrants' being hunted down, abused, or beaten with flashlights. Groups or individuals get in their pickups or ATVs, detain groups at gunpoint, and then call in the Border Patrol."[12] What interests us in terms of this discussion is both parties' decision to employ extralegal enforcement techniques to uphold the law. In the case of vigilante groups, we have to ask why they do not join the Border Patrol if in fact they want to uphold the "rule of law," particularly given the anti-militia law currently on the books in Arizona.[13] Since these vigilante groups are militia-like in their zeal to have the law enforced, they come close to breaking the letter of the law.

It is of critical importance to understand that the present "border wars" that vigilante groups and Sheriff Joe are fighting were directly engendered by an act of war by the U.S. government when it militarily invaded the sovereign country of Mexico. By the time the United States was preparing to invade Mexico in the mid-1830s, it had forged an American identity that posited white Americans as socially, culturally, and economically superior to Native Americans, Blacks, and Mexicans. And the violence and wars that historically have driven the territorial and economic expansion of the United States are part of this racialized identity. For example, the belief that people who are nonwhite are "uncivilized and barbaric" justified U.S. colonialism and the invasion of Mexico. Political leaders who agitated for the invasion often represented the coveted lands of what are now Texas, Arizona, California, Nevada, New Mexico, and Colorado as "lawless" and underdeveloped.[14] While the United States carried out numerous attacks against villages during the U.S.-Mexican War — massacring men, women, and children — U.S. political leaders and non-state actors insistently characterized, and continue to adamantly decry, Mexican people as posing a threat to law and order.

It is not coincidental that the prototype for today's vigilante groups was created during the lead-up to the U.S. invasion of Mexico. In 1823 Stephen Austin created the Texas Rangers to protect the "pioneers" from "hostile elements," "renegade Indians," "outlaws and Mexican bandits."[15] The Texas Rangers were not state-sanctioned law enforcement, but were an extralegal group of civilians who organized and led posses to police Mexican people. The Rangers often targeted completely innocent people, sometimes lynching them and leaving their dead bodies on the side of the road as a warning to other Mexicans that they had better "stay in line."[16] The Rangers have a folkloric place in the U.S. imagination. One Ranger was said to be worth a hundred militia,[17] and countless books, short stories, television programs, and movies recount their legendary feats.

Given the history of rationalizing — and celebrating — hostility and violence against Mexicans, we can examine the recent history of contemporary vigilante groups, which also justify their actions as protecting and defending "the homeland" against imminent threats. Congressman J. D. Hayworth, a former representative from Arizona, echoed the sentiments of many Americans when he said, in reference to a town in his constituency:

> When you go to Douglas, Arizona, you step into a town that is literally on the front lines of illegal immigration. And it is a town where just under the surface of civility, it is being torn asunder by costs, by criminal elements, and by the strain of law-abiding Americans getting up every day, trying to live their lives, trying to do their jobs, trying to educate their children in an atmosphere that is growing increasingly hostile.[18]

What is striking in this quote is the congressman's reliance on martial language such as "front lines," "torn asunder," "illegal," "hostile," and "criminal elements," juxtaposed with words like "civility," "law-abiding Americans" who "live their lives," "do their jobs," and "educate their children." The logic of this statement follows the bifurcated structure identified by scholars like Takaki[19] and Limerick[20] in which white America is coded as virtuous, and people of color are coded as embodying vice. Does Hayworth really think that undocumented migrants are *not* trying to live their lives, do their jobs, and educate their children? This logic aligns whiteness with American goodness and juxtaposes it with Mexican depravity. The essential objective of this form of discourse is to rationalize or disavow white supremacy by ignoring U.S. hostility and domination and projecting it onto its victims.

Taking a cue from the political success of California governor Pete Wilson and Proposition 187 — and its expansion to other states — in 1996 Congress passed the Illegal Immigration Reform and Immigrant Responsibility Act (IIRIRA), the most restrictive immigration policies the nation had seen in more than seventy-five years. This legislation recategorized a number of petty crimes — including shoplifting and drunk driving — as aggravated felonies. These, in turn, now served as grounds for revoking an immigrant's legal status in the country. This reclassification resulted in the immediate detention and deportation of thousands of green-card holders, the vast majority of whom were people of color, predominantly Latino/as. Because undocumented migrants are portrayed as "lawbreakers" who have entered the United States illegally, it is generally understood that a punitive posture should be taken toward them. Exacerbating the perceived need for vigilance against undocumented immigration is the popular tendency to racialize many of America's social ills, including crime, drugs, and poverty. Thus, undocumented immigration is easily understood as another threat from people who are "not white" and who should be contained using the criminal justice apparatus.

It is not coincidental that the Minuteman Project, Ranch Rescue, Proposition 187, and IIRIRA all emerged in the ten years or so after the conclusion of the wars in Central America. Proposition 187 and IIRIRA effectively denied the responsibility of the United States in the creation of immigration flows with its support of repressive regimes in Central America and the violation of its own laws. Anti-immigration rhetoric and discourses of criminalization place culpability solely on immigrants for coming to the United States. This prevailing rhetoric does not recognize that the U.S. government has had a direct hand in creating the circumstances that cause refugees to flee their countries in the first place.

CONCLUSION

There are two images of undocumented migrants that are widely disseminated in popular culture. One image portrays a group of dark, shadowy figures sneaking across the U.S.-Mexico border. Along Interstates 5 and 805 in California are neon yellow signs depicting what is presumably an undocumented family—a male, a female, and a child; the purpose of the sign is to caution drivers to watch out for undocumented migrants, and the graphic has become a popular T-shirt. The other image is of undocumented immigrants in detention, handcuffed or shackled, or being escorted into the back of a Border Patrol truck. Countless television broadcasts, newspaper articles, documentaries, and films keep these images in popular circulation. While considered extreme by some, Arpaio's parade of immigrants and the vigilante groups patrolling the border are not far from the prevailing images about immigration that circulate in the media today. Viewing migrants through the lens of criminalization, these images deflect attention away from structural and institutional violence.

Vigilante groups and law enforcement agents like Joe Arpaio perform discourses of criminalization, thus consolidating U.S. national identity. Sheriff Arpaio and vigilantes justify their actions by claiming that they are doing the job of law enforcement that the nation refuses to do. They position themselves as being better law enforcement or "citizens" than everyone else. The exceptionalism they claim for themselves parallels the American exceptionalist national identity, which recalls the history of U.S. expansion and war as virtuous rather than colonialist and imperialist.

Our contention that their punitive and spectacle-driven tactics are not extreme nor out of the ordinary is reflected in the dramatic escalation in Immigration and Customs Enforcement raids and in the detention of immigrants. Highly publicized raids in Iowa, North Carolina, and Tennessee in 2008 generated images like the ones we have described here. Racialized logic underwrites vigilante groups and is mirrored in ICE raids and detention, while the escalation of immigrant detention corresponds to the more general expansion of prisons in the United States. Entire groups of people are subject to racial profiling by law enforcement, the courts, and citizen groups.

Because this certainly belies U.S. national myths that espouse equality, social mobility, and opportunity, dominant discourses must disavow and justify racialized inequality and structural violence. These prevailing discourses criminalizing Latino/as, such as on undocumented immigration, effectively deflect attention from U.S. structural racism and violence. Sheriff Joe's parade of shackled migrants, the spectacles of vigilantes patrolling the border, and Congressman Hayworth's vitriolic condemnation of undocumented immigrants' threat to "law-abiding citizens" are analogous to what Dolores Huerta witnessed at the State of the Union speech. Perhaps the largest concentration of power gathered in one building at the time remains overwhelmingly white. Yet, under white supremacy, violations of the law by those charged to uphold it are rendered invisible by the shadowy figures of undocumented migrants. The actions of people like Sheriff Joe and vigilante groups emerge from and are empowered by hundreds of years of wealth, power, and privilege predicated upon the conquest, domination, and exploitation of people of color.

One of the primary objectives of mainstream pro-immigrant activist organizations is to generate and disseminate discourses that will cultivate a favorable opinion of migrants and pro-immigration law in the general public and political leaders. Typical examples of popular pro-immigrant narrative are Sonia Nazario's *Enrique's Journey* and the films *De Nadie*, *The Visitor*, and *Under the Same Moon*. All of these evoke sympathy for individual cases and characters, but fail to ask the audience to think about the structural violence and racism that has existed historically in the United States. While it is crucial to recognize, acknowledge, and analyze the struggles of individual undocumented migrants, we encourage pro-immigrant activists to speak about immigration on a structural level. More specifically, we urge activists to think through and disseminate knowledge about the very real connections between social, economic, and political value and privilege and racialized criminalization. This has the potential to shift how the general public talks and thinks about immigration and the "rule of law." Indeed, activist groups that underscore the ways that immigration law—similar to criminal law—disproportionately targets people of color for economic and political gain may effectively push groups and individuals in the general public to join the collective struggle for social, racial, and economic justice.

NOTES

1. Tequida, "Arpaio dando circo, maroma y teatro."
2. Anti-Defamation League, *Border Disputes*.
3. Chavez, *The Latino Threat*.
4. Cornelius, "Death at the Border"; Massey, Durand, and Malone, *Beyond Smoke and Mirrors*; Hondagneu-Sotelo et al., "There's a Spirit That Transcends the Border."
5. Romero, "Racial Profiling and Immigration Law Enforcement."
6. Minuteman Project, http://www.minutemanproject.com.
7. Anti-Defamation League, *Border Disputes*.
8. Minuteman Civil Defense Corps, http://www.minutemanhq.com/hq.
9. Arpaio, website biography.
10. Ibid.

11. "U.S. Investigating Sheriff's Office."
12. Rosas, "The Thickening Borderlands," 342; Anti-Defamation League, *Border Disputes*.
13. Border Action Network, petition no. P-478-06.
14. Acuna, *Occupied America*.
15. Texas Rangers, http://www.texasrangers.org.
16. Johnson, *Revolution in Texas*.
17. Paredes, *With His Pistol in His Hand*.
18. Quoted in Knoblock, *Border War*.
19. Takaki, *Iron Cages*.
20. Limerick, "Making the Most of Words."

BIBLIOGRAPHY

Acuna, Rodolfo F. *Occupied America: A History of Chicanos*. New York: Pearson, 2007.

Anti-Defamation League. *Border Disputes: Armed Vigilantes in Arizona*. Anti-Defamation League, 2003.

Arpaio, Joe. Interview with *East Valley Tribune*. April 18, 2008. http://www.eastvalleytribune.com.

———. Website biography. 2009. http://www.mcso.org/index.php?a=GetModule&mn=Sheriff_Bio.

Border Action Network. Petition no. P-478-06. 2006. http://www.law.arizona.edu/depts/iplp/advocacy/border/Border%20Action%20Network%20Response%20to%20USA.pdf.

Chavez, Leo. R. *The Latino Threat: Constructing Immigrants, Citizens, and the Nation*. Stanford, Calif.: Stanford University Press, 2008.

Cornelius, Wayne. "Death at the Border: Efficacy and Unintended Consequences of U.S. Immigration Control Policy." *Population and Development Review* 27, no. 4 (2001): 661–89.

Detention Watch Network. "About Detention." 2009. http://www.detentionwatchnetwork.org/aboutdetention.

Hondagneu-Sotelo, Pierrette, Genelle Gaudinez, Hector Lara, and Billie C. Ortiz. "'There's a Spirit That Transcends the Border': Faith, Ritual, and Postnational Protest at the U.S.-Mexico Border." *Sociological Perspectives* 47, no. 2 (2004): 133–59.

Johnson, Benjamin Heber. *Revolution in Texas: How a Forgotten Rebellion and Its Bloody Suppression Turned Mexicans into Americans*. New Haven, Conn.: Yale University Press, 2005.

Kahn, Robert. *Other People's Blood: U.S. Immigration Prisons in the Reagan Decade*. Boulder, Colo.: Westview, 1996.

Knoblock, Kevin, dir. *Border War: The Battle over Illegal Immigration*. 2006. Genius Entertainment.

Limerick, Patricia Nelson. "Making the Most of Words: Verbal Activity and Western Americans." In *Under an Open Sky*, edited by Jay Gitlin, 168. New York: Norton, 1992.
Massey, Douglas S., Jorge Durand, and Nolan J. Malone. *Beyond Smoke and Mirrors: Mexican Immigration in an Era of Economic Integration*. New York: Sage Foundation, 2002.
Paredes, Americo. *With His Pistol in His Hand*. Austin: University of Texas Press, 1958.
Romero, Mary. "'Go after the Women': Mothers against Illegal Aliens' Campaign against Mexican Immigrant Women and Their Children." *Indiana Law Journal* 83 (2008): 1355–89.
——. "Racial Profiling and Immigration Law Enforcement: Rounding Up the Usual Suspects in the Latino Community." *Critical Sociology* 32, nos. 2–3 (2006): 447–73.
Rosas, Gilberto. "The Thickening Borderlands: Diffused Exceptionality and 'Immigrant' Social Struggles during the 'War on Terror.'" *Cultural Dynamics* 18, no. 3 (2006): 335–49.
Takaki, Ronald. *Iron Cages: Race and Culture in 19th-Century America*. New York: Oxford University Press, 1979.
Tequida, Rosa. "Arpaio dando circo, maroma y teatro: El sheriff Arpaio está usando a los inmigrantes indocumentados para publicitarse." *La Frontera Times*, 2009. http://www.lafronteratimes.com/indexrosarpaio.php.
"U.S. Investigating Sheriff's Office." *Los Angeles Times*, March 11, 2009. http://www.latimes.com/news/nationworld/nation/la-na-briefs11-2009mar11,0,7881698.story.

Resisting the Security-Industrial Complex

Operation Streamline and the Militarization of the Arizona-Mexico Borderlands

BORDERLANDS AUTONOMIST COLLECTIVE

Every day, beginning at 1:30 p.m., on the second floor of the DeConcini Federal Courthouse in downtown Tucson, the U.S. government assembles before a judge seventy people arbitrarily singled out for special prosecution. Those being prosecuted here have been taken into custody by the U.S. Border Patrol for entering the territory of the United States without inspection. They wear the grunge and sweat from days spent crossing a remote and barren desert. For many of these individuals, this was their first time entering the United States; others have lived here for years and are trying to return to homes and families scattered throughout the country. None of the accused is granted more than an hour to meet with an attorney; they are brought here shackled and cuffed, shuffling in and out of the courtroom, their chains a constant clatter throughout the proceedings. The courtroom bustles with prosecutors, defenders, marshals, Border Patrol agents, and court clerks. The judge asks, one by one — or sometimes to the whole group, in order to save time:

"Are you a citizen of Mexico?"

"Do you have papers to allow you to enter the United States lawfully?"

"Did you enter the United States of America at a location other than a port of entry, without inspection?"

The judge then declares: "These defendants are guilty of illegal entry."

All seventy are sentenced to up to 180 days in prison. This is Operation Streamline, one of the latest in a series of punitive enforcement policies unleashed by the Department of Homeland Security (DHS) as part of a larger expansion of boundary enforcement practices and infrastructure in southern Arizona. Implemented in the U.S. Border Patrol's Tucson Sector in January 2008, Streamline is an "enhanced enforcement operation" designed to apprehend and prosecute people whose only offense is unauthorized entry into the United States, thus officially designating them as existing outside the national polity and reclassifying them as "criminal aliens."[1]

In this contribution from the Borderlands Autonomist Collective, we use the example of Operation Streamline to discuss how U.S.-Mexico border enforcement and immigration policy produce criminality and drive the expansion of state power and its dispersal through the private prison and security industries. With its assembly-line mass prosecution, Streamline is exemplary of the policies and mechanisms driving an emergent security-industrial complex, a confluence of state power and private industry that mirrors — and partially overlaps with — the prison-industrial complex and the racialized criminalization upon which it is built.[2] In addition to the production of criminality, both complexes hinge on the necessity of failure — the need to maintain a perpetual threat that escapes the apparatus of control in order to legitimize their activities and justify their expansion.[3]

In exploring Operation Streamline as a process of criminalization, we begin with an overview of U.S.-Mexico border militarization, and then outline our understanding of how the mechanics of this type of criminalization and legitimization function. We continue by exploring the challenges involved in building resistance to this apparatus of criminalization, and how its legitimacy and infrastructure can, should, and have been resisted using a diversity of tactics. We end by defining and advocating for a no-borders politics. Our collective joins an ever-growing chorus of voices calling for the abolition of nation-state borders, as part of a larger project of dismantling the colonial project in North America and its expression in the security- and prison-industrial complexes, and moving toward the realization of a more free and just society.

HOMELAND SECURITY AND BORDER MILITARIZATION, 1990S–PRESENT

Since the late 1990s, southern Arizona has been the nation's epicenter for both federal boundary enforcement practices and unauthorized cross-boundary migration. Following the 1994 launch of Operations Gatekeeper and Hold the Line in San Diego and El Paso, respectively, the ecological and cultural communities divided by the border have been militarized through an ever-expanding enforcement apparatus that includes surveillance cameras, walls, roads, checkpoints, and facilities for detention and prosecution. Under Gatekeeper and similar initiatives, which sought to block unauthorized migrants' access to densely populated urban areas, this traffic began to concentrate in the more remote desert areas of Arizona — first in Cochise County, and then steadily progressing westward into the Altar Valley and the Tohono O'odham nation southwest of Tucson.

In 1996, the Border Patrol launched Operation Desert Safeguard, building the first series of sheet metal walls between Arizona and Mexico's state of Sonora, which are seen today in Nogales, Naco, and Douglas/Agua Prieta. Safeguard also increased the number of agents deployed in the Tucson Sector. In the wake of the coordinated terrorist attacks against U.S. military and financial interests in September 2001, twenty-two federal agencies, including the U.S. Border Patrol, the Immigration and Naturalization Service (INS), and the Customs Service, were consolidated into the Department of Homeland Security (DHS).[4]

From 1992 to 2006, the Border Patrol tripled its total number of agents.[5] By the end of fiscal year 2008, the agency numbered more than seventeen thousand agents, with a mandate from President Barack Obama to meet the goal of twenty thousand agents by the end of 2009. In addition to increasing funding for traditional boundary enforcement tactics, the ongoing expansion of DHS and the Border Patrol has led to the deployment of more high-tech surveillance and interdiction tools, such as Predator unmanned aerial vehicles.[6] One of these enforcement programs is the Secure Border Initiative, where at least $8 billion has been contracted to private companies to produce and implement "virtual fencing" technologies, including high-tech towers, ground sensors, and infrared technology.[7]

This expansion of agents and infrastructure along the border, as well as the channeling of unauthorized migration away from urban areas, is premised on what DHS calls a "strategy of deterrence" — the belief that making the journey into the United States as difficult and treacherous as possible will deter would-be crossers. In order to produce the desired effect, the Border Patrol uses the terrain, including natural barriers such as remote desert and mountain areas, to maximize its "tactical advantage."[8] The consequences of this strategy have included a dramatic increase in the number of migrant deaths along the border and the growth of violence and organized crime as human smuggling becomes more lucrative (the Border Patrol points to the latter as one indicator of the strategy's success).[9]

The Border Patrol's Tucson Sector expanded the implementation of the deterrence strategy by launching its version of Operation Streamline, a "limited zero-tolerance enforcement" strategy called the Arizona Denial Prosecution

Initiative, on January 14, 2008.[10] While the initiative began with the aim of criminally prosecuting forty eighteen- to thirty-five-year-old, single Mexican men daily, by January 2009 it had expanded to seventy people daily (including women, married men, individuals older than thirty-five, and many from elsewhere in the Americas).

In an op-ed piece published in the *Arizona Daily Star* on January 25, 2009, Tucson Sector chief Robert Gilbert stated that the Border Patrol intended to expand Operation Streamline, with the goal of ending administrative voluntary return for all Mexican nationals apprehended by the Border Patrol, and to instead detain and prosecute all unauthorized migrants arrested along the 262-mile-long Tucson Sector. However, as of this writing, the available infrastructure prevents such prosecution. Already, southern Arizona's judicial system is overstretched. Immigration prosecutions more than quadrupled nationwide since 2001, reaching close to eighty thousand in 2008.[11] Deterrent strategies like Streamline have caused federal prosecutors to redirect their attention away from other cases involving transborder drug smuggling, white-collar crime, and Native American reservations, which are then dumped onto county-level prosecutors. In an article that appeared in the *New York Times* on January 12, 2009, Pima County prosecutor Barbara LaWall threatened to stop taking on what would otherwise be federal cases, unless the Justice Department either changed its priorities or offered the county financial compensation.[12]

The expansion of Operation Streamline has necessitated a major increase in both Homeland Security and prison infrastructure in order to deal with the thousands of people who are *daily* apprehended by DHS. Thus Streamline and its proposed expansion feed directly into the costly and growing nexus of immigration enforcement and the prison-industrial complex; DHS awarded contracts worth $385 million for the construction of new immigration prison facilities[13] and paid more than $250 million to private companies to house prisoners in 2008 alone.[14]

Approximately 36 percent of unauthorized migration across the U.S.-Mexico border takes place in the Border Patrol's Tucson Sector,[15] and an army of nearly three thousand agents is stationed in the sector to impede this crossing. Among the primary results of these efforts has been the channeling of unauthorized migration to ever more difficult and remote terrain, leading to hundreds of deaths each year (at least 183 bodies were recovered in the Tucson Sector in fiscal year 2008).[16] While the Border Patrol publicly bemoans these deaths as "unfortunate," they fit squarely within the stated logic of DHS's deterrence strategy, which publicizes these deaths as graphic illustrations to discourage other would-be crossers. However, the fact that fatalities and unauthorized crossings continue in such large numbers is evidence that this strategy has never worked — people continue crossing regardless of the difficulty or risks incurred[17] — prompting the question of why the federal government continues to pursue this policy in spite of its failure.

RACIAL EXCLUSION AND THE PRODUCTION OF CRIMINALITY

The security-industrial complex justifies its existence by proclaiming the presence of a perpetual threat that is imagined to exist "outside" the nation, necessitating DHS's intervention. Boundary enforcement policy is not intended to address the root causes of migration, but rather is used to perpetuate an industry devoted to the constant management of manufactured threats.[18] It is an institutional, strategic continuation of the colonial project in the U.S. border region.

When Border Patrol sector chief Robert Gilbert speaks about his agency's mandate for protecting "national security" and improving "the quality of life in communities across Arizona,"[19] he necessarily excludes large sectors of Arizona's population whose communities have been destabilized and made *less* safe by Homeland Security initiatives. The abuse of and disregard for the people of the borderlands go beyond those individuals who are explicitly targeted by the enforcement apparatus, affecting families and communities who are terrorized by surveillance, raids, random detention, racial profiling, violence, deportation, and associated social tension. These communities include indigenous peoples like the Tohono O'odham on whose nation's lands hundreds of federal agents, National Guard soldiers, and associated enforcement infrastructure are deployed, as well as border towns and rural areas whose populations are made up of families whose immediate ties span both sides of the international boundary.

While discourses of multiculturalism point to an ongoing struggle over the meaning of national identity, the normative ideal of U.S. nationality — shaped around a white, English-speaking, heterosexual community — belies the diversity of identities and cultures long present in what is today the U.S. Southwest. The militarization of the border and its consequences for southern Arizona's residents builds on a history of conquest and occupation, itself the basis for the territorial annexation of this region by the United States between the years 1848–1854. Measures like Arizona's 2006 Proposition 300 (limiting access of noncitizens to state-funded services) and English-only laws are not simply attempts at excluding the "newcomer" or the "migrant," but also point to an unfinished colonialist project serving to erase recognition of those outside the circled wagons of a definitively Anglo national imaginary — repressing those whose cultures and histories territorially predate and coexisted in what is today the state of Arizona. Effectively, those who are non-Anglo and non-English-speaking become coded as "alien." This status as cultural outsider is easily transformed into legal outsider, whereby, through the enforcement and judicial apparatuses, racialized "outsiders" become "criminals."

Operation Streamline is one of the mechanisms deployed by the state to produce this criminality: these "criminals" then become a target that the state can claim to be "cracking down" on. Most immigration violations are administrative, rather than criminal, violations. However, the discourse of "illegality" has served to confuse these distinctions in the popular imagination. Thus, the criminal prosecution of unauthorized migrants represents a convergence between the formal state sanctioning of racialized discourses of national belonging and illegality.

The somewhat arbitrary nature of Operation Streamline prosecutions in the Tucson Sector reflects the degree to which legal categories and popular discourse are blurred; to distinguish between who will and who will not be detained and prosecuted under Streamline, the Border Patrol establishes "designated zones" in the desert. These designated zones move, expand, and contract until seventy individuals have been apprehended on any given weekday. Those apprehended outside of these zones, or after the quota is filled, are subject to "normal" administrative removal procedures.[20]

Border Patrol agents treat Streamlined migrants as guilty from the point of their capture, placing handcuffs (and sometimes even leg shackles) on people at the moment of initial contact; this is often a signal to repeat crossers that something other than voluntary repatriation and immediate removal is going to occur. They are then taken to a detention center in Tucson where they are held in a cell with limited access to food, water, and medical aid until their court date, usually within seventy-two hours from when they arrived.[21] Most receive sentences of between 7 and 45 days with a possibility of up to 180.[22] Many who are prosecuted will inevitably be separated from friends and family members because of gendered prisons and varying lengths of sentences. One woman, upon her encounter with Border Patrol, was shackled along with her companions for over ten hours without any food, water, or breaks. She recounted that the handcuffs were so tight around her wrists that they caused a good deal of pain and left marks.[23] Reflecting on the experience later with a member of this collective, she exclaimed, "Why did they treat us like this? We are not bad people."

The Streamlining of due process rights communicates the state's ability to arrest, detain, and otherwise violate people's rights and well-being with impunity. The thirteen thousand people who were forced through this process in 2008 have federal misdemeanors on their records, with repeat offenders receiving felonies and eligible to be sentenced to up to twenty years in prison. Not only do such charges affect the possibility of legally entering the United States or normalizing one's immigration status at some point in the future, they also work to rationalize the growth and perpetuation of the security-industrial complex, reflected in such claims as "[a]pproximately 10 percent of all illegal aliens arrested have criminal records"[24] — records that are themselves arbitrarily doled out by DHS. By producing "illegal" subjects, by creating "criminals," Streamline exemplifies how the state and the security-industrial complex institutionalize social marginality, resulting in the potential for still-greater exploitation by employers, landlords, and companies contracted to run detention, transportation, legal defense, and interdiction efforts.

The security-industrial complex is incapable of succeeding in fulfilling its stated mission and eradicating the threats upon which its legitimacy is based[25]; indeed, it must never succeed. Both DHS and private contractors justify their existence and activities in terms of their own failure. They need more funding because they are failing, and they are failing because they need more funding. This is why boundary enforcement policy, epitomized by Streamline, is always limited and never successful. Even if the policy managed to achieve its goal — eliminating unauthorized migration in the Tucson Sector (at a tremendous cost in terms of infrastructure for prosecution and detention) — like Operation Gatekeeper, it would merely shift unauthorized migrant traffic to other sectors of the two-thousand-mile-long border.[26]

Despite the criminalization and prosecution of greater numbers of unauthorized migrants, DHS's ability to detect and apprehend those crossing in the Tucson Sector remains limited. A UC San Diego study from 2007 demonstrated that 97 percent of those who intend to cross the border are ultimately successful.[27] Asked if many are actually deterred by this process, one Streamlined migrant responded, "Of course we will cross again; we have families on the other side." While the Border Patrol claims that a part of its aim is to break the "revolving door of smuggling," what is seen instead is the very limits of the state's capacity to prohibit unauthorized entry. Some potential unauthorized migrants are deterred, but the vast majority are not.

The selective prosecution and deterrence of a few means that those who do cross remain vulnerable and exploitable, yet still fully "threatening" to the nation. The state is able to use this threat to justify expanding its reach, while the security and prison industries are able to transform this threat into profits. Rather than having a revolving door of smuggling, there is an ever-growing, quickening cycle of perceived threat and institutional limitations that legitimizes an expansion of security measures and prison infrastructure. Among the questions prompted by the above scenario, we must ask: What kind of society is being produced by such policies? In addition to the racial inequality and segregation suggested by the term "global apartheid,"[28] we see a spiral of violence, criminalization, fear, and exploitation. The next question becomes: How can we resist this Leviathan?

DIRECT RESISTANCE TO STREAMLINE: A WRENCH IN THE OPERATION

In the spring of 2008, a group of activists and lawyers called a meeting with the contract lawyers and public defenders brought in to represent Streamline clients. At times, the conversation was full of tension. The representatives of the public defender's office explained their attempts, before the program was even in place, to ensure that it would not be implemented as problematically as it had been in other Border Patrol sectors. Their efforts resulted in more time with clients and a smaller attorney-to-client ratio, among other aspects. Despite this, the activists and community members reminded the Streamline lawyers, the defenders are the grease on the wheels of this criminalization machine. Their willingness to limit their arguments, encourage their clients to accept plea deals, and avoid making arguments to reduce detainee sentences is necessary for moving the seventy or so men and women through the system each day.

While these efforts have not elicited the wholesale walkout of participating lawyers, they have been a potential wedge in the process. After these conversations began, we saw more lawyers making stronger cases for their clients—using their specific biographical information to confront the undifferentiated alienation represented by Streamline, sharing the detainees' personal stories, such as having to choose between the well-being of their families and the danger and hardship of crossing the border for work. The quick movement of detainees through the Streamline process is essential to allowing this program to operate under the restraints of the existing infrastructure; while activists' efforts have by no means ended Streamline nor the injustices involved, slowing down the system by insisting that defendants be granted due process is a first step toward broader legal and political strategies to fight the expansion of this program.[29]

In March 2008, in an effort to expand Streamline prosecutions to a hundred people per day, the Border Patrol proposed moving court proceedings from the federal courthouse (which was operating at capacity) to the Border Patrol processing center located inside the Davis-Monthan Air Force Base. Isabel Garcia, of the Tucson-based Coalición de Derechos Humanos, observed at the time:

> It is a very dangerous precedent to permit the criminal justice system to diminish meaningful rights and the court environment for those facing convictions and prison terms. It is equally frightening to limit accessibility to the public to observe and monitor our courts. Presently, accessibility is already limited to small areas for the public, and the move would dramatically diminish our ability to witness the most-unknown aspect of the "Border Security"/militarization measures — the criminalization of migrants in federal courts.[30]

Numerous local residents and community organizations held protests and raised public pressure based on principles of transparency, accountability, and public access to court proceedings. Due to this pressure, Homeland Security and the Justice Department chose not to move the Streamline hearings, freezing the expansion of these prosecutions. This victory, however, was temporary, as an expansion of the federal courthouse was proposed as an alternative.

In addition to the above, humanitarian organizations like No More Deaths / No Más Muertes and the Tucson Samaritans / Los Samaritanos[31] have increased efforts to document human and civil rights abuses suffered by Streamline defendants while in custody. These community groups have also begun a project to return confiscated belongings to Streamline defendants.[32] Other groups work to maintain a presence and witness during Streamline proceedings. These efforts are part of ongoing resistance strategies on the part of numerous individuals and community groups (including our collective) to tie up the growing security-industrial complex through advocacy, support, and direct action.

ABOLITION: TOWARD A WORLD WITHOUT BORDERS

Between November 9 and 13, 2007, more than five hundred people gathered in Calexico, California, and Mexicali, Baja California, for the first ever North American No Borders Camp. Participants created a temporary autonomous space along the international boundary to engage in workshops, skill sharing, film screenings, art, networking across the border wall, and demonstrations against migrant detention and border controls. This week-long action had been timed to coincide with the eighteenth anniversary of the fall of the Berlin Wall, with simultaneous actions taking place at immigrant detention centers in Tacoma, Washington, and Montreal, Canada.

This camp was part of a larger constellation of struggles against borders and immigration controls that has developed since the late 1990s in Europe, Oceania, North America, and Palestine/Israel. Actions have included blockades against the separation wall in Palestine and No Borders Camps along the Poland-Ukraine-Slovakia border, the Polish-German border, the "blue border" around Sicily,[33] and detention facilities in the United Kingdom and in Australia. This movement has developed in opposition to the twin policies of the militarization of daily life through extended networks of surveillance and control (such as the Schengen Information System in Europe) and neoliberal economics, which has devastated the integrity of people's livelihoods and communities across the planet. However, while No Borders Camps and protests are spectacular manifestations of resistance, to be effective they must be part of larger, strategic, day-to-day struggles grounded in movements and communities.

The Borderlands Autonomist Collective came together in 2006 in Tucson, Arizona, out of a shared desire to be involved in this movement and to initiate a more radical and political approach to the issues we had been discussing in our communities. We propose an abolitionist approach to the border regime.[34] We advocate a politics built not merely around opposition to the most pernicious effects of nation-state boundary enforcement, but around the rejection of the broader territorial, economic, and sociocultural claims such efforts project. Like the prison abolition movement that has developed around Critical Resistance,[35] we believe that an abolitionist struggle must embrace a multiplicity of tactics and sites of action, embracing short-term victories while avoiding any compromises that expand the life or scope of the border regime and the security- and prison-industrial complexes that help give it form.

It is not enough just to fight against the criminalization of unauthorized migrants. Rather, the discourse of criminality itself must be opposed.[36] We believe that anti-border and anti-prison struggles are well positioned to jointly articulate their resistance within a wider anticapitalist/antistate framework. We view the state and the security-industrial complex as bound in a system of domination and alienation that affects all of us who live in North America. National borders and the discourse of (in)security perpetuate the colonial project by fostering nationalism, inequality, and racist exclusivity. Likewise, the militarization required to enforce this colonial project is not merely targeted at the border regions, but targets many facets of our everyday lives. Thus, we see border abolition as a necessary component of a larger emancipatory struggle for a free society and self-determination.

We propose a politics that follows dual strategies of pushing back against the material infrastructure that allows the state to impose criminality and pushing back against the discursive and political legitimacy of this project itself. We thus view a no-borders politics as an approach, rather than as a conclusive set of positions or tactics. Certainly, this is a project that none of us can realize alone.

In our three years of collective efforts, we have engaged in multiple forms of direct confrontation with the border regime and coalition work with others whose struggles are grounded in different contexts of community, culture, and status. In 2006, we infiltrated and disrupted a private border security contractors' meeting and trade fair in Tucson. We have worked against the expansion of the border wall through critical wildlife habitat along the San Pedro River, and engaged in solidarity work with comrades in Mexico and indigenous communities in Arizona who are among the most deeply affected by expanding boundary enforcement efforts.[37]

Our participation in this struggle has in no way been unproblematic. The process of articulating and embodying an abolitionist politics can lead to many detours and dead ends. Understanding abolition as a long-term struggle, we are constantly faced with the question: How do we build and actualize an emancipatory politics in our everyday lives? As a predominantly Anglo collective, we have struggled to articulate our role vis-à-vis the struggles and communities with which we collaborate; while working to undermine colonialist dynamics of power and privilege, we must be careful not to reproduce them. We have to hold one another accountable for the ways we unwittingly participate in systems of oppression and militarization daily; while less romantic than more combative forms of struggle, the decolonization of interpersonal relationships and everyday life is fundamental to building sustainable communities and movements.[38] Dialogue, reflection, self-critique, and collaboration are critical to the process, and we make no claim to have mastered these. Yet the challenges are worth embracing.

It is our conviction that border abolition efforts and struggles against the prison-industrial complex need to be connected in both discourse and practice, though we do not seek to reduce the variety of voices that speak in opposition to systems of violence and oppression. There is at least a vision of the future that in some way unites us, and that is a future without walls, oppression, prisons, and borders. "Criminality" and "illegality" are political constructs fueling state power and for-profit industries that increasingly work in both prison and Homeland Security operations. The struggles against criminalization, against prisons, and against militarization are ultimately connected to the larger struggle against the legacy of colonialism in North America and against all systems of domination and apartheid.

Through our discussion of Operation Streamline, we have attempted to demonstrate how borders are mechanisms that produce criminality and how the production of criminality validates and reproduces the security-industrial complex and the socioterritorial claims of the state. However, while Streamline is exemplary of this system, it is by no means exceptional; to merely target Streamline would be, at best, to cut a branch off a tree — but this tree needs to be uprooted. This joint struggle can make concrete gains when it is grounded in day-to-day resistance to the security-industrial complex, the prison-industrial complex, and the border regime, targeting both the infrastructure and the legitimizing that make them possible. By uniting our struggles we can come ever closer to the world we desire.

POSTSCRIPT, FEBRUARY 2011

On April 23, 2010, Arizona governor Jan Brewer signed Senate Bill 1070, dramatically expanding the mandate for state and municipal police agencies to collaborate with federal immigration enforcement. Just one week before SB1070 was signed into law, one of the largest coordinated federal immigration raids in recent history was launched against communities in Arizona, involving more than eight hundred federal agents from the Border Patrol, FBI, DEA, ICE, and U.S. Customs and Border Protection. The media reports stated that the raids were a sting operation on a human smuggling network with participants in Nogales, Rio Rico, Tucson, and Phoenix; however, these reports by and large failed to mention that many innocent workers and random passersby were also swept up in the raids, in some cases with parents being pulled out of their homes in front of their screaming children.

SB1070 marked a vitriolic apex in the national discourse about "immigration." While many progressives and liberals likened the legislation to Nazism (a comparison with which we agree — in an entirely sober, nonhyperbolic way), it emboldened nativist demands to "secure the border first"[39] and encouraged the rapid expansion of additional anti-immigrant policies and infrastructure at the local, state, and national levels. Not wanting to be outdone by the state of Arizona, on May 25, 2010, President Obama ordered twelve hundred National Guard troops to be deployed on the U.S.-Mexico border,[40] and on August 13, 2010, he signed a $600 million border security bill providing a thousand new Border Patrol agents, unmanned drones, communication technology, and partial expansion of Operation Streamline in the Tucson Sector. Simultaneously,

DHS secretary Janet Napolitano continued to argue that the border "is more secure than ever" — claiming that this is due to a departmental emphasis on the removal of "criminal aliens."[41]

In December 2009 the U.S. Ninth Circuit Court of Appeals had ruled that Operation Streamline violated Rule 11 of the Federal Rules of Criminal Procedure due to the practice of having multiple defendants plea in unison and waive their right to a jury trial. This ruling came in response to a legal challenge filed by a small group of defense attorneys representing Streamline clients. But although a moral victory, the impact of this ruling on Streamline procedure was relatively minor: instead of having all defendants plea at once, they are now instructed to plea individually, merely extending the length of the hearings by about an hour. Otherwise, the character of Operation Streamline remains the same.

Although a number of additional legal challenges to Operation Streamline continue to be filed, the Constitution itself grants Congress plenary power over immigration, thus removing many of the juridical tools that might otherwise have traction against the racism and violence implicit in the convergence between immigration enforcement and criminality. Furthermore, the outcome of the Ninth Circuit ruling suggests the limitations of relying too heavily on legal avenues for combating the processes of criminalization discussed in this chapter, and points to the need for a diversity of resistance strategies that exceed those with which many nonprofit organizations are comfortable.

In Arizona, SB1070 has been a catalyst for the rejuvenation of grassroots organizing, community mobilization, and direct action politics. Throughout the summer of 2010 hundreds of thousands of Arizonans took to the streets, including coordinated direct actions on July 29 that blockaded a Maricopa County jail (disrupting one of Sheriff Joe Arpaio's immigration raids) and blocked rush-hour traffic along major intersections and freeways in Phoenix and Tucson. Thousands of businesses, homes, and institutions in and around Tucson announced publicly that they would not comply with the law nor allow it to be enforced on their premises.[42] Like the 2006 nationwide immigration uprising, high school and junior high students have been at the forefront of these struggles, launching spontaneous walkouts, occupations, and other direct actions, and organizing sustained resistance to HB2281, the state law banning ethnic studies curricula in public schools.

Although many in Arizona celebrated the court injunction that blocked the implementation of much of SB1070, many of the law's provisions remain in effect as a matter of federal policy. Through raids, police discretion, and programs like 287(g) and Secure Communities, migrant detentions and deportations have surged to historic levels under the Obama administration, increasing 9.5 percent in 2009 alone.[43] Despite the creative and courageous opposition from communities around the country, these policy trends are clearly troublesome and suggest that the racist exclusion, violence, and insecurity long concentrated at the border are now becoming commonplace throughout the interior of the United States.

We may be beyond the point where calls for "immigration reform" are sufficient or proportional to these attacks. Indeed the barely hidden racist and white supremacist attitudes driving these laws and policies suggest that it may be prudent to abandon "immigration" as a framework for our struggles, recognizing that the very term reinforces the territorial divisions and identities that we have inherited from conquest. Instead, perhaps, we should begin grounding these struggles in terms that refuse a distribution of belonging and exclusion that relies on abstract categories such as citizenship or status. "Immigration" is a red herring. The real question is whether the future of our communities and of our country will be one that maintains the structural features of apartheid and white supremacy that have, for so long, been characteristic of life in the United States and constitutive of our polity.

As we write this postscript, the situation appears dark: the disenfranchising enclosure of fiscal austerity alongside the ever-expanding entrenchment of the security-industrial complex at times threatens to overwhelm our capacity to sustain resistance and hope. Yet there is reason for nurturing hope, not the least being the world historical events unfolding in the Middle East and North Africa, and threatening to engulf the wider world. Like the cloudburst of a great storm, the first few months of the new decade have exploded the geopolitical and ideological contours of post–September 11 *pax Americana*, and here's hoping these winds spread to the four corners of our own desert home, overturning the prisons and walls that divide us and the everyday violences that have become tolerated and normalized. Together, we have a long way to go.

NOTES

The collective members who contributed to this chapter are Geoffrey Boyce, Samantha Herr, Sarah Launius, Sandy Marshall, and Maryada Vallet.

1. Most immigration violations are civil, administrative violations. The vast majority of Mexican nationals taken into custody by the Border Patrol sign a "voluntary removal" or "voluntary departure" form and are repatriated — a civil, rather than a criminal, procedure.

2. See Gilmore, *Golden Gulag*.

3. Martin and Simon, "A Formula for Disaster"; Foucault, *Security, Territory, Population*.

4. For an institutional overview of this organizational reshuffling, see Department of Homeland Security, "Who Became Part of the Department?"

5. McCombs, "Border Patrol Out to Hire 6000 Agents."

6. U.S. Customs and Border Protection, "U.S. Customs and Border Protection Selects the 'Predator B.'"

7. The SBInet program was permanently abandoned on January 14, 2011, in response to ongoing software and technology failures that rendered the project unworkable. Yet prior to March 2010, Boeing and DHS continued to claim that these problems were only minor, justifying several extensions of the initial contract. For an example of this type of discourse, see Lipowicz, "DHS, Boeing Move Closer to SBInet Rollout." The U.S. Government Accountability Office later determined that the technological failures that Boeing encountered were of a systemic nature, and remained so throughout the program's "development."

8. U.S. Border Patrol, *Border Patrol Strategic Plan*; for more discussion of the development and implementation of Border Patrol strategy in the 1990s, see Nevins, *Operation Gatekeeper*.

9. Nevins, *Operation Gatekeeper*.

10. The process and consequences for defendants are identical to those in Operation Streamline — which was first introduced in the Yuma, Del Rio, and Laredo Sectors in 2005 — however, the Tucson Sector is calling the Arizona Denial Prosecution Initiative an "enhanced enforcement operation" until it becomes more comprehensive, according to Tucson Sector spokesperson Jesús Rodriguez.

11. Transactional Records Access Clearinghouse, "Bush Administration's Immigration Prosecutions Soar."

12. Moore, "Push on Immigration Crimes Is Said to Shift Focus."

13. Lovato, "One Raid at a Time."

14. See Business of Detention, "Detention."

15. Terrazas, "Immigration Enforcement in the United States." The Tucson Sector has had the largest number of apprehensions since 1998.

16. See Coalición de Derechos Humanos, http://www.derechoshumanosaz.net.

17. See Government Accountability Office, *Illegal Immigration*.

18. For more discussion on this, see Loyd and Burridge, "La Gran Marcha."

19. *Arizona Daily Star*, January 25, 2009.

20. *Douglas Dispatch*, February 28, 2009.

21. No More Deaths, *Crossing the Line*.

22. U.S. Customs and Border Protection, "Operation Streamline Nets 1,200 Plus."

23. Testimonial information in this chapter was collected firsthand by the authors.

24. *Arizona Daily Star*, January 25, 2009.

25. The fantastic nature of the threats used to justify the Homeland Security ap-

paratus was hinted at, for example, in former Vice President Dick Cheney's insistence on the success of Bush-era security policies based on the failure of Al Qaeda to realize additional attacks on the United States because of the policies adopted following September 11, 2001. Following this line of argument, security efforts are justified by the presence of a threat *or* its absence. See Cheney's May 2009 speech to the American Enterprise Institute.

26. See Gathmann, "Effects of Enforcement on Illegal Markets."

27. Cornelius and Salehyan, "Does Border Enforcement Deter Unauthorized Immigration?"

28. Joseph Nevins in *Dying to Live* uses the phrase "global apartheid" to refer to the entrenchment of global racial and class disparities that result from a combination of the legacies of colonialism and new forms of control over movement between states (and the rights delineated therein).

29. For a list of additional tactics that have been suggested to expose and fight Streamline, see American Civil Liberties Union and National Immigration Forum, *Operation Streamline Fact Sheet*.

30. Quoted in Coalición de Derechos Humanos, "Operation Streamline Action Alert."

31. See No More Deaths (http://www.nomoredeaths.org) and Tucson Samaritans (http:// http://www.tucsonsamaritans.org).

32. During the Border Patrol process of detention, personal items are confiscated in the field. They remain in the hands of the Border Patrol until the moment of repatriation, at which time they are supposed to be returned to their owner if the individual files a request (a requirement that many detainees are unaware of). But the Border Patrol only holds onto personal belongings up to forty-five days. People who are put through the Streamline process are shifted from the custody of the Border Patrol to that of the state of Arizona, and finally into a corrections facility. Those forced to serve more than forty-five days have previously had no way of retrieving their personal possessions, often including their state-sponsored ID. Without such identification they cannot access health care nor seek formal employment. While our collective sees returning belongings as a state responsibility, and not necessarily a resistance strategy, we recognize its importance in relieving the harsh consequences of the Streamline process.

33. The "blue border" is a term that has been used by activists and officials to describe the use of the Mediterranean Sea and Atlantic Ocean as barriers to unauthorized migrants' and refugees' access to continental Europe. The International Centre for Migration Policy Development estimates that more than ten thousand migrants have drowned while attempting to cross the Mediterranean. Nevins, "Boundary Enforcement and National Security."

34. We use the phrase "border regime" to indicate the broader ideological, structural, and territorial projects through which nation-state borders are (re)produced, rather than representing borders as simple geographic or political markers.

35. The Critical Resistance mission statement can be accessed at http://www.criticalresistance.org/article.php?id=36.

36. For a much more developed discussion on this point, see Escobar, "No One Is Criminal."

37. Other groups with which we've worked and which we support include No More Deaths; Border Action Network, a membership-based human rights organization that works to elevate the voices of Southern Arizona residents and engages in a myriad of policy struggles (www.borderaction.org); and Tierra y Libertad Organization, a youth-led collective that reclaims community land to redevelop traditional agriculture practices and build grassroots power.

38. For a helpful discussion of some of the issues involved, see Koopman, "Imperialism Within."

39. On April 10, 2010, Arizona senators Kyl and McCain launched a ten-point border security plan. First in the plan was a call for the deployment of three thousand National Guard troops and a fully funded expansion of Operation Streamline. Included among the suite of controls put forth in the duo's plan is expansion of Operation Stonegarden, completion of seven hundred miles of border fence, expansion of Predator B unmanned aerial vehicles (drones) for border surveillance, one full-time federal magistrate in Cochise County, Arizona, and a host of new technology aimed at increasing infrastructure and capacity along the Arizona-Sonora border. Proponents argued its necessity for gaining "operational control" of the border. See KVOA, "McCain, Kyl Announce Border Security Plan."

40. MSNBC, "Obama Orders 1,200 Guard Troops to Border."

41. In an August 17, 2010, report, DHS secretary Janet Napolitano stated that the administration would focus the country's border strategy on criminals who have entered the United States illegally. Currently, half of deported illegal immigrants were convicted of a crime, she said. That compares with 34 percent of those deported in June 2009. See Immigration and Customs Enforcement, "Setting the Record Straight."

42. For more on the historical context of SB1070 and organized resistance to the law, see Boyce and Launius, "Normalizing Noncompliance."

43. Secretary Napolitano has announced that participation in Secure Communities will be mandatory for all state and local law enforcement agencies by 2013. See http://www.deportationnation.org for more.

BIBLIOGRAPHY

American Civil Liberties Union and National Immigration Forum. *Operation Streamline Fact Sheet*, 2009. http://www.immigrationforum.org/images/uploads/OperationStreamlineFactsheet.pdf.

Boyce, G., and S. Launius. "Normalizing Noncompliance: Militarization and Resistance in Southern Arizona." *Bad Subjects* 81 (2011). http://bad.eserver.org/issues/2011/81/boyce-launius.htm

Business of Detention. "Detention." August 26, 2008. http://www.businessofdetention.com/?p=74.
Cheney, Richard. Speech to American Enterprise Institute. May 2009. http://www.weeklystandard.com/weblogs/TWSFP/2009/05/text_of_cheneys_aei_speech.asp.
Coalición de Derechos Humanos. "Operation Streamline Action Alert." March 14, 2008. http://www.derechoshumanosaz.net/images/pdfs/operation%20streamline%203-14-08.pdf.
Cornelius, W., and I. Salehyan. "Does Border Enforcement Deter Unauthorized Immigration?: The Case of Mexican Migration to the United States of America." *Regulation & Governance* 1, no. 2 (2007): 139–53.
Department of Homeland Security. "Who Became Part of the Department?" [n.d.]. http://www.dhs.gov/xabout/history/editorial_0133.shtm.
Douglas Dispatch. February 28, 2009. http://www.douglasdispatch.com/articles/2009/02/28/news/doc4991ecebaad68272023815.txt.
Escobar, M. "No One Is Criminal." In *Abolition Now!: Ten Years of Strategy and Struggle against the Prison Industrial Complex*, edited by the cr10 Publications Collective. Oakland, Calif.: AK Press, 2008.
Foucault, Michel. *Security, Territory, Population: Lectures at the Collège de France 1977–1978*. New York: Palgrave, 2004.
Gathmann, C. "Effects of Enforcement on Illegal Markets: Evidence from Migrant Smuggling along the Southwestern Border." *Journal of Public Economics* 92 (2008): 1926–41.
Gilbert, Robert W. "Curbing 'Voluntary Return.'" *Arizona Daily Star*, January 25, 2009.
Gilmore, R. W. *Golden Gulag: Prisons, Surplus, Crisis, and Opposition in Globalizing California*. Berkeley: University of California Press, 2007.
Government Accountability Office. *Illegal Immigration: Border-Crossing Deaths Have Doubled since 1995: Border Patrol's Efforts to Prevent Deaths Have Not Been Fully Evaluated*. Washington, D.C.: GAO, 2006.
Immigration and Customs Enforcement. "Setting the Record Straight." 2010. http://www.ice.gov/doclib/secure_communities/pdf/sc-setting_the_record_straight.pdf.
Koopman, S. "Imperialism Within: Can the Master's Tools Bring Down Empire?" ACME 7, no. 2 (2008): 283–307.
KVOA. "McCain, Kyl Announce Border Security Plan." April 19, 2010. http://www.kvoa.com/news/mccain-kyl-announce-border-security-plan.
Lipowicz, Alice. "DHS, Boeing Move Closer to SBInet Rollout." *Washington Technology*, February 6, 2009. http://www.washingtontechnology.com/Articles/2009/02/06/sbinet-update.aspx.
Lovato, Roberto. "One Raid at a Time: How Immigrant Crackdowns Build the National Security State." 2008. http://www.publiceye.org/magazine/v23n1/immigrant_crackdowns.html.

Loyd, J. M., and A. Burridge. "La Gran Marcha: Anti-Racism and Immigrants Rights in Southern California." ACME 6, no. 1 (2007): 1–35.

Martin, Lauren, and Stephanie Simon. "A Formula for Disaster: The Department of Homeland Security's Virtual Ontology." *Space and Polity* 12, no. 3 (2008): 281–96.

McCombs, Brady. "Border Patrol Out to Hire 6000 Agents." *Arizona Daily Star*, February 19, 2007.

Moore, Solomon. "Push on Immigration Crimes Is Said to Shift Focus." *New York Times*, January 12, 2009. http://www.nytimes.com/2009/01/12/us/12prosecute.html.

MSNBC. "Obama Orders 1,200 Guard Troops to Border." May 25, 2010. http://www.msnbc.msn.com/id/37340747.

Nevins, J. "Boundary Enforcement and National Security in an Age of Global Apartheid." *Dissident Voice*, July 2006. http://dissidentvoice.org/July06/Nevins18.htm.

———. *Dying to Live: A Story of U.S. Immigration in an Age of Global Apartheid*. San Francisco: City Lights, 2008.

———. *Operation Gatekeeper: The Rise of the "Illegal Alien" and the Making of the U.S.-Mexico Boundary*. New York: Routledge, 2002.

No More Deaths. *Crossing the Line: Human Rights Abuses of Migrants in Short-Term Custody on the Arizona/Sonora Border*. Tucson, Ariz.: No More Deaths, 2008.

Terrazas, Aaron. "Immigration Enforcement in the United States." *Migration Policy Institute*, October 2008. http://www.migrationinformation.org/U.S.Focus/display.cfm?ID=697#14.

Transactional Records Access Clearinghouse. "Bush Administration's Immigration Prosecutions Soar: Total of All Federal Filings Reaches New High." 2009. http://trac.syr.edu/tracreports/crim/201.

U.S. Border Patrol. *Border Patrol Strategic Plan: 1994 and Beyond*. Washington, D.C.: U.S. Border Patrol, 1994.

U.S. Customs and Border Protection. "Operation Streamline Nets 1,200 Plus." July 24, 2007. http://www.cbp.gov/xp/cgov/newsroom/news_releases/archives/2007_news_releases/072007/07242007_3.xml.

———. "U.S. Customs and Border Protection Selects the 'Predator B' as Unmanned Aerial Vehicle Platform to Guard our Nations [sic] Borders." August 30, 2005. http://www.cbp.gov/xp/cgov/newsroom/news_releases/archives/2005_press_releases/082005/08302005.xml.

Detention and Access to Justice
A Florence Project Case Study

CHRISTOPHER STENKEN

I step into the visitation room and see the long-tired faces packed around kindergarten-style lunchroom tables. I greet my coworker and we look over the court list for the day.

"The two buses were late and they barely got in for court," Marcelo comments. "I had to do the talk in ten minutes, but I think they got it."

Marcelo is an attorney for the Florence Project and gives know-your-rights presentations every morning for detainees who have their first court appearance. The Florence Project is a small nonprofit that has been providing free immigration legal services in Arizona detention centers for over twenty years. I have been a paralegal with the project for a year now, and I meet Marcelo at the center when he's done with his talk to prepare people for their future court appearances.

I look over the 8:30 court list and note how many people have told us that they are asking for more time to fight their case to stay in the United States. "Not too many people asking for more time to go over their case, but we have five 10:30s and two final hearings to prepare today. They have everyone in here for dental exams as well," Marcelo says.

We start calling names based on the court list the clerks gave us yesterday. The room is packed. We've been doing our presentations and court preparations in the visitation room for a couple of months now. We used to have a semi-private setting with cubicle walls where there was some sense of privacy, but when construction began on a new court we were given the boot and had to find a new place where we could work. Here, the guards and all the other detainees are sitting in the same room as we speak with clients. On some days, there is no talking except our conversations so legal confidentiality does not exist.

I begin my days by talking with people who are scheduled for their second hearing. We have an hour to speak one-on-one with typically eight people before they go to this second court hearing. I grab a file, look at the name, and call out, "Mr. Ortega-Sanchez." Everyone stops talking.

"Ortega-Sanchez?" I ask again. The orange-jumpsuited crowd looks around.

"Ortega-Sanchez!" one of the more boisterous detainees repeats to the crowd.

"Baño," someone else responds. The guards have taken him to the bathroom, as they do every hour or so for anyone who asks.

I grab another file and try again. "Mr. Theodore Lee," I call out, though I immediately recognize Mr. Lee and walk across the room to him as he stands up. It's then that I can recall the details of his background and the first time we met.

I came to know Mr. Lee in a different manner than most of our clients, whom we screen before their first hearing. I first met Mr. Lee through a letter he sent from the local county jail. Pinal County Jail in Arizona had been leased for bed space under a multimillion-dollar contract from Immigration and Customs Enforcement (ICE), so we had been accustomed to working with detainees there. In his letter, Mr. Lee explained his story about coming into ICE custody. He wasted no time with formalities and got right to the point. He explained that he came to the United States with his parents when he was seven and became a permanent resident of the United States when he was seventeen. He married, had kids, and worked over twenty years at the U.S. Postal Service. When his marriage fell apart, he started using drugs. One night he was walking home, and was stopped by police. He was searched and found with methamphetamine, a drug he had been using for the past six months. He was taken to jail, had a trial, was found guilty, and served a six-month sentence in a California state prison.

When the day came that he thought he would be able to begin his life anew, an ICE agent arrived at his cell and told him that he was now deportable from the United States under the 1994 Immigration and Nationality Act. He was transferred to Florence and eventually ended up in a cell in the Pinal County Jail, serving time again. He had a small amount of savings, so he got a lawyer for his first hearing. But like many of our clients, who find the cost of keeping their lawyers through a lengthy process is far too much money, he dropped his lawyer after one appearance. He had read one of our know-your-rights packets in the jail's legal library and used a typewriter to prepare all of his own documents. I had gone to visit Lee after reading his letter, and found him sitting in the library with his application and legal documents ready for submission.

I smile when I see him in visitation because I know he is an example of the few cases where someone will succeed in immigration court. Mr. Lee is well educated and has experience dealing with the U.S. legal system. He's interested in the law, which will help him win his own case. This is a bittersweet process to witness as most persons in his situation, for various reasons, do not have the skills and luck to fight an uphill battle to win their case in detention. He is an exception to my usual work. In contrast, his peers will spend the next couple of months in detention only to find themselves deported after battling through the arduous process.

A MODEL OF THE EXPANDING IMMIGRANT DETENTION SYSTEM

Florence is a town in southern Arizona with just over seventeen thousand residents, the majority of whom are incarcerated. The history of oppression and incarceration in Florence dates back to World War II when the town hosted a prisoner-of-war camp for Italian and German people, most of whom were captured in a North African campaign. The first Arizona state prison was built in Florence in 1908 and housed all of the state's criminal convicts. As criminal law enforcement and punitive law sentences grew more popular, the Arizona Department of Corrections expanded its operations and Florence became a "company town" in the nation's fast-growing system of industrial-scale imprisonment. There are now three Arizona state prisons, seven county and federal prisons, and two private prison facilities in Florence. Needless to say, the town is a poster child for the expansion and profitability of the prison-industrial complex.

Four of the six major ICE detention centers in Arizona are in Florence. While ICE uses its own federal processing centers to house over one thousand detainees in the town, it also contracts with two private Corrections Corporation of America (CCA) facilities and the county jail for bed space. Altogether ICE holds nearly three thousand persons in Florence on any given day. These ICE-funded facilities account for more than one-sixth of the prison-industrial complex facilities in one small town, and give a glimpse into the expansion of the system nationwide.

THE FLORENCE PROJECT: PROVIDING ACCESS
TO JUSTICE IN DETENTION

The absence of a system of public legal defense in immigration court may affect someone in more drastic ways than a criminal sentence. If people lose their removal hearing, or lose their residency status for minor legal infractions, they may be returned to a country where they face persecution or torture. Deportation from the United States for some people means lifetime separation from family, with no hope for visits or reunification, as well as forced relocation to a country they may never have known.

To address the inequities in immigration court proceedings, Chris Brelje established the Florence Project in 1989. Immigration court judge John J. McCarrick, who was concerned that indigent people in removal proceedings were in danger of having their constitutional and statutory rights disregarded, had publicly urged Phoenix area attorneys to fill these needs for representation in a system lacking public defense. So Brelje spent a year, with the encouragement and support of Lewis and Roca, his law firm, creating what was originally named the Florence Asylum Project. It is now named, in reflection of the range of detained immigrants' legal issues, the Florence Immigrant and Refugee Rights Project (FIRRP). FIRRP expanded its reach to offer legal services at the Eloy Detention Center in 1998, and in the cities of Phoenix and Globe for detained children in late 2000.

The Florence Project consists of three separate teams providing services to different detained populations. Each team consists of two attorneys and a paralegal, and is also assisted by a shared legal director, a pro bono attorney, and a social services coordinator. The team that serves the detainees in Florence works with a population of over fourteen hundred persons. In order for three people to most effectively give legal orientation and advice to such a large number of detainees, the Florence Project developed a model of legal rights presentations and orientations that does not strive to represent people but to empower them to represent themselves in court, which is known as *pro se* representation.

The Florence Project provides in-person know-your-rights presentations, which outline legal relief and basic court procedures, before detainees' first removal hearings. Through these presentations the project is able to connect with detainees without representation and later provide a one-on-one case intake and orientation session to further explore legal remedies. Through this method, the project is able to track individuals with possible relief and provide intensive assistance to those with particularly compelling cases. The project attorneys rarely represent detainees and the project's basic services are minimal compared to a public defender system.

The model of the Florence Project has been successful in providing basic services to large populations. The project's model of *pro se* assistance has been replicated by the federal government across the country in the Legal Orientation Programs (LOP). The LOP grants do not provide representation or legal advice to clients. They exist to maximize the efficiency of the immigration court systems and provide bare bones information to persons who have no experience in the U.S. court system.

In January 2001, FIRRP developed the Integrated Social Services Program to address the diverse mental health and social needs of its clients. The psychological and emotional stress placed on detainees and their families is an extreme burden. ICE detainees commonly face being shipped across the country to unspecified locations where they are not able to be visited by family members, they can only make high-priced collect telephone calls, and their time spent outdoors and access to daylight are tightly regulated. Some are the breadwinners for their families, and so their children may have to drop out of school to support themselves and the family, or other family members may need to take on additional jobs. Some lose custody of their children for life to Child Protective Services, or divorce from their partners after the stressful separation of detention. While it is by no means comprehensive, FIRRP's Integrated Social Services Program is able to address some of these needs by connecting detainees and their families to outside service providers.

THE SCARCITY OF SUCCESS

The Florence Project is able to assist and succeed with very few cases. Connecting detainees to resources and legal knowledge is FIRRP's most prominent accomplishment. FIRRP may aid in cases of the cancellation of removal for permanent residents, asylum, and special immigrant juvenile status (SIJS) for minors. The cancellation of removal for permanent residents refers to a type of "pardon" in immigration court where persons who have been residents of the United States for seven years and don't have certain serious criminal convictions may be given another shot to live in the United States. In cases such as asylum and SIJS, FIRRP may help people identify a remedy they did not otherwise have knowledge of, and help them find the tools they need to pursue legal relief. In the cancellation of removal for permanent residents, as in these other special cases, FIRRP assists the few persons who have legal relief and provides legal orientation and advice. If no relief for clients exists under current immigration law, there is nothing FIRRP can do.

Without a shift in immigration law and a decrease in government funding for aggressive immigration enforcement, the system of migrant detention across the nation will continue to expand. Success for immigrants in detention will continue to be an anomaly unless federal enforcement agencies are defunded. Unfortunately, even if comprehensive immigration reform is passed in

Washington, D.C., it will likely only shift the demographics of the people being detained. For instance, undocumented workers or students may acquire legal status, but it's likely that enforcement will simply shift to detaining permanent residents with criminal convictions more aggressively. A banner that hangs in one detention center reads, "It is ICE's mission to 'deport all deportable aliens.'" With the federal government's money and resources behind them, ICE agents are successfully removing from the United States nearly everyone they get their hands on.

Community, Identity, and Political Struggle
Challenging Immigrant Prisons in Arizona

ZOE HAMMER

This chapter offers a glimpse into a campaign to fight the construction of new immigrant prisons in the state of Arizona. It highlights the strategies and tactics activists used to challenge the state's capacity to cage, kill, and criminalize poor people of color in the United States. Stopping the expansion of prisons is one of many fronts in a larger abolitionist struggle examined throughout this volume. My analysis begins with a consideration of the relationship between identity and political struggle in building social movements. I will then analyze ways in which anti-prison and immigrant rights activists, working together, reimagined community identities as part of the work of opposing the construction of immigrant prisons.

In *The Darker Nations: A People's History of the Third World*, Vijay Prashad writes, "The anticolonial nationalist movement produced a series of gatherings and a language of anticolonialism that elicited an emotional loyalty among its circle and beyond. This historical struggle made the identity of the Third World comprehensible and viable. The identity gained credence through trial and error, while participation and risk in the struggle produced the trust that gave the term social legitimacy."[1]

For Prashad, building the identity of the third world was part of the process of creating an expansive political agenda, a powerful ideology, and institutions that enable the powerless "to hold a dialogue with the powerful, and try to hold them accountable."[2] Contemporary mass movements fighting neoliberalism across the globe have the potential to produce "a genuine agenda for the future,"[3] suggesting that such an agenda is a prerequisite for once again challenging regimes that derive authority from the violent social problems they claim to solve.

Developing comprehensible, viable identities is of political importance because "moving beyond walls and cages" is an ambitious project that confronts problems that are as deeply entrenched as the challenges that were taken on in the global struggle against neocolonialism. Making political identities and projects legible and viable is a project that is crucial to both the prison abolition and immigrant justice movements; hopes for linking these movements in the United States and for making this combined movement part of the global social justice agenda depend on crafting political identities based in political practices that draw people in, engendering trust and legitimacy through participation in struggle.

Another reason I begin this analysis with Prashad's historical account is his clarity around the complexities of what it takes for ordinary people to challenge powerful regimes of social control in a world of vast inequalities of wealth and political power. The Third World project was able to create and wield new capacities that shaped and limited neocolonial forces on a global scale. Grounded in a critical rejection of colonialism, its development of a positive new agenda and a new ideology and, crucially, its strategic engagement with and transformation of political institutions (both national and international) were the basis of political empowerment.

As an active participant in the prison abolition and border justice movements for more than a decade and as a college professor teaching student activists, I confront barriers to this historical understanding of how power is built in two related arguments. The first argument is that "demand politics," or engaging in campaigns to change laws and policies, is always already "giving power to the state" and thus the state should be abandoned as a site of struggle. The second and, I think, related argument is that "horizontalism," the creation of local, radically democratic forms of self-governance, is sufficient to challenge violent regimes of social control. While these arguments offer important insights, the juggernaut of prison growth and border militarization insists that the state is a crucial site of struggle if politics are to be transformed and alternatives made possible.

A campaign conducted in 2000 to stop the construction of an immigrant-only prison in Arizona brought immigrant rights and anti–border militarization activists, prisoner families, ex-prisoners, environmentalists, and youth of color together in a struggle that would eventually also draw migrant unions, ranchers, formerly imprisoned immigrants, local chambers of commerce, university and high school students, anarchists, and anti-Walmart activists. It fostered the conditions in which the contemporary abolition movement extended its reach into Arizona, and activists have been able to prevent the construction of at least five new prisons there since 2001. And the project produced a loose alliance of people newly able to start imagining community economies without prisons.

The strategies and tactics used in the 2000 campaign were directly inspired by the work of two California-based organizations, Critical Resistance (CR), a national prison abolition organization with chapters throughout the United States, and the California Prison Moratorium Project (CPMP), an organization that fights the construction of new prisons in California. As CR emphasizes, the abolition of anything requires the building of something in its place. Prisons claim to control the violences they actually exacerbate, but abuse, inequality, and violence are rampant in our society, so eliminating the "need" for prisons requires addressing these problems in ways that do not depend on prisons.

CPMP's rural organizing work demonstrates that forming alliances across complex identities is needed to do the collaborative, creative, grassroots work of opposing the expansion of regimes of coercive control. It requires thinking beyond race-to-the-bottom economic development models that encourage people in depressed rural towns to believe that prisons are their only hope for building local economies.

THE PROBLEM

In November 2000, the federal Bureau of Prisons (BOP) proposed Criminal Alien Requirement 3 (CAR-3), the construction of three private, fifteen-hundred-bed "criminal alien" prisons in southern California and Arizona. CAR-3 would warehouse migrants, the majority of whom were expected by the BOP to be Mexican. Of the twelve proposed sites, nine were in small, depressed, rural towns in Arizona, including Willcox in Cochise County, a border community that has experienced mass migration, militarization, and anti-immigrant backlash.

The Arizona Prison Moratorium Coalition (APMC), composed of southern Arizona organizers, launched a statewide prison abolition campaign aimed at stopping CAR-3. The APMC was formed in January 2001 following a December 2000 Border Summit gathering in Tucson, Arizona, that brought together over six hundred social justice organizers from across the United States and Mexico to develop coordinated campaigns to fight border militarization. Like many problem-centered political gatherings, as Prashad notes above, the Border Summit created a platform for diverse organizers and activists to produce new analyses, new alliances, and a number of campaigns and ongoing organizing projects that continue to challenge border militarization in Arizona.

One of the issues that emerged during the conference was the CAR-3 proposal. The December meeting planted the seeds for an abolitionist coalition organized primarily by the Arizona American Friends Service Committee's (AFSC) Criminal Justice Project, a Quaker-led, international peace and justice organization that organizes prisoner families and opposes prison expansion, and the Border Action Network (BAN), a local, immigrant-led human rights organization based in Tucson and the border towns of Douglas and Nogales, Arizona. Caroline Isaacs and Jennifer Allen, respectively, coordinate these groups. Also in attendance were representatives from CR and CPMP, who encouraged our campaign and advised us on strategies for fighting new prison construction.

The new Arizona coalition was predicated on the understandings that immigration and prison issues are interrelated, that migrant and prisoner rights can't effectively be won when they are imagined in competition, and thus, that opposing CAR-3 could only be effective if the strategies used did not extend the life or scope of border militarization *or* prisons. Coming to these understandings was not easy.

BUILDING A BASE

Several months before the APMC was formed, prisoner families in Tucson were devastated when the Arizona Department of Corrections (ADC) moved their inmate family members out of Tucson, and into state prisons throughout Arizona, in order to concentrate prisoners of Mexican nationality in two wings of the Tucson facility. Many families had moved to Tucson specifically to be near their loved ones, and the sudden, unannounced moves created new hardships for already struggling families. People showed up for visitation one Saturday and were told that their family members had been moved to other facilities (it took them weeks to find out where). The explanation offered by prison officials was that the new segregation policy was a response to dangerous gang warfare: a "security" issue. Many of the AFSC-organized prisoner families aimed their anger at the Mexican prisoners, just as the ADC had encouraged them to do. Many felt that "protecting" prisoners of Mexican nationality at the expense of prisoner families with U.S. citizenship was a violation of those citizens' rights. An identity-based competition was thus established.

At the same time, a number of immigrant rights organizations were insisting on differentiating migrant prisoners from U.S. prisoners on the grounds that "the immigrants are innocent!" because immigration laws are unfair. Again, these advocates imagined their constituency in isolation and migrants' unjust subjugation to imprisonment as independent from the larger culture of punishment. Both groups initially imagined their own group identity as fixed and discrete; they saw each other as the "enemy"; and they were convinced that their community's worthiness of fair treatment was somehow dependent on defining their perceived enemy as unworthy.

Allen and Isaacs called a large meeting in Tucson specifically for prisoner families, Latino youth from Tucson, ex-prisoners, migrants, and immigrant advocates to talk through these issues. Almost everyone who walked into the El Rio Community Center was surprised by the number of people who had chosen to attend, about sixty, including people who had driven more than a hundred miles. The turnout engendered a drive for cooperation among the attendees I spoke with because most of them had felt that not many people cared about their particular issues, and they were excited to see so many faces. Isaacs explained the CAR-3 proposal, and Allen facilitated conversation, asking people to talk about what they thought was most important about fighting the construction of the prison. People's concerns kept building upon one another.

- "They're never going to change immigration policy if they keep building immigrant prisons and filling them up."
- "My school counselor is already sure that I'll end up in prison. It's like a plan."
- "They're building prisons for immigrants because they know they can get away with it."
- "Oh, they can get away with anything! Trust me."

By the close of the meeting there was a unanimous vote to work together to fight CAR-3. One of the high school students in attendance said, "We should tear down all the prisons," and the room erupted in agreement. Two groups of people, migrants and prisoner families, both highly impacted by prison expansion, who had previously imagined themselves as enemies, now started to imagine themselves and their struggles as interdependent. The meeting established a new coalition of allies, ready to fight the construction of CAR-3.

THE CAMPAIGN: EXPANDING COMMUNITY

On May 8, 2001, the Cochise County Board of Supervisors met to consider the rezoning of fifty-eight acres of land just southeast of the Willcox city limits in order to make it available to build an immigrant prison should their town become one of the CAR-3 sites. People representing a diversity of interests participated in the meeting, including the mayor of Willcox and the three Cochise County supervisors; representatives from the Willcox Chamber of Commerce; a representative speaking on behalf of Cornell Companies, a private prison corporation; immigrant rights activists from the town of Bisbee; and four members of the Arizona Prison Moratorium Coalition, including myself (a University of Arizona graduate student and new volunteer in the CAR-3 campaign); Caroline Isaacs and Jennifer Allen, co-coordinators of the APMC; and Gustavo Lozano, an APMC volunteer and longtime Arizona political activist and artist. We had heard about the meeting at the last minute and were the only people from the APMC available to drive to Willcox that day.

Because the term "prison abolition" sounds radical and dangerous to the ears of U.S. audiences living in the contemporary culture of fear, it is a very challenging idea to communicate, but APMC attempted to meet this challenge in a number of ways: by listening to and starting with the visions of local audiences; by introducing multiple perspectives into the discussion; and by broadening local definitions of community to include all groups of people impacted by prisons. In the process, it became clear that visions of economic development and ideas about community are significantly intertwined.

The supervisors meeting in Bisbee was a small but significant site of regional political decision making. About ten miles north of the militarized U.S.-Mexico border, it became a stage where several forces came together: those representing national prison expansion and border militarization, networked community organizing, and various local groups seeking sustainable community development.

Knowing that the APMC representatives were likely to be discredited as "professional activists" and outsiders, we decided to divide up the points we would make. We wanted to define ourselves as partial community *insiders* because we are Arizona residents, inhabitants of the NAFTA economic "free zone," organizers working in border communities, U.S. dwellers, and subjects of the world economic system with clear stakes in any further expansion of the prison-industrial complex. By questioning narrow definitions of "community" that exclude diverse interregional, transnational, and local relationships, we hoped to expand notions of community belonging—and hence legitimate political decision making—in ways that might recast prisons as engines of rural *under*development.

We were also concerned that the anti-migrant sentiment in the region (exacerbated since 1999 by massive daily migration through Cochise County's rangelands and backyards) and local Anglo traditions of socially conservative libertarianism might make people more supportive of an immigrant-only prison. We didn't want to lose any chances to develop local alliances (since we were trying to organize in nine towns simultaneously) and wanted to avoid arguments that would encourage people to fear prisoners or migrants, since such fears manufacture popular demands for more prisons and more border militarization.

THE MEETING

After approval of the previous meeting's minutes, a young man from the mayor's office gave a presentation based on his communications with Cornell Companies. Though he was not from the corporation, he conveyed their argument that prisons are a viable, attractive form of economic development. He assured the audience that the prison would be outside of town, very safe, and barely noticeable — except that it would bring $18–$20/hour jobs to Willcox residents and that this income might stimulate further economic growth. He had questioned Cornell extensively, but had not done any research into the company or its claims about the economic benefits of prisons. His emphasis on community safety and on the social and physical invisibility of the prison foregrounded the extreme outsider status of prisoners in his description of "community." According to his story, this was a group whose lives would not figure into the equation of the town's future.

The mayor spoke next and explained that he and his administration had been working hard for years to bring economic development and jobs to Willcox. Speaking as a humble, entrepreneurial "community patriarch," Mayor Marlin Easthouse spun a narrative of sustainable community development that drew on a local sense of community. First, he described his trip to the BOP in Washington, D.C. The BOP representatives told him how impressed they were that he had come so far, in person, to ask for a prison. As he stood before the meeting with his large white cowboy hat held against his chest, the mayor's story of his journey to Washington evoked emotions including rural southwestern residents' frustration with regional invisibility and resentment of urban condescension.

The mayor's story did not recognize any link between the policies of a global system that impoverishes the residents of Willcox and the policies that displace and immobilize Mexican migrants. The disavowal works because it invokes an idea of community that consists of an implicitly white public sphere of U.S. citizens, protected by well-intentioned white patriarchs, in which prisons affect only "enemies of the state."

Easthouse went on to tell about touring five private prisons that provide the bulk of employment for a small Texas town's residents. He emphasized that the prisons were "modern, clean, and quiet. Not like what you hear about. The prisoners had clean cells and activities. It was a nice place. A good place to work." He continued: "We would all like to live in a town with good enough jobs and wages that our children might choose to stay here and raise families of their own." The mayor's emphasis on prisons as workplaces, rather than as warehouses for human beings, tells a story of benevolent corporate development and reinforces the idea of community that excludes prisoners and immigrants. Further, his concern for the future of the town evoked residents' fears that their children will need to move away to survive if the economy remains stagnant. These concerns again erase prisoners and migrants from the notion of community.

Five members of the Willcox Chamber of Commerce, all white, male small-business owners, attended the meeting expecting to support the proposal, but were not yet committed to the idea of competing with other towns for the construction of a new prison. They supported invigoration of the local economy, but were not convinced that all development schemes would necessarily work to the advantage of local commerce. The executive director of the Chamber of Commerce and two other prominent local businessmen took turns describing their meetings with Cornell Companies.[4] Where the mayor's vision was primarily protective and focused on bringing high-wage jobs to unemployed community residents, the businessmen were more interested in the possibilities for personal partnerships with successful corporations.

Following this show of support for the immigrant prison by Willcox's economic developers, five white residents of Bisbee spoke against the prison. Their arguments centered on humanitarian concerns for the plight of poor Mexicans and Central Americans crossing the border. None of them referenced the tattered state of the Willcox economy nor suggested any alternatives to the prison as economic development. Their story about community created a narrative of competing oppressions — "Which group of poor folks are most worthy of our help?" — in which Willcox's mayor and developers were encouraged to turn their attention to the plight of migrants crossing the border *instead of* providing assistance to struggling Willcox residents.

The speakers' competing narratives of white paternalism reflected the class differences between white Bisbee residents and white Willcox residents. While the relatively affluent businessmen could be understood as legitimate stakeholders in community economic development, the Bisbee contingent could not, in part because of the failure of their narrative to recognize issues of unemployment in Willcox. The story of community told by the Bisbee humanitarians also echoed assumptions that powerful white people are the appropriate rescuers of less powerful Others, reiterating a vision of community decision making that excludes the voices and political agency of migrants *and* less powerful white people.

The chairman's insistent dismissal of anyone opposed to the prison as "outsiders" cast the town of Willcox as an Anglo island, disconnected from neighboring towns and cities, and distinct from its own Latino/a, migrant, Native American, and other nonwhite residents. His implicit description of the community as a discrete, monoracial space shut down any vision of development that might grow out of existing regional economies. In this view, the local economy can only be rescued by what is imagined as "global capital," effectively disconnecting Willcox from any regional allegiances, alliances, or responsibilities.

He had similar responses to the comments of the Tucson speakers, emphasizing our "outside agitator" status. When Jennifer Allen suggested that the Latino population of Willcox might be less comfortable with a migrant-only prison than the town residents sitting in this particular meeting, the chairman blew up, interrupting her speech with the claim that "the residents of the city of Douglas — which are mostly Hispanics — are very much in favor of the prisons which are in or near Douglas." Allen pointed out that prisons are built in poor communities of color for the same reason that toxic waste is dumped there: because other communities have the political power to keep environmental liabilities out of their backyards. She then discussed some of the environmental problems that new prisons create, emphasizing their heavy water use, a particularly important issue in arid southern Arizona. She interpreted new prison construction as a practice that victimizes the communities in which prisons are built, aligning Willcox and Douglas residents across racial lines, instead of setting them in competition with migrants over who has the greatest entitlement to victim status.

"I don't see that that has anything to do with this," responded the supervisor, again distancing "his" community from Douglas.

Isaacs launched into a laundry list of Cornell's conflicts with local communities around the United States in which the company operates prisons, including overcharging for incarceration "services," raising suspicions about the corporation's claim that local economic development is its first priority. Her description of Florence, Arizona, home to five prisons and no grocery store, was evidence that prisons do not grow local economies, a point that aligns the interests of rural Arizonans *against* the interests of corporations.

When it was my turn to speak, I raised further doubts about Cornell's promise of jobs by pointing out that new prisons hire the vast majority of their staffs from a national pool of trained and seasoned employees. I ended with an environmental justice argument: if prisons were really an unobtrusive yet lucrative form of community development, they would be sited in the wealthy areas of Scottsdale and eastern Tucson, not in poor rural towns like Willcox and Eloy.

While I was speaking, the local businessmen who had spoken glowingly of Cornell as a good corporate citizen had begun asking Isaacs and Allen about their research. The mayor also thanked us for coming to the meeting. We gave them the documentation we had brought and contact information for BAN and AFSC. The people from Bisbee also thanked us. They knew Jen Allen from her organizing on the border, and said they were interested in working with us on the campaign to fight CAR-3 elsewhere.

Not only did most Willcox residents have no input during this fast and quiet rezoning hearing, but prisoners and immigrants had no possibility for a voice. In subsequent hearings in other targeted towns, APMC would advertise the meetings, encouraging local community members to attend. Though it was never possible for former immigrant prisoners to speak in person (because they are deported upon release), later in the campaign BAN conducted interviews with recently released and deported migrants in Mexican homeless shelters in an attempt to bring their experiences and analysis into the negotiations.

When the vote on the rezoning took place, the county supervisor from Bisbee voted against it. He had entered the meeting planning to vote for the proposal, but his constituents had opened his eyes to the ethical and human rights problems of prison construction. Although he wanted very much to support economic development in Willcox, he felt that building an immigrant prison was "not the right thing to do." The other two supervisors voted in favor of the rezoning, and it passed.

In March 2002, the federal Bureau of Prisons withdrew the CAR-3 proposal. The people involved in the nationally networked, trans-Arizona, and transborder APMC celebrated the cancellation (BOP later called it a "postponement"). The work done during the CAR-3 campaign enabled AFSC to mobilize coalition members again in 2003 against the construction in Marana, Arizona, of what would have been the world's largest women's prison. This campaign was also successful.

REFLECTIONS

While successful, the work of the anti-CAR-3 campaign could have been more effective. We did not achieve our goal of swaying a majority of supervisor votes at the Cochise meeting, but we made progress toward developing some new alliances and strategies. We were tossed into what seemed like a frenzy of work, in nine towns, with little time to achieve our goal, learning as we went. When the BOP suddenly canceled the proposal, we felt almost as if the agency was plotting to stop the coalition that CAR-3 had inspired. We had been improving our tactics, getting more former prisoners and young people of color involved in leading the campaign, and had made alliances across the region with migrant labor unions, a statewide anti-Walmart campaign, ranchers, former U.S. prisoners in Mexico, LGBT organizations, and student groups (Young Democratic Socialists, United Students against Sweatshops, Anarchist Black Cross Network, Young Uprising Radicals, to name a few). And crucially, we had gained and benefited greatly from the mentorship, guidance, and support of CR and CPMP.

The task ahead of us involved working to develop a statewide community of abolitionists, especially including the people most directly affected by prison expansion. We knew that stopping the construction of this set of prisons in Arizona and southern California would not prevent prison construction someplace else. Our campaign represented the expansion of a network that was born in California, and it was clear that this network needed to expand nationwide. It was also clear that linking anti–border militarization, immigration justice, and prison abolition work would be more complicated in settings where the linkages appeared less obvious, and where migrant prisoner and citizen prisoner communities were increasingly being encouraged to view each other as threats rather than potential allies.

I had started to experience the fact that visions of development and the politics of alliances are intertwined and inseparable from abolition. The work of reorganizing community and economy — imagining community development to address real human needs — is the work of reorganizing complex social hierarchies by creating new community identities through political struggle. Such imaginative work requires the acknowledgment of social interdependencies — as they really exist and as they might be reorganized.

Recognizing social interdependencies requires understanding that localities are not discrete, and communities are not solely local. People inside, beyond, and passing through local territories and social groups all work together to reproduce entrenched inequalities, and so, together, they have the power to challenge and transform them. This work has the potential to build the capacity to hold the powerful accountable and to substantively transform the decision-making processes and institutions in which power is consolidated.

The lessons I have learned in this process include:

Connect to and learn from experienced activists. It is crucial to seek out and learn from the experiences of activists and organizers who have developed effective strategies. Building bridges between immigrant justice and prison abolition work can be facilitated by developing projects and campaigns around issues that draw on the existing analyses, goals, and ongoing projects of each movement.

Ignoring the state will not make it go away. If we had pursued strategies aimed at "going around" the state in an attempt to remain unsullied by state power, there would be tens of thousands more prisoners in cages in Arizona today.

Visions of community matter. Activists and organizers fighting prisons and militarization need to understand the ways decision makers and potential allies envision community, and then act in ways that can expand the parameters of who defines these visions. This requires strategic alliance building among criminalized and otherwise excluded communities, creative communication with powerful social actors, and direct participation in decision-making processes about the expansion of prisons and other apparatuses of coercive social control.

Think long term. Abolishing prisons and militarized borders requires long-term strategies, broad alliances, and the development and facilitation of communication across large-scale networks.

Activists can change the way decisions are made. A key task in challenging the expansion of the state's coercive capacities is to broaden social decision making to include the perspectives of directly impacted communities. Rather than "giving power to the state" (which implies that the state is a being, rather than a continually constructed set of collective social capacities), such actions can limit and challenge the state's capacity to cage by (a) transforming the criteria used to determine who makes decisions, and (b) keeping potential decision makers out of cages.

A critical analysis of power and a historical understanding of struggles for social justice will allow organizers to identify fronts, utilize and reinvent effective strategies, and imagine movements with the capacity to challenge violent regimes of domination and coercive social control.

The capacities of states to militarize borders, and to criminalize, cage, and kill people, shape and are dependent in part on decision-making processes grounded in unchallenged notions of community that make coercive regimes coherent and viable. These include an understanding of personhood that segregates groups of people into small, culturally and geographically homogeneous islands, and that encourages us to imagine community development in terms of competition, exploitation, and exclusion rather than creative cooperation. To return to Prashad, making gatherings, new language, and new identities are key practices in building powerful agendas capable of challenging unjust regimes of walls and cages. The Border Summit, and the coalitions and strategy and base-building meetings that emerged from it, built new configurations of community. The CAR-3 campaign that emerged from these meetings began to put that new community into practice, struggling to bridge the archipelago of identities whose isolation is both an effect and a cause of walls and cages.

NOTES

1. Prashad, *The Darker Nations*, 13.
2. Ibid., xviii.
3. Ibid., 281.
4. The chief supervisor of Cochise County, who was in charge of running the meeting, was a member of Concerned Citizens of Cochise County. The CCCC is reminiscent of the spirit (and the abbreviation) of the White Citizens Councils that were popular in the southeastern United States before desegregation (when they became Concerned Citizens Councils), which acted as boosters for the activities of the Ku Klux Klan. The CCCC has also held anti-immigrant rallies in support of white nationalist vigilante activity on the border.

BIBLIOGRAPHY

Prashad, Vijay. *The Darker Nations: A People's History of the Third World*. New York: New Press, 2007.

"Live, Love, and Work"
An Interview with Luis Fernandez
AUGUST 2010

JENNA LOYD

JENNA LOYD (JL): I'm glad to be talking with you in Arizona at such an important and rapidly changing time. Arizona Senate Bill 1070 just went into effect. Can you give us a sense of where SB1070 fits in the longer history of Arizona and migration politics?

LUIS FERNANDEZ (LF): The most important element of SB1070 is the intentionality of what's happening in Arizona. And by this I mean the "self-attrition" strategy.

There's the longer history of white supremacy and colonization, of course, but this particular wave started in 2003 or 2004 as part of a very deliberate white supremacist strategy. In 2003, white supremacist militia groups began to point to Arizona as their new battleground. Members from the Center for New Community, based in Chicago, came to us saying, "Hey listen, these white supremacists are talking about Arizona as the next site of struggle for them. So they are going to be shifting their focus away from the traditional white supremacy thing in the South, and focusing on the border and immigration as the new struggle for their movement."

The anti-immigration wave started in Arizona with Prop[osition] 200 in 2004. Groups connected to FAIR [Federation for American Immigration Reform] and PAN [Protect Arizona Now] were pushing for Proposition 200, which requires proof of citizenship before an individual can register to vote or apply for public benefits. If you look at the records, in twenty-five years there were only two incidents of voter fraud in Arizona, so this was not a big problem. You can't get normal citizens to vote, let alone undocumented citizens!

It was about scaring undocumented people enough so that they would leave the state, really a form of ethnic cleansing.

Proposition 200 was quickly followed by a law requiring proof of citizenship when applying for a state driver's license. This was the start of the criminalization of undocumented people and allowing the police to stop people for minor offenses. By *not* giving people access to a driver's license, the state turned these folks into criminals. They created an entry into the criminal justice system that was not present before this law, casting a wide "criminal" net that served as the excuse to capture undocumented people.

The Minutemen quickly followed. It was like a one-two-three punch. First there was Proposition 200, then the driver's license law, and then Minutemen at the border. The Minutemen arrived with that weird perspective: "Let's go to the border and somehow aid the government in a job that they are really not doing." Their antics resulted in enormous media coverage that fueled anti-immigrant sentiment in Arizona, resulting in attracting other anti-immigrant folks to Arizona.

Then we saw the anti-immigrant movement start to run their candidates, and we began to see them elected. Russell Pearce and a number of other legislators made their way to power riding an anti-immigrant message. These folks are connected to white supremacist groups, in some cases directly. Once they got in power, they made immigration the central issue. However, these laws were kept at bay for several years because they were vetoed by Governor Janet Napolitano.

But when Napolitano left, we got SB1070. When people ask, "How did Arizona get to this point?," the answer is that not enough people from outside and inside the state took these anti-immigration folks seriously in 2004 when other folks were saying, "This is a *racial* issue. This is a fight, and you need to understand it that way."

To understand the criminalization of immigrants, we can look at the parallel way in which the state criminalizes homeless people. Randall Amster, who does work on homelessness, suggests that if you look at the criminalization of the homeless, you see the state criminalizing all the actions required to *be* homeless. You can't make a human being a criminal (at least in this instance), so you instead criminalize all the activities that are required to live as a homeless person. Thus, to eliminate homelessness from your streets, the state criminalizes all of those behaviors separately under different ordinances at the city level, such as public camping laws, sitting on the sidewalk, urination [in public], etc. As a homeless person, you have to live in public. If you criminalize what is required for a homeless person to exist, such as sleeping in public, then you eliminate the human being. This erases the possibility of existing as a human being in public without the state having to say, "That homeless person is illegal."

When I look at the criminalization of undocumented people, it's similar to what is done to the homeless. It is also a little different because an undocumented person *can* be made into a criminal at the *being* level. But perhaps we can think of this as a two-level process. The federal laws make being undocumented an illegal act, making the person inherently illegal: their entire *being* is breaking the law. While at the local level, the laws make all that is required to exist as an undocumented person illegal so as to capture them. To go back to the driver's license example, when legislators in Arizona made it so that undocumented people could not get a driver's license without proof of citizenship, they created the crime of driving without a license, an act that is required in Arizona since our public transportation is lacking. This act, then, turns into the excuse to capture a person for a minor traffic violation, then triggering federal laws that make this person's *being* illegal.

If the above is correct, then we can see that the strategy is to target all those things that make undocumented life possible: work, education, family life, health care, home, etc. The tactic of "enforcement through attrition," then, targets the essence of undocumented life, making it very difficult for undocumented people to meet their needs. For instance, nativists are trying to pass laws that take away the possibility of primary or secondary education for undocumented people. On health, they are trying to make hospitals request documentation for non-emergency cases. In work, they are forcing employees to request papers. This makes hiring undocumented people risky, which eliminates access to work.

To sum up, we can see the targeting of education, health, and work, things required to sustain life. But one other provision that's more obscure is the one requiring proof of U.S. citizenship for a marriage license. What they were trying to do was make love impossible, so that if you are undocumented the state tells you who you can marry and who you cannot. So you begin to see the closing of all the possibilities of what it means to become an undocumented person.

If you go back and look at the actual strategy of the right, they talk about the strategy of self-attrition. And that means that you make it so difficult to survive that undocumented people choose to leave Arizona. People have equated this with ethnic cleansing. Generally, ethnic cleansing involves violent acts aimed to induce fear or terror to rid an area of "undesired" ethnic or racial groups. In the case of Arizona, we see a neo–ethnic cleansing that is more nefarious, since it uses a little less violence and uses the noncitizenship status of an individual as the excuse to terrorize. It then relies on the fear of being caught, the difficulty of getting a job, the terror of having your children left behind, to produce a self-cleansing outcome. That is, people leave Arizona en masse. So that's a key point in the criminalization of undocumented people; it's a neo–ethnic cleansing policy aimed to whiten Arizona.

JL: How do you talk with people in terms of organizing around such commonsense understandings of crime? How do you tackle "They are criminals, so they deserve to be locked away or deported"?

LF: Yeah, this question is difficult because it opens important theoretical spaces. When one speaks about immigrants not being "criminal," then it naturally reinforces the notion that there are real criminals out there who deserve the treatment they are getting. As any critical criminologist will tell you, crime enforcement serves many functions, including the maintenance of class and race divisions. For instance, if you look historically you can see that the segregation laws made it difficult for a white person and a Black person to marry. Thus, in this sense people in integrated marriages were "criminals" who broke the law. If one held a strong law stance in this instance, then you would support segregation. The same is true with immigration. We know that immigration is a minor crime, which the nativists want to criminalize. If we try to distinguish the criminal from the noncriminal, we run the risk of reinforcing, for instance, the atrocities committed under the war on drugs, where young Black men are being sent to jail for minor drug offenses.

This logic of criminal versus noncriminal can lead to nonliberatory struggle because it becomes a situation where we can fix things for a certain group of people and leave everything else intact for other groups of people. If we are not careful, this is not a liberatory fight; it's actually a momentary or sectional fight that helps certain groups but not other groups.

Recently, a group of young African American students visited the Repeal Coalition, the organization I work with. They were in town from different parts of the United States looking to understand the immigration issue more directly. The meeting we had with these young people is a good example of how to link issues across racial boundaries. One of the students said, "I'm from Oakland, and in Oakland the police beat me up, they hurt me. I was beat up by a police officer and I was going to lodge a complaint, and the police officer told me that it wasn't in my best interest to do that. Meaning that he was threatening me, so I didn't."

One of the persons from the undocumented community here replied (in Spanish), "Oh, I see! So you are treated really badly and you *have* papers." That's the important link, that some populations (with papers or without) are treated badly in our system, repressed in similar ways.

So when I talk to people about criminality, I have to unpack all of that. I have to start talking about systems that oppress and cleanse in different kinds of ways, in different locations, with different populations, and about how they are all interlinked.

JL: Do you frame the work you are doing as immigrant rights work, or do you use a frame of decriminalization, or a frame of demilitarization?

LF: We use the framework of liberation. We say we want freedom. In the Repeal Coalition, the slogan is: "We fight for the right to live, love, and work, wherever you please." And the idea is to open up different kinds of struggle, and not just about "I want in," because that has the potential to just say, "Hey, can you just let me in and give me the rights?" And then, once you come in and you have the rights, the structure—the political structures and the racial hierarchies—remains in place.

We say we are fighting for the right to live, love, and work wherever you please, meaning the freedom of movement. So I can live here or there, I can live on this side of the border or that side of the border, and the government should not be involved in that. By "work," we should have as human beings the right to work in any location, and work should not be something that is criminalized. The notion of work also opens up struggles around labor issues that are happening all around, just like the "live" part opens up the struggles around mobility. The part about "love" refers to marriage licenses. Our claim that people need the right to love whoever they please is empirically based. Politically, it opens up a link between immigrant movements and queer movements, since that is another location where legislators are trying to prevent people from loving each other.

The "live, love, and work" slogan broadens politics, rather than narrowing them down to the right of citizenship or the bracero-like labor policies. The idea is an important step toward making links between immigration and other movements and struggles. In immigration, we see a potential to unravel business as usual, meaning that the contradictions that are in place between citizen and noncitizen come into sharp contrast in this struggle. And this citizen-noncitizen split is closely linked to class and racial subjugation. Thus, the struggle itself has potential to open up in interesting ways.

If you think of the civil rights movement as a movement of Black people trying to get into the polity, trying to get access to the rights from which they were being excluded — and the exclusion was blatantly a racial exclusion — what they did is create situations and movements that unraveled their system of oppression, that is, segregation. For example, SNCC (Student Nonviolent Coordinating Committee) began with a simple claim: Black people in the South have the right to register to vote. And in trying to register Black people to vote in places they couldn't, they began to unravel the entire white supremacy system because the contradictions in what they were asking, the system itself just couldn't match. And it really undid segregation; they were successful in undoing segregation.

If you think of immigration today, it's not precisely the same thing because the distinction is between citizens and noncitizens. This citizen issue is fundamental to the nation-state itself, in a similar way that segregation was important in maintaining the racial divide before 1964. We are currently in an unstable system, where old concepts of clearly defined nation-states are becoming difficult to maintain. The clearly defined inside and outside classifications are becoming more complicated given the movement of people resulting from globalization. The global economic system itself is presenting challenges to boundaries, borders, and territoriality as it pushes for a global, integrated flow of goods and resources (of course, unevenly).

In this context, we see the rise of a nativist movement trying to reinforce those boundaries and borders that the economic system itself no longer wants. And the fact that they are resorting to police enforcement suggests that this citizen-noncitizen distinction is no longer hegemonic: nativists are having to intentionally reinforce things that were taken for granted just a few years ago. To me, this indicates that we are in a moment of transition, with old systems being weak and new systems looking to emerge — because when something is hegemonic, you don't have to reinforce it. But as soon as they try to reinforce the old system in an unstable moment, it also opens up the possibility of its opposite.

But what is happening here, unlike the civil rights movement, is that the issues and themes are bigger than the nation-state. They are now about mobility, transnationalism; they are about what it means to be human in the global age, what it means to have the right, the working ability. What does it mean to exist in this other world where borders are more problematic? What is being debated here is what the nation-state might look like in the next fifty to a hundred years.

JL: I wonder if you could give us a sense of the organizing you do on the ground when people are dealing with an everyday form of state terrorism.

LF: I think our tactic is simple. The way I would frame it is through standpoint theory, which means that you start with the people who are the most affected. That is, when people exist in an uneven power relationship, the people upon whom power is operating are likely to understand that relationship much more quickly than the people who actually have power. Power distorts and when you have it, it is harder to see its effects. But when you are on the less powerful side of an unequal and subjugating relationship, the power dynamics are much clearer to see.

Coming from that framework, our idea was to be as close to the ground as possible and work with the people who are likely to have a better understanding of these power relationships. More specifically we work with undocumented people, who are likely to directly feel the effects of anti-immigrant attacks.

In Flagstaff, our tactic was to go door knocking in the community, talking to people face-to-face. This is a very difficult thing because trust takes a long time to develop, and who are we to just come knocking and saying, "We want to help"? So we had to prove ourselves to people. And some people said to us, "You are just the latest people coming in here. Every three months, there is someone coming in here saying that they are going to stick around, and then they disappear. So why should we believe you?" And we say, "That's right, you are perfectly right, but just watch and you will see that we won't go anywhere."

So we held some meetings, and the night of one of these meetings, where eighty people showed up, ICE raided Flagstaff. Coincidence? I don't know. But they raided that very same night. The meeting ended at 10 p.m., they raided at midnight. It created a huge uproar in the community because Flagstaff had never been raided before.

What came out of that raid is that we had to follow people through the court system and try to find lawyers, and then follow the people that were inside jail through the system, trying to call them, trying to find them, trying to figure out what's happening. Then, we tried to educate people about what to do if they run into a police officer, what to say, what not to say, what kinds of things to do.

JL: So, know-your-rights and raid-response types of work?

LF: Right, but also going with them to the courts because the criminal justice system is difficult to negotiate. And it is scary for someone who is undocumented to have their husband inside — because usually it is the wife and the kids left behind — to feel like they can actually go to court without them being grabbed.

All those interactions led to the creation of deep bonds, but it took time. We created not just political relationships but also family-like bonds. For example, today I need to go visit one of the people we work with at the hospital because the family had a baby. The second part comes when we ask them to do political work. We can support each other, but we also have to push politically. I learned this lesson from reading about the SNCC organizers in the South, such as James Forman. Recently, this political work has developed into a noncompliance campaign, similar to the one that Tucson people are running, asking local businesses, schools, and churches to sign a pledge that they will not cooperate with law enforcement seeking to deport undocumented people. This is a moral stance against immoral practices that target people. Folks in the community, undocumented people, are grabbing Repeal signs and going to businesses in the Latino communities and saying, "Hey, will you sign our noncompliance form? Would you support us? Would you do these things if the cops show up? Will you put the sign in your window?" And businesses are replying, "Absolutely!" It is undocumented community members who are doing this.

This political aspect is what makes this strategy interesting. Generally, you think about the undocumented populations as non-Political, with a capital P, meaning that these are not people who can vote. They cannot go to their councilman and say, "Hey, can you represent me?" because they are nonrepresented people. They are literally outside of the political system, and their abuse relies on the fact they are outside of this system. . . . Well, the question is: How do we make these individuals political beings? How do we encourage groups to make political claims in locations where they think they can't make political claims? This is similar to, but not the same as, the work that civil rights activists like SNCC were doing to destroy segregation. We partnered with a few other groups in Flagstaff and flooded the city council—five hundred people attended the city council meeting, many of them undocumented. They went up to the city council and said, in Spanish, "Hey, I'm undocumented, and I think that what you are doing is really bad for me." And they did this over and over again.

In the moment, I remember thinking, "This is it. This is what we have been looking for, when an undocumented person who is not supposed to be a political subject becomes one. This has the potential to turn the system inside out, to transform the polity. It is the moment when the impossible might become possible."

That would be the key for this movement to really become a gigantic movement. It would require that some kind of political *identity* develop around these particular individuals—undocumented people—that allows them to link and begin to make really, really loud, broad claims. An example is the Sans Papiers [Without Papers] movement in France, where individuals embrace their undocumented status. This "without papers" terminology has become almost an identity. You go to Paris and there's a march almost every other day, and those that are marching are the Sans Papiers themselves. And it is like, "I am this person, but I am still a being that is asking for all these things."

Another example where it crystallized for me was with the Dream Act. So when the Dream Act young people got arrested in Tucson, I had spoken with them and I was really amazed because their politics were about intentionally claiming the undocumented identity as a *political* stance. They were undocumented people, and would get to a meeting and start with, "Hi, my name is ———, and I am undocumented. My parents brought me to this country." They all do that, and then they explain, "Listen, the reason that we are doing this is because we know that people don't claim the identity of 'undocumented,' but this is who we are. This is our being, and we are going to be proud of that because, one, we can't help it. Our parents brought us here, these weren't our choices, so we need to claim it and be proud of that. And two, we need to lose our fear because our fear is of being deported, and if we lose that fear we are very powerful." And I remember thinking that this is the start of a potential political identity, making new political claims that are difficult to meet without unraveling the current system of exploitation. And three, we lose the fear of confrontation. There it is. There is the movement. This may not work for all undocumented people because this is about a particular set of young people, but for the larger movement we need those three things.

JL: What do you think have been the most important things to come out of the last few weeks and months leading up to the July 29, 2010, mobilizations in Arizona, and where do you think we go from here?

LF: That's tough because I have no crystal ball. And these things are dynamic and dialectic processes, so they change quickly. What was important over the last couple of weeks for me was that the acts of civil disobedience that occurred on July 29 in Phoenix, in Tucson, were . . . I don't want to say they were *unprecedented*. I want to put it this way: I've been here almost twenty years, and I don't remember seeing that here. I study social movements, so I study confrontation, I study the policing of protest. I usually have to travel to other places to see how that operates. This is the first time that I went, "Whoa! It's here! It arrived in Arizona." And what I mean by arrived is that a number of individuals just said, "Hey, listen, this just got to an unacceptable spot, and we are willing to take arrest, and willing to do some particular things in order to identify and name this particular problem."

This thing is going to spread nationally. It is going to come from Arizona outward. It is already starting to do that, and it's probably going to do that more. So what I have been telling people here is — people keep calling me and saying, "I want to come to Arizona and help. What do you think we should do?" And I say, "If you want to help us, stay put, start organizing there, because Arizona is coming to you. You don't have to come to Arizona."

Some of the folks behind SB1070 took a couple of punches, and they are not happy. Mainly because the courts temporarily suspended the law; the federal government intervened forcefully; people were in the streets protesting and gaining international attention; the news made it *global*; and this was not necessarily the kind of publicity that some of these folks were aiming for. So, what is their next move? My guess is that things are going to mellow out in the next couple of weeks and then heat up again. People are going to try to outdo each other in how much of an anti-immigrant person they can be. When politicians begin to do that, it has reverberations for communities because they anger people and people yell at other people. So we are going to see some of that.

Internally in Arizona, what is likely to happen is that these particular individuals are going to retaliate by trying to eliminate the Fourteenth Amendment, trying to come around what has been called the "anchor baby" theory — the notion that some individuals are going to throw an anchor, and the anchor is a child, and somehow they will . . . I don't know what! But that is the image that they are using. They are going to try to eliminate the Fourteenth Amendment to make it so that at least one parent has to have U.S. citizenship.

Now the issue about the Fourteenth Amendment is that it unravels a whole bunch of things. I am not sure they even understand what they are about to unravel, but one thing that you begin to unravel by questioning the Fourteenth Amendment is emancipation itself. And this is emancipation from slavery. That is the way they tried to give freedom to Black former slaves. Undoing the Fourteenth Amendment might unravel all sorts of historical issues and connections of other communities. I think Black communities are going to understand that, and will make the link between the Black-Brown communities and the white supremacy behind this stuff a little bit clearer.

JL: Yes, even a staunch conservative like Alan Keyes warned that "the Fourteenth Amendment is not something one should play with lightly."

LF: My prediction is that the law will be proposed, but never implemented, going to the courts immediately. But it doesn't matter because again, this is about the attrition tactic, which aims to increase fear in the undocumented populations; it seeks to terrorize. It also seeks to galvanize a particular group of white people to vote for nativists and at the same time increase racial tensions. Unfortunately, this strategy has worked to some extent. Fortunately, it has also galvanized movements of undocumented and working-class people in Arizona.

JL: I think we are at a crossroads. The 2006 immigrant rights mobilizations were so amazing and had so much energy, but they were very much directed at immigration reform. But Arizona, and states like Georgia and Alabama doing copycat bills, Secure Communities, the ICE ACCESS [Agreements of Cooperation in Communities to Enhance Safety and Security] programs, etc., all make criminalization a much clearer issue. So, while I feel like the movement paradigm is still overly oriented toward getting rights through the existing system, I think it's at a turning point.

LF: I'd say that there is some potential for that shift. It's hard to predict, but the thing I find most interesting about social movements is that they can't be reduced to a group or to a person or to a leader. Social movements are large collective multitudes that move in these strange patterns, which are sometimes contradictory, but always flowing and moving. You can always enter the flow, but you don't necessarily control it, or guide it or push it. Or you can, maybe momentarily, but if people decide to do something else, then . . .

So the question is: Will this organic thing rise out of the immigration struggle? It's unpredictable. But it does happen. I mean, it happened with the gay movement, right? The gay movement, before it was "the gay movement," was homosexuals being arrested in bars and persecuted by the police. Then we had the Stonewall riot that became a working-class revolt with gay people shouting, "Enough! Enough of this!" It quickly transcended into claiming a strong gay identity, an identity that led to many political struggles with liberatory claims.

The question is: Will it happen here in Arizona? I think it already has. We already have working-class movements of undocumented people making liberatory claims. The real question is: Can we recognize them as such? And what are you doing to support them?

Part V

Speaking Up! Standing Up!
Local Struggles against Walls and Cages

Part V can be read as a series of antiwar protests. These chapters make vividly clear that the harms that security wars inflict on families, neighborhoods, and communities are not received passively. People who are most directly impacted by prison and border regimes, and their allies, are resilient and determined to create real safety and well-being for themselves, their families, and their communities.

The contributors to this part document political struggles and resistance to walls and cages in local organizing efforts across the United States. They recast political questions of security, home, and citizenship in eminently human terms. Their case studies focus on building power to challenge prison and migration regimes, and thus to end the harms these do to families and communities. These chapters offer concrete examples and frank discussions of the difficulties of abolitionist organizing, whether to transform conditions at a local jail or close a detention center. They also discuss how organizing and creating power at the urban scale offer possibilities for building the kind of power that creates social justice.

A Politics for Our Time?

Organizing against Jails

JOSHUA M. PRICE

This chapter is about a community-led effort in a town in New York state to advocate for people held in our county jail. Under the auspices of the local NAACP, civil rights activists, formerly incarcerated people, local students, and other community members came together to form a coalition to stop abusive and neglectful health care at the jail. As the coalition expanded, we noticed that the jail is also used for detained immigrants. We took tentative steps to form a coalition with groups that were working to end U.S. imperialism and the abuse of people held in U.S. custody both here and overseas.

I describe what we did in order to explore the possibilities for coalition work against incarceration and for justice for immigrants. How can a local campaign based around medical conditions and accountability at a local jail broaden its scope and the radicalism of its demands? What are the possibilities for organizing to change local conditions and oppose the prison-industrial complex and imperialism? My hope is that sharing this appraisal may be instructive and helpful for similarly minded projects elsewhere and for our own future efforts.

It may seem quaint to focus on the inner workings of a county jail in Binghamton, a town four hours from New York City. Prisons, especially men's penitentiaries, and big cities get more attention than provincial towns. But large immigration raids in Greenville, South Carolina, and Postville, Iowa, underscore the importance of small towns to grasping the scope of immigrant detention in the United States. The burgeoning number of townships and counties that contract with the federal government to hold migrants in local facilities points to their importance in the landscape of an expanding punishment state. Local jails capture the convergence between militarization, immigration policy, penal policy, and multiple economic dislocations.

BACKGROUND

Binghamton is a deindustrialized working-class town in upstate New York. A "depressed" city implies a place that has been hit hard economically, a temporary condition. But in this case, "depressed" must include the full emotional coloration of the persistently gloomy horizon, the blight, the lethargy, and the defeat.

Binghamton sprang briefly into national headlines in the spring of 2009 when, in a horrific massacre, a disaffected Vietnamese immigrant gunned down other immigrants and staff at a downtown immigrant assistance center. For a few years before 9/11, Binghamton was a favored site to resettle immigrants, and so we have larger pockets of Lao, Somali, Kurdish, Afghani, Iraqi, Ukrainian, and other Eastern European migrants than one might expect in central New York. That resettlement stopped abruptly after the towers fell and border security tightened. Immigration and Customs Enforcement (ICE), the successor to the Immigration and Naturalization Service (INS), makes occasional sweeps.

Binghamton has long been a destination for Italians, Poles, Arabs, Puerto Ricans, African Americans, and others who made their way from New York City. From the Great Migration of the 1910s through the end of the economic boom in the 1970s, African Americans migrated here in waves from small towns in Georgia, the Carolinas, Tennessee, and other points south. But the history goes back much further; African Americans have lived and traded with the local indigenous peoples since the seventeenth century, before the area was settled by white English colonists, who massacred the indigenous populations. The local chapter of the NAACP is one of the oldest in this part of the country.

ORGANIZING AGAINST HEALTH CARE ABUSE
AT THE COUNTY JAIL

In July 2004, I attend a meeting of the NAACP where participants are discussing complaints they've received from prisoners about health care in the county jail. The meeting is attended by seven or eight people, most of them septuagenarians from the civil rights movement. One elderly African American woman is introduced with great formality as the daughter of the founder of the local branch of the NAACP.

I say I am from the university, but this feels almost unnecessary. With my frayed blue oxford shirt, they take me for a student. Once they learn I am a social scientist, they invite me to document the prisoner abuse. A few days later Stan Gluck, the branch secretary, presents me with a folder full of letters and documents on the health care provider at the Broome County Correctional Facility, which is run by the sheriff's department. County jail inmates are generally people being held before trial, people arrested who have not made bail, or people sentenced to less than a year. The NAACP learned that the jail's health care is contracted to Correctional Medical Services (CMS), a multibillion-dollar corporation that administers health services in prisons and jails in twenty-seven states and employs over six thousand people. CMS has lost numerous lawsuits across the country, and has several pending, for inadequate care, malpractice, neglect, and participating in cruel and unusual punishment.

After attending a few meetings, I decide to enlist students from my research methods class to help with the interviews. In consultation with members of the NAACP, we design a set of questions for open-ended interviews with current and formerly incarcerated people. The first people we interview in the jail let me know that they are speaking to me only because someone they trust has put in a word for me. People are suspicious of outsiders, especially university people, so having these connections is important.

The interviews turn out to be the core of the project and the source of its organizing potential. We start with just one or two a week, but word gets out quickly, and soon we are doing eight or ten interviews a week. One man went into a diabetic coma when denied his insulin shots. A woman shows me her scarlet, swollen limb, and tells me she is worried she has gangrene but cannot get medical attention. Other people were forced to languish in their cells for days with a burst appendix or a fractured vertebra before they received anything other than Pepto-Bismol or Advil. We interview many women who are denied routine prenatal care.

As time goes on, more and more people come to our weekly meetings, including family members of people in jail, formerly incarcerated people, and concerned community members. From 2004 through 2007, we have about twenty-five to thirty-five people attend our meetings on the jail. The resulting working group, which I call a coalition, involves members of a civil rights organization with deep ties to the community; anti-prison activists; African American and white people; immigrants from the Caribbean, Africa, Latin America, and the Middle East; Christians, Muslims, and Jews; young mothers bouncing babies in their laps; retirees; and working-class and middle-class students. Some people have served only short stints in jail, while others spent the last thirty years in prison; others have never been near a jail before.

Many involved are transient and this affects the character of our organizing. Incarcerated people are often transferred, released, re-incarcerated, or deported. Students move on to other things. The families — especially the spouses and mothers — are the most constant participants in the coalition, joined by a small handful of community advocates and activists. The "we" of the coalition represents this fluidity.

What collaborations are possible? The participants hold various understandings of political action, strategy, tools, and concepts. Some see the project as legal and pragmatic, trying to force the jail to provide adequate health care, framed within the terms of the modern liberal state and its institutions of punishment. Others are prison abolitionists and embrace socialist, anarchist, or other radical politics. Some are just beginning to have a political understanding of the world and come to this work because they have an assignment for class. Some see the research in instrumental terms; others see it as a form of consciousness raising. Some seek change only on the level of the institution; others look for incremental changes in people and their relationships. Some focus on their individual needs, others on the town; still others have links to activists throughout the state and to counterhegemonic movements throughout the world.

As we organize ourselves to improve jail conditions in this conservative, working-class town, we begin hearing terrible stories from across New York of people disappearing and being held incommunicado. The police are stationing officers outside mosques; it is not clear if they are protecting the mosques or monitoring them. We move in a climate of fear and trepidation that preceded but intensified after 9/11. When we begin to discuss how to stop the racial profiling and religious persecution, several Muslims caution me that some Muslim leaders and imams in the community may not be ready to take this on. I invite some friends from antiwar and anti–Israeli occupation organizations to join our work. I hope this team can analyze the connections among local prisoner abuse, the abuse of other detainees within the United States, including Arab and Muslim detainees, and overseas detainees, and develop a politics that ties anti-prison work to anti-imperialist and anti–immigrant detention work.

Here are some moments, or scenes, that capture the convergence of forces in our work on the jail, in the community, and in our own efforts.

1. I am in the dayroom of a homeless shelter, accompanied by my good friend Mohamed, who is a certified court interpreter for Arabic-speakers. I know him from organizing against the Israeli occupation of Palestine and from anti–U.S.

imperialism and antiwar activism. He is older than me and is an immigrant from the Middle East. I am a middle-class American Jew.

We are interviewing a shelter resident who just got out of jail. We describe our project and explain that we are just gathering information, not preparing a legal case. Though we have a set of questions typed out for the interview, the conversation is difficult at first, as we stumblingly get to know a bit about each other. The man asks Mohamed if today is the first day of Ramadan, but Mohamed is not an observant Muslim and doesn't recall. I take it the man is identifying himself to Mohamed as Muslim.

The interviewee tells us that in the jail it is standard practice to collect and reissue prison jumpsuits, moving them from prisoner to prisoner, without washing them. Because of this practice, he developed a bad rash for which he was denied adequate care. He also tells us that he suffers from acute arthritis in his spine. Nevertheless, he was forced to mop as his chore or face solitary confinement. He would like to sue the jail, but he also wants the conditions to change for prisoners.

At the end, we thank the man, give him our names again, and write down numbers he can call if he has anything else to say. The encounter feels too brief somehow, not exactly perfunctory but not satisfying, and maybe not useful for the interviewee in the way he might have anticipated.

The three of us — our class backgrounds, our ways of thinking and acting out masculinity, our hopes and expectations, the perils we face in living in a racialized state, our political horizons — are different from one another. Yet we have been brought to this point of contact with manifestly political aspirations. What brings us to this place: a set of ethical convictions, a need to survive, a desire for recognition from another, personal or collective injury, fear, rage, love, friendship?

In order to understand and support any coalition, it is important to take honest stock of oneself and one's allies, to inventory one's motivations, desires, and limits. Mohamed and I have an interest in thinking about how jail practices are tied (conceptually, legally, politically, institutionally) to the detention of Muslims and Middle Easterners within the United States and in the custody of U.S. troops abroad, and even more widely to colonial and neoliberal forms of detention, incarceration, and mistreatment in places like Colombia and Egypt. Several of the U.S. soldiers who pled guilty to abuse at Abu Ghraib and elsewhere are now corrections officers in the United States. Our interviews show us that the abuse of prisoners is also occurring in correctional facilities within the United States. It is an ongoing challenge to figure out how to capture the widespread disgust and outrage at the Abu Ghraib abuses and engender a wider and deeper consciousness of state violence, including its very real local manifestations. What, in other words, could be a transnational resistance against these global structures of oppression?

2. I get a phone call at home from a man from Long Island. I do not know how he got my number, but by now we've interviewed over a hundred currently and formerly incarcerated people, and talked to as many family members, so there are lots of ways he could have gotten my name. He asks me to look in on two Tunisian people he knows who are being held at our jail until they are deported. He sounds worried. I agree and hang up.

I ask Mohamed to accompany me in case I need an interpreter. We go out to the jail the next day, and as we kill time in the waiting room, I amuse myself by watching some of the small children run around. Eventually we are called and make our way through the metal detector, past the guard who frisks us, through the sliding sally port and two electric doors into the visiting room, where we face a row of men in orange jumpsuits across the counter from us. The guards motion Mohamed and me to chairs opposite a Middle Eastern man about my age.

I needn't have worried about his English. In his seven months at the jail, he has picked up jail lingo, which peppers his speech. Still, I am glad for Mohamed's company, since he can be counted on for his perspicacity and political insight. The man tells us that he and his friend both married Americans. But their wives had grown tired of them, he says, and denounced them to the authorities for marriage fraud — unjustly, he is quick to add. I do not evaluate this description. I am concerned about his treatment at the jail, about making sure he is okay now, and not what he has or has not done.

The man assures us that he has been in fairly good health. On the other hand, the guards taunt him constantly. They ask him over and over if he is a terrorist. When he first came in, they made him strip an extra time to examine him for bombs and to make sure he wasn't a "suicide bomber." After more than seven months at the jail, he has given up fighting to remain in the United States. Most of all, he is tired and just wants to go home to Tunis. When we offer to check on him the following week, he tells us he would appreciate that. He also wants us to check on his friend.

In the parking lot on our way out, I see the kids from the waiting room, who glance at me. I try to make a funny face, but suddenly the kids get stony and unresponsive. One of the women rushes up to our car, enraged, screams a string of obscenities and tells me to stop looking at her kids and to go back to "Arabia." I am mortified and shaken. I had nothing but playful intentions.

Mohamed stiffens, and tells me just to ignore her, that her anger has nothing to do with us. I feel bad she took us, or me, to be potentially predatory—but I am also struck that she took me to be a foreigner. I am angry that her defensiveness has a xenophobic edge to it. I understand that most people who visit the jail are under enormous pressures. I have talked to enough people to know how devastating the circumstances can be. In the waiting room, people sometimes strike up conversations, share advice, lightly commiserate. So I am dismayed again that we who visit people in the jail for various reasons—all of them unhappy—cannot find the basis for a little less suspicion and more generosity, if not solidarity. But I am not so naive to think that these common straits would be enough by themselves to build an oppositional politics. Too many histories, too much mutual suspicion. Imperialism and racism divide people who otherwise share remarkably similar conditions.

When I get home, I call the Tunisians' friend on Long Island and give an update on the detained man. But when we return to visit the jail the following week, we find that both men have been transferred. The jail will give us no more information on their whereabouts or whether they have been deported.

3. I am in the sheriff's office in Broome County with Stan and Billie, long-time NAACP staffers well known in the community. We have come to see the sheriff about our research into the jail's health care. The jail administration has begun to dock the time of our visits from the prisoners' allotment of two hours of weekly visits. This effectively pits a prisoner's desire to speak with us against his or her need to see relatives and friends. We and the people held at the jail interpret the new rule as an obstacle to our monitoring of the jail's conditions. We have decided to take up the new rules with the sheriff.

The sheriff is a large, pink-faced man. He starts with a tale of the time he got his hand caught in a wood chipper. I wonder if the small talk is to annoy us, or because he is a bit nervous. I am impatient. Finally, Billie and Stan raise some of our concerns. The sheriff seems unperturbed. He is confident that the medical care is fine: "One always finds some complainers." I know there are several lawsuits pending against the jail for poor health care. I cannot read if he is cynical or dissimulating. The Teflon sheriff.

He gives us a statistical rundown of the jail. The magnitude of the organization is enormous; the jail employs hundreds, it costs millions of dollars to run, and the medical contract alone is over $1 million. The sheriff speaks with pride about the money the jail generates for this relatively impoverished upstate county through leasing beds to other counties and the federal government for immigrant detainees and other federal criminals (almost $100/day per prisoner). He has begun a well-publicized campaign to expand the jail. He tells us that he gets a call every year from the county executive (often a Democrat) about the possibilities of making revenue from the jail. He makes a point of mentioning the current executive, as if to imply her hypocrisy, since she has gone on record opposing the jail expansion.

Stan and Billie try to bring the conversation back to the question of the visits. The sheriff listens and nods idly and says he will take the question under consideration, but he must consult with the jail administrator, his direct subordinate. I know then that nothing will change.

Weeks later, the NAACP gets a perfunctory note from the jail that the new restrictions will remain in place. While I am disappointed, I am not surprised that they do what they can to restrict our access. They are accustomed to acting with impunity. Soon, the other shoe drops. The jail administrator demands that we have written permission from each inmate's lawyer before we will be given clearance to conduct interviews. Many of the people held at the jail do not have legal representation. Moreover, because we are sometimes critical of the lackluster public defenders who are cozier with the district attorney's office than with their own clients, many local defense lawyers distrust us or are openly hostile to our efforts. This will be a difficult bar to leap.

But we have learned something else. In a bloodless and unruffled way, the sheriff has alerted us to how incarceration is literally part of the *business* of governance: he seemed to relish reciting how much money the county could make. In fact, the potential revenue-producing capacity serves as his rationale for expanding the jail; he does not give even lip service to a law-and-order argument. This local process reflects national trends. In purely economic terms, the record-breaking boom in the incarceration industry drains more than $49 billion nationally a year. What Marc Mauer has termed the "race to incarcerate" has been a boon for some government agencies and for private industry. Incarcerated people serve rural communities through their quadruple status as "raw material," workers, consumers, and "three-fifths" citizens.[1]

The tremendous expansion in the scale and types of imprisonment represents the opportunity for not just capital growth, but also state expansion: "The state criminalizes, detains and deports immigrants in the name of the war on terror, while disenfranchising, criminalizing and incarcerating people of color and poor whites in the name of the war on crime and the war on drugs. In this way, the state updates the social infrastructure of state-generated racist practices."[2]

In a circular logic, the significant increase since 9/11 in the number of criminal prosecutions, detentions, and deportations of immigrants has provided political capital for ICE officials trying to justify their swelling budgets and aggressive enforcement.[3] ICE policies, like the practice of shipping prisoners between counties and across state boundaries, keep local jails full. Most contracts with ICE and the Department of Justice for detaining immigrants are with local governments.[4] Indeed, in Binghamton, the sheriff's economic rationale for jail expansion is bolstered by the enthusiasm to detain and deport migrants and the jingoism that accompanies our overseas wars.

MISSED POSSIBILITIES AND FUTURE GOALS

Once the sheriff effectively blocked our ability to interview people in the jail, we faced a practical dilemma of what to do. Assessing the project's current limits and possibilities is therefore useful, though evaluating the successes of a political project is never easy. Did we succeed in what we set out to do? Are the changes tangible? Are they lasting? Were we able to take on the more ambitious goal of linking local anti-jail work to advocacy for migrants?

We involved hundreds of people in our work. Activists from across the state took notice and sent notes of support. A whistleblower from the jail told me that all of the jail guards and administrators were aware of what we were doing and felt on the defensive — a good thing. Almost all the incarcerated people we spoke with told us they felt accompanied, even if temporarily, and urged us to continue. Families had a place to work with others and a way to channel their rage and frustration and to voice the harm to which they, too, were subject. Dozens of students, most of whom had never been to a jail before, made weekly trips to listen to incarcerated people recount their experiences. In this way, we aided in making jail conditions more transparent, which many incarcerated people thought was crucial. "Rot can't grow where there's a bright light shining," as one man put it.

Just as important were new and transformed relationships. Before we started, many in the coalition would have never encountered one another, or we would have only met in atmospheres of hostility, exploitation, or violence. Through our work, we created the possibility for new relationships based on collaboration. The coalition was fluid and unstable, but the work we did was democratic, even if messily and unevenly so. The decision-making power was largely in the hands of those most oppressed: people who had been incarcerated and their families. But most of these people moved on, were sent elsewhere, or were deported. Thus it is not easy or even possible to find out what lasting difference we made, especially in the lives of those individuals. This is especially true of the intangible parts of political work: the changes in people's consciousness, the new directions people take with their lives, the transformation away from hate, fear, private shame, despair, and grief into something more affirming and sustaining.

At the same time, we must acknowledge some possibly unavoidable contradictions in our work:

- We did not fully integrate local anti-prison efforts, advocacy for immigrants held at the jail, and anti-imperialism work. Maybe we underestimated the difficulty, maybe we were not dogged enough, or maybe we had a failure of imagination. Because we were so results-oriented, and because we did not want to get spread too thin, we missed opportunities for creating a crucial coalition against the incarceration of *all* people.
- We face an ongoing contradiction between pressing for incremental changes in agencies and institutions, on the one hand, and a deeper belief that the structure itself is rife with abuse and racism, on the other. This is a classic dilemma, sometimes posed as reform versus revolution.

Writing this chapter has helped me reach two conclusions. First, the initial design of the project, with its focus on local incarcerated people, kept us in tune with the life of our community in its concreteness, and provided a good basis for organizing. On the other hand, its emphasis on crisis took up too much of our energy. In a similar situation, if we're not careful, we could find ourselves pushing only for better health care or lobbying only to ease access to inmates. On the other hand, our focus on health care alerted us to many deep structural problems in society, which led to many detainees' involvement with law enforcement in the first place.

Put in positive terms, we need to find the political energy to take on the ambitious task of decarceration of all people, both migrants and non-migrants. I have learned that an advocacy group for transgender people in prison in California has a rule of thumb: the members only advocate for changes that will not expand the prison-industrial complex. So, for example, they do not push for new, separate facilities for transgender people. This is an example of what André Gorz, Avery Gordon, and others have called nonreformist reform, or "abolition reform." As a practical and philosophical question, we did not and do not accede to the existing arrangement of punishing people or detaining them by putting them in cages. Our work does not reinforce, expand, rationalize, or provide an apology for the current correctional arrangement, nor for the ethos of punishment, cruelty, retribution, and vengeance which backs it. We aim to accompany people well, to build horizontal solidarity, and to create transparency in jail conditions. This does not solve the problems of prisons or immigrant detention, but it does enhance community participation.

This leads me to a second conclusion. We found a tension developing in our coalition between those who wanted to advocate *against* the jail and the excesses and petty tyrannies of the small-time brokers of power in our town, and those who began advocating working *with* them. This marked a political turning point. Our coalition faces a split between people who, in my estimation, are willing to join those who hold small-time power in Binghamton, and thus are willing to subordinate their own power and desires to the existing power arrangement, and those who advocate putting people who are under the thumb of the law at the center of political analysis and planning.

Because I came to see the concrete harms of migrant detention through anti-prison work, rather than through immigrant rights struggles, I notice the extent to which the immigrant rights movement argues in terms of "We are not criminals."[5] Framed in this way, we miss a crucial opportunity for coalition among peoples who are caged by the state.[6] In contrast, anti-imperialist struggles engender conceptualizing prisons as part of larger imperial ambitions over subject populations, including Puerto Ricans (in the States or on the island), African Americans, Colombians, Iraqis, Afghanis, and so on. Put another way, we must constantly struggle to overcome a provincialism not only born of our geographic locations outside of the metropolis, but also engendered by the urgent local problems, including individual problems, which need to be addressed.

Health care at the jail provides too narrow a framework if it does not encompass the making and remaking of citizenship, including state and populist-nativist cultural exclusion of migrants who face detention and deportation. Participating in what Du Bois called an abolitionist-democracy means crossing distances and de-provincializing our political work. For those of us for whom the depredations of the prison system and the racial state are a daily condition, we must explore how to use these meetings, these incipient ties, these coalitions, to articulate the condition as a problem and try to struggle out of it. In our case, the work started with an investigation of a private medical provider at the Broome County Correctional Facility, but it launched a political project that ties the global with the local, and that experiments with a politics for our time.

NOTES

Many people in Binghamton contributed to this chapter, especially Mohamed Aly and Rozann Greco. I appreciate the thoughtful and challenging queries and suggestions by the editors. I would also like to thank the James Weldon Johnson Institute, which hosted me during the writing of this piece.

1. See Allard and Muller, *Incarcerated People and the Census*; Wagner, "Phantom Constituents in the Census"; Marantz, "The Five-Fifths Clause."
2. Gilmore and Gilmore, "Restating the Obvious," 142.
3. See Camayd-Freixas, "Statement of Dr. Erik Camayd-Freixas."
4. See Barry, "The New Political Economy of Immigration."
5. Fran Ansley provided a critical reading of this tendency in a public lecture at Emory University in March 2009.
6. See Bhattacharjee, "Private Fists and Public Force."

BIBLIOGRAPHY

Allard, Patricia, and Chris Muller. *Incarcerated People and the Census*. New York: Brennan Center Publications, 2005.

Barry, Tom. "The New Political Economy of Immigration." *Dollars and Sense*, January–February 2009.

Bhattacharjee, Anannya. "Private Fists and Public Force: Race, Gender, and Surveillance." In *Policing the National Body: Race, Gender and Criminalization*, edited by Anannya Bhattacharjee and Jael Silliman, 1–54. Cambridge, Mass.: South End, 2002.

Camayd-Freixas, Erik. "Statement of Dr. Erik Camayd-Freixas, Federally Certified Interpreter at the U.S. District Court for the Northern District of Iowa Regarding a Hearing on 'The Arrest, Prosecution, and Conviction of 297 Undocumented Workers in Postville, Iowa, from May 12 to 22, 2008,' before the Subcommittee on Immigration, Citizenship, Refugees, Border Securing and International Law." http://judiciary.house.gov/hearings/pdf/Camayd-Freixas080724.pdf.

Gilmore, Ruth Wilson, and Craig Gilmore. "Restating the Obvious." In *Indefensible Space: The Architecture of the National Insecurity State*, edited by Michael Sorkin. New York: Routledge, 2007.

Marantz, Andrew. "The Five-Fifths Clause: How We Count, and Use, Our Prisoners." *Slate* (November 6, 2006). http://www.slate.com/id/2152994." *Slate*, November 6, 2006.

Wagner, Peter. "Phantom Constituents in the Census." *New York Times*, September 26, 2005.

"A Prison Is Not a Home"
Notes from the Campaign to End Immigrant Family Detention

BOB LIBAL, LAUREN MARTIN, AND NICOLE PORTER

While mainstream American history understands the internment of Japanese families during World War II as a lapse, a paranoid moment pardoned by the anxieties of war, the war on terror has exhumed and institutionalized these practices to round up a new group of supposed enemies: immigrant and asylum-seeking families. Beginning in March 2001, the Immigration and Naturalization Service (INS) began to hold families in a former nursing home in Berks County, Pennsylvania. In 2006, Immigration and Customs Enforcement (ICE), part of the Department of Homeland Security (DHS), expanded family detention to the T. Don Hutto Correction Center in Taylor, Texas. Hutto was opened as part of the Secure Border Initiative, which combined new immigration enforcement policies with unprecedented levels of funding, surveillance technology, fencing, and staff. Representative of the massive expansion of detention through SBI, Hutto multiplied ICE's family detention capacity *sevenfold*, from Berks County's 84 beds to 592. Family detention only became institutionally necessary, however, because SBI also expanded the expedited removal program from its focus on Mexican citizens to include "other than Mexicans." Immigration officers retain exclusive authority to place noncitizens in expedited removal, putting them in detention and deeming them deportable with no immigration court review. Calling it a shift from "catch and release" to "catch and return," DHS's Secure Border Initiative is based on a presumption of detention and deportation, with little regard for the claims to asylum and immigration relief migrants may have.

Immigration law grants ICE the authority to change immigration enforcement procedures and practices, including who is detained where and for how long. The majority of Hutto's detainees are asylum seekers from Central America, Africa, Eastern Europe, and Iraq—people who would not have been detained without the SBI's expansion of expedited removal and mandatory detention. Working from the assumption that *everyone* must be detained, ICE opened Hutto to reconcile two problems of its own creation. First, prior to SBI, families were exempted from detention (since the detention infrastructure consisted entirely of correctional facilities unfit for children), and ICE argued that this "loophole" encouraged smugglers to "rent" children. According to ICE, smugglers assumed that if they were apprehended with children, they could be released under the pretense of being a family.[1] No examples of such a practice, which would have been prosecutable under criminal law, have been provided to date.

ICE's initial solution was to separate parents from their children and detain them separately, which created the second problem: public outrage over unnecessary family separation. Congress, for example, told ICE, "Children who are apprehended by DHS while in the company of their parents are not in fact 'unaccompanied'; and if their welfare is not at issue... the [House Appropriations] Committee expects DHS to release families or use alternatives to detention such as the Intensive Supervis[ion] Appearance Program whenever possible. When detention of family units is necessary, the Committee directs DHS to use appropriate detention space to house them together."[2] Unfortunately, these comments were part of an appropriations bill and do not carry the force of law ascribed to enacted legislation. ICE ignored Congress's call for "appropriate" detention space and alternatives, a failure that has since haunted the agency.

FROM PRISON TO "FAMILY RESIDENTIAL FACILITY"

The T. Don Hutto Family Residential Facility (as it has been known since its external sign was changed in 2006) is a former medium-security prison built for male prisoners in 1997 by the Corrections Corporation of America. Once the largest town in Williamson County and home to the largest railyard and cotton gins in Central Texas, Taylor was a vital hub of the cotton and grain economy in the state. The automation of the railroads and the mechanization of agriculture reduced the need for manual labor in Taylor. The deregulation of agricultural markets led to falling prices and the consolidation of family farms into massive factory farms, which sent towns like Taylor into a long recession in the 1970s, 1980s, and 1990s. Despite the rapid growth of Williamson County's technology sector, these investments were focused thirty miles away in Austin's suburbs. Taylor's officials expected the prison to bring $4 million to the local economy (though they neglected to explain how) and a significant increase in taxes paid to the Taylor Independent School District. Hutto opened in 1995 with contracts to house prisoners from Oregon and Texas, and eventually became a federal pretrial detention center. By 2003, CCA's contracts did not supply enough federal detainees to make Hutto profitable. CCA planned to close the prison, and was saved only by a late night agreement with the U.S. Marshals to house adult male immigrant detainees. In 2006 this contract was amended to include a new group of inmates: families.

Despite Hutto's shift from a prison to an immigration detention center to a "family residential facility," CCA's contracts stipulated no changes in the facility's operating procedures. To CCA, one group of prisoners is like any other: they bring payments for bed space. Thus, a failing private prison corporation was saved by the expansion of migrant detention, which filled its half-empty prisons and provoked a building frenzy across rural West Texas to capitalize on the "expanding market" for immigrant detention. Thus, the for-profit prison model served as the basis for *speculation* on increased immigration enforcement, a strategy investors evidently approved as CCA stock prices rose after 2003. By the fall of 2006, Hutto had come to represent the worst of a disturbing trend throughout Texas: the speculation on and rapid construction of privately owned detention centers in remote locations, with little governmental oversight.

THE CAMPAIGN TO CLOSE HUTTO: MAKING DETENTION VISIBLE

Hutto reopened as a family detention center rather quietly in May 2006, advertised by a single ICE press release. Alarmed by the drastic increase in detention throughout Texas, organizers against for-profit incarceration and immigrant rights advocates began meeting to discuss the issue in September 2006. This Detention Working Group included the ACLU of Texas; the Texas Civil Rights Project; Grassroots Leadership; the Texas Criminal Justice Coalition; and University of Texas professor Michele Deitch and faculty and staff of the University of Texas Immigration Law Clinic.

Seeking to highlight the complex issues of prison privatization, raids, detention, and abuses of executive power, the group decided to focus on Hutto and family detention policy. While the geographic proximity of Taylor to Austin played a major role in the decision to focus on Hutto, so too did the sympathetic population targeted by family detention policy. Many organizers viewed Hutto and family detention as an entry point into the larger, and admittedly more complicated, issues of detention and deportation. Others were angered by the incarceration of innocent children. However, the group worried that focusing on children's innocence implied that the other thirty-three thousand detained adults were criminals, a strategy that might have silenced deeper questions about criminalization, racism, and militarization. While closing Hutto was the working group's central campaign, organizers developed a broader message that identified problems that plague the immigration detention system generally: the rights of asylum seekers, the lack of enforceable standards and independent oversight, long and indefinite detention periods, and ICE's continued refusal to use nonpenal alternatives to detention.[3]

ORGANIZING AGAINST FAMILY DETENTION: A FOUR-TIERED STRATEGY

Utilizing the diverse skills of its members, the Detention Working Group, which later became known as Texans United for Families (TUFF), developed a four-tiered campaign strategy: litigation, grassroots organizing, media advocacy, and legislative advocacy.

Litigation

As local organizers protested outside Hutto, attorneys were shocked by what they found inside. Detained mothers reported appalling conditions to their attorneys:

> My daughters and I share a small cell. We all have to use the toilet in front of each other and right next to our beds. [My daughters] are forced to wear prison clothes. . . . They wear the same clothes all day, including to sleep and to recreation.[4]
>
> They wake us at 5:45 or 5:30 a.m. And at 6 a.m. we have to have finished bathing ourselves. After that we have to eat in 20 minutes, then return to the pod to do nothing, they don't allow us to sleep, only to sit and wait for the hours, days, months to pass.[5]
>
> We have lost our religion in here. Our religion requires that we pray at certain times of the day, but we have to go to rec[reation] or chow at each of those times. The guards rush my children through meals. When Bahja was having problems with another girl at rec time, the guards and our social worker told me that they would take my children away from me if I could not control them.[6]
>
> At Hutto it is difficult for me to take care of Sherona the way a mother should. The family here is destroyed. We live in a prison. It is a prison. There is no freedom.[7]

When you're in Hutto, you feel like [you're in] prison, you are a criminal, that you did something bad, that people are after you, they put you in these clothes. These guards they treat you like you are in prison.[8]

Conditions at Hutto violated nearly every right granted to children in ICE custody by *Flores v. Reno*, a 1997 settlement that stipulated immigration procedures and conditions of custody for all minors in INS (now ICE) custody. Family detention did not enter into the imaginations of either the federal government or children's advocates at that time, indicating the twenty-first-century novelty of detaining families in the United States. As attorneys learned more, they found that CCA had not altered its operating procedures when it transitioned to a "family residential facility." The same tactics of intimidation and surveillance familiar to critics of the prison-industrial complex were daily practices at Hutto. Automatic doors and laser-monitored doorways prevented families from moving freely around the facility and placed small children in danger. CCA's use of prison-style headcount procedures required families to remain in their cells during counts, which confined them to their rooms for eleven to twelve hours a day.

In February 2007, Michelle Brané of the international human rights organization Women's Refugee Commission published a detailed report on family detention at Hutto and Berks, which drew international media attention.[9] In March, the ACLU, the University of Texas Immigration Law Clinic, and a private law firm sued the Department of Homeland Security for the release of twenty-six children detained in Hutto. Arguing that the conditions at Hutto caused irreparable harm to detained children and that the *Flores* settlement stated that both release and family unity should be ICE policy, the attorneys sought to close Hutto by showing that it was grossly out of compliance with existing law.

Unfortunately, the judge refused to interfere with ICE's ability to detain the plaintiffs' parents, and the parties settled for improvements to conditions. The stipulations of the settlement revealed massive compliance failures, ranging from inadequate education, medical care, and nutrition, to dangerous living quarters for toddlers and infants, to lack of attorney-client confidentiality. While the settlement required the creation of family residential standards, which ICE published in January 2008, these were non-binding guidance documents that did not guarantee compliance with *Flores*; in any case, the settlement expired in August 2009. Ultimately, ICE's discretionary power to detain noncitizens, an authority granted by Congress and affirmed in numerous court decisions, came into conflict with existing laws for children, and the compromise was continued detention, albeit under improved conditions.

Grassroots Organizing

Tucked away from large population centers or in warehouse districts, detention centers often are invisible both to the communities affected by immigration enforcement and to the wider American public. Organizers have often accused ICE of purposefully contracting with centers in remote locations to avoid scrutiny. And during the Hutto lawsuit, an anonymously leaked ICE memo stated that Hutto was not an ideal location for immigrant family detention precisely because of its close proximity to "immigrant legal services" and "Austin's empowered immigrant rights community."[10]

Seeking to highlight the presence of detention centers in Central Texas, the Detention Working Group organized a vigil outside Hutto in December 2006. The event captured the attention of activists around the state, and "border ambassador" Jay Johnson-Castro led a three-day walk from the Texas capital to Taylor.[11] The vigil brought out nearly a hundred protesters. The resulting media coverage proved that family detention captured public attention, and there were near-monthly vigils for the next year and a half. A coalition of existing groups converged around the issue, forming the Austin-based Texans United for Families, which shared the grassroots organizing efforts with the Texas Indigenous Council (from San Antonio), Free the Children, the League of United Latin American Citizens, and a growing group of Williamson County residents calling themselves the WillCo Family Justice Alliance.

When ICE requested proposals for three new family detention centers in June 2008, activists with Grassroots Leadership, TUFF, and other organizations recognized the need to broaden the campaign's focus from Hutto to the nationwide policy of family detention. This led Grassroots Leadership to start a national campaign against family detention in early 2009. Beginning with "100 Events in 100 Days," Grassroots Leadership and TUFF collected fifty-five thousand petition signatures, organized toy and book drives, screened documentaries, performed radio interviews, and reached out to faith-based organizations. Grassroots efforts continue to focus on pressuring Congress and Homeland Security secretary Janet Napolitano to mandate the use of noncarceral options for families, a policy change that does not require major legislation and would have wide support from pro-immigrant and pro-family groups alike.

Media Advocacy

While media coverage was initially limited to stories in the local and alternative press (such as the *Austin American-Statesman*, *Taylor Daily Press*, *Democracy Now!*, and *CounterPunch*), the ongoing vigils at Hutto, a grassroots media campaign, litigation, and authoritative reports brought the issue to a broader media audience. *Democracy Now!* was one of the first national media outlets to cover Hutto with its story about a nine-year-old detained Canadian in February 2007.[12] In the subsequent eighteen months, the story of family detention was covered on National Public Radio and in the *Los Angeles Times*, the *New York Times*, and the *New Yorker*. The lawsuit created regular opportunities for legal and academic experts to describe the indignities of family detention to a wide audience. These reports offered critical authoritative support to the passionate arguments of advocates and activists, whose continuing vigils created a social change narrative utilized by many media sources. Each brought attention to the other, a synergy that worked to keep family detention in the national spotlight for months.

The grassroots media strategy has utilized email lists, print, web media (including *La Nueva Raza* and the *Texas Civil Rights Review*), and film. The T. Don Hutto blog proved vital to publicizing vigils, providing photos and videos of events, and consolidating information for journalists covering family detention. In 2007, filmmakers Matt Gossage and Lily Keber produced *Hutto: America's Family Prison*. Running seventeen minutes, the film has been highly effective in two senses. First, it raises an immediate awareness about family detention; and second, it usually provokes a wider discussion of migrant detention, prison privatization, and their interconnections. To facilitate Grassroots Leadership's national campaign, TUFF developed a DVD toolkit that included the film and Hutto-related videos, documents, and pictures. The toolkit was distributed at conferences and to allies across the country. During the spring of 2009, Austin's South by Southwest film festival screened the world premiere of *The Least of These*, a feature-length documentary about the ACLU's lawsuit against ICE. Shown at international film festivals and — most important — to an audience of congresspeople in Washington, D.C., *The Least of These* drew attention to the August 2009 expiration of the lawsuit settlement and raised awareness at a national level.

Since the Hutto lawsuit settled in August 2007, ICE has been more aggressive in its public response to criticism, inviting the League of United Latin American Citizens and some media representatives on tours of Hutto. In 2008, ICE began to insist that changes occurred before the lawsuit was settled and that because of this, the settlement was redundant and unnecessary. In response, our message shifted to emphasize a few key points:

1. Hutto was still a restrictive facility. Both *Flores v. Reno* and Congress mandate that children be held in the least restrictive settings pos-

sible. In the federal magistrate's final report on ICE's compliance with the Hutto settlement, the judge questioned the suitability of a former prison as a family facility and noted that, even with drastically improved conditions, Hutto never fully complied with *Flores* or the settlement itself.

2. Alternatives to incarceration exist. The Vera Institute piloted a supervision program in which 93 percent of immigrants in proceedings appeared for their court dates. The program combined legal, employment, housing, and social support, demonstrating that high rates of court appearance can be achieved without detention, at a much lower cost, and without sacrificing the rights of noncitizens to due process.

3. There is no clear regulatory framework for family detention. The Hutto settlement expired in August 2009, leaving only the Family Residential Standards as guidance documents for ICE oversight. Since they are based on adult corrections and detention standards, the Family Residential Standards ensure neither "home-like" facilities nor compliance with *Flores*, which remains the overarching legal framework for ICE custody of children.

Facilitated largely by TUFF, these arguments have been publicized through letters to the editor and op-eds, a national sign-on letter, a petition, statements from faith communities, press conferences, and radio appearances, all of which have been posted at the T. Don Hutto blog.

Legislative Advocacy

Advocates based in both Texas and Washington, D.C., have remained in frequent contact since 2006, but have not planned a long-term legislative strategy outside of existing immigration reform discussions. This was a major limitation of the campaign, but is being addressed through Grassroots Leadership's national campaign, which seeks to raise the profile of family detention in national policymaking discussions. During the 2008 Texas Democratic presidential primary, more than twenty-five precincts across five counties passed resolutions calling for non-penal alternatives to Hutto. Submitted by members of TUFF and other organizers living in these districts, this strategy was an effort to join grassroots activism and electoral politics. While the resolution was not ratified at the state Democratic convention and was not passed on to the national

Democratic convention, the resolutions raised political awareness of detention across Texas.

In response to TUFF members' ongoing advocacy, Texas state representative Rafael Anchia filed a resolution in the Texas House of Representatives calling for the use of noncarceral alternatives in place of Hutto. By the end of the legislative session in 2009, thirteen state representatives supported the resolution.[13] Due to an agreement to table *all* immigration-related bills and resolutions, HCR95 did not receive a hearing, but it did serve as an organizing tool for anti-Hutto activists at the state capital. Finally, as Barack Obama's administration has taken office, national-level immigrant rights advocates have now placed detention reform, including family detention, at the center of Homeland Security policy and immigration reform discussions.

CONCLUSION

While family detention is a relatively new policy, the biggest obstacle to organizing public support has been the question: What's the alternative? In the political climate of enforcement-led immigration policy, the fact that families have never before been detained in such numbers has failed to be a convincing argument for ending the practice. The American public has become incapable, it seems, of understanding immigration outside of a crime-and-punishment framework.

Originally, TUFF materials included information on ICE's Intensive Supervision Appearance Program as a desired alternative to family detention. Based on the Texas advocates' lack of experience with ISAP — no such program has been implemented in the state — this decision took a cue from DHS materials and from other immigrant rights advocates. In working with organizers with direct experience of ISAP, such as the New York–based Families for Freedom, however, these alternatives have proven more restrictive than their early advocates in the immigrant rights community expected. The programs use ankle bracelets, random visits from ICE, and curfews to restrict the mobility of migrants. Ankle bracelets require two hours to charge each day, are cumbersome and often painful to wear, and stigmatize the migrant since many people assume that the wearer is on parole for criminal activity. In addition to their frequent interruptions of daily life, "alternatives to detention" work more like new forms of detention than true alternatives. Furthermore, these programs have been used more often to surveil people who would otherwise be ineligible for detention. Rather than operating as an alternative to detention, they operate *in addition* to detention and allow ICE to surveil more people than ever before.

The emergence of these mixed reports has forced us to remove the references to ISAP and replace them with calls for nonrestrictive, noncarceral, and nonpenal alternatives to detention, though we have refrained from naming specific programs.

Texas remains home to the majority of U.S. for-profit immigrant detention centers, an outgrowth of twenty years of prison privatization in the state. Repurposing failing prisons like Hutto and speculating on the rise in detention demand from programs like Operation Streamline and Secure Communities, migrant detention has been a boon to the private prison industry. Fortunately, the movement to close Hutto and to fight private detention corporations has spawned protests at other detention centers across the state. Before Hutto opened, these protests were small and sporadic. Today, they are better connected, more visible, and have a more cohesive criticism of enforcement, privatization, and the impact of detention on human rights. Groups such as the Inter-American Commission on Human Rights, the United Nations, Amnesty International, the ACLU, Human Rights First, and others have visited detention centers in Texas, including but not limited to Hutto, making the issue of detention more prominent in immigrant rights and human rights circles.

As mentioned above, focusing on family detention has also focused on the noncriminality of children, on the unfair punishment of children for their parents' actions. These arguments worked to bring new people into the movement to close Hutto, but do not always translate into broader arguments against the detention of adults. The detention of children, in particular, has captured the public imagination in ways that a decade of mandatory immigration detention did not. It has become clear that focusing on family detention is a powerful strategy for publicizing both migrant detention and family separation in general. The strategy carries long-term risks for the broader anti-detention and anti-prison movements, however. On the one hand, arguing that children should not be detained because they are *not* criminals can imply, first, that detention and imprisonment *are* legitimate punishments for crimes, and, second, that adults *are* criminals. But on the other hand, arguing that children have the right to family unity and a stable childhood provides a powerful case against the deportation of undocumented parents. As more and more children find themselves in "mixed-status" households, with parents and other relatives facing deportation, the trauma of detention and deportation is in danger of becoming an epidemic. Family unity remains, however, ICE's core justification for detaining families. Advocating on the basis of collective rights for families has allowed us to demonstrate the inconsistencies in immigration enforcement and to build stronger linkages to other grassroots organizing efforts. As the country continues to await immigration reform, rolling back ICE's enforcement system rests on the power of coalition building, creative organizing, and critical resistance.

EPILOGUE

On August 6, 2009, Immigration and Customs Enforcement announced that the T. Don Hutto Family Residential Facility would no longer house families. As the *New York Times* wrote, "Hutto, a 512-bed center run for profit by the Corrections Corporation of America under a $2.8 million-a-month federal contract, was presented as a centerpiece of the Bush administration's tough approach to immigration enforcement when it opened in 2006. The decision to stop sending families there — and to set aside plans for three new family detention centers — is the Obama administration's clearest departure from its predecessor's immigration enforcement policies." In essence, the government admitted what activists had been saying for years: Hutto was wholly inappropriate for detaining families. Over the following weeks, media outlets, including the *Washington Post* and the *Economist*, covered the policy changes at "the infamous" T. Don Hutto.

Clearly something had changed. In the months leading up the announcement, we had gained momentum in all four areas of our strategy. In the "First 100 Days Campaign," we argued that closing Hutto and ending family detention was an easy way for the Obama administration to differentiate itself from the Bush administration. *The Least of These* highlighted the impact of the lawsuit on conditions at Hutto and drew attention to the impending expiration of the settlement. The federal court's final inspection report stated that, even though "use of [Hutto] as a family detention center may not violate the Settlement Agreement [that] does not mean that doing so is good public policy. . . . it seems fundamentally wrong to house children and their non-criminal parents this way. We can do better" (*In re Hutto Family Detention Center*, "Report to Parties of Final Periodic Review of Facility," case no. A-07-CA-164-SS). In Williamson County, residents pressed the County Commissioners' Court to end its contract with CCA, and met with significantly less resistance than in the past.

Immigration detention as a whole continues to be under attack from immigrant rights advocates, and the Obama administration's appointed special investigator, Dora Schriro, has critically evaluated the state of the detention system. Washington-based advocates met with her repeatedly in the months leading up to the announcement and pushed hard for the release of families from detention. It is hard to measure which aspect had the most impact, but we know that three years of grassroots organizing, litigation, media advocacy, and legislative efforts have paid off.

So what now? ICE released some families from Hutto and transferred the rest to the Berks County Family Care Shelter. While the policy change reduced family bed space by 75 percent, returning family detention to pre-9/11 levels, ICE director John Morton has continued to assert that ICE will *not* end family detention as a policy. In addition, Hutto has remained open and now detains women without children, leaving some activists to question the extent of the "change" and whether it's a victory at all. ICE's announcement of Hutto's changes preceded a broad description of a reorganization of the entire detention system. It is difficult to tell, at this point, whether this will truly make detention more humane, or whether it will expand the detention system as a whole.

Combining these multiple layers of advocacy arguably made Hutto the most controversial detention center in the United States. Linking a specific detention center to a recent policy change — the expansion of family detention — allowed us to form both a focused and a multifaceted campaign centered around humanizing those in detention. This strategy allowed us to repeat the message — "End family detention at Hutto" — in numerous locations and media outlets. As we take our strategy to the next Texas detention center, we look forward to retooling for the bigger fight: ending migrant detention in the United States.

NOTES

1. Department of Homeland Security, "DHS Closes Loophole."
2. House Committee on Appropriations, *Department of Homeland Security Appropriations Bill, 2006*.
3. While the authors of this chapter are members of Texans United for Families, we recognize that Hutto has catalyzed a diverse opposition. The following portions of the text outline TUFF's organizing strategy, but readers should note that groups in San Antonio, Dallas, Houston, and the Rio Grande Valley have been very active and have organized around a variety of messages. Please see www.tdonhutto.blogspot.com for a complete archive of the organizing against Hutto.
4. Second Declaration of Rasa Bunikiene, in *Saule Bunikyte v. Michael Chertoff, Julie Myers, John Torres, Marc Moore, Gary Mead, Simona Colon, and John Pogash*. March 18, 2007. http://www.aclu.org/immigrants/detention/31504lgl20070826.html.

5. Declaration of Elsa Carbajal, in *Richard Anderson Tome Carbajal and Angelina Juliet Tome Carbajal v. Michael Chertoff, Julie Myers, John Torres, Marc Moore, Gary Mead, Simona Colon, and John Pogash.* March 1, 2007. http://www.aclu.org/immigrants/detention/31504lgl20070826.html.

6. Second Declaration of Deka Warsame, in *Mohammed Ibrahim, Bahja Ibrahim, and Aisha Ibrahim v. Michael Chertoff, Julie Myers, John Torres, Marc Moore, Gary Mead, Simona Colon, and John Pogash.* March 18, 2007. http://www.aclu.org/immigrants/detention/31504lgl20070826.html.

7. Declaration of Delourdes Verdieu, in *Sherona Verdieu v. Michael Chertoff, Julie Myers, John Torres, Marc Moore, Gary Mead, Simona Colon, and John Pogash.* March 18, 2007. http://www.aclu.org/immigrants/detention/31504lgl20070826.html.

8. Quoted in Keber and Gossage, *Hutto: America's Family Prison.*

9. Women's Refugee Commission, "Locking Up Family Values."

10. Barbara Hines, personal communication, March 2, 2009.

11. Johnson-Castro has led walks along the U.S.-Mexico border to protest the Secure Fence Act and other border security measures. For more on his work, see Texas Civil Rights Review, "Our Hero Jay Johnson-Castro Walks Again."

12. Democracy Now!, "I Want to Be Free."

13. State of Texas, House Concurrent Resolution 95.

BIBLIOGRAPHY

Democracy Now! "'I Want to Be Free': 9-Year-Old Canadian Citizen Pleads from Texas Immigration Jail." February 23, 2007. http://www.democracynow.org.

Department of Homeland Security. "DHS Closes Loophole by Expanding Expedited Removal to Alien Families: New Facility in Texas Opens Today for Illegal Alien Families." May 16, 2006. www.dhs.gov.

House Committee on Appropriations. *Department of Homeland Security Appropriations Bill, 2006: Report Together with Additional Views (to Accompany H.R. 2360).* 109th Cong., 1st sess., 2005, H.R. 109-79.

Keber, Lily, and Matt Gossage, dirs. *Hutto: America's Family Prison.* http://tdonhutto.blogspot.com.

State of Texas. House Concurrent Resolution 95. http://www.legis.state.tx.us/BillLookup/Text.aspx?LegSess=81R&Bill=HCR95.

Texas Civil Rights Review. "Our Hero Jay Johnson-Castro Walks Again." http://www.texascivilrightsreview.org/phpnuke/modules.php?name=News&file=article&sid=683.

Women's Refugee Commission. "Locking Up Family Values." http://www.womenscommission.org/pdf/famdeten.pdf.

Fighting for the Vote
The Struggle against Felon and Immigrant Disenfranchisement

MONICA W. VARSANYI

Casting a vote is often considered, perhaps next to military service, to be the premier act of membership in the American polity. Yet there are three groups of adults in the United States who do not have that right: citizens convicted of felony crimes, legal immigrants, and undocumented migrants. The number of adults impacted by this disenfranchisement is significant. Approximately 5.3 million adult citizens have lost the right to vote as a result of state criminal disenfranchisement laws. One-quarter of these individuals are currently serving prison terms for felony crimes, one-third are on probation or parole, and 40 percent are *former* felons who have fully completed their sentences and rehabilitation.[1] Similarly, there are currently 11.6 million legal permanent residents — legal immigrants — living in the United States, all of whom do not have the right to vote in local, state, or federal elections.[2] Finally, there are an estimated 11.2 million undocumented residents currently living in the United States.[3] Barring the passage of comprehensive immigration reform by the federal government which includes a pathway to legalization, these residents — many of them living in the United States for five, ten, and even twenty years — are permanently barred from voting.

While having a significant number of adults in the United States unable to vote casts a broad shadow over the nation's commitment to universal democracy, felon and immigrant disenfranchisement also sounds a number of social justice alarms, given the disproportionate impact of disenfranchisement on people of color. With the shift since the 1970s toward a "law-and-order," "tough on crime" society, including the expanding "war on drugs," crime rates have been falling for several decades while rates of conviction for felony crimes have continued to climb.[4] This paradox can be explained by the increasing criminalization of drug trafficking and possession, the vast expansion of mandatory minimum sentences, the proliferation of three-strikes laws, harsh drug sentencing policies, and rising conviction rates. As Fellner and Mauer reported in 1998, "In California . . . more than 40,000 offenders have been sentenced under the state's 'three strikes' law as of June 1998. As a result of the law, 89 percent of these offenders had their sentences doubled, and 11 percent received sentences of twenty-five years to life. Only one in five of these were sentenced for crimes against persons; two-thirds were sentenced for a nonviolent drug or property crime. Seventy percent of the sentenced offenders were either African American or Hispanic."[5]

These trends have continued in the twenty-first century.[6] Furthermore, these racial disparities cannot be explained as the result, for instance, of the illicit drug habits of African Americans and Latinos. Rather, law enforcement strategies associated with the war on drugs have targeted street-level drug dealers and predominantly poor and minority neighborhoods.[7] Even though an estimated two-thirds of crack users are white or Latino, the vast majority of those convicted of crack-related crimes — 85 percent — are African American.[8] These inequities are further exacerbated by highly disparate sentencing policies: the possession of and intent to distribute *five hundred* grams of powder cocaine carries a five-year sentence, while the possession of and intent to distribute only *five* grams of crack cocaine carries the same five-year mandatory sentence — on the first offense.

One of the consequences, nationally, is that an estimated 13 percent of all African American men have lost the right to vote as a result of state-level felon disenfranchisement laws.[9] While a national average of 13 percent is already significant, patterns of residential settlement and racial segregation result in considerably higher concentrations of disenfranchised individuals in certain states, cities, and neighborhoods. Florida leads the nation in the number of people permanently disenfranchised due to past felony convictions: 1.1 million people, or approximately 10 percent of the adult population. In fourteen states, one in ten African Americans is disenfranchised due to state law, and in five of these states, over 20 percent of the African American population cannot vote due to prior felony convictions.[10] In the state of Georgia, one out of eight African American men has lost the right to vote due to felony convictions (one-third of which are drug offenses), and in Atlanta, the number creeps up to one in seven.[11]

Citizenship and voting are also a distant dream for many legal immigrants. Officially, legal immigrants may become citizens, or naturalize, five years after being legally admitted to the United States, thereby gaining the right to vote. However, in practice, immigrants wait much longer to naturalize due to a combination of personal, bureaucratic, and financial reasons. For example, the cost of the naturalization application has increased significantly over the years: in 1990, the application fee was $90, but in the twenty-first century, this fee has climbed to $595. The most recent increase, which went into effect in July 2007, represented an 80 percent hike over the prior fee and places naturalization financially out of reach for many working immigrant families.[12] Processing backlogs have also prevented many legal permanent residents from naturalizing in a timely manner. Not only is the U.S. Bureau of Citizenship and Immigration Services receiving record numbers of naturalization applications, but documentation and background check requirements put into place after September 11, 2001, have increased application processing times from seven months to eighteen months.[13] As a result of these delays, immigrants generally take more than five years to naturalize. And while they wait, they are not able to vote. Immigrants from Africa, Asia, and Europe naturalize most quickly, after six to seven years. But legal immigrants from North America (Canada and Mexico) take twelve years, on average, to naturalize.[14]

According to the 2000 U.S. Census, approximately 77 percent of the foreign-born residents in the United States (22 million of 28.4 million) self-identify as people of color (black, Hispanic, or Asian/Pacific Islander), and just over 50 percent (14.5 million) of all foreign-born residents are not yet U.S. citizens.[15] These figures, combined with the numbers of disenfranchised African Americans and Latinos, add up to a significant proportion of people of color in the United States without a formal voice in the political process.

FELON DISENFRANCHISEMENT: HISTORY AND CONTEMPORARY CONTEXT

Contemporary felon disenfranchisement in the United States has roots in the concept of "civil death," which was first developed and practiced in medieval Europe: persons convicted of certain crimes would be stripped of their civil rights, such as the right to inheritance, the right to vote, and so forth.[16] During the nineteenth century, various state constitutions and laws continued this practice and disqualified persons convicted of certain crimes from voting: eleven states enacted such laws prior to 1821 and eighteen more states between 1821 and 1868.[17] However, the vast majority of contemporary state felon disenfranchisement laws have their roots in the post–Civil War Reconstruction era, a period in which African Americans were nominally guaranteed personhood, citizenship, and the right to vote by the Fourteenth and Fifteenth Amendments to the U.S. Constitution. Despite the overarching civil rights emphasis of the amendments, state legislatures took advantage of a clause in the Fourteenth Amendment that permits states to deny the vote to those guilty of "participation in rebellion, or other crime" (section 2). Only 35 percent of states disqualified felons from voting in 1850, but by 2002, 98 percent of states (with Vermont and Maine the only exceptions) had broad-based felon disenfranchisement laws on the books.[18]

Various analyses have demonstrated the overtly racist justifications for the passage of state-level criminal disenfranchisement laws in the post–Civil War era.[19] For example, John B. Knox, the president of Alabama's constitutional convention in 1901, urged the attendees to pass felon disenfranchisement laws to "'establish white supremacy in this State' to any degree permissible under the United States Constitution."[20]

While overtly racist laws became less socially and politically acceptable throughout the twentieth century, laws that were at face value racially neutral but had similarly discriminatory outcomes became more prevalent. Mirroring this trend, two Supreme Court cases have set the tone for contemporary legal challenges to felon disenfranchisement laws.[21] First, in *Richardson v. Ramirez* (1974), the Court overturned a California State Supreme Court decision holding that the state's felon disenfranchisement laws were racially discriminatory and therefore unconstitutional under the Equal Protection Clause of the Fourteenth Amendment. Justice William Rehnquist delivered the opinion of the Court and upheld California's felon disenfranchisement law based on a narrow textual interpretation of the "rebellion, or other crime" section of the Fourteenth Amendment. In contrast, in *Hunter v. Underwood* (1985), the Court held that state felon disenfranchisement laws (in this case, Alabama's) that were racially biased—in other words, that targeted specific crimes so as to intentionally disenfranchise the state's African American community—were unconstitutional. However, courts have been generally unwilling to rely upon this precedent to overturn other state disenfranchisement laws, leaving *Richardson* as a formidable barrier to enfranchisement efforts via the courts.

In the wake of the *Richardson* decision, the bulk of reform efforts have turned to state legislatures. Due to the concerted activism and advocacy of groups such as the Sentencing Project (Washington, D.C.) and the Brennan Center for Justice (New York City), efforts to overturn felon disenfranchisement laws have gained steam. Since the mid-1990s, eleven states have scaled back or eliminated their felon disenfranchisement laws.[22] Currently, only two states permanently disenfranchise *all* people with felony convictions, eight states permanently disenfranchise people with *certain* felony convictions, twenty states reinstate voting rights upon full completion of the sentence (including parole and probation), five states permit former felons to vote after they have completed parole, fourteen states allow those on probation or parole to vote, and two states permit those with felony convictions — even those currently serving sentences — to vote.[23]

It's important to note that these victories have relied heavily both on a well-trained and dedicated legislative staff and on the concerted activism and organizing of grassroots and community groups. As Darryl McMiller details, the successful campaign to restore voting rights to former felons in Connecticut took seven years of effort by state representative Kenneth P. Green.[24] During the final two years of the campaign, organizing efforts were made by more than forty groups under the umbrella of the Connecticut Voting Rights Restoration Coalition, including civil rights and faith-based organizations, social service agencies, and democracy reform groups (such as Common Cause). Prior to the legislation, approximately fifty thousand people were disqualified from voting while serving sentences, on parole, and on probation. As a result of the legislation, thirty-six thousand of them — those on probation — became eligible to vote.[25]

While the bulk of reform activity is taking place at the state level, members of Congress have also proposed laws that would prevent state-level felon disenfranchisement laws nationwide. In October 2008, Senator Russ Feingold (D-Wis.) and Representative John Conyers (D-Mich.) proposed the Democracy Restoration Act, which would restore voting rights in federal elections to all those released from prison, including those on probation and parole, as well as notify people of their right to vote upon their release from prison.[26]

IMMIGRANT DISENFRANCHISEMENT: HISTORY AND CONTEMPORARY CONTEXT

Though not widely known, throughout much of the nineteenth century, noncitizens had the right to vote in local, state, and national elections in forty states and federal territories across the union.[27] "Alien suffrage" was the result of various dynamics, offered particularly as an inducement for the immigrant settlers moving across a nation deep in the throes of "manifest destiny" and rapid westward expansion. Though not the case in the earliest years of the practice, as noncitizen voting became more commonplace in the mid-nineteenth century, states increasingly required that immigrants signing up to vote also declare their intention to become citizens of the United States, also known as a "declarant alien qualification."[28] Since women citizens could not vote until the ratification of the Nineteenth Amendment to the Constitution in 1920, the nineteenth and early twentieth centuries marked a time when not all citizens of the United States could vote, yet in many states, male noncitizens *could* vote.

Due to a number of factors that varied state by state, including the advent of universal male citizen suffrage (de jure, if not de facto), women's suffrage, the rising xenophobia associated with the "first great wave" of immigration between 1880 and 1920—during which tens of millions of migrants arrived in the United States, predominantly from Europe—and World War I, the practice of alien suffrage slowly disappeared in states across the nation. Georgia was the first state to abolish the practice (1877), and Arkansas was the last (1926).[29] Crucially, however, noncitizen voting has never been declared unconstitutional. Rather, because voting is controlled by states, states have the right to reinstate the practice at any time should they choose to do so.

The changing immigrant landscape of the United States over the past several decades has brought back discussions of immigrant voting. Racially restrictive and national-origin-focused immigration laws passed in the 1920s significantly restricted the numbers of migrants admitted to the United States each year, leading to an all-time low in the number of noncitizens living in the United States by 1950: 1.4 percent. With numbers so low and no foreseeable end to this trend, data on noncitizen status were not even collected during the 1960 Census.[30] However, reflecting the imperatives of the civil rights era and the Cold War, the Hart-Celler Act of 1965 dramatically shifted the nation's immigration policies, and the number of foreign-born residents in the United States has climbed steadily ever since. Currently, the number of foreign-born residents is at a high level—28.4 million—though relative to the entire United States, this still only represents 10.4 percent of the total population, which is less than the historical high of 13–15 percent reached between 1860 and 1920.[31]

Given the growing numbers of resident noncitizens in the United States and the long waiting periods for naturalization, some immigrant rights groups have started advocating to reinstate noncitizen voting. In contrast to the felon voting rights movement, which centers its activism at the state level, the immigrant voting rights movement has been most focused on cities across the nation. Six cities in Maryland have allowed noncitizens to vote in local elections for a decade or more.[32] A number of cities in Massachusetts have passed immigrant voting rights bills—Cambridge, Amherst, Newton, and Somerville, among them—but they await approval of the state legislature, which hasn't yet been forthcoming. Noncitizen parents of school-age children, legal and undocumented migrants alike, were permitted to vote and run for leadership positions in New York City school board elections from 1969 to 2003, when school boards were dissolved by Mayor Bloomberg. And in Chicago, noncitizens — again, both legal and undocumented residents — are still permitted to vote in school board elections.[33] Efforts to restore noncitizen voting continue in a number of cities, including New York City; Hartford, Connecticut; San Francisco; and Boston; and various states, including Minnesota, North Carolina, Texas, Wisconsin, and Maine.[34] Measures to pass noncitizen voting were only narrowly defeated in San Francisco in 2004 and in Boston in 2008.[35] And the struggle continues.

CONCLUSION

Given the myriad ways in which the nation's electoral system is corrupted by special interests, outdated and antidemocratic institutions such as the electoral college, and so forth, gaining the right to vote does not, of course, mean that social justice has been attained. There are many citizens who are *legally* entitled to vote who are disenfranchised by various means. Take, for example, the notorious purging of state voter rolls by Katherine Harris, the Florida secretary of state, prior to the 2000 presidential election. Or the shortage of voting machines in predominantly African American voting precincts in Ohio during the 2004 elections. Or states such as Arizona that have passed laws requiring voters to present certain forms of identification, which have mainly had the effect of disenfranchising poor, homeless, elderly, and Native American voters who do not have ready access to those acceptable forms of identification. However, despite the de facto limitations of suffrage, simply attaining the right to vote still holds highly symbolic and meaningful value for thousands who do not currently hold that right, as evidenced by the increasing energy of the immigrant and felon voting rights movements.

Generally speaking, despite common grounds and aspirations, the felon and immigrant voting rights movements have labored independently, although there have been occasional efforts by parties in each camp to combine energies.[36] Those fighting against felon disenfranchisement tend to focus their arguments on the fact that *citizens* are being denied the right to vote, and are hesitant to hitch their wagons to a movement arguing that noncitizens should have the right to vote. Those in the immigrant voting rights movement focus more broadly on the importance of the expansion of democracy to all long-term residents, regardless of citizenship status, and some within that movement are hesitant to combine forces with former and current felons, as they fear that people will then associate migrant status with criminal status. Additionally, as mainly grassroots movements, often operating independently in cities and states across the United States, both are limited in terms of resources, financial and otherwise. The movements are bound together in spirit, however, by the reality that disenfranchisement excludes a significant number of people of color from having a formal voice in politics across the United States, as well as by an enduring commitment to social justice.

NOTES

1. Manza and Uggen, *Locked Out*, 77.
2. Rytina, "Estimates of the Legal Permanent Resident Population and Population Eligible to Naturalize in 2004."
3. Passel and Cohn, "Unauthorized Immigrant Population: National and State Trends, 2010."
4. Manza and Uggen, *Locked Out*, 96.
5. Fellner and Mauer, *Losing the Vote*, 11.
6. Chen, "The Liberation Hypothesis and Racial and Ethnic Disparities."
7. Fellner and Mauer, *Losing the Vote*.
8. See Sentencing Project, "Crack Cocaine Sentencing Policy." See also Provine, *Unequal under Law*.
9. Mauer, "Mass Imprisonment and the Disappearing Voters," 51.
10. Manza and Uggen, *Locked Out*, 78–79.
11. King and Mauer, *The Vanishing Black Electorate*, 3.
12. Bergeron and Banks, "Behind the Nationalization Backlog."
13. Ibid.
14. Lee and Rytina, "Naturalization in the United States."
15. Schmidley, "Profile of the Foreign-Born Population in the United States."
16. Ewald, "Civil Death," 1060; Schepperle, "Facing Facts in Legal Interpretation."
17. See Ewald, "Civil Death," 1063–64. See also Keyssar, *The Right to Vote*, table A.15.
18. Behrens et al., "Ballot Manipulation and the 'Menace of Negro Domination.'"
19. Ibid.; see also King, "Jim Crow Is Alive and Well in the 21st Century."
20. King, "Jim Crow Is Alive and Well in the 21st Century," 9–13.
21. Ibid.
22. Ibid.
23. Permanent disenfranchisement of all with felony convictions: Kentucky and Virginia. Permanent disenfranchisement of some with felony convictions: Alabama, Arizona, Delaware, Florida, Mississippi, Nevada, Tennessee, Wyoming. Voting rights restored upon completion of full sentence: Alaska, Arkansas, Georgia, Idaho, Iowa, Kansas, Louisiana, Maryland, Minnesota, Missouri, Nebraska, New Jersey, New Mexico, North

Carolina, Oklahoma, South Carolina, Texas, Washington, West Virginia, Wisconsin. Voting rights for those on probation: California, Colorado, Connecticut, New York, South Dakota. Voting rights for those on probation and parole: District of Columbia, Hawaii, Illinois, Indiana, Massachusetts, Michigan, Montana, New Hampshire, North Dakota, Ohio, Oregon, Pennsylvania, Rhode Island, Utah. No disenfranchisement: Maine, Vermont. See Wood, *Restoring the Right to Vote*.

24. McMiller, "The Campaign to Restore the Voting Rights of People."
25. Ibid., 646.
26. Brennan Center, "Democracy Restoration Act Fact Sheet."
27. Hayduk, *Democracy for All*, 15. See also Raskin, "Legal Aliens, Local Citizens."
28. Neuman, *Strangers to the Constitution*.
29. Keyssar, *The Right to Vote*, 138, 168–69.
30. Varsanyi, "Stretching the Boundaries of Citizenship in the City," 50.
31. Schmidley, "Profile of the Foreign-Born Population in the United States," 8.
32. Harper-Ho, "Noncitizen Voting Rights."
33. Hayduk, *Democracy for All*, chapter 5.
34. Immigrant Voting Project, www.immigrantvoting.org.
35. Ron Hayduk, personal communication with author, June 18, 2009.
36. Ibid.

BIBLIOGRAPHY

Behrens, Angela, Christopher Uggen, and Jeff Manza. "Ballot Manipulation and the 'Menace of Negro Domination': Racial Threat and Felon Disenfranchisement in the United States, 1850–2002." *American Journal of Sociology* 109, no. 3 (2003): 559–605.

Bergeron, Claire, and Jeremy Banks. "Behind the Naturalization Backlog: Causes, Context, and Concerns." *Migration Policy Institute*. Last updated February 2008. http://www.migrationpolicy.org/pubs/FS21_NaturalizationBacklog_022608.pdf.

Brennan Center. "Democracy Restoration Act Fact Sheet." Last updated 2009. http://www.brennancenter.org/content/resource/democracy_restoration_act_of_2008.

Chen, Elsa Y. "The Liberation Hypothesis and Racial and Ethnic Disparities in the Application of California's Three Strikes Law." *Journal of Ethnicity in Criminal Justice* 6, no. 2 (2008): 83–102.

Ewald, Alec C. "'Civil Death': The Ideological Paradox of Criminal Disenfranchisement Law in the United States." *Wisconsin Law Review* 5 (2002): 1045–1137.

Fellner, Jamie, and Marc Mauer. *Losing the Vote: The Impact of Felony Disenfranchisement Laws in the United States*. Washington, D.C.: Human Rights Watch and the Sentencing Project, 1998.

Harper-Ho, V. "Noncitizen Voting Rights: The History, the Law and Current Prospects for Change." *Law and Inequality Journal* 18 (2000): 271–322.

Hayduk, Ron. *Democracy for All: Restoring Immigrant Voting Rights in the United States*. New York: Routledge, 2006.
Hunter v. Underwood. 471 U.S. 222 (1985); 105 S.Ct. 1916.
Keyssar, Alexander. *The Right to Vote: The Contested History of Democracy in the United States*. New York: Basic, 2000.
King, Ryan S. "Jim Crow Is Alive and Well in the 21st Century: Felony Disenfranchisement and the Continuing Struggle to Silence the African-American Voice." *Souls* 8, no. 2 (2006): 7–21.
King, Ryan S., and Marc Mauer. *The Vanishing Black Electorate: Felony Disenfranchisement in Atlanta, Georgia*. Washington, D.C.: Sentencing Project, 2004.
Lee, James, and Nancy Rytina. "Naturalization in the United States: 2008." Office of Immigration Statistics, Department of Homeland Security, 2008. http://www.dhs.gov/xlibrary/assets/statistics/publications/natz_fr_2008.pdf.
Manza, Jeff, and Christopher Uggen. *Locked Out: Felon Disenfranchisement and American Democracy*. New York: Oxford University Press, 2008.
Mauer, Marc. "Mass Imprisonment and the Disappearing Voters." In *Invisible Punishment: The Collateral Consequences of Mass Imprisonment*, edited by Marc Mauer and Meda Chesney-Lind, 50–58. New York: New Press, 2002.
Mauer, Marc, and Tushar Kansal. *Barred for Life: Voting Rights Restoration in Permanent Disenfranchisement States*. Washington, D.C.: Sentencing Project, 2005.
McMiller, Darryl L. "The Campaign to Restore the Voting Rights of People Convicted of a Felony and Sentenced to Probation in Connecticut." *American Behavioral Scientist* 51, no. 5 (2008): 645–58.
Neuman, Gerald. *Strangers to the Constitution: Immigrants, Borders, and Fundamental Law*. Princeton, N.J.: Princeton University Press, 1996.
Passel, Jeffrey, and D'Vera Cohn. "Unauthorized Immigrant Population: National and State Trends, 2010." Pew Research Center, 2011. http://www.pewhispanic.org/2011/02/01/unauthorized-immigrant-population-brnational-and-state-trends-2010.
Provine, Doris Marie. *Unequal under Law: Race in the War on Drugs*. Chicago: University of Chicago Press, 2007.
Raskin, Jamin B. "Legal Aliens, Local Citizens: The Historical, Constitutional, and Theoretical Meanings of Alien Suffrage." *University of Pennsylvania Law Review* 141 (1993): 1391–1470.
Richardson v. Ramirez. 418 U.S. 24 (1974); 94 S.Ct. 2655.
Rytina, N. "Estimates of the Legal Permanent Resident Population and Population Eligible to Naturalize in 2004." Office of Immigration Statistics, Department of Homeland Security, 2004. http://www.dhs.gov/xlibrary/assets/statistics/publications/LPRest2004.pdf.
Schepperle, Kim Lane. "Facing Facts in Legal Interpretation." *Representations* 30 (1990): 42–77.

Schmidley, A. Dianne. "Profile of the Foreign-Born Population in the United States: 2000." U.S. Census Bureau, Current Population Reports, 2002. http://www.census.gov/prod/2002pubs/p23-206.pdf.

Sentencing Project. "Crack Cocaine Sentencing Policy: Unjustified and Unreasonable." [n.d.]. http://www.sentencingproject.org/Admin/Documents/publications/dp_cc_sentencingpolicy.pdf.

Varsanyi, Monica W. "Stretching the Boundaries of Citizenship in the City: Undocumented Migrants and Political Mobilization in Los Angeles." Ph.D. diss., UCLA, 2004.

Wood, Erika. *Restoring the Right to Vote*. New York: Brennan Center for Justice, 2009.

¡La Policía, la Migra, la Misma Porquería!

Popular Resistance to State Violence

MARIANA VITURRO

Millions of immigrants, documented and undocumented, rose up fearlessly to confront the state and demand justice and equality on International Workers Day in 2006. They were successful in stopping federal bills that proposed to further criminalize immigrant communities. They inspired students to walk out of schools in support of their communities, and inspired workers to put down their hammers and brooms and pick up picket signs with handwritten slogans like "Legalización Ahora" (Legalization Now) and "Alto a las Redadas" (Stop the Raids).

The character of the mobilization quickly changed. One week immigrants were confronting the state to demand equal rights, and the next they were appealing to the state to be recognized as "good" Americans. One week the sky was filled with mostly Mexican and Central American flags, and the next they had been replaced by a sea of red, white, and blue. I wrote this chapter to help understand the mass spontaneous dissent, the response on the part of the state, and different forces in the immigrant rights movement. Our goal is to bring clarity to our work in building resistance to state violence and advancing the movement for justice in San Francisco and beyond.

After the 2006 mobilizations, the state deliberately increased internal migration enforcement activities, intensified border security, and developed new methods to crack down on undocumented workers. Rural towns were some of the worst hit; ICE would temporarily occupy and then hold towns under siege, creating virtual war zones. One of the largest immigration raids in the country occurred in Postville, Iowa, where ICE deported over three hundred workers from a meatpacking plant and displaced an entire community. Afterward, the town's population was half of what it once was.¹ Nor were urban areas spared. In the San Francisco Bay area, on May 2, 2008, just one day after the annual immigrant rights May Day marches, ICE conducted concurrent raids at eleven restaurants in the Taqueria El Balazo chain, detaining over sixty workers in six cities.²

The response on the part of immigrant rights organizations has varied based on their vision, analysis, and strategy. The more mainstream national organizations, which sought to capture and harness the rallying masses, were set on reaching a compromise immigration reform bill at any expense. The more militant and radical groups attempted to radicalize the national immigration debate and build resistance to state violence. Hundreds of organizations sprang to life across the country to respond to state repression in their communities. They were somewhat successful on a local level in building community resistance to ICE and the Border Patrol and organizing for reforms to challenge the increased criminalization, but for the most part they were unable to influence the national debate.

The immigrant rights mobilizations and what came out of them are very telling. They expose the role of the state in the repression and co-optation of immigrant dissent. They reveal the contradictions within the immigrant rights movement and migrant communities. They bring to light opportunities to advance an agenda against state violence and for economic and racial justice.

THE STATE: A REPRESSIVE AND IDEOLOGICAL FORCE

I find useful Lenin's definition of the state — a coercive force that secures the interests of the ruling class — and Antonio Gramsci's conception of the role of civil society and the ways the state and civil society together create, maintain, and reinforce hegemonic notions of criminality.³ In defining and redefining what constitutes a criminal, criminal activity, and safety, the state gains both legitimacy and active support for its repression from the majority in the interest of a dominant minority. The state is able to exert dominance not only by coercion but also by making its laws and definitions of criminality seem commonsensical.

Current immigration policy fits within the U.S. legacy of extreme violence and racism. From the theft of tens of millions of Africans from their homeland for slave labor to the ban of Chinese immigrants in the 1880s once their work in the mines and railways was no longer needed, the state has controlled the movement of workers to advance explicitly racialized economic and political interests.

Since the 1970s, the United States has aggressively imposed neoliberal economic policies in order to facilitate the accumulation and movement of capital and to resolve its and the elite classes' fiscal difficulties.[4] Neoliberalism includes the liberalization of trade, privatization of public assets, deregulation of the market, and fiscal austerity. The impact has been devastating in the third world and to a lesser extent in working-class communities of color within the United States. Wages and employment dropped while the cost of living rose. National industries closed their doors when they couldn't compete with transnational companies. Debt deepened. Critical services like education, housing, health care, and infrastructure were cut. People were dispossessed from their lands and livelihoods and were moved to provide a source of cheap and exploitable labor.

With the overall deterioration in living conditions for the overwhelming majority, the few who benefit increasingly rely on aggression and violence. There has been an immense increase in capacity and resources allocated to military, police, and paramilitary groups to secure U.S. hegemony. The use of force globally is also mimicked within the United States as the state increases the construction of prisons and detention centers, adopts criminalization and antiterrorist laws, and expands law enforcement entities and capacity.

Since 9/11, repression and militarization have intensified for migrant communities. Latino and Muslim, Arab and South Asian communities have been particularly subject to anti-immigrant rhetoric and targeting, with the former used to maintain a cheap and exploitable labor force, and the latter as justification for the "war on terror" and U.S. imperial projects in the Middle East. In San Francisco in October 2008, numerous Latino families with children suffered an ambush when ICE agents carrying shotguns threw gas bombs into their homes and then proceeded to break all their windows and kick down doors as part of Operation Community Shield. One of our clients, Rosa, was threatened with eviction because of the damage caused by ICE, and her grandchildren suffered from nightmares and were unable to sleep because of the traumatic incident.

In conjunction with such repression, the state has carried out an ideological project to legitimize and build consent for its use of force against migrant communities. The state and its enforcement agencies are not alone in upholding the U.S. imperial project. The racialized notions of criminality give legitimacy to the use of force and also create a culture of racist fear and repression. Thanks to its ideological project, the state is accompanied by the society at large regardless of whether there is explicit consent. As Gramsci writes in the *Prison Notebooks*, "The 'normal' exercise of hegemony on the now classical terrain of the parliamentary regime is characterized by the combination of force and consent, which balance each other reciprocally, without force predominating excessively over consent. Indeed, the attempt is always made to ensure that force will appear to be based on the consent of the majority, expressed by the so-called organs of public opinion — newspapers and associations — which, therefore, in certain situations, are artificially multiplied" (248). Community institutions, organizations, and spaces outside of the state apparatus, referred to as civil society, play a role in reinforcing and reproducing the dominant ideology and repression.

During the height of the 2006 street mobilizations and congressional negotiations, the main rhetoric in the mainstream media equated migrants to criminals, terrorists, and leeches of the country's resources, which rightfully belong to "hard-working Americans." There was specific messaging targeted toward the white population, and to a lesser extent to other Americans, to rally their support for the xenophobic hate speech and nationalist project. We regularly heard that there was a Mexican invasion to pillage "our" resources and riches without contributing to society, without paying taxes, and that English was threatened as the "official" language of the United States.

White supremacist groups outside of the state apparatus took up arms to defend this white settler nation. For example, the Minuteman Project, a nationalistic white supremacist organization, took advantage of the anti-immigrant sentiment coming out of the government and carried out recruitment drives, organized anti-immigrant actions in more progressive and "sanctuary" localities throughout the country, and expanded its vigilante projects: minutemen have been known to shoot people crossing the border.

Most important, analyzing civil society and its role in reproducing hegemony clarifies the contradictions within the immigrant rights movement. This analysis helps explain why some immigrant communities have supported the economic interests and racist ideology of the state and the ruling minority. The immigrant rights movement and immigrant communities are not immune to these ideologies. And at the end of the day, they do give legitimacy to the state project of reproducing hegemony. During the many immigrant rights marches, the main slogans and rhetoric heard from the stage or written on picket signs included "We Are Not Terrorists," "We Are Not Criminals," "We Are Not a Public Burden," and "This Is a Country of Immigrants."

Instead of uniting against the unjust disappearances and detentions of Arab, Muslim, and South Asian immigrants in the war on terror, or the police brutality and incarceration of African Americans, Latinos differentiated themselves from these communities and upheld the state's definition of "good" and "bad" migrant or citizen. Instead of uniting with the African American community for economic and racial justice, Latino immigrants highlighted their work ethic and rejection of social welfare, which they more commonly refer to as handouts or a public burden.

These messages and their underlying ideology appeal to the state and the white nation at the expense of other communities of color and their struggles for racial justice and against state violence. This approach not only deepens divisions between communities of color, but also deliberately removes racism and white supremacy from the immigrant rights debate and fight. These messages also intensify the divisions within the Latino community itself, such as between documented and undocumented migrants or between those who have lived in this country for many years and those who are more recent newcomers.

The assimilationist and whitewashed slogans are more than mere rhetoric. They reflect a strategy to appeal to the state and to appease racist anti-immigrant sentiments in order to push forward a reformist immigration policy agenda. As the national organizations continue to lobby, compromise, and wait for immigration reform from Washington, popular dissent has been harnessed and directed toward an agenda that does not place economic and racial justice at the center. The 2006 tactics had a mass character, but were for the most part nonconfrontational, did not disobey the state, and were not part of a long-term liberatory vision.

As exemplified by the mass mobilizations, civil society is not homogeneous or static, and it contains the potential to challenge hegemony. Immigrants took to the streets to challenge the state in solidarity with all other migrants regardless of their status and with class consciousness as workers. They spoke out against the unjust repression imposed on their communities. They created a newly contested terrain with an opportunity for building power and a movement against racism and state violence.

COMMUNITY RESISTANCE AND POWER

Given the role that Latino migrants can and do play in the resurgence of the immigrant rights movement and as a workforce in the economy, they have the potential to be a radicalizing political force in challenging state violence and racism. It is critical that the movement not resort to reforms and strategies that reinforce state repression and white nationalism and instead fight for an agenda inclusive of worker rights, civil rights, and racial and social justice. The immigrant rights movement should continue to demand full legalization and just immigration reform, but do so without obstructing the radical potential of the migrant working class. It must also respond to the increased repression and militarization of our communities and build strategic alliances with other communities confronting state violence and racism to further the struggle for equality and justice.

Given the main contradictions of the state—the need for a hyper-exploitable labor force contradicts the desire to preserve a white nation—the immigrant rights movement should place antiracism and worker exploitation at the center of the debates on migration. Alliances should be built with the African American community in its struggle against economic dispossession and the prison-industrial complex; with the Arab, Muslim, and South Asian communities against increased repression from ICE; and with workers, employed and unemployed, for just solutions to the economic crisis.

In responding to state repression, the main tasks for the immigrant rights movement are twofold: to confront the state and its repressive laws and to push for policy reforms that alleviate some of the conditions for migrants and open more space for resistance. A central component of this strategy is to build community resistance. Immigrant communities do not need to wait for the state to defend our rights, but can follow the example of the civil rights or Black power movements, disobey the state, and build the community's capacity to defend itself against state violence. At St. Peter's Housing Committee, we can support community members' sentiments of solidarity with our know-your-rights workshops, and we can support them when they purposefully disobey state orders and do not identify their status nor open the door for ICE agents. While we arm the community with their rights, we should also deepen the community's analysis of the role of the state, the root causes of migration, and white supremacy to build a consciously counterhegemonic political force to challenge state violence.

Campaigns for policy reforms provide an opportunity to positively impact the lives and conditions of migrant communities. They also expose the contradictions of the state and its repressive apparatus, and provide opportunities for building strategic alliances with other movements. For example, St. Peter's Housing Committee's campaign for a city ID in San Francisco won government-issued photo identification for all residents regardless of immigration status. Through this campaign, an alliance was built between the immigrant and transgender communities as they were both denied identification documents. The campaign ultimately reframed the concept of citizenship and political rights to be based on the municipality where people live and work.

Similarly, our efforts to reform and strengthen the San Francisco sanctuary ordinance have the potential to build an alliance between the immigrant rights movement and the movements against racial profiling, police brutality, and the prison-industrial complex. The sanctuary ordinance is primarily violated through the collaboration of ICE and the San Francisco Police Department. Regardless of whether an undocumented migrant is charged or convicted, the person will be handed over to ICE authorities and, in almost all cases, deported. The demands in our efforts to strengthen the sanctuary ordinance cannot reinforce the hegemonic notions of criminality and instead should expose the state's racism and classism in its definitions of criminality and criminal activity.

CONCLUSION

In order for the immigrant rights movement to win true immigration reform, we should ensure that our demands and tactics remain consistent with our analysis. This is particularly important given the current crisis in the economy and its impact on working-class communities of color.

With the economic crisis and massive debt facing most states and localities, working-class communities of color and migrants in particular are denied basic services as the states slash their public spending. Unemployment and underemployment will continue to rise, divisions between poor communities will deepen, and anti-immigrant sentiments and attacks will increase unless key grassroots forces seek to build alliances and advance a united antiracist agenda that will benefit all working-class people and people of color. This means that immigrant rights cannot be divorced from worker rights, especially when we consider the migrant labor force in the agriculture, food production, and service industries.

While we continue to organize and put pressure on President Obama to ensure just immigration reform, the immigrant rights movement should also expose the repressive and racist state and society. The Obama administration has expanded immigration enforcement in the prisons and militarized security on the border. In fiscal year 2006, the year of the historic immigrant rights marches, the budget for Customs and Border Protection was $7.1 billion and ICE's budget was $3.9 billion. For fiscal year 2013, Obama has requested $12 billion for Customs and Border Protection and $5.6 billion for ICE.[5] The immigrant rights movement should continue to build resistance to this repression and demand an end to detentions and deportations and a reallocation of government spending toward education, health care, housing, employment, and other services as part of the demands for legalization.

This economic and political moment calls us to build a racial and economic justice movement that is grounded in the grassroots, that has a sharp analysis, that is broad enough to mobilize working-class sectors, and that is bold in its demands. The immigrant rights movement has the opportunity to be a conscious political force that can build solidarity with communities of color and the working class and advance the movement for true justice.

NOTES

1. Olivo, "Immigration Raid Leaves Damaging Mark on Postville, Iowa"; Hsu, "Immigration Raid Jars a Small Town."
2. Knight, "Immigration Raids at 11 El Balazo Restaurants."
3. Gramsci, *Selections from the Prison Notebooks*; Lenin, *The State and Revolution*.
4. Harvey, *A Brief History of Neoliberalism*.
5. Gorman and Nicholas, "Obama Budget Puts Security First at the Border"; http://www.dhs.gov/xlibrary/assets/Budget_BIB-FY2007.pdf (20); http://www.dhs.gov/xlibrary/assets/mgmt/dhs-budget-in-brief-fy2013.pdf (34).

BIBLIOGRAPHY

Gorman, Anna, and Peter Nicholas. "Obama Budget Puts Security First at the Border." *Los Angeles Times*, May 6, 2009.
Gramsci, Antonio. *Selections from the Prison Notebooks*. New York: International, 1971.
Harvey, David. *A Brief History of Neoliberalism*. New York: Oxford University Press, 2005.
Hsu, Spenser S. "Immigration Raid Jars a Small Town: Critics Say Employers Should Be Targeted." *Washington Post*, May 18, 2008.
Knight, Heather. "Immigration Raids at 11 El Balazo Restaurants — 63 Seized." *San Francisco Chronicle*, May 3, 2008.
Lenin, Vladimir. *The State and Revolution*. Kila, Mont.: Kessinger, 2004.
Olivo, Antonio. "Immigration Raid Leaves Damaging Mark on Postville, Iowa." *Los Angeles Times*, May 12, 2009.

Part VI

Ending Border Wars
Building Abolitionist Futures

The work of building and maintaining borders and prison walls is also about creating and policing social difference. This part focuses on how prison and migration regimes are gendered, racialized, sexualized, and classed institutions that reproduce and police dominant relations of power. Put another way, state policing practices are bordering practices that violently enforce heteronormativity and hierarchies of race, gender, and class. Finally, this section shows how prisons enact violence within the prison walls and transmit harms to already vulnerable communities.

If societies can be militarized, they can also be demilitarized. The intersectional analyses and organizing strategies found in this part do the hard work of demilitarizing the understandings of violence that shore up categorical oppression. These include gender binaries, nationalist enemy-friend relations, and the ideology of domestic policing as maintaining the peace rather than exercising (often socially sanctioned) state violence. Such understandings obscure the violence of everyday hunger, degradation, and oppression and code them as normal and natural, rather than as the unacceptable consequences of cumulative domination and power.

These contributors centrally discuss the importance of challenging the ways in which our social movements often reproduce lines of social and civil exclusion and abandonment. As the authors compellingly show, trading away the rights of the least powerful for the "good of the majority" effectively does the work of the state (and capital and empire), but only has the potential of being a temporary and partial reprieve for the most privileged. Such tactics should be seen as creating pyrrhic victories that simply rely on racism, sexism, and heteropatriarchy to legitimate state policing. Once policing is normalized for one group, it doesn't stop at the border of that group, but normalizes the use of the tool, making it available for the expanded policing of other people and practices. Thus, this part offers important intersectional analyses and concrete examples of how organizing can challenge interlocking forms of violence simultaneously. This involves the long-term work of building relationships and shared understandings, and building vehicles for organizing and mobilizing power. It also means that the vision of another possible world can be put to work in building that world.

Mapping Black Bodies for Disease
Prisons, Migration, and the Politics of HIV/AIDS

RASHAD SHABAZZ

> Prisons, although more hidden from public view, are yet another arena where the AIDS epidemic is being allowed to spread because the authorities don't give a fig about human life when it comes to gays, [people of color], and the poor.
> — DAVID GILBERT, *No Surrender*

Few could have predicted the role prisons would play in the expansion of HIV/AIDS. The rapid explosion of prisons in the 1970s and 1980s, which relocated tens of thousands of poor urban Blacks to rural landscapes, crossed paths with a growing "secret epidemic" that was devastating "gay spaces" in cities like San Francisco, New York, and Los Angeles.[1] This collision resulted in a rapid growth of the disease among the most marginalized elements of Black life. The anti-Black, antipoor, and antigay policies of the Reagan administration were stirred together in a cauldron of silence and conservative policymaking. This political climate enabled the growth of the disease among not only gay men, but marginalized Blacks as well. Bedrock Black political institutions — institutions that historically have been the first and only opposition to Black suffering — allied with the conservative opposition to funding HIV/AIDS prevention, research, and treatment, reinforcing the political tone and silence of the Reagan Republicans.

Silence and conservative policymaking provided fertile political space for the disease to grow. One of the places the disease began to swell was inside America's prisons. Though HIV/AIDS is spread through sex and sharing needles, prison policies have actively encouraged transmission by banning condoms, denying access to clean needles, providing substandard health care, denying mandatory testing, and providing little if any AIDS education. Perhaps the most devastating element of this matrix is the impact it has had on Black communities. As men "come home" from prison, and most do, they are in many cases unaware of their HIV status. Returning home presents a double-edged sword. Leaving prison is a welcome day for prisoners and their loved ones. Yet it also means the possibility of moving the disease from prison to the communities from which they came, and where they can unknowingly pass the disease to others. This has had significant implications for Black women's health. Of the over one million women who are infected in the United States, half are Black. Black women are the fastest growing group to test positive, they have the highest rate of infection, they get treated the least, and they subsequently die from the disease at higher rates than whites.[2]

Blending the research of prisoners, geographers, epidemiologists, and political scientists, this chapter maps the spatial, migratory, and political interconnections between Black bodies, prisons, and the rise of HIV/AIDS. I argue that the rise of HIV/AIDS among Blacks has been significantly influenced by three factors: the warehousing of Black men in prison; the subsequent migration of these men back to their communities; and a conservative political calculus unable and unwilling to grapple with this danger. This chapter also seeks to clarify the ways in which the practice of incarceration produces and reproduces migration. In the post-9/11 world, Americans and the global community have become increasingly aware of the exercise of U.S. power through carceral punishment. Yet, paradoxically, one of the unique abilities of the prison-industrial complex is to make borders — social, epidemiological, geopolitical — *porous*. Therefore, in demonstrating the vulnerability Blacks have to HIV/AIDS, I conclude by arguing that de-incarceration is the most effective strategy to combat the AIDS crisis in Black America.

Comprehending the prison's function of internal forced migration provides us with a new conceptual lens to think through the roles prisons play in the United States. The tragedy of Hurricane Katrina, which produced what one scholar called the "biggest resettlement in American history," reminds us that internal migration is an ever-present reality in the United States.[3]

BLACK POLITICS OF HIV/AIDS

Black political organizations like the church, the NAACP, and the Urban League played a contradictory role in the rise of HIV/AIDS in Black communities. In effect, their silence undermined their ability to actively engage the epidemic. And they were not alone. Ronald Reagan's conservative politics set in motion

HIV/AIDS policies that exacerbated the problem. His administration's disavowal of the disease and those affected by it summarily offered a death sentence to thousands living with HIV/AIDS. Reagan cut funding to nonprofits that were educating the public about the disease, and he dismissed research by the CDC, which discovered the relative ease with which the disease could spread. Because HIV/AIDS was associated with gay men (it was known as the "gay cancer"), Reagan could not even bring himself to talk about AIDS. His only public statement about HIV/AIDS was a racist lamentation that Haitians were bringing the disease into the country, reasoning that continues to inform immigration restrictions against Haitians and HIV-positive individuals.[4] (The formal ban on admitting HIV-positive people to the United States was only lifted in January 2010.)

Reagan's reactionary politics were in lockstep with the conservative wings of the Black political mainstream. Their unwillingness to engage HIV/AIDS worked to create a context where Black people with the disease had little institutional assistance to curb its disastrous effects. Much of this stemmed from the framing of AIDS as a non-Black issue, which placed AIDS politics on the margins of Black political life. The response to HIV/AIDS by Black political institutions illuminates the complex ways oppression affects Blacks. Even more, it illustrates how the most marginal elements of Black communities are left out in the cold in favor of conservative politics and illusory "consensus" issues.[5]

"To discuss AIDS in Black communities," argues political scientist Cathy Cohen in *The Boundaries of Blackness*, "is to discuss a multiplicity of identities, definitions of membership, locations of power, and strategies of the political, social and economic survival of the community" (8). HIV/AIDS has affected the most marginal members of Black communities: gays and lesbians, women, the poor, and prisoners. According to Cohen, mainstream Black politics has been reluctant to rally around these groups for two reasons. First, conservative Black organizations are hostile to what they consider "cross-cutting" issues, meaning issues like HIV/AIDS, that cut across or "stand in contrast to consensus issues which are understood to constrain or oppress with equal probability all identifiable marginal group members" (13). (Things like housing and affirmative action come to mind.) Furthermore, cross-cutting issues are often situated among the "subpopulations of marginal communities." Not coincidentally, the vulnerability of these subpopulations is often linked to "questionable" morality, such as identifying with non-normative sexualities or drug use (14).

The second reason that the Black political establishment is reluctant to rally around marginal segments of Black communities, according to Cohen, is because a cross-cutting issue like HIV/AIDS "threatens a perceived unified

Black group identity" (16). Because issues like HIV/AIDS affect the subgroups of marginal communities, they cast a light on the fact that Blacks are not a monolithic group and that reductive politics excludes segments of Black life. One reason unification has and continues to be important in Black politics is because it simplifies the political landscape by connecting Black identity with education, health care, employment, police brutality, and discrimination. In George Lipsitz's generative formulation, this political formation is based on identities rather than a "political project aimed at creating identities based on politics."[6]

Sex also troubles the Black political establishment's ability to grapple with HIV/AIDS. It is no secret that the association of HIV/AIDS with gay men or with men who have sex with men seriously delimits the ability of Black political organizations like the church to engage with AIDS. While Black Americans are by no means the only people to express homophobia, the antigay rhetoric that can often be heard from the pulpit illuminates the ways the church is complicit in fostering sentiments that marginalize AIDS within Black America. Part of the reason that Black organizations like the church have taken a vow of silence on AIDS (other than so-called biblical reasons), Cohen argues, is because some Black communities see non-normative sexuality as "mitigating" racial subjectivity.[7] One must choose whether to elevate racial *or* sexual identity because current formulations of Black identity do not allow for Blackness to exist outside of heteronormativity (14).

These forces greatly limit the scope and possibility of what is considered important for Black political mobilization and who should have the privilege of drawing on the resources of Black churches, the NAACP, and the Urban League. While there is no one way to characterize these institutions' responses to HIV/AIDS, when the epidemic first emerged the response was "mixed, limited, and often reluctant," to say the least. In cases where programs were created, they were designed to "fit within a constrained moral and political framework, where anything from a lack of expertise on this issue to the word of God were offered as reasons for doing less," argues Cohen (256). This political framework has also made being Black and living with HIV/AIDS extremely difficult. Homophobia, hostility, and paternalism place Black people living with AIDS within what Cohen calls an advanced form of marginalization (63). In many cases, advanced marginalization works to ostracize and alienate these Black people from mainstream Black communities. For some, being silent about their HIV status or their sexuality is the route of least resistance.[8]

The politics around HIV/AIDS is also deeply racialized. Despite Reagan's silence, by the 1990s gay white activists had convinced elected officials — particularly the Arkansas governor, Bill Clinton, who was running for president — that action had to be taken to combat the disease. And in the early 1990s, popular culture helped to change minds about HIV/AIDS. The nation was swept up in the life of AIDS activist Pedro Zamora, a roommate on MTV's reality show *The Real World*. Zamora's charisma, character, and struggle to survive helped to push the debate on HIV/AIDS away from the disavowal of the 1980s. Moreover, the death of Ryan White (an Indiana teenager who contracted HIV via blood transfusion whose death spawned the Ryan White Foundation, which was backed by the late Michael Jackson) helped to set the stage for a new direction on HIV/AIDS. Against the backdrop of Zamora and White, elected officials, particularly then-governor Bill Clinton, put political capital and money behind efforts to stamp out the growth of HIV/AIDS. Overnight, there was a change in how HIV/AIDS was addressed: public service announcements championing condom use were broadcast, money for research and development emerged, and there was an overall commitment by the government to save the lives of those dying.

But race was an underlying element that shaped the changing attitudes of HIV/AIDS. Black AIDS activist Phil Wilson contends that the whiteness and maleness of AIDS infection, death, and activism encouraged political elites — who are largely white and male — to deploy resources to save white lives. Yet, as HIV/AIDS became a Black disease in the early 2000s, a new silence around the disease emerged. Because whites were no longer the signifier of the disease, it was no longer a problem that warranted attention, political resources, and compassion. As quickly as funds had emerged to combat HIV/AIDS, they began to dry up; the condom public service announcements disappeared; and popular culture moved away from the topic. The Black bodies now carrying the disease did not warrant the same compassion and concern that white bodies had just a decade earlier.

PRISONS AND THE EMERGENCE OF HIV/AIDS

From its earliest appearance in the United States, HIV/AIDS and prison have been linked. One significant explanation of this link is that in the 1980s HIV/AIDS emerged against the backdrop of massive prison expansion, which stretched from coast to coast. The rapidly growing AIDS epidemic and the expansion of prisons formed an alliance that worked to silently spread the disease among prisoners, many of whom were Black.

California's prison expansion was termed by one elected official as the "biggest . . . in the history of the world."[9] This statement is not hyperbole.

California, Illinois, New York, Florida, Arizona, Georgia, and Texas dumped billions of dollars into what Mumia Abu-Jamal called one of America's largest economic growth industries.[10] Rural landscapes across the country were prisonized through the rapid building of new facilities. With the evacuation of industrial, agricultural, and resource extraction jobs, prisons became the new industry, an industry built on the backs of poor people and people of color.[11]

The expansion of the prison-industrial complex was made possible in part by a continued disinvestment in urban communities, which occurred in tandem with Black migration from the U.S. South between World Wars I and II and the emergence of the hyper-ghetto in the years after the Second World War. Even in the years following the civil rights movement, Blacks in urban centers had few prospects for employment or decent education. Under these conditions the underground drug economy emerged as the most viable option for decent pay. The Reagan and Bush administrations' cruel and unwarranted war on drugs, which focused its attention on street-level dealers and not suburban consumers, effectively created a war zone in many urban communities and placed hundreds of thousands behind bars.[12]

Elected officials ran campaigns on the promise of being the toughest on crime, and this rhetoric dominated both the conservative and liberal factions of the political establishment. They promised their mostly white, middle-class, and suburban constituents that they would curb the imagined insatiable criminal appetites of poor people of color through military incursion and mass warehousing. This throw-them-away logic has left individuals and entire communities on the brink of destruction.[13] President Bill Clinton bowed to the pressure of law and order and placed another million police officers on the street. This resulted in a ballooning of the numbers of people arrested, but never reduced crime.[14]

As the prison population burst at the seams in the early 1980s, prisoners, activists, family members, and some scholars raised concerns about overcrowding, increasing violence, and substandard medical care in prisons. It was under these conditions that AIDS entered prisons, which were mostly populated by Black men. By the early 1990s, thousands of prisoners had already died from it and many more were infected.[15] The disease, which had been discursively mapped onto the spaces of gay white men, was now affecting a space in which Black men moved. Against the backdrop of substandard health care and neglect, prison administrations fomented the growth of HIV/AIDS among prisoners. This not only mortgaged the futures of an entire generation of poor people of color, it also gave rise to a series of closed and isolated spaces where HIV/AIDS festered.

PRISON POLICY AND THE WHIRLPOOL OF RISK

Prisoners were the first ones to realize the threat HIV/AIDS posed to their health, and they were organizing to combat the growing threat before outside researchers began talking about it. For example, in the 1980s, women at the Bedford Hills Correctional Facility in New York established the first ever prison-based HIV/AIDS organizing platform.[16] In his collection of writings from prison, former Weather Underground member and political prisoner David Gilbert created a proposal for a peer prison education project. His insightful analysis illustrates the ways in which prisons are a "whirlpool of risk" for HIV/AIDS infection:

> While drugs and sex are officially prohibited, these activities are not uncommon. The conditions of prison mean that those who use hard-to-come-by needles are likely to share them widely and without much access to proper sterilization. Sexual activity is likely to occur without proper safeguards and often with multiple partners. These realities indicate that the ongoing spread of the deadly disease is a very grave problem. . . . Furthermore, in the closely packed and nonvoluntary prison community, the rise of the disease is likely to cause increasing fear, panic and violence.[17]

With seroprevalence (the number of people in a population who test positive) steadily rising, HIV/AIDS is turning prison into a "potential death sentence."[18] Consider this: as the inmate society has matured and the prison-industrial complex has expanded, the rates of infection for Black Americans have grown significantly. This secret epidemic which first took root in the early 1980s found a foothold in prisons.[19] Part of the reason it found fertile ground in prisons is because the policies and spatial order encourage transmission. Most federal and state prisons do not have mandatory testing, they have inadequate medical facilities, condoms are not allowed, and neither are clean needles or cleaning agents like bleach. Moreover, thousands of men are forced to live in hyper-confined and hyper-aggressive spaces where sanitation is often compromised. Under these conditions HIV/AIDS was able to embed itself in this population and grow exponentially. Gilbert's analysis underscores how important condoms and clean needles are in the fight against HIV/AIDS, but most prisons in the United States ban both. By doing so, the state is actively taking a let-them-die approach.

Prison officials argue that prisoners having condoms means that they are having sex, and they do not want to admit what is obviously true. For example, the Tennessee Department of Corrections fended off advocates and doctors who argued prisoners should have access to condoms by citing the exorbitant cost of medications to treat HIV/AIDS patients and the significant number of men with HIV/AIDS in prison. The Tennessee DOC rebuffed advocates' claims, arguing that providing prisoners with condoms would "send the wrong message." The department's reasoning attempted to derail providing condoms because, it argued, this would legitimize sex among prisoners. However, the administration's silence on sex among prisoners and the growing rates of HIV/AIDS have done already what the DOC claimed providing condoms would do.[20]

In contrast, Vermont has distributed condoms to prisoners (in some prisons, they even distribute lubrication). The deputy superintendent for one of Vermont's prisons argues, "[G]ood public health policy is good correctional policy."[21] Further, AIDS researchers Braithwaite and colleagues state that "in systems with condom availability, there have been few if any problems with condoms being used as weapons for smuggling contraband, despite suggestions by opponents that this would occur" (85). Providing condoms to prisoners does not encourage sex among prisoners; rather, it protects prisoners against disease, which has implications that stretch beyond prison walls.

Clean needles are also important in stopping the transmission of HIV/AIDS. Currently, no prisons in the United States provide prisoners with clean needles. However, clean needles in prison are not unheard of; according to Braithwaite and colleagues, one prison in Switzerland started a needle exchange program in the late 1990s (86). The fact that needle exchange programs are rare outside prison walls makes it incredibly difficult to get these programs started inside prisons. Prison officials do not allow even the use of bleach to clean dirty needles, another method proven to significantly reduce rates of infection between those that share needles.[22]

The U.S. Supreme Court ruled in 1976 that prisoners have a constitutional right to adequate health care while incarcerated, arguing, "Deliberate indifference to serious medical needs in prisons constitutes the unnecessary and wanton infliction of pain." But states have been unwilling to follow the Court's decision.[23] In many cases, the reason is financial. The prison administration does not want to incur the costs of treatment (antiretroviral), and often uses excuses (it's too costly, prisons are places where people should be punished, and providing health care defeats the point of punishment) to deny paying for treatment. Ineffective care on the part of the prison medical staff further complicates matters. By the mid-1990s, prison administrations' intractable position on medical coverage had fostered the deaths of over five thousand prisoners due to HIV/AIDS–related illnesses.²⁴

The lack of education on HIV/AIDS in prison also significantly impacts the ability to combat the disease. States continue to delay implementing HIV/AIDS education programs while a wealth of research indicates that the disease has killed and will kill thousands of people in prison. Only a few states (California, New York, and Vermont) have programs in place to educate prisoners about the disease. In 2005, the Chicago AIDS Foundation issued a call to action, demanding that the state provide funds to educate, test, and provide resources to prisoners about HIV/AIDS. In 2007, Representative Barbara Lee and Mayor Ron Dellums, both of Oakland, put forth legislation to have local jails provide education, counseling, and testing to prisoners.²⁵ But these are exceptions; low levels of investment — time and money — in AIDS education are the norm.

This negligence has prompted those inside to create programs to address their specific needs. For example, in April 1987, with the assistance of activists Kuwasi Balagoon, Mujahid Farid, and Angel Nieves, David Gilbert helped to write one of the first prisoner education programs on HIV/AIDS. The project was prompted by numerous prisoner deaths from AIDS-related illness, including that of Kuwasi Balagoon. Balagoon was a long-time freedom fighter and Gilbert's co-defendant. The program was ahead of its time in understanding the impact of HIV/AIDS on prisoners and on the larger communities from which prisoners come.

The Prisoner Education Project on AIDS began in 1987 at Auburn Correctional Facility in Auburn, New York. It was prompted by the deaths of 124 prisoners from HIV/AIDS in 1986.²⁶ The program stressed the importance of peer counseling for those struggling with the disease; peer education on HIV/AIDS, sex, and drug use; and the creation of a counseling program to provide mental and emotional support for infected prisoners.

In spite of obstacles, the Prisoner Education Project had some success. But while the prison administrators agreed the program was important, they refused to see the importance of prisoners running it. Two outside AIDS professionals who worked on the project agreed with the prison administration that prisoners were not capable of organizing the program, and suggested that professionals should run it instead. By denying prisoners the ability to run the program, the administration and the professionals removed the most important element: peers. According to Gilbert, "The peer aspect is doubly important in prison, where inmates tend to distrust the authorities and are unlikely to discuss proscribed activities with staff."

HIV/AIDS AND THE POLITICS OF COMING HOME

The impact of HIV/AIDS in prisons has implications that stretch beyond prison walls. The overwhelming majority of people released will "come home," will return to their communities. And when they return, they bring back any diseases they have contracted. In this way, prison walls stretch into the community.

The consequences this has had for Black communities are devastating. Black people constitute the majority of state and federal prisoners. Each year over seven hundred thousand people are released from state and federal prisons, and the vast majority leave prison with no idea of their HIV status. And those who do know their status will be sent back to their communities with almost no financial, emotional, or institutional support.[27] With no mandatory testing of prisoners, no condoms, no clean needles or bleach to clean needles, little peer education, and inadequate care for those who know their status, prisons create a whirlpool of risk for the wider Black community. In many cases, this lack of support enables a context where those released may continue drug use or have unprotected sex with partners, despite being HIV-positive.

Indeed, the growing rate of seroprevalence among Black Americans since the 1990s is strongly linked to mass incarceration. As HIV/AIDS has moved from being a white gay male disease to becoming a disease of poor Blacks, it has grown in the spaces where hundreds of thousands of Black Americans live — prisons and Black communities. Oakland, Chicago, New York, Baltimore, Los Angeles, Detroit, Atlanta, and Washington, D.C., all suffer from high incarceration rates and high seroprevalence among Black people.[28]

One way to get a clear sense of the risk that mass incarceration poses to the health of Black communities is to look at the skyrocketing rates of Black women who are HIV-positive. While men constitute the majority of people in prison with HIV/AIDS, Black women outside prison are the fastest growing population of people infected.[29] Because most women are infected via heterosexual contact, some researchers think that men become infected while in prison and unknowingly spread the virus to their female partners after they are released. Jim Thomas, an AIDS researcher who has studied sexually transmitted diseases in prisons in North Carolina, discovered that counties where incarceration rates were the highest had high rates of sexually transmitted diseases, including HIV.[30]

Thomas's research implicitly reveals the importance of space as a "dynamic actor" in the expansion of HIV in Black communities.[31] Feminist geographer

Susan Craddock writes that disease plays a "critical role in the production of places as lived, seen (built), and cognitively mapped" (8). In other words, the expansion of HIV/AIDS in prisons makes the disease part of prisons' punitive practices. Prisons are closed, tightly guarded archipelagos, physically cut off from society. But isolation and restricted spatial confines also have enabled prisons to become conveyor belts where the disease migrates into Black living spaces via Black bodies (9). The forced migration of Black bodies into this space that is mapped and built for disease traps them in prisons' whirlpool of risk.

Carceral punishment is no longer simply about isolation and containment. Prisons are not only places to send those who break the law; they are also sites where disease grows. Indeed, the circulation of Black bodies through carceral institutions—institutions that refuse to acknowledge how prison spaces and prison policies predispose prisoners to sexually transmitted disease—places them and the communities to which they return into a widening whirlpool of risk.

CONCLUSION

Unpacking the spatial, migratory, and political forces that have helped to create Black America's AIDS crisis reveals the complex ways these realities impact Black health. It also reveals the need to rethink the United States' overreliance on prisons as a way to address social problems. Conservative conventional thought might suggest that not going to prison at all or, even worse, longer stays in prison, and better sexual responsibility might stifle the spread of HIV/AIDS among Black communities. However, these answers normalize prison punishment; they do not address the ways in which Black bodies are marked as criminal nor the profound economic realities that land many Blacks in prison. Furthermore, they make conservative ideas of sexual responsibility the arbiter of ending the surge of HIV/AIDS. Sex is not what produces HIV/AIDS; rather, poverty, instability, and exclusion are the culprits.

Testing, condoms, bleach, and clean needles are necessary and can reduce the spread of the disease among prisoners and save lives. Yet we must not lose sight of the fact that warehousing people is bound to give rise to other diseases that affect prisoner health and subsequently that of their communities. As long as Black bodies continue to be the raw material in the production of the prison industry, their migration from urban ghetto to rural prison and back again will continue to map Black bodies for disease. What we need, therefore, is not incarceration that is more "humane" but, ultimately, de-incarceration. We must oppose incarceration and place more emphasis on addressing the social forces that produce the race to incarcerate.

De-incarceration pushes against Black criminalization, against Black forced migration to rural prisons. Indeed, de-incarceration does what condoms, clean needles, cleaning agents, and education programs cannot; it works to unhinge Black folks from the deadly disease by severing the ties that bind them to the social forces that enable HIV/AIDS.

NOTES

1. Levenson, *The Secret Epidemic*.
2. "The Age of AIDS"; "Out of Control."
3. Grier, "The Great Katrina Migration."
4. "The Age of AIDS."
5. Cohen, *The Boundaries of Blackness*.
6. Lipsitz, *The Possessive Investment in Whiteness*, 67.
7. Cohen, *The Boundaries of Blackness*, 18.
8. On silence, alienation, and AIDS, see *Tongues Untied*; Johnson and Henderson, *Black Queer Studies*; Roberts and White, *If We Have to Take Tomorrow*; Bailey, "The Labor of Diaspora"; "Out of Control."
9. Quoted in Gilmore, *Golden Gulag*, 5.
10. Abu-Jamal, Live from Death Row.
11. James, *The New Abolitionists*; Gilmore, *Golden Gulag*; Davis, *Are Prisons Obsolete?*; Rose, *Black Noise*; Marable, *How Capitalism Underdeveloped Black America*.
12. Parenti, *Lockdown America*.
13. Abu-Jamal, "Actin' like Life's a Ball Game," in his *Live from Death Row*.
14. Parenti, *Lockdown America*; Gilmore, *Golden Gulag*.
15. Braithwaite et al., "Inmates, HIV, and AIDS," in their *Prisons and AIDS*.
16. This organizing platform educated prisoners about how HIV is spread, what it is, and how it causes AIDS. See ACE, *Breaking the Walls of Silence*.
17. Gilbert, *No Surrender*, 123; see also Sabo et al., *Prison Masculinities*, 173.
18. Rowe, "Death Row."
19. Levenson, *The Secret Epidemic*.
20. Demsky, "Tennessee: Condoms No Way to Fight HIV in Prison."
21. Quoted in Braithwaite et al., *Prisons and AIDS*, 85.
22. See Braithwaite et al., *Prisons and AIDS*; Gilbert, *No Surrender*.
23. Anne-Marie Cusac, "The Judge Gave Me Ten Years. He Didn't Sentence Me to Death," in Herivel and Wright, *Prison Nation*, 195.

24. Braithwaite et al., *Prisons and AIDS*, 5.

25. AIDS Foundation of Chicago, "A Call to Action"; Gokhman, "Lawmakers' Bill Would Boost AIDS Education in Jails."

26. I was unable to determine if the Prisoner Education Project on AIDS is still in existence. No information is given in Gilbert's book, which was published in 2004, and there is no online presence for the project.

27. AIDS Foundation of Chicago, "A Call to Action."

28. According to the Centers for Disease Control, in 2007 Black people made up roughly half (46 percent) of people living with HIV/AIDS, which amounted to over 230,000 people. See Centers for Disease Control, "AIDS among African Americans."

29. According to the CDC, Black women are twenty-three times more likely to be diagnosed with HIV than white women. See CDC, "AIDS among African Americans."

30. See "Out of Control."

31. Craddock, *City of Plagues*, 8.

BIBLIOGRAPHY

Abu-Jamal, Mumia. *Live from Death Row*. Reading, Mass.: Addison-Wesley, 1995.
ACE [AIDS Counseling and Education]. *Breaking the Walls of Silence: AIDS and Women in a New York State Maximum-Security Prison*. Woodstock, N.Y.: Overlook, 1998.
"The Age of AIDS." *Frontline* episode directed by William Cran. Chicago: WGBH, PBS, 2006.
AIDS Foundation of Chicago. "A Call to Action: Addressing the Intersection of HIV/AIDS and Prison." Chicago: AIDS Foundation of Chicago, 2005. http://www.aidschicago.org/pdf/advocacy/2005_policy_priorities.pdf.
Bailey, Marlon. "The Labor of Diaspora." PhD diss., University of California, Berkeley, 2005.
Braithwaite, Ronald L., Theodore M. Hammett, and Robert M. Mayberry. *Prisons and AIDS*. San Francisco: Jossey-Bass, 1996.
Centers for Disease Control and Prevention, Division of AIDS. "AIDS among African Americans." 2008. http://www.cdc.gov/hiv/topics/aa/index.htm.
Cohen, Cathy. *The Boundaries of Blackness*. Chicago: University of Chicago Press, 1999.
Craddock, Susan. *City of Plagues*. Minneapolis: University of Minnesota Press, 2000.
Davis, Angela Y. *Are Prisons Obsolete?* New York: Seven Stories, 2003.
Demsky, Ian. "Tennessee: Condoms No Way to Fight HIV in Prison, Officials Say." July 1, 2005. http://www.thebody.com/content/art25264.html.
Gilbert, David. *No Surrender*. Montreal: Abraham Gillen Press, 2004.
Gilmore, Ruth Wilson. *Golden Gulag: Prisons, Surplus, Crisis, and Opposition in Globalizing California*. Berkeley: University of California Press, 2007.
Gokhman, Roman. "Bill Would Boost AIDS Education." *Oakland Tribune*, March 13, 2007.

Grier, Peter. "The Great Katrina Migration." *Christian Science Monitor*, September 12, 2005. http://www.csmonitor.com/2005/0912/p01s01-ussc.html.
Herivel, Tara, and Paul Wright, eds. *Prison Nation*. New York: Routledge, 2003.
James, Joy, ed. *The New Abolitionists*. Albany: State University of New York Press, 2005.
Johnson, Patrick, and Mae Henderson, eds. *Black Queer Studies: A Critical Anthology*. Durham, N.C.: Duke University Press, 2005.
Levenson, Jacob. *The Secret Epidemic*. New York: Pantheon, 2004.
Lipsitz, George. *The Possessive Investment in Whiteness*. Philadelphia: Temple University Press, 2006.
Marable, Manning. *How Capitalism Underdeveloped Black America*. Boston: South End, 1983.
"Out of Control: AIDS in Black America." ABC News, August 24, 2006.
Parenti, Christian. *Lockdown America : Police and Prisons in the Age of Crisis*. New York: Verso, 2000.
Roberts, Frank Leon, and Marvin K. White, eds. *If We Have to Take Tomorrow: HIV, Black Men and Same Sex Desire*. Los Angeles: AIDS Project Los Angeles, 2006.
Rose, Tricia. *Black Noise*. Middletown, Conn.: Wesleyan University Press, 1994.
Rowe, Harmeen. "Death Row: AIDS Is Turning a Prison Term into a Potential Death Sentence." *California Lawyer* 7, no. 9 (1987): 49–51.
Sabo, Don, Terry A. Kupers, and Willie London, eds. *Prison Masculinities*. Philadelphia: Temple University Press, 2001.
Tongues Untied: Black Men Loving Black Men. Directed by Marlon T. Riggs. San Francisco: Frameline, 2007.

The War on Drugs Is a War on Relationships

Crossing the Borders of Fear, Silence, and HIV Vulnerability in the Prison-Created Diaspora

LAURA MCTIGHE

> Sometimes even the stories we ourselves tell dissolve before us as if a mist were momentarily lifting, and we glimpse in that instant our own participation in the myths and constructions of our societies.
> — LEILA AHMED, *A Border Passage*

The rain was coming down in sheets across Philadelphia. As we sat waiting for the Frances Myers Recreation Center doors to open, all of us were getting a bit worried. Teresa, Waheedah, Ben, and Eddie had been covering the surrounding blocks for weeks — reaching out to halfway houses, parole offices, barber shops, laundromats, welfare offices, corner stores, bus stops, and service organizations to find individuals struggling under the fear and silence of perpetual dislocation. Their message was simple: Do you have a loved one in prison? Did you just come home? Do you need support? *This is a day for you.*

This was the third in a series of neighborhood speak-outs organized by the Support Center for Prison Advocacy (SCPA), a citywide criminal justice network committed to building a resource and organizing center without walls. As the clock struck 10 a.m., over a hundred community leaders and families with loved ones in prison had assembled in the main room. And the group was serious about getting to work. Through discussions on expanding mentoring and support networks, navigating the ins and outs of prison systems, dealing with the hurdles of having families separated by prison walls, and gaining access to everything from jobs to housing, West Philly residents made plans not only for addressing the immediate needs of loved ones who were the casualties of the "war on drugs," but also for stepping up community advocacy efforts to challenge the policies of forced migration through mass imprisonment.

We all left Frances Myers Recreation Center that day knowing that our community restoration work was just beginning. A partnership of Philadelphia FIGHT and Kingdom Care Reentry Network, the SCPA was launched in 2008 as a deeply self-critical organizing project to interrogate the persistent borders of fear and silence in American society and to envision a methodical process by which the freedom that currently/formerly imprisoned communities have fought to retain in their minds might also be lived in their bodies and their lifeworlds.[1] We realized that this organizing vision meant connecting with the people who had slowly and stubbornly been trying to keep their neighborhoods thriving; providing space to talk through the pains that there were often not ears to hear; developing plans for neighborhood-directed community restoration; and establishing neighborhood resource teams to implement these plans and provide support to residents in crisis.

It was a tall order. But these were goals that Teresa, Waheedah, Ben, Eddie, and so many others whose lives had been punctuated by periods behind the walls, whose lives had been forever changed by being diagnosed with HIV, had dedicated themselves to. We needed to embrace uncertainty — not knowing what *would* happen next. But we also needed to embrace possibility — wondering what *could* happen next if we came together, dealt with the things in front of us, and pushed forward day after day.

THE LONG ROAD TO COMMUNITY ORGANIZING

HIV and imprisonment are connected — in the lives of the one in four people with HIV who pass through correctional facilities every year and in the very fabric of our communities.[2] I learned that lesson from Teresa, Waheedah, Ben, Eddie, and so many others with whom I have worked in struggle in Philadelphia. Each of their days had been marked by a continual process of wrestling with the structural forces marginalizing their lives and the messages of shame they heard from within and outside their communities; coping in the midst of these challenges; their attempts to find their voices amid the fear and silence; and their work to support other people living with HIV. While there is a tremendous amount of pain in their stories, there is also humor, vigor, and brazen creativity.

Teresa has pulled herself through a lot in her nearly forty-eight years — from her own diagnosis with HIV in 1997, to the loss of her sister to the virus, to her relentless care for her only son in the midst of her struggles with addiction. But there was little that could have prepared her for the day when her boyfriend cut his own hand and called the cops, claiming she had attacked him. It was weeks before Teresa's son was able to track down someone to visit her in a Philadelphia jail, but that visitor, John Bell, changed her life. First, he believed her when she said she was innocent. And second, he had connections with TEACH Outside, a community organizing class where she met other people with HIV. Three years later, Teresa founded her own group, which she named Reaching Out: A Support Group with Action. This group has become the driving force behind the SCPA's neighborhood outreach work.

In 2003, Waheedah's life changed forever when she was diagnosed with HIV in a room in a Philadelphia county jail with no curtains. She was crying and everyone was walking by. She told me many times that she felt like killing herself. This is still where Waheedah's head was most days when Bell and I first met her. She has an undeniable spark, but it often felt to us like she was acting, just hoping things would be okay. If you did not know her, you might have thought that things were fine. She had one of the best parole officers in Philly, her health was good, and she still had her family's support. Not long after her release, Waheedah fell into our emerging community, and started doing activist work to change the health care in the Philadelphia jails. She found hope in this struggle for justice, and she found her voice beyond the threads of HIV and imprisonment that had once entwined her. That struggle has taken her far and wide, working alongside other HIV-positive women nationally and internationally, but it is in Philadelphia, in prison organizing work, that this fifty-five-year-old community elder still finds her home.

Ben is the young'un of the group at forty-four, but he was diagnosed with HIV a decade prior to Waheedah, in 1993, in a similar curtainless room in a Philadelphia jail. That was a very different time in Philadelphia AIDS work. There was no John Bell to visit Ben in jail, and there was no TEACH Outside to provide a community of support. So the next fourteen years were a blur — in and out of jail, in and out of programs. When in 2007 Ben met Bell behind the walls, he wanted to make sure that that arrest would be his last. Working his way up the Philadelphia housing ladder, he got his first apartment on his forty-second birthday. Soon after, he met Teresa, whose Reaching Out group was just getting off the ground. Today, there is a lot that keeps him pushing on in the SCPA's neighborhood work, but it is mostly his knowledge of the many people who were there for him, the people who never gave up on him, and his hope that he might be able to do that for someone else.

Now forty-eight, Eddie can almost taste the day when he will finally be off parole. It is perhaps that more than anything else that led him to pick the probation and parole offices as his SCPA outreach spots. Home two years now after his parole officer sent him back to jail for not updating his address, the ground Eddie feels under his feet is in large part because of his family's support. Although he is the eldest sibling and a grandfather of three, that family support was hard for him to hold through the years of his addiction. But his daughter was stubborn, and made sure that when her dad came home in 2007 he landed in a vibrant self-help community in the northeast of the city and that he reconnected with the TEACH Outside activist team. With the other Reaching Out members and with his partner, Waheedah, self-help is his mantra and community uplift is his life's work. And, in a few short months, when his parole is finally up, he will be able to turn in his janitorial job for a position at that same self-help community that has been his refuge and jumping-off point.

By inviting people into their lives, Teresa, Waheedah, Ben, and Eddie are first and foremost asking to be seen. Their stories are often excluded from the public discourse, hidden in the broken neighborhoods they call home, hidden in the prison cells that kept each of them captive for stretches of time. And while much has been written about the poverty and imprisonment holding their communities in bondage, statistical attention to their social realities often serves to further obscure their voices, treating them as an undifferentiated group rather than as a dynamic community of individuals struggling to cope and thrive in a time of mass imprisonment. In the SCPA, these organizers ask people to resist these two silences, to step closer to them so as to understand their lives as fully and humanly as possible, with all their varied and often maddening complexities intact.

In sharing their personal stories, in reaching out to others in their communities, they have asked people to bring a different, fuller attention to the structural forces marginalizing their lives. Teresa, Waheedah, Ben, and Eddie are all acutely aware of the danger in discussing the particularity of their lives to the exclusion of the context in which they are living: the risk that *they* might become the focus of the change that needs to happen, instead of the injustices they and others are moving through daily. They are not asking for people to help them cope better with their social realities. Rather, they are asking people to join them in their respective balancing acts — to hold together their social realities and their personal experiences, the beautiful, the horrible, and the mundane. They want people to join them in challenging the structural forces marginalizing their lives, in healing the severed threads of communities in diaspora, and in supporting the people who are still pained by fear and silence.

IMPRISONING COMMUNITIES THROUGH THE WAR ON DRUGS

Under the auspices of the "war on drugs," legislators in the late 1970s and early 1980s began pushing imprisonment over treatment and crafting laws designed to restrict the rights of people once they are released from prison.[3] Currently more than one out of every hundred adults is confined in American jails and prisons; in this system of forced migration, the daily census exceeds 2.3 million.[4] The fivefold jump in prison population since 1980 is the direct result of increased policing, more zealous prosecution, and mandatory sentencing for drug-related crimes.[5] These policies have formed a multidimensional process of exclusion from participation in social activities, further institutionalizing the structures of racism and classism already woven into the fabric of U.S. society and history.[6] In 2009, more than 7 million people were in prison, on probation, or on parole.[7]

The hallmark of drug-related "reforms" has been mandatory minimum sentencing laws, including the 100–1 sentencing disparity for crack cocaine versus powder cocaine, which was enshrined in the 1986 Anti–Drug Abuse Act; this was reduced to a disparity of only 18–1 when Congress passed the Fair Sentencing Act in 2010. A further outgrowth of mandatory minimums has been three-strikes laws, mandating life in prison for a third felony conviction, without eligibility for parole until a considerable time into a person's sentence, generally twenty-five years. The effect: more people are serving longer sentences for mostly nonviolent crimes that could arguably be better addressed through drug treatment programs. About 80 percent of the people in U.S. prisons report histories of addiction, and only about 15 percent of them are receiving drug treatment.[8]

Teresa, Waheedah, Ben, and Eddie all tell people that the war on drugs has always affected poor people of color the most. While drug use is equal across racial lines, people of color are arrested, convicted, and sentenced at dramatically higher rates than white people.[9] With 35 percent of Black men between the ages of twenty-five and thirty-four currently imprisoned, on probation, or on parole,[10] it is hardly an overstatement to say that an entire generation is behind bars. The impact of these racial disparities on communities has been further intensified by the disproportionate toll that the war on drugs has taken on women. Since 1980, eight times as many women have been imprisoned (compared to the fourfold increase for men), most of them for petty drug crimes, theft, or self-defense against abuse. Seventy-five percent of these women are mothers; two-thirds have children under the age of eighteen. An estimated 1.5 million children have at least one parent in prison.[11]

Alarming as these statistics might be, they cannot provide a picture of the lived experience of communities that are rapidly losing their fathers and mothers, their caregivers and providers. Families are too often unable to make ends meet and thus find themselves on the move, shuffling from temporary home to temporary home, always trying to stay one step ahead of the piercing stigma of having a loved one in prison.[12] Nor do these statistics tell the stories of the loved ones who have been shipped to correctional facilities eight or more hours from their family homes, sometimes for disciplinary infractions or on the whims of wardens. What these statistics do give us, however, is an understanding of the magnitude of imprisonment in the United States. To express the enormity of the migration of prisoners, mirrored by migration in the communities left behind, I call this the "prison-created diaspora."

MAPPING HIV VULNERABILITY IN A TIME OF MASS IMPRISONMENT

Just as the war on drugs was gaining speed in the 1980s, the AIDS crisis broke. And while AIDS is still tracked by behaviors that can transmit HIV, research is starting to document what Teresa, Waheedah, Ben, and Eddie — people in communities hardest hit by the war on drugs — knew from the start of the epidemic: HIV vulnerability is driven by the structural forces that disrupt family and social networks; weaken emotional, financial, and political support systems; and make it more difficult for people to prioritize their long-term health over their daily survival.[13] Mandatory minimums, racial profiling, and other criminal justice policies are the mechanisms that imprison extraordinary numbers of people of color, fueling HIV vulnerability inside and outside of prison by endangering individuals' lives and their communities. The connection between these two crises is caused by and, in turn, creates a web of social, political, and economic disparities, showing that HIV is much more than just a virus.

The war on drugs has been a war on relationships, a war on people's parents, their spouses, their partners, and their caretakers. These are precisely the relationships that form the basis of strong and vibrant communities; these are the relationships people depend on for assistance and support in times of need. In the wake of a partner's imprisonment, a mother may suddenly be saddled with the impossible burden of making ends meet alone, trying to keep a roof over her children's heads and food in their bellies. Sex work may feel like her only viable source of income, and immediate needs like feeding her children and having a safe place to sleep are likely to take priority; long-term health consequences — like increasing her risk for HIV infection — might not even register in the midst of such pressing crises.[14]

As the war on drugs has progressed, more and more people have been put in the position of making such impossible decisions. And because of the racial bias that has infused the increased policing, prosecution, and sentencing since the 1980s, the health crises have most impacted communities of color, particularly Black communities. Thus, the new sentencing laws and post-imprisonment punishments ushered in by the war on drugs have become primary forces fueling the Black AIDS epidemic in the United States. A 2006 study by Rucker Johnson and Steven Raphael found that the connection among race, incarceration, and HIV is so strong that it almost completely explains the disproportionate impact of HIV on Black communities.[15]

BUILDING A RESOURCE CENTER WITHOUT WALLS

Both HIV and prison are lonely, painful realities. That is a truth I have learned from Teresa, Waheedah, Ben, Eddie, and so many others with whom I have worked over the years. Whether in prison or on the streets, they often had only two options: *give in and everyone sees me*, or *resist and no one sees me*. Before finding each other, all of them had huge emotional walls up, walls that were so impenetrable that they could not perceive the looks or comments or actions of those around them. Those walls had been built because of too many small abuses to count, and because of great and incomprehensible abuses. Their descriptions — of the thin veil of HIV secrecy that always threatened to fray in prison, of the lengths they had gone to get money for drugs, of the sex work that was sometimes their only companionship for months, of the people following behind them, bleaching toilets and showers after learning of their HIV diagnoses — only gestured at the years of accumulated pain that threatened to break them most days.

Through TEACH Outside and Reaching Out they have been able to walk with each other as they grapple with their most distressing moments. And in the midst of this participation in each other's lives, they have felt their despair begin to lift; they have seen hope break through. Perhaps this transition simply came when the direct pressure of their suffering relented a bit. Perhaps it came when they were able to help each other see the stubbornness and strength that persisted inside them even at their lowest points. Perhaps this transition will never be complete. But they are all certain that it is only in communion, and by pushing forward together, that they will have any chance of holding onto the power that now guides their lives.

Each of them came to the understanding that the SCPA was not just a next step, but was the only possible step forward. Each of them came into the others' lives as people living with HIV, through communities only open to people living with HIV. While those communities have been vital for enabling them to cross the borders of fear and silence to the lives they now lead, they also believe that no one should have to become HIV-positive to find that power. They know, as all of us who founded the SCPA know, that mass imprisonment has been a key structural driver of the domestic AIDS epidemic, taking root in precisely those same fears and silences that fuel the prison-created diaspora. We envision that building the power of those hardest hit by mass imprisonment might also be a way of reducing HIV vulnerability for entire Philadelphia neighborhoods. Together, we can be emergency support for one another, holding each other's pain. Together, we can make the plethora of reentry programs in Philadelphia work for those coming home and for their loved ones, so that the road is a little easier. And together, we can push for the policy changes needed to dismantle the walls and cages of mass imprisonment. We do not need to have all the answers. We only need to be willing to walk with one another to figure them out.

To walk with one another, we have to get close — beyond the fear, beyond the silence — and build trust in the neighborhoods bearing the brunt of the city's prison reentry crisis. So, in preparation for neighborhood speak-outs, Teresa, Waheedah, Ben, and Eddie, along with the member organizations of the SCPA, mapped the neighborhood block captains, civic groups, local agencies, faith leaders, drug treatment programs, mental health programs, nail salons, and laundromats. And then the street outreach began: "Hi! I'm Teresa with the Support Center for Prison Advocacy. We are trying to bring about a positive change for all people who are in prison now or ever have been in the past. And to do that, we need your help." We asked people to identify the issues they were seeing in their neighborhoods, the issues they were experiencing in their families, and those issues set the agenda for the Saturday morning neighborhood speak-outs.

At 10:30 a.m., the mic opened in the Frances Myers Recreation Center, and the speakers were a chorus from diverse zip codes, street addresses, and neighborhood affiliations.

> There was a young man from a local recovery house who had been home just two weeks. He had been passing in and out of jail since his early teens, as had his brothers. He not only wanted that cycle to stop for himself, but he also wanted support in figuring out how to get his family home and together again.

There was a mother who had been trying to get legal help for her son, who had already been away for three years on a false charge. She had been through too many legal offices where people tried to pressure her for sexual favors when she could not meet that month's fees, and was starting to feel like she would never see her son come home.

There was a man who had just been diagnosed with HIV while behind the walls, who was outraged that everyone kept talking to him about recovery from addiction. *But what about recovery from injustice?* He told the room that if he had found this kind of support the first time he came out of prison, he might not be HIV-positive today.

There was a man from the state representative's office who did time back in the day, but he had been home and thriving for years now. His message was that folks coming home do not need to be shuffled from agency to agency, having to bow their heads down and beg for services; they need jobs and a life with dignity.

There was a father whose undocumented son had been arrested two days prior to the speak-out. Their family was counting down the days until they received word of his deportation to Mexico. They were terrified that if they posted his bail they too might face the same penalty.

And there was a neighborhood leader who, after coming home, built up his own community resource center to be that place with dignity.

The room seemed to expand with each person who spoke, making space to hold the experiences of pain, the stories of struggle, and the visions for resilience and resistance.

Next came the breakout discussions hosted by staff from the core member organizations of the SCPA: one conversation focused on Philadelphia-based mentoring programs working behind the walls and in the community; a discussion led by a local attorney focused on the legal barriers to reentry; one session explored options for securing sustainable employment with a record; another was a time for families with children in prison to band together; a skills-sharing session discussed navigating the ins and outs of the prison systems to support loved ones; and another gathering highlighted housing programs in the city that had available beds open to people with records. In most cases, the breakout discussions only scratched the surface of the issues people were dealing with. But the point was not to fix everything on the spot. It could not be. The point, rather, was to ensure that West Philly folks had the names and phone numbers of people who would be there through the pain and in the triumphs, be those people working at SCPA organizations or those living in their own communities. And that message was echoed throughout the speak-out's closing: Stand up if you can offer a resource for those in the room. Stand up if you can be a source of comfort for your neighbors. Stand up if you will not rest until our city gets the healing and justice it needs.

The importance of this community-led resource center without walls was immediately apparent as the city's budget crisis mounted in 2009. Our first SCPA action brought this growing network of individuals and organizations to the mayor's community budget forums to highlight the impact of mass imprisonment on the city's budget crisis and to push for a scaling-up, rather than a scaling-down, of prison prevention services like mentoring, housing, treatment, and jobs. These same four demands guided the SCPA in advocacy efforts during Philadelphia's strategic planning process on reducing recidivism. The forceful advocacy of Teresa, Waheedah, Ben, and Eddie ensured not only that the concerns of those most impacted by imprisonment were heard during the city's three-day retreat, but also that people who had spent time behind the walls were present as key stakeholders. As this strategic planning process has continued, the SCPA organizing efforts continue to mobilize hundreds of city residents to speak the truth of their lives, demanding a refocusing of criminal justice priorities in Philadelphia.

ORGANIZING FOR COMMUNITY HEALING AND RESTORATION

My work with Teresa, Waheedah, Ben, Eddie, and all those who have come together in the SCPA's resource center without walls has demonstrated time and time again that in community and by fostering hope, the promise of a future beyond imprisonment can become real to people here and now. The process of community organizing holds the potential not only to dismantle the prison-created diaspora, but also to break the cages of fear and silence that permeate community experiences of injustice at the hands of the criminal justice and immigration systems. For it was in organizing with the SCPA that Teresa, Waheedah, Ben, and Eddie each found the capacity to make use of the power of rage, which both arises from their refusal to accept that they should become "productive members" of a society that tolerates their structural suffering and also motivates the societal transformation they envision. As individuals marked, but not bound, by the policies of mass imprisonment, their truths give voice to the potential for freedom and humanity in a hostile world, for their own communities and for those who have historically benefited from their subjugation.

The policies ushered in through the "war on drugs" have created a logic that focuses on problems, with resolutions only being possible ten, twenty, thirty years down the road. Countering this logic requires not only focusing on the solutions to the imprisonment crisis, but also demanding that these solutions are possible *now*. Like others in the one-third of people who are *not* rearrested within three years of their release from prison, Teresa, Waheedah, Ben, and Eddie have not seen the reformation of the policies that have paved the way for mass imprisonment in the United States. But by being part of a movement working toward social change, they have crossed the borders of the prison-created diaspora to gain support and hope. Through their involvement in this work, they have set their hands to changing the systems they once found inescapable and to rebuilding their communities so that the next generation can imagine a future beyond mass imprisonment. Just as their work has moved through the streets of Philadelphia, so too has the work of countless others moved through cities across this country and other countries across the globe. Theirs is the decisive and deliberate work of people determined to live in love, openness, health, and well-being. Or, to use the words of Teresa, Waheedah, Ben, and Eddie, community organizing *is* a reentry program. And *that* is real HIV prevention.

NOTES

1. Philadelphia FIGHT was formed in 1991 as a partnership of individuals living with HIV/AIDS and clinicians, who joined together to improve the lives of people living with the disease. Now a comprehensive AIDS service organization providing primary care, education, advocacy, and research, FIGHT has been a leader in prison health advocacy. Kingdom Care Reentry Network was founded in 2002 to significantly reduce the rate of prison recidivism in the greater Philadelphia area and beyond. KCRN works to mobilize, organize, and empower the considerable resources of the Philadelphia area faith community, focusing on prison ministry in general and reentry aftercare in particular.

2. Hammett et al., "The Burden of Infectious Disease among Inmates," 1791.

3. The often-permanent legal restrictions people face simply for having a criminal record limit their access to public housing, welfare benefits, employment options, voting rights, and student loans. See Travis, "Invisible Punishment."

4. Pew Center on the States, "One in 100."

5. Mauer, *Race to Incarcerate*, 91.
6. Fullilove, *Root Shock*.
7. Pew Center on the States, "One in 31."
8. Maddow, *Pushing for Progress*, 25; Mauer and King, "A 25-Year Quagmire."
9. Mauer and King, "A 25-Year Quagmire."
10. Drucker, "Drug Prohibition and Public Health," 21. Black males born in 2001 or later have a 32 percent likelihood of imprisonment at some point in their lifetime. See Mauer, *Race to Incarcerate*, 138.
11. Mauer, *Race to Incarcerate*, 204–5.
12. Braman, "Families and Incarceration," 117–18, 121–22, 122–23, 131.
13. Fournier and Carmichael, "Socioeconomic Influences," 214–17; Singer, "AIDS and the Health Crisis of the United States Urban Poor."
14. AMFAR, "HIV in Correctional Settings," 2.
15. Johnson and Raphael, "The Effects of Male Incarceration Dynamics." According to the Pew Center on the States, one in nine Black men between twenty and thirty-four is in prison, but only one in thirty of the general population. See "One in 100," 6. The Centers for Disease Control, "HIV/AIDS among African Americans," reports that Black men comprise only 13 percent of the population, but account for half of new HIV diagnoses.

BIBLIOGRAPHY

Ahmed, Leila. *A Border Passage: From Cairo to America — A Woman's Journey*. New York: Penguin, 2000.

AMFAR. "HIV in Correctional Settings: Implications for Prevention and Treatment Policy." Washington, D.C.: American Foundation for AIDS Research, 2008. http://www.amfar.org/uploadedFiles/In_the_Community/Publications/HIV%20In%20Correctional%20Settings.pdf.

Braman, Donald. "Families and Incarceration." In *Invisible Punishment: The Collateral Consequences of Mass Imprisonment*, edited by Marc Mauer and Meda Chesney-Lind, 117–35. New York: New Press. 2002.

Centers for Disease Control and Prevention. "HIV/AIDS among African Americans." 2008. http://www.cdc.gov/hiv/topics/aa/resources/factsheets/pdf/aa.pdf.

Drucker, Ernest. "Drug Prohibition and Public Health: 25 Years of Evidence." *Public Health Reports* 114, no. 1 (1999): 14–29.

Fournier, Arthur M., and Cynthia Carmichael. "Socioeconomic Influences on the Transmission of Human Immunodeficiency Virus Infection — The Hidden Risk." *Archives of Family Medicine* 7 (1998): 214–17.

Fullilove, Mindy. *Root Shock: How Tearing Up City Neighborhoods Hurts America, and What We Can Do about It*. New York: One World/Ballantine, 2004.

Hammett, Theodore M., Mary Patricia Harmon, and William Rhodes. "The Burden of Infectious Disease among Inmates of and Releases from U.S. Correctional Facilities, 1997." *American Journal of Public Health* 92 (2002): 1789–94.

Johnson, Rucker C., and Steven Raphael. "The Effects of Male Incarceration Dynamics on AIDS Infection Rates among African-American Women and Men." Ann Arbor: National Poverty Center, 2006. http://www.npc.umich.edu/publications/working_papers?publication_id=84&.

Maddow, Rachel. *Pushing for Progress: HIV/AIDS in Prisons*. Washington, D.C.: National Minority AIDS Council, 2002.

Mauer, Marc. *Race to Incarcerate*, rev. ed. New York: New Press, 2006.

Mauer, Marc, and Ryan S. King. "A 25-Year Quagmire: The 'War on Drugs' and Its Impact on American Society." Washington, D.C.: Sentencing Project, 2007. http://www.sentencingproject.org/Admin/Documents/publications/dp_25yearquagmire.pdf.

Pew Center on the States, Public Safety Performance Project. "One in 100: Behind Bars in America 2008." Washington, D.C.: Pew Center on the States, 2008. http://www.pewcenteronthestates.org/uploadedFiles/8015PCTS_Prison08_FINAL_2-1-1_FORWEB.pdf.

———. "One in 31: The Long Reach of American Corrections." Washington, D.C.: Pew Center on the States, 2009. http://www.pewcenteronthestates.org/uploadedFiles/PSPP_1in31_report_FINAL_WEB_3-26-09.pdf.

Seddon, Toby. "Drugs, Crime and Social Exclusion: Social Context and Social Theory in British Drugs-Crime Research." *British Journal of Criminology* 46 (2006): 680–703.

Singer, Merrill. "AIDS and the Health Crisis of the United States Urban Poor — The Perspective of Critical Medical Anthropology." *Social Science and Medicine* 39 (1995): 931–48.

Travis, Jeremy. "Invisible Punishment: An Instrument of Social Exclusion." In *Invisible Punishment: The Collateral Consequences of Mass Imprisonment*, edited by Marc Mauer and Meda Chesney-Lind, 15–36. New York: New Press, 2002.

Immigrant Justice from a Trans Perspective

An Interview with Gael Guevara

MAY 2009

JENNA LOYD

JENNA LOYD (JL): Let's start with a history of the Sylvia Rivera Law Project.

GAEL GUEVARA (GG): The Sylvia Rivera Law Project [SRLP] started off as a one-person fellowship. Dean Spade, who founded the organization, is a white trans man and lawyer. When SRLP was created over seven years ago, there was a great need in New York City to provide basic free legal services to low-income trans communities. The services included everything from advocating to obtain public assistance benefits, to changing your name on your identity documents, to working with people who had issues in their workplace and in their living spaces, including pervasive discrimination in the shelter system. People were being kicked out of their apartments and homes due to transphobia, and trans youth were facing discrimination in the foster care system for being trans. So there was just a huge range of legal issues and a great need for legal representation, especially for transgender and gender-nonconforming people of color who are low income.

We are a collective organization, so we have a nonhierarchal governing structure that makes decisions using a consensus process and involves the active participation of collective members and volunteers. The reason for becoming a collective was to expand the capacity of the organization to do the work, and to develop a structure with multiple access points where members have an active role in the decision-making process of the organization. We recognize that the power dynamics that exist within a hierarchical structure would make it impossible for our members to feel they could participate effectively and have ownership of the organization, so we wanted to create an organization that is governed by the people most directly impacted by the issues we were trying to address.

JL: Can you tell us about some of the policy work that the Sylvia Rivera Law Project does and the groups that you work with?

GG: In addition to providing direct legal services, we do a lot of public policy work that impacts the lives of low-income transgender people's access to basic needs. We work in coalition with organizations in the city and nationally on different kinds of issues, everything from birth certificates to public benefits, foster care, criminal justice, and immigration.

One important issue is identification documents. Identity documents often require people to identify their gender; however, the process of obtaining identification that truly reflects one's identity can become very difficult for someone who is transgender and who is also low income. There is a range of rules and regulations that varies depending on the agency that grants these identity documents. Social Security has a different list of requirements to prove one's gender than, say, the Department of Motor Vehicles, the welfare office, or the passport agency. So when individuals go through the process of changing their identity documents, there is a lot more money expenses, paperwork, and verification hurdles they need to go through to prove who they are. And if you are low income and you have no money and no resources, the process of getting your ID becomes ten times more difficult.

We live in a time when we no longer question when the government implements sophisticated forms of surveillance and tracking systems to document our identities and use them in negative ways to further restrict our mobility and access to essential services. However, we continue to witness how these restrictions and increased security measures — disguised as the "war on terror" for the sake of our "security" — have had a very direct impact on the criminalization and growing xenophobia that affects immigrant communities who come to this country. And what many people don't realize is that it has also had a huge impact on transgender communities' lives and ability to obtain the proper documentation they need to be safe and get the essential services they need to survive.

We are also working in coalition with a number of activists and organizations in New York City to pass a policy within the NYPD that addresses the proper treatment of transgender individuals whom they come in contact with. There is currently no best practices procedures or guidelines that address the treatment of transgender people in their patrol guide; currently, the placement and treatment of transgender people who get arrested is at the discretion of the individual police officer. This exposes the individual to all kinds of violations and abuses without any recourse to hold the police officer accountable. There are many transgender people who experience police brutality in the hands of the NYPD. Many of these incidents are underreported or simply not reported at all for fear of retaliation or no action at all.

We have also been part of the HRA Review Committee, which has been responsible for reviving the campaign to implement a best practices policy that will allow New York City's Human Resources Administration to have respectful and competent services for all of their clients, including trans people. [The Human Resources Administration is the body overseeing every kind of welfare benefit: food stamps, housing assistance, Medicaid, drug treatment programs, employment programs, HIV/AIDS services, and others.] This campaign, if successful, would help implement trans sensitivity training for all HRA workers as well as establish concrete guidelines for caseworkers to follow and offer respectful and adequate services to all transgender clients.

We've also done work on policy around the homeless shelters in NYC with the Department of Homeless Services to provide respectful services for transgender folks going into the homeless shelter system. Together with a number of [other] organizations that worked on the policy, we were successful in implementing a best practices policy stating that folks should be placed based on their gender identity and the individual's safety. However, we continue to work to provide political consciousness in trans communities to ensure they know their rights, and to hold the Department of Homeless Services accountable when there are complaints of discrimination in the shelters.

JL: Part of what makes SRLP unique is its commitment to services and to organizing.

GG: In addition to direct legal services and policy [work], we also [provide] a lot of organizing support to organizations that are doing base-building organizing work, and that are led by and/or building the leadership of transgender people who are low income and/or people of color. We also support the development of our community members' leadership and political involvement by connecting our clients to educational resources, trainings, internships, volunteering opportunities, and other services they can benefit from. Some of the organizations that we work with closely are the Audre Lorde Project, FIERCE, and Queers for Economic Justice.

SRLP recognizes that it has a particular expertise in the field of trans legal rights and advocacy that can be used most effectively to support the organizations that are doing base-building work with the people most directly impacted by transphobia. Our role as a legal organization is to provide our community with essential legal services that provide them with their basic needs and to bring some sense of stability in their lives so that they can participate fully and effectively in community organizing and long-term change. To do this, we provide community organizing projects with know-your-rights trainings for their members, create materials that inform members about their legal rights, and organize on-site clinics where we provide legal services for their members. During direct actions, we train and coordinate legal observers and provide any further legal representation/coordination if needed.

JL: Do you consider yourselves an abolitionist organization? How did you come to focus on prison abolition as a queer issue, and likewise migration as a queer issue?

GG: We are an abolitionist organization because we don't see the prison-industrial complex—all of the businesses and organizations that promote the expansion of prisons—as a solution to society's problems. The PIC is a business that profits from the targeted criminalization and disenfranchisement of people of color who are disproportionately young, poor, queer, and differently abled.

For example, we strongly oppose hate crimes legislation because we believe it is not the long-term solution to ending discrimination and violence against our communities. We know it would only result in giving the system *more* power to put *more* people in jail and expand prisons. Raising the punishment for committing a hate crime is not going to actually stop those things from happening, especially when there are no programs or trainings in place for people to raise their consciousness about what they have done when they get locked up. People continue to replicate transphobia and homophobia inside prison walls without facing any consequences, and are even encouraged by correctional officers to do so. Both inside and outside of prison, people will not gain consciousness unless there is strong support for expanding equal rights for transgender people in every aspect of society.

Time and time again, we have heard that trans people feel that police do not protect them. Many times, we've heard people talk about calling the police, either for a domestic violence situation or when they are being harassed or assaulted, and when the police show up, trans folks are the ones who are getting arrested just because they are trans. No questions asked.

The prevalence of how often trans people are arrested and incarcerated is often invisible because trans people are not recognized by the system. If the system doesn't recognize people as trans people or respect their identities, then they don't exist. We don't really know what the statistics are on how many trans people have been incarcerated or who have encountered some form of police brutality. We know that the numbers are high because of the frequent testimonials of incidents of police brutality in our communities, but I'm sure if there was a way to track these incidents more effectively within these institutions we could show an even larger percentage of transgender people reporting violence. I think that tracking in the context of ID documents is different from documenting incidents like violence, statistics that would be beneficial as a tool to better advocate for services, rights, or showing how the system is not effective.

JL: It seems that the conundrum you're discussing is how to distinguish between reformist reforms that make the system stronger and nonreformist, or abolitionist, reforms. How do you make those decisions in terms of what reforms SRLP chooses to organize and campaign around and those that you don't?

GG: When we choose to work to make reforms within the prison system, it is with the purpose of improving the living conditions and wellness for our clients, to make it more tolerable during the time that they are incarcerated.

In terms of making the decision about what policies to work on, we receive direct feedback and guidance from our incarcerated clients through our Prison Advisory Committee. PAC, as we call it, is a group of about twenty to twenty-five trans folks and allies who are being held in various prisons throughout New York state. They have come together to provide us with feedback and direction as to how we can best support them and advocate for their rights. We also provide support to trans prisoners through the prisoner pen pal program, which currently serves over seventy trans and gender-nonconforming prisoners.

JL: How do you see immigration policy and the PIC working together?

GG: Both of these systems are all about the control of profit and control of people. Big businesses profit from cheap labor that they extract from sweatshops in Latin America in the same way they benefit from cheap labor inside prison walls and the labor of immigrant workers who work for below minimum wage in the United States. The U.S. government simultaneously criminalizes the lives of people who are just trying to survive and looks the other way when [the government has] systematically failed to implement institutions and services that support people's everyday basic needs.

So in terms of linking trans-related issues to immigration: simply, trans people are also immigrants. SRLP provides direct legal services to trans immigrants and provides consultation for attorneys taking on immigration cases in this field. We developed a trans immigration flow chart [figure 11] as a way to explain visually how different barriers affect the lives of our immigrant clients and to explain the specific experiences of trans people when they go through the system. Being an immigrant who is also trans presents another layer of obstacles in order to obtain the basic necessities like shelter, legal, health, and other support services. The options are even more limited when you do not speak English.

On the left side of the chart we point out the general barriers trans people might face in getting any kind of legal immigration status. First, because of widespread employment discrimination, trans people have a very hard time getting any sort of employment-based immigration into the United States. In addition, family-based support is often lacking, and since marriages to trans people are not validated, that option is pretty much off the table.

On the right of the chart we explain how trans people are criminalized on the basis of their identities, and how trans people must engage in criminalized behavior, such as prostitution, jumping turnstiles, living on the street, loitering, etc., in order to survive.

The bottom of the chart breaks down how once someone is detained or deported, the individual might face even greater danger and discrimination because of their gender identity or expression. Transgender people face and fear the pervasive harassment and violence that are perpetuated by correctional officers that operate detention facilities. This type of violence affecting trans people often falls under the radar because transgender people are not identified/recognized as such, and therefore are invisible when it comes to documenting the extensive violence and discrimination they face inside these facilities. Trans folks often have no recourse for filing a complaint because of a great fear of retaliation. Trans women are placed with non-trans men, where they are often both physically and verbally raped and abused. Often, trans folks are also denied access to hormones and forced to conform to traditional gender norms, denying them garments or products that reflect their gender expression, causing trans people a lot of psychological harm. Finally, trans people often try to

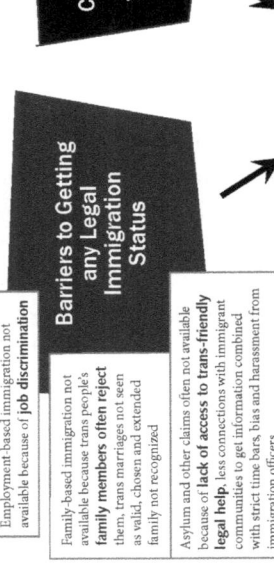

FIGURE 11. Some of the gender-related harms experienced by trans immigrants during detention and deportation procedures. Courtesy of the Sylvia Rivera Law Project.

seek asylum and migrate here because of fear of persecution in their home countries or because of the need to seek better medical treatment for HIV/AIDS.

Sometimes, trans folks who are not immigrants are also affected by the restrictions and scrutiny of identity documents and the restriction of mobility. As I have explained, obtaining identity documents that reflect one's gender identity is one of the most common challenges people face when going through their transition. The overall increased vigilance and policing at airports and other public spaces as well as additional restrictions in acquiring identity documents has had a big impact on trans communities in general. When you have documentation that does not match your presenting gender identity or you have documents with different information, this raises the level of scrutiny whenever you try to use them.

Here's another example of the intersections between transphobia, migration policy, and the PIC. Imagine a trans person who might have come here fleeing persecution in their country for their gender identity or expression. They get to New York City, where they need shelter and have needs for health care. And let's say that person is HIV-negative. So they come to the city thinking, "Hey, they have so many things! There must be something here." One of the obstacles that they might face in terms of health care is that there aren't a lot of resources for people who are HIV-negative. A lot of the health care services that are respectful to trans people revolve around people who are HIV-positive. So if you're not HIV-positive, because of a lack of information trans people either don't get health care or prefer to get HIV so that they can get health care. It's also really tough for trans people to find a place where they feel respected as trans people, and are able to access services that are knowledgeable about what their needs are.

Another obstacle they might face in terms of health care is that there aren't a lot of resources for people who are undocumented to get health care. They often don't have insurance, so a lot of folks either don't get any care or get their medication and hormones on the street. They also often engage in prostitution or some other criminalized activity due to the lack of other employment opportunities. This raises many health concerns as well as the likelihood of getting deported.

If you're undocumented, you *should* have access to the shelter system in New York City; however, many people do not know about this. Homeless shelters *should* allow people to go to the shelter based on their stated gender identity, but we see repeatedly that it takes a really long time to move from policy to practice. So trans women *should* be able to access women's shelters, but unfortunately that's not always the case.

JL: How do you see bridges being built between prison abolition and immigrant justice movements?

GG: The prison abolition and immigrant justice movements are already interconnected in a lot of ways. Both address the need to end the caging and control of communities of color for the profit of a few who are in power. In terms of how trans rights connect to immigration justice, it's about recognizing that trans people are part of the movement. Often, trans and queer folks have been excluded from the migrant justice and prison abolition movements because of widespread transphobia and homophobia. I think we need to stand in solidarity with each other and build on the intersections of our common experiences that in the end make us stronger.

JL: One place I could see this conversation progressing would be around the issue of family reunification in the immigrant justice movement. How does that idea get advanced without shoring up heteropatriarchy and normative views of sexuality, gender, and the family?

GG: When we talk about family reunification in the context of immigration, people often forget that trans people have families too. And some have supportive families, which becomes one of the ways they seek legal immigration status in the United States. Often, trans people are seen as sexually active but not as people who have children and create families of their own. "Family" is not heteropatriarchial if we think of family as more than just a straight heteronormative couple.

JL: What are you excited about in terms of abolitionist organizing, and what are some of the challenges you see in terms of people organizing at cross-purposes to one another?

GG: I'm really excited about the work we've been doing through Transforming Justice. Transforming Justice is a network of over two hundred participants, including activists and grassroots organizations from all over the country, who came together in Oakland, California, in 2007 to bring visibility to trans rights issues within the abolitionist movement and to bring visibility to prisoner issues within the mainstream LGBT movement. It has sparked a lot of energy around the country to bring prisoner issues to the center of conversations when talking about pressing LGBT issues. And I feel that there has been an increased awareness about what is really happening to trans people inside prisons like there wasn't before. I'm not saying this came about only through Transforming Justice's work, but I definitely think more people take notice when a large group of people and organizations come together to strategize and form collaborative efforts to increase the impact and importance of this work.

I think that Transforming Justice was unique and empowering for many people because the conference centered the leadership of folks who were directly impacted every step of the way, from the initial concept and planning of the gathering, to local and national outreach, to the facilitation and planning of the agenda for the weekend. Many people highlighted how important it was for them to be in a room with people who were also survivors of the prison system.

It was also important because it brought together a lot of allies and people in the prison abolition movement and in the LGBT movement who either had not thought about trans prisoners as part of their work or who hadn't really known how to articulate it. And it brought together LGBT organizations that have or were starting to talk about trans rights issues in their work, but hadn't really thought about doing trans prisoners rights work.

We then organized to bring this work to Critical Resistance's tenth-anniversary conference, which was really important for us. I think the exciting thing about it is the dialogue and collaboration that have continued from that work in terms of bridging the abolition movement to be more aware and more inclusive of trans prisoners, and for trans and gender-nonconforming people to feel that they are part of that prison abolition movement, and not being hidden or in the closet about it.

We are really trying to open those bridges between movements, to have those conversations and open up the possibility of working together instead of separately. For example, we wouldn't want an abolitionist trans movement; we want to be part of the abolitionist movement as transgender people. As well as the immigrants rights movement; we are immigrants as well. We can't just focus on trans immigrant rights issues without working alongside and in solidarity with other immigrant justice organizations. We need to work together in order to do this work well and not exclude people from our movements, and hold each other accountable to that idea.

RESOURCES

Audre Lorde Project. http://alp.org.

FIERCE. http://www.fiercenyc.org.

"It's a War in Here." SRLP report that documents the experiences of trans women in New York state prisons. http://srlp.org/resources/pubs/warinhere.

Making It Happen. Short documentary film of the Transforming Justice gathering in 2007; includes a list of contacts in different regions of the United States. www.transformingjustice.org.

Queers for Economic Justice. http://q4ej.org.

Sylvia Rivera Law Project. http://srlp.org.

Descado en Los Angeles
Cycles of Invisible Resistance

IRINA CONTRERAS

HASTA LA VICTORIA: A BORDER HYMN FOR VICTORIA ARELLANO

Tell us something we don't already know about borders.

Show us a line we haven't already crossed.

Your walls, your fences, your bullets, your holding cells cannot keep us from our destinations.

We have been planning our outfits for this journey for years.

We cross though we already long for home, a kiss blown backwards, a sashay skyward, a prayer to someday return.

We cross though the borderlands get smaller and smaller with each passing day, the earth embedded with mines, sinister and unrecognizable, a landscape as lifeless and terrifying as theme parks. Though steel bar barriers twist through like roller coasters. Though the stomach drops. Though the mouth hangs open in fear.

In our minds we have traveled back and forth daily, danced a cumbia one foot in, one foot out, a tipsy dance across this space slim as highwire, leading us wherever we want to go.

We cross and the borderlands on the Gringo side stink sterile as hospitals. White vans, white trailers and even whiter barricades appear like apparitions, ghosts in white sheets haunting the desert.

There is no room for subtlety here; the sun shines too bright and our bodies are all too human.

Be warned:

These border places, these crossroads places are ours. When we die here, it is the blood of angels that has fallen. When we die here, the earth is blessed and fed and those that kill us are cursed.

May your soul be damned to roam, lost, alone, and thirsty. May your soul be damned to die across infinite miles of empty desert.

May your red, red heart be wrapped with the barbed wire you use to keep us out and slowly cease its beating.

May you bleed past the borders of your skin and know that each drop lost is one of us, crossing to the other side.

— NICO DACUMOS

WHAT I REMEMBER . . .

In 2007, a former roomie died in Los Angeles's Daniel Freeman Hospital after a brief battle with pneumonia and sarcoma resulting from HIV. The nurses at Daniel Freeman ignored Shaun, or Shauna as we lovingly called her in our home (both names are pseudonyms). Shauna's brother called the nurses for everything from medication to medical attention to requests for clean sheets, which were all repeatedly ignored.

Shauna was magnetic. She loved Missy (as in Elliott), big sequins, Destiny's Child, little sequins, Tom of Finland, big hugs, and an afternoon cocktail hour that was announced with a cheer and a chiming bell. She had a butch side too: she prided herself on being able to woodwork, mosaic, and fix things around the house even though they were rarely ever completed. Most of all, I'll always remember the way she fell asleep out in the common spaces with the buzz of *The L-Word* on the television next to her. She said she wanted to be around us, her presence known even while she slept.

Two months later, when I was still reeling from losing Shauna, Victoria Arellano's name popped up in the news. Well, not quite. Victoria, a trans woman, died in a San Pedro immigrant detention center after being denied her HIV medication, Dapsone.

Shauna and Victoria are connected by their deaths, by the way their deaths affected me and maybe a handful of others. Yet, in most ways, their lives were completely unconnected. They shared a disease, but not the same gender identity. Both were varying degrees of trans, one more gender fluid than the other; one was undocumented, one documented; they had different desires and goals, which were never fully realized.

Looking at both of them, it becomes more apparent the ways in which the code of gender privilege has walked hand in hand with the privilege of documentation since this land was "settled." With my best intentions, I assume that many of us (it can't just be me, right?) walk holding our heads up high even though we are angry, so often tired of worrying about family and friends and the cycles of violence that our families and communities have been through. I have walked numb from the ricochet of violence centuries old that has never truly touched this skin.

Ultimately, Victoria and Shauna are connected by two related systems that disregarded their lives. Victoria was detained while returning from Mexico, a trip she had completed a number of times since her initial crossing. Even though she was female-identifying, she was placed in an all-male cell and began to experience her illness fairly quickly without her meds. Upon requesting the proper medication, she was instead given amoxicillin, which is used to treat mild bacterial infections, and became more ill. While other detainees in her cell rallied for her to receive treatment, she was eventually shackled to her bed. Her health deteriorated even more quickly, and she was taken to the clinic where she again asked for her meds.

And again, was refused.

She died in her cell a few days later.

I received emails about the injustice of Victoria's detention and death from friends as far away as South Africa and Brazil who work in the world of AIDS nongovernmental organizations. At the same time, the large majority of folks I spoke to in Los Angeles about Victoria's death were people I work with on issues related to queer people of color. This demonstrated to me the possibilities of how quickly our networks can connect. At the same time, it showed the ways in which, locally, we fail to connect with people working on other issues, or those who are not involved but self-identify as queer people of color, or those who do not have access to the information that travels between organizations.

Feminist media sources were called to account because other feminists felt that Victoria's death should have been reported. Local immigrant rights organizations were seen as having failed because they were focused on policy reform but neglected people like Victoria. And the mainstream gay movement seemed to only be thinking about marriage.

I headed to Victoria's vigil but discovered it had been canceled because a different vigil was planned for the same time.

THE OTHER ARELLANO

Elvira Arellano was a young, undocumented mother who sought sanctuary in a Chicago church in 2007 before going on a tour to speak about migrant rights. At Placita Olvera in downtown Los Angeles, she and, eventually, her son were detained and then deported. For this to happen while she was being protected under sanctuary was a slap in the face. And the symbolism of La Placita struck many even deeper.

On February 26, 1931, another raid occurred at La Placita: at least four hundred men, women, and children, both documented and undocumented, were rounded up. The raid and the interrogation process were said to last around an hour and a half. La Placita was a place where families spent time, where politicos and anarchists shared ideas and action, and where people openly argued, kissed, and ate. Much of downtown at this time, while already heavily surveilled, had a rich history of public space used for speech, alternative or barter models for income, and public sex or prostitution. In February and March 1931 alone, there were three thousand to four thousand deportations.[1]

From 1930 to 1935, over four hundred thousand people were "repatriated" to Mexico, many of them U.S. citizens.[2] We know that these raids and "removals" were attempts to cleanse the United States of its "immigration problem."[3] To conduct an open place raid, as in 1931, by putting two guards each on the entrances/exits was a calculated tactic. It was one successfully designed to echo in Angelenos' minds.

Victoria's death, the silence around it, and her vigil felt like Shauna all over again. The rescheduled vigil was small, yet powerful, taking place downtown in front of the Federal Building on Los Angeles Street. I heard Victoria's mother, Olga, and Bamby Salcedo speak while I mostly stood alone. In contrast, when Elvira was deported, groups sent media blasts all over Indymedia, MySpace, and the Pacifica radio stations.

At Victoria's vigil I saw people from qteam, a collective of individuals who self-identify as queer and trans youth of color; most have complex identities rooted in various traditionally marginalized and oppressed communities in Los Angeles. They had signs and wore stenciled T-shirts, but a lot of what I could have seen was clouded by invisible bureaucracy. The qteamers stuck in my mind mostly because they seemed pissed and young. At the time, I had no knowledge that the low attendance was because of a decisive move by immigrant rights organizations to separate the two vigils, and that this was the reason for the young and angry queers.

And Victoria's name disappeared.

WE REMEMBER THE INVISIBLE

I began researching immigration law for a documentary, looking for the earliest laws that led to the present-day detention centers and prisons and, particularly, how they're connected to gender. Each day, I needed to look even further back, and at some point I was far from what had initially motivated my search.

The 1875 Page Act, the first federal law that prohibited "undesirable" migrants, built on California state legislation such as the 1862 Act to Protect Free White Labor (or the Anti-Coolie Law), which challenged whether the immigration of any Chinese, Japanese, or other Asian person was free and voluntary. It placed sexual and "obnoxious" behavior at the center. Page predates the Chinese Exclusion Act (1882) by several years and mandated the exclusion of Asian women who were thought to be coming to the United States for "lewd and immoral purposes." The Page Act ruled that people could not migrate specifically for the purpose of prostitution or polygamy or if they already had a record of such crimes in their home countries. While it wasn't aimed just at Chinese women, it primarily affected them since poor, unmarried Asian women often arrived in the United States as promised wives or as part of polygamous marriages, or they ended up working as prostitutes since they had few other ways to support themselves.[4]

There are ways in which the rigor of research and storytelling reclaims something. This work cannot fix everything, but it feels like part of a process, a step toward healing. Investigating this history feels like proof that Shauna and Victoria existed. Victoria and Shauna are connected via the Page Act, a flimsy sheet of paper that forever changed the way we wear ourselves, our hearts, and our sexualities on our sleeves.

COOPERS DOUGHNUTS, LOS ANGELES, 1959

Communities of color know from our past experiences, from history, and from friends that we are most certainly always under attack. We are on guard even when we are careless and free. The year 1959 was not much different, but it has been historicized as a period in which upper-class, white gay males (often in heterosexual marriages of convenience) were consistently attacked and arrested. Then or now, the stories of queer folks of color are mostly absent.

Coopers Doughnuts was nestled in a block at Sixth and Main near two queer and trans spaces called Harold's and the Waldorf, where most club-goers were people of color. As folks would leave these spaces, many would crowd into Coopers for a late night snack or hustle. The Los Angeles Police Department would do a nighttime routine, picking up hustlers, queers, trans people, and chasers alike in downtown Los Angeles. During these routine stops, cops were reported to have chanted things like "One, two, three, four / We're coming back for more."[5]

As the story goes, or at least the one I would like to believe, one transfabulous sistah decided she had had enough of the shit; she was tired of constantly being picked up and arrested and then picked up all over again the next night. One person was pulled into the backseat of a squad car after a fed-up sistah decided to throw her doughnut and then some more doughnuts at the cops. Others joined in, not just with doughnuts, but with their bodies. They attempted to free the person from the squad car by blocking the car, by running around, circling the paddy wagon, and generally causing chaos. They were successful, and their presence and resistance temporarily won the battle of the night.

This is where the fantasy ends, or at least mine. It is likely that the momentarily successful queer struggle that night ended with a vengeance, including more police and more police brutality, more cars and paddy wagons and harassment. In spite of this, I think that many of us look to these kinds of stories of our chosen ancestors/community to provide a reason to continue. I don't mean continue to work either, but continue to look for reasons to survive.

The oppression experienced at Coopers Doughnuts in 1959 was widespread and ongoing, and it would be another six years before the Black Cat Tavern riot/uprising at the Silver Lake gay bar. How were people preparing and organizing for attacks which they knew were going to happen? Is it at all similar to how we plan, organize, or hide now?

PREPARING FOR THE UNKNOWN

In my lifetime, it is a combination of immigration raids, police brutality, and hate crimes, not events exactly like Coopers Doughnuts, that has affected my friends and family. Raid response networks have developed out of concerns around a specific geographic region where Homeland Security vans might be seen or where raids have already taken place. In Illinois, Mississippi, California, Massachusetts, New York, and Pennsylvania raid response networks have developed so that people are prepared, alert, and ready for Immigration and Customs Enforcement. There is a history for these actions from the Underground Railroad to the sanctuary movement of the 1980s. Like those movements, today's raid response was developed to provide basic needs for one another and to build our own forms of community policing.

I met with Nenu, a friend from qteam, to discuss issues around Victoria, the two vigils, community, and the work that qteam has done or promoted. I asked Nenu to share a story of crossing the border:

The trip started in el D.F. [Mexico City] and went to Tijuana. In Tijuana, I spent a whole week because the person that was supposed to help us cross backed down. That whole week was spent trying to figure out who was gonna help us out. It was my sister, myself, and my aunt who was there just to be with us. Finally our coyote took us to a house and told us what we had to do. "You have to dress this way and you have to learn this script." The script was in English, so we memorized everything we needed to, like our name, our age, our parents' names, and our address.

All of these things were made up obviously, because we pretended to be something that we were not. My character was two years older and my twin sister's was two years younger. We weren't even supposed to be related. Our fictional characters were two girls that our neighbor was driving over. My sister's was the most dramatic as they made her cut her hair very, very short. She was the feminine one, the one that couldn't wait to have long hair down to her waist. But, because of her character, she became eight years old and had hair to her ears.

Our grandmother had made us these beautiful matching orange with white polka-dotted dresses for our trip, but the coyote wasn't diggin' it. They told us to get rid of them in order to look more American. So my aunt took us to get these stupid Mickey Mouse shirts with shorts and tennis shoes. We left our grandmother's handmade dresses for these ugly-ass used Mickey outfits. I remember thinking, "Damn, this is how the U.S. kids look like, for real?" It was then that I realized that a lot of what we had and valued would have to be put to the side.

In some texts, Nenu might be presented as either queer or immigrant, but Nenu holds both of these spaces. And while theirs certainly isn't my reality, it is also one that is simultaneously silenced and romanticized. Nenu owns both of those experiences in the ways that they note the dresses, the walk, the clothing distinguishing the U.S. kids, and the labor that went into creating these characters.

There are a few things I learned during that time of public and not-so-public mourning, about myself, about qteam, and about the various groups and communities we traverse. The exclusionary measure of the Page Act plays out daily in how we cannot remember that a 1931 raid at La Placita can lead to Coopers Doughnuts, and then back again.

One way single-issue organizing plays out is that the two vigils were held separately when the memorializing of their lives really should have been held together. Nenu and Byron Perez, another qteam member, expressed their experiences with the mainstream immigrant rights groups during the weeks after Victoria Arellano's death and Elvira Arellano's deportation. Perez saw that what was being said was: "A single mother is more important. Victoria's vigil was postponed for Elvira Arellano. Victoria was not just a trans woman. The day she died, she was also an immigrant. The day she was detained, she was an immigrant. The day she got sick, she was an immigrant."

Perez and Nenu attended Elvira's vigil in support, but also to ask its organizers why the two events were not combined. "Descado," Perez says. It's a word you use when you have no shame. "That is what these organizers did: they were at the table when the decision was being made [to keep the vigils separate or hold them together], and they decided it was time to move on. It wasn't up for discussion, it was said and done."

He continued, "They wanna have a plate on the table. The folks that are consistently marginalized are told to wait their turn. It's like, let's talk strategy: 'incremental gains to include everyone.' But for me it's easy to say that when it's always the same people that are always left behind."

My biggest fear as a teacher or doer of any sort is when our organizing replicates the very structures we fight against. We can surf through history and see where mobilizing campaigns have been contingent on proving that some folks deserve rights more than others. As Perez stated, *incremental gains are necessary for change for all.*

Looking at history, we see much of the same pattern and power struggles. Before the Page Act, many states regulated their own migration processes. In fact, the Page Act is almost identical to the "moral certificates" already on the books in California in which persons wanting to migrate needed to provide paperwork from their home countries stating their upstanding citizenship. The moral certificates were eventually upheld by the federal courts, and many states also attempted to tax Chinese immigrants on property and land owned.

The very birth of these laws and acts suggests that there was an ideal American that is still in place today in a number of forms: male, white, heterosexual, with a family, healthy, and able-bodied. The Page Act set the stage for the same gender policing that is embedded in today's immigration policies. However, little work has been done to analyze the ways in which poor, female-bodied people of various diasporas, genders, and sexualities have been affected or to make practical suggestions about how we can address this policing. These are the same reasons we don't have accurate statistics on the queers picked up in raids.

With each group that has resisted, fought, or worked with these laws, what is forgotten is that the public baiting of the most marginalized groups simultaneously ensures that even larger groups of people will be ensnared. Making gender and sexuality invisible, even in the name of group protection or solidarity, disengages people from the political process.

BILLS, BILLS, BILLS; OR, GREEN IS THE COLOR OF SINGLE-ISSUE ORGANIZING

The passage of two laws in 1996, under President Bill Clinton, simultaneously pushed our work into a single-issue focus. One was the Illegal Immigration Reform and Immigrant Responsibility Act, a two-hundred-page revision to immigration law, which included more funding and staffing for the U.S. Border Patrol, and raised civil and criminal penalties for immigration law violations. The second was the Personal Responsibility and Work Opportunity Reconciliation Act (welfare reform), which made both undocumented and *legal* permanent resident immigrants ineligible to receive most forms of federal assistance, including many types of Social Security benefits and federally insured student loans. These new laws sent a clear message: there is no room for the poor, whether documented or not. Liberal and progressive America needs reform.

The immigrant rights movement contributes to the same exclusionary idea of the perfect citizen (productive, hetero, white, male, etc.) that other single-issue organizing does when movements fail to respond to the public baiting of people who are "imperfect" citizens: poor, queer, and outspoken. One of the organizers responsible for deciding whether Victoria's and Elvira's vigils would be held together was called out at a symposium centering on queer women of color, but the larger issue was ignored. Even in a queer-centered space, a single mother was somehow more relevant, more important, and more romantic for these organizers than Victoria, although both were immigrants.

When I asked Perez what he thought was gained by keeping Elvira's vigil separate from Victoria's, he noted that the crowd was largely made up of organizers, members of a few organizations, and the media. "They are trying to show numbers. I'm not dismissive, but the organizers often push their agenda so much that they don't talk, they are not allowed to have their own analysis. You are not being effective if you are breaking up issues. People accuse the immigrant community of being transphobic and that's not true. That community [an undocumented trans community] exists in L.A., and it's a lie to suggest it doesn't."

THE PAST, PRESENT, AND FUTURE OF NOW

Twelve years after IIRIRA, Proposition 8, the California Marriage Protection Act, passed. And so in retrospect it made sense that something like the separation of Elvira's and Victoria's vigils could have happened. After all, the model citizen needed to be not only a citizen, but a married one.

When the fight against the passing of Prop 8 began on November 4, 2008, people in Los Angeles were hysterical. Ironically, I was hiding in Desert Hot Springs, near Palm Springs, California, wrapped in a thick white terrycloth robe that said "Hope" on the back (for Hope Springs). My boyfriend had decided to take matters into his own hands and get us away from the endless rants of "hope" and marriage and other things we thought were a sham. It seemed perfect: we could be alone, get massages, fuck, eat, fuck more, and swim if we wanted in peace and quiet — away from the people sending endless text messages for us to "stonewall" in West Hollywood.

People in the media and folks we knew talked as though the fight against Prop 8 was the civil rights issue of our time. Any talk of how the Gay and Lesbian Task Force might have failed could lead one to feel quickly ostracized within one's own supposed — make that truly imagined — community. There were some who said that the initiative failed because of a lack of outreach to the poor and people of color. In Los Angeles, for example, this meant a lack of organizing in South Central and the Southeast. Meanwhile, the farthest east the outreach traveled was to areas populated with varying degrees of outness, such as West Hollywood, Silver Lake, and other areas of "gay ghetto" comfort. When outreach did happen in other spaces, as Jasmyne Cannick pointed out in her *L.A. Times* blog, it happened in Leimert Park, thanks to the comforts of gentrification.

Cannick was blasted by various queer people of color for selling out her so-called community, mimicking much of what happened with the vigils. I heard friends say that she needed to be more positive, that she wasn't really an activist because she was only a blogger, and she needed to stop being a hater. Much like qteam checking other Brown folks for perpetuating trans invisibility, Cannick was doing the same within her own queer community. The task force did not go to South Central, while ideas spun around that people of color (both Black and Brown) are homophobic, perpetuating the myth that there aren't any queers living in South Central.

When we came back from Hope Springs, there was a celebration to commemorate the historic monument induction at Le Barcito, formerly known as the

Black Cat Tavern, where there had been a gay uprising within a few years of the events at Coopers Doughnuts. The space was packed with people who all seemed to want to gawk at councilman Eric Garcetti, who was called "one of our own." There were even gay cops from West Hollywood to model progress of some sort.

That night we also stopped at the Wildness dance party at the Silver Platter bar. Despite both being near ultra-gentrified Silver Lake, Le Barcito and Silver Platter are very different places. Silver Platter rides some weird balance of being packed one day a week with mostly artists and queers who don't necessarily live in the neighborhood, while the rest of the week it is more Centroamericana/o or Latina/o, like most of MacArthur Park.

Some of us working on raid response were angry that the Wildness party didn't have a plan for what to do should the cops or sheriff show up and ask folks for documentation. In L.A. County, the sheriffs can turn a situation over to ICE, or at times act *as* ICE. It is all too common in places where real estate is booming, such as here, that the sheriff and police abuse their full power, enforcing gang injunctions and "quality of life" offenses.

A place to dance, Prop 8, and raid response may not seem connected, but the club provided a context for us to think about the ways that we can hold each other accountable, solve conflicts, or lose ourselves to conflict. That night, we walked with different eyes in the same alleys in which we had haphazardly made out or finished a cigarette, trying to figure out where we could hide bolt cutters, or running shoes if an undocumented attendee in glitter spike heels might need to make a run for it.

There are many possibilities for building coalitions locally, nationally, and transnationally. More than ever, events painful as these seem to echo, they seem to repeat; things get better, things get worse.

Histories, whether personal or collective — painful histories, as most often they are — can be like blankets of warmth and comfort when we want them to be. When we claim them to be. Sometimes they are ours — and sometimes they are certainly not. But there is always power in these stories and words.

NOTES

1. Ruiz, "South by Southwest," 25.
2. Ngai, *Impossible Subjects*, 8.
3. Koch, "U.S. Urged to Apologize."
4. "Asian Pacific Americans and Immigration Law."
5. Faderman and Timmons, Gay L.A., 1–2.

BIBLIOGRAPHY

"Asian Pacific Americans and Immigration Law." http://academic.udayton.edu/race/02rights/immigro5.htm.
Faderman, Lillian, and Stuart Timmons. *Gay L.A.: A History of Sexual Outlaws, Power Politics, and Lipstick Lesbians*. New York: Basic, 2000.
Koch, Wendy. "U.S. Urged to Apologize for 1930s Deportations." *USA Today*, April 5, 2006. http://www.usatoday.com/news/nation/2006-04-04-1930s-deportees-cover_x.htm.
Ngai, Mae. *Impossible Subjects: Illegal Aliens and the Making of Modern America*. Princeton, N.J.: Princeton University Press, 2004.
Ruiz, Vicki L. "South by Southwest: Mexican Americans and Segregated Schooling, 1900–1950." *Magazine of History* 15 (2001): 23–27.

Winning the Fight of Our Lives

SUBHASH KATEEL

If the immigrant rights movement doesn't understand raids, detention, and deportation in the context of the greater prison-industrial complex, and organize accordingly, we will lose the fight of our lives — a fight we can and must win.

During the immigration debates and protests of 2006–2007, a small but significant chorus of organizations — those working with families facing deportation — spoke out strongly against many of the immigration reform legislative proposals. What many inside the beltway were calling "comprehensive immigration reform" wasn't comprehensive enough to fix the detention and deportation system that had eaten up and spit out almost 2 million people and destroyed nearly as many families. Instead, the grand bargain for reform was stricter immigration enforcement in exchange for a normalized status for some undocumented workers.

In the limited scope of those debates, the primary question was whether that normalized status would lead to green cards (legalization) for those immigrant guest workers. It seemed the folks inside the beltway, some of them dear friends of ours, felt the need to accede to the anti-immigrant forces' thirst for more enforcement in order to obtain some semblance of legalization. However, the survivors of immigration enforcement — those facing deportation and those affected by the deaths of loved ones and by the militarization of the border — were being made into sacrificial lambs for an elusive blessing of limited legalization riddled with unwanted curses.

Our intentions weren't based solely on self-interest. Fighting for justice for our brothers and sisters who died in detention, for our children who lost parents to deportation, and for our families whose sole income provider suffered in the desert terrain alongside the border wasn't a trivial struggle. But, like our colleagues backing comprehensive immigration reform, we were also fighting for the future of migrant communities.

EMERGING APARTHEID

In 2006 I wrote in *Left Turn* about the fight of our lives.[1] Back then, my colleagues and I had highlighted to our friends in the immigrant rights movement that we were witnessing the emergence of immigrant apartheid in the United States. A system was developing that would criminalize and attack migrants, people of color, and working people. This emerging apartheid would use the criminal justice, prison, and deportation systems — and any other system at its disposal — to make the lives of immigrants, both legal and undocumented, as hard as possible. What we would see, whether we won reform or not, would be more arrests, more raids, more detentions, and more deportations. In sum, more destruction of our communities.

Many people in the mainstream of the immigrant rights movement thought that we were blowing things out of proportion. Some mocked our characterization of what was happening to migrants as "apartheid." Some allies labeled our work against deportation, detention, and the excesses of the criminal justice system as "boutique issues" — sexy, but not as substantive as the fight for legalization. Others were far too enchanted with portraying immigrants as hard-working and law-abiding. They saw nothing wrong with focusing the ire of immigration enforcement on the "bad" migrants nor saw anything cynical about alluding to rights as something that "good" immigrants deserve. They sure as hell weren't going to sacrifice a potential win just to benefit the "bad" migrants, namely those in the deportation and criminal justice systems. We would keep insisting, in vain it seemed, that this fight had to be about more than just green cards in an era when green cards were losing their significance. It also had to be about more than the "good" immigrants in an era when the "good" immigrants could easily be recast as "bad."

We were speaking from experience. We had seen how the FBI had taken a young, hard-working, legal immigrant and pizza deliverer named Anser Mahmood and recast him, first, as a suspected terrorist. When that didn't work, the small financial assistance he gave to migrant friends was defined as "alien smuggling," making him a criminal alien and mandatorily deportable to Pakistan, despite pleas from his upstate New York neighbors and more than a dozen members of Congress. We had seen U.S. Army veteran and legal immigrant Warren Joseph's posttraumatic stress from the first Gulf War cause him to run afoul of the law and into an Immigration and Customs Enforcement detention center for three years, facing deportation to Trinidad. We had seen post–September 11 raids tear apart the lives of over fifteen hundred working families from South Asia and the Middle East under the guise of the "war on terror."

The anti-immigrant far right (and not-so-far right) had no such illusions of a difference between good and bad immigrants. They talked openly about a "war of attrition" against immigrants. Late night pundits like Pat Buchanan spoke candidly and favorably about going after all unwanted immigrants under the guise of going after the "worst." Those of us who had worked with families facing deportation since the mid-1990s understood this strategy.

MOVEMENT MISCALCULATION

A major miscalculation of some of the immigrant rights movement was the assessment that the immigration system was attacking only migrants' undocumented status. So once immigrants had their papers — a path to legalization, not to be confused with actual legalization — they would be fine. This ignores the fact that the value of a green card had diminished since the passage of the so-called reforms in 1996. It also ignores the fact that even documented immigrants still lead their lives as low-income working people of color.

Many of our friends in the immigrant rights movement simply couldn't see that the forces creating apartheid against migrants were attacking the ideas and institutions of migrants — those that allowed them to rise above subsistence (and in some cases flourish) — as much as they were attacking migrants and their status. In the process, immigrants — and the ideas and institutions of their everyday lives — were being criminalized. This criminalization had become far easier in a period marked by "wars" on drugs, "wars" on terror, and other "wars" meant to have an elusive target and a beginning with no end.

Some of us had the blessing of knowing elders who fought for civil rights, and those who carried the struggle beyond civil rights to the Black liberation movement. And historical reflection impressed something upon us. Just maybe, for all the rhetorical linkages that the immigrant rights movement drew with the civil rights movement, we had failed to see what happened in the Black community after the peak of the civil rights movement.

The victories of African American integration were followed by an explosion in the prison system and mass incarceration in the Black community. Communities that had survived poll tests, poll taxes, and grandfather clauses to gain and then preserve their right to vote were processed through the criminal justice system — and disenfranchised again. The vibrant businesses and civic associations that had endured decades of Jim Crow were replaced by extreme capital flight and a criminalized informal sector — a criminalized political economy. What the civil rights struggle forced the government to give back to Black folks through the narratives of its "best" (Rosa Parks, Dr. Martin Luther King Jr., etc.), the government would later take by pushing narratives of the Black community at its "worst."

OPEN EYES

Hindsight is only 20/20 when our eyes are open. The difference between that period and this period is that the clues of what was next for the Black community were not as readily available to our freedom fighters of that era. President Nixon's crime strategy, articulated behind closed doors, was to direct the criminal justice system primarily at the Black community without publicly saying so. This only became public knowledge after one of Nixon's closest aides' personal experiences with the prison system exposed him to its evils.

By comparison, the blueprint for the criminalization of migrants was made readily available to the public. The much-touted and -hated Sensenbrenner-King bill of 2005–2006, which passed the House of Representatives, left little encrypted in its desire for the wholesale criminalization of immigrant communities. Even earlier, plans like the quickly recanted PATRIOT Act II, crafted in 2002 by then–attorney general John Ashcroft, proposed to criminalize the very ways migrants made their livings and lived their lives.

During the civil rights movement, there was a whole chorus of freedom fighters who cried that the struggle couldn't just be about integration. The expansion of the prison-industrial complex in the Black community and its subsequent wars (on drugs, for example) were that era's tragic "We told you so." In 2006, many of us were screaming, "This can't just be about green cards!" The expansion of ICE raids was our tragic "We told you so."

On May 12, 2008, ICE agents arrested 389 workers during a raid at the Agriprocessors meatpacking plant in Postville, Iowa. Within weeks, nearly 300 mostly Latino workers were charged by federal prosecutors with crimes ranging from identity theft to illegal entry. Where a typical ICE raid would result in mostly administrative immigration charges, these workers were railroaded through federal criminal court, receiving up to six-month sentences in federal prison. In dramatic fashion, ICE instantly made this group of migrant workers into criminal aliens — the "bad" immigrants.

We felt no satisfaction when government tactics confirmed our worst fears. No one wants to be right when predicting the destruction of our communities. However, we were surprised by the response from the previously conservative mainstream of our movement. People who would have never been open to understanding the injustices of the criminal justice system and the deportation process saw clearly the need to tackle these systems with a newfound vigor. Over and over again, we heard new voices in immigrant communities come out and say, "Let us fight for legalization, but let us fight for more than legalization." Organizers and activists who had rarely spoken publicly about a family member's incarceration or deportation began to come forward. Old adversaries began talking about strategies to tackle the deportation system.

SO, WHERE AND WHY ARE WE LOSING?

1. Fighting the expanding immigration enforcement system — the linchpin of migrant apartheid — has always taken a backseat to the greater dream of comprehensive immigration reform. As a close colleague of mine has pointed out, organizing against Arizona's SB1070 would have never become so popular if Sheriff Joe Arpaio and his 287(g) agreement with ICE (an agreement that gives local police the power to enforce immigration laws) were not allowed to go unchecked. Groups in Arizona had been organizing against Arpaio and the 287(g) program for years, but were never given the outpouring of support they needed until after SB1070 was passed. Florida was the first state to sign a 287(g) agreement in 2002.

But 287(g) programs are just the tip of an ICEberg known as ICE ACCESS. Most of the programs under ICE ACCESS have been operational since before I started doing this work. But there was always a tendency within the immigrant rights movement to think that the bigger, more important fight was for comprehensive immigration reform as opposed to local battles, enforcement battles, or local enforcement battles. At the same time, ICE was extending its reach into communities by pushing ACCESS programs into every corner of the country, until Secure Communities, for example, made it into every county in Florida. The rationale for ignoring the local battles was always that comprehensive immigration reform would fix the other systemic problems, but that was never true. Which leads to my next point.

2. The "grand compromise" was never grand and never a compromise. In the immigration reform fight, there was always an implicit understanding of a compromise between increased enforcement and a path to legalization. In the process, our side often conceded important arguments on enforcement. For example, repealing or reforming the basic pieces of the 1996 immigration laws — the strictest immigration laws in decades, including mandatory detention, mandatory deportation, restricted judicial review, 287(g), and expanded

local enforcement — has often been left out of the immigration reform debate entirely. The idea that thousands of people dying at the border is a bad thing has been largely left out of the policy debate. When I say "debate" here, I mean the debate among policymakers, who are crafting the parameters of the discussion — because the immigrant rights movement has always had a vibrant and vocal debate about these issues. But enforcement policy was based on what lawmakers and the successive presidents from Clinton to Obama thought they could get away with. So what we have today is more enforcement without a roadmap or pathway to legalization.

3. We have succeeded in moving some leaders, but leaders have lost their luster. The immigrant rights movement has done a remarkable job of moving major institutions and the leaders of those institutions to their side. Whether it be church leaders, business leaders, or labor leaders, the immigrant rights movement has been impressive on this front. However, and this is an educated hunch (not empirical), I think that while we have been able to move these leaders, the political climate (that we often have no control over) has become so volatile that winning leaders hasn't led to winning the hearts and minds of the people who would typically listen to leaders. People are extremely angry right now for a lot of really good and bad reasons. And people from all sides of the political spectrum are openly and actively challenging even the most well-respected leaders. If you look at the struggles that politicians, religious leaders, and other leaders have had to go through to maintain any relevance and credibility, it is startling.

4. Communication, communication, communication. I feel like the immigrant rights movement has become really good at communicating to elected officials, to immigrants themselves, and to people who nominally care about immigrants. However, we have not been able to effectively communicate to people who are legitimately on the fence or falling off the fence to the other side. One example is the whole "immigrants are good for the economy" argument. I don't care how good the numbers are, a lot of Americans, even those who would believe it when we are not in a recession, just don't believe it. If you work in the construction or restaurant industries, it is really hard to believe. I could write a whole article on how our message framing has alienated some folks in African American communities. We have to be able to communicate the idea that both migrants and non-migrants are hurting right now, and it is neither's fault.

As organizers we know that exploitation is the problem. Exploitation hurts immigrants, hurts non-immigrants, and pits us against each other. How do we communicate that in a way in which we don't sound like "commies"? Just as the other side has one message — "What part of illegal don't you understand?" — we should be just as effective at saying "What part of exploitation don't you understand?" Plus, I feel like we haven't been as good at fighting xenophobia and racism *while* showing that we are feeling other people's (read: citizens') pain. To put things in perspective, there are citizens literally killing themselves and their families because of this economy. Why would folks treat the Other (read: migrant) any better than they are treating their own families in this economy? We all know that any economic problem that citizens feel, immigrants often feel more intensely, but just demonstrating empathy in messaging may move mountains for us.

REASONS FOR OPTIMISM

Although the road ahead for the immigrant rights movement is really rocky, it is still by far the biggest and most organized social movement in the country. With every loss, it gets smarter and its organizers become more conscious of the root causes and their solutions.

1. Arizona has made everyone think local and think enforcement. Since the passage of SB1070, real attention is being focused on local enforcement, on ICE's reach into our communities, and on the spread of anti-immigrant legislation at the state level. The energy isn't just filtering into the fight against SB1070 in Arizona; there are pitched battles being waged in states trying to replicate SB1070. As of this writing, a massive statewide campaign called We Are Florida! successfully beat back a nasty Arizona copycat that was being pushed by the most powerful politicians in the state. It feels like *everyone* is trying to understand ICE ACCESS, 287(g), and Secure Communities. And I truly believe that different sectors of the immigrant rights movement are finally getting a grasp on how immigration enforcement happens and how to stop it.

2. Uncovering the truth. Secure Communities, ICE's flagship enforcement program, seemed like a bulletproof vest. A program that purports to go after the most "dangerous criminal aliens" seems too hard to fight, especially when ICE is aggressively marketing it as the best enforcement program. In Florida, our first attempts to fight Secure Communities ended with ICE marketing heavily to editorial boards, winning them over, and effectively casting us as sympathizers for violent illegal aliens. But it seems like the shell is slowly beginning to crack. And it seems like our work has touched a nerve with ICE. Information about

what ICE's flagship program really means in communities is slowly starting to get out and raise eyebrows. Illinois decided to pull out of Secure Communities, a major blow to the program. It is too early to declare victory yet, but the fact that news outlets that thought Secure Communities was great are now asking questions is really good news for our work.

3. No more Mr(s). Nice Immigrant. The year 2010 marked a turning point for migrants and civil disobedience. I don't think I am exaggerating when I say that January alone probably had more acts of civil disobedience than all of the immigrant rights movement the year prior. Since then, from sit-ins, to mass arrests, to flash mobs, the tactics in the immigrant rights movement are getting more direct and more confrontational. To be clear, there is also a greater desire to specifically target the Obama administration to do more to protect the rights of migrants. I believe the press has made the outcomes look better than they really are, but the efforts have had some pointed results, not least of which is virtually forcing the administration into a lawsuit against SB1070.

4. It's the Latino vote, stupid. No matter how much anti-immigrant hysteria is drummed up, it ends up creating diminishing returns for the politician or party that is anti-immigrant. On a personal level, I have always been skeptical that voters have the electoral power to improve the lives of people who don't have the right to vote. However, with the notable exception of Joe Arpaio and some other Arizona Republicans, anti-immigrant politicians have ignored the Latino vote to their own detriment. In Florida, attorney general and gubernatorial hopeful Bill McCollum switched from denouncing the idea of an SB1070 in Florida to actually authoring a Florida version of the bill that is probably worse. In the process, he alienated much of the Latino Republican leadership and his crusade probably cost him the nomination. There seems to be a trend among anti-immigrant politicians of ignoring the Latino vote, but the Latino vote seems to have a real ability to punish anti-immigrant politicians.

MOVEMENT BLUEPRINT

Predicting the emergence of migrant apartheid is far easier than identifying how a movement can defeat it. But individuals and organizations around the country are developing a blueprint for how we might begin to win.

1. We must make this bigger than green cards. We are fighting for the future of our communities. We cannot act like the path to legalization is a path flowing

with milk and honey. It is simply one necessary step toward a greater vision of social justice.

2. We must focus on building power in migrant communities. Organizers such as Juan Pablo Chávez of the Florida Immigrant Coalition have instructed us at great length on the need to organize rather than mobilize. We cannot be a movement of mobilizations and talking heads. We must build real leaders in real communities to bring about real change.

3. We must organize in the migrant communities most directly impacted. We must stop talking about "good" and "bad" immigrants and build connections with those most affected. This is the only way to build a movement with more depth.

Families that have survived the prison-industrial complex are not sob stories and charity cases; they have survived one of the most sophisticated systems this society has for marginalizing someone. Their knowledge and determination make our movement stronger. The difficult work to build the leadership of the families most directly affected by deportation must be supported and incubated in earnest.

4. We must build the capacity of grassroots organizations to create the solutions to their own problems. Policies inside the beltway must be grounded in the wisdom and intellect of communities on the ground. But that can only happen when migrant communities develop the faith and the capacity to create those solutions. Otherwise, "solutions" will be made for immigrants, not by immigrants.

5. We must identify the ideas and institutions in migrant communities that we need to protect, and protect them vigorously. The things that enable a detainee to represent himself in immigration court and win his freedom, or enable an immigrant family to survive the desert and support family members on two continents are the same things that will enable us to build real alternatives to the world we live in today. When we forsake what our communities have already built, we forsake our real power.

6. We must confront the Department of Homeland Security more directly. From Hurricane Katrina, to the ICE raids, to corrupt agents along the border, the Department of Homeland Security has survived numerous investigations and audits only to see its budget increase even more. If we don't find more

creative and strategic ways to confront ICE, we will see even more destruction of our communities and have no one else to blame but ourselves.

Recently, I spoke with a family friend, a young Caribbean woman whose husband was detained by ICE. Nearly everyone had told her that her husband would be deported. Despite this, through her persistence, he was released a month after being detained. After picking him up, she told me, "I said my prayers and knew if I fought hard enough, I would see us together again." With that spirit, if we fight smart and fight hard, our communities, our families, and our loved ones will win this fight.

NOTES

This chapter reprints with permission articles that were published originally by *Left Turn* magazine and *Organizing Upgrade*. See Kateel, "Winning the Fight of Our Lives"; Kateel, "Diminishing Returns."

1. Kateel, "Immigrant Apartheid."

BIBLIOGRAPHY

Kateel, Subhash. "Diminishing Returns." *Organizing Upgrade*, September 1, 2010. http://www.organizingupgrade.com/2010/09/subhash-kateel.

———. "Immigrant Apartheid: Immigrant Rights Movement at the Crossroads." *Left Turn* 20 (June–July 2006): 70–73.

———. "Winning the Fight of Our Lives: Immigrant Rights and the Prison-Industrial Complex." *Left Turn*, October 1, 2008. http://www.leftturn.org/winning-fight-our-lives-immigrant-rights-and-prison-industrial-complex.

Contributors

OLGA AKSYUTINA is a senior research fellow at the Institute for African Studies of the Russian Academy of Sciences, Moscow.

CYNTHIA BEJARANO received her PhD from Arizona State University in the School of Justice Studies. She is currently an associate professor in the Department of Criminal Justice at New Mexico State University. She is the author of *"Qué Onda?": Urban Youth Cultures and Border Identity*, and the co-editor (with Rosa-Linda Fregoso) of an interdisciplinary anthology, *Terrorizing Women: A Cartography of Feminicide in the Américas*. Bejarano is an advocate for farmworkers' access to postsecondary education, and is also the co-founder of Amigos de las Mujeres de Juarez, an organization working to end violence against women in Chihuahua, Mexico, and the borderlands.

ANNE BONDS is an assistant professor of geography at the University of Wisconsin, Milwaukee. Her current research examines the recruitment and siting of prisons in rural areas experiencing deep poverty in the American Northwest as a strategy for local economic development.

BORDERLANDS AUTONOMIST COLLECTIVE was an anarchist, no-borders collective in southern Arizona active from 2006 to 2009. During this period the collective worked to confront the homeland security state through creative direct action and through participation and intervention in broader social movements. Although the group is currently on hiatus, various members remain involved in no-borders, anti-occupation, and immigrant rights struggles in Palestine, Arizona, and Kentucky.

ANDREW BURRIDGE completed his PhD in the Department of Geography at the University of Southern California in 2009. Burridge has worked alongside migrant rights and humanitarian aid groups, including No More Deaths in southern Arizona, and with immigration raid response networks based in downtown Los Angeles. He has also been involved with the no-borders movement in the United States and the United Kingdom. He is currently a research associate at the International Boundaries Research Unit at Durham University.

IRINA CONTRERAS is a Pacoima girl at heart. Her work as an interdisciplinary artist, fake-ademic educator, and writer engages language, public sites, and info dispersal. A former editor for LOUDmouth magazine, she writes and has made media for *make/shift* magazine, the anthology *Nobody Passes*, KPFK Pacifica's *Radioactive*, and *Clamor* magazine. While not currently working in the PIC, she still volunteers legal information for youth and adults.

RENEE FELTZ and STOKELY BAKSH conducted an award-winning investigation into the profitable business of immigration detention while fellows in the Stabile Center for Investigative Journalism at the Columbia Graduate School of Journalism (www.BusinessofDetention.com). They have produced www.DeportationNation.org (supported by the Soros Criminal Justice Fund), which critically examines the Secure Communities program and the increasing detention of innocent and low-level immigrant offenders. Feltz is a former news director for KPFT-FM in Houston, Texas, and currently a producer for *Democracy Now!* Baksh is a freelance writer and graphic artist residing in Baltimore, Maryland.

LUIS A. FERNANDEZ is an assistant professor in criminology and criminal justice at Northern Arizona University. He is the author and editor of several books, including *Policing Dissent* and *Shutting Down the Streets: Political Violence and Social Control in the Global Era* (with Amory Starr and Christian Scholl). His research and teaching interests include protest policing, social movements, globalization, immigration, and issues in the social control of late modernity.

RUTH WILSON GILMORE, a professor of geography in the doctoral program in earth and environmental sciences at the City University of New York, is an activist as well as an intellectual and is a past president of the American Studies Association (2010–2011). She examined how political and economic forces produced California's prison boom in *Golden Gulag: Prisons, Surplus, Crisis, and Opposition in Globalizing California*, which was recognized by ASA with the Lora Romero First Book Award. She holds a PhD in economic geography and social theory from Rutgers University.

AMY GOTTLIEB is the program director of the American Friends Service Committee Immigrant Rights Program in Newark, New Jersey, a nonprofit organization dedicated to promoting the rights of immigrants and refugees through legal services, community organizing, and advocacy. Gottlieb graduated in 1996 from Rutgers Law School, where she is an adjunct professor of immigration law. She chairs the steering committee of the Detention Watch Network and is a board member of La Fuente and Houses on the Moon Theater Company.

GAEL GUEVARA is a former collective member and former community organizing coordinator of the Sylvia Rivera Law Project, an organization that provides free legal services and community organizing support to low-income and people of color who are transgender, intersex, and gender-nonconforming. Guevara is an organizer with Transforming Justice, a national coalition that works to address the root causes of imprisonment, criminalization, and poverty in transgender and gender-nonconforming communities.

ZOE HAMMER is a faculty member in the Program in Cultural and Regional Studies at Prescott College. She earned her PhD in comparative cultural and literary studies at the University of Arizona in 2004. Hammer is active in social justice movements in Arizona and nationally, sitting on the board of directors of the Border Action Network and serving as a member of the Southern Border Communities Coalition. She has also served on the boards of the Criminal Justice Steering Committee of the American Friends Service Committee, the Progressive Communicator's Network Criminal Justice Working Group, the Institute for Restorative Justice, and the National Security States Working Group.

JULIANNE HING is the editorial assistant at *Colorlines* magazine. Before joining *Colorlines* she served for two years as an editor of *Jaded* magazine, an award-winning progressive publication at the University of California, Irvine. Hing came to journalism by way of campus organizing around labor and access issues. She has written about detention and deportation, the politics of globalization, pop culture and consumerism, and food. Her work has appeared on AlterNet, WireTap, and other outlets.

SUBHASH KATEEL is a cofounder and codirector of Families for Freedom, a multiethnic network of immigrants facing deportation. He has worked at Jesuit Refugee Services and the American Friends Service Committee (Wayfarer House), and initiated and coordinated the Detention Project for Desis Rising Up and Moving. Kateel has received various honors for his organizing work, including a Soros New York Community Fellowship and the Volunteer of the Year Award from the Detention Watch Network. He earned an MS in social work from Columbia University and now lives in Miami, Florida, where he works with the Florida Immigrant Coalition to help develop community-based responses to ICE raids, detentions, and deportations.

JODIE M. LAWSTON is an associate professor of women's studies at California State University, San Marcos. Her research interests include women's incarceration, prison expansion, immigrant detention, and social justice movements. She coedited *Abolition Now!: Ten Years of Strategy and Struggle against the Prison Industrial Complex* (as part of the CR10 Publications Collective) and *Razor Wire Women: Prisoners, Activists, Scholars, and Artists* (with Ashley Lucas). She serves on the boards of several nonprofit organizations and is active in grassroots movements against prison and immigrant detention.

BOB LIBAL is a senior organizer for Grassroots Leadership, and coordinated its national Campaign to End Immigrant Family Detention. He was a founding member of Texans United for Families and serves on the steering committee of the national Detention Watch Network. Libal edits the *Texas Prison Bid'ness* blog and has authored or co-authored many articles and reports for Grassroots Leadership, including *Progress or Profit: Positive Alternatives to Privatization and Incarceration in Shelby County, Tennessee* and *Operation Streamline: Drowning Justice and Draining Dollars along the Rio Grande*.

JENNA M. LOYD is a scholar and activist who studies the political geographies of violence and health. Her book *Freedom's Body* traces the health activism of the Black freedom, women's, and antiwar movements in Los Angeles during the 1960s and 1970s. She is working on a book with Alison Mountz on the post-1980 history of the U.S. immigrant detention system in the context of racialized Cold War geopolitics, U.S. military restructuring, and the growth of the prison system.

LAUREN MARTIN worked with Texans United for Families from 2008 to 2011, and was a scholar-in-residence with Grassroots Leadership. She helped to start the Hutto Visitation Program. She has published opinionated editorials, blog posts, and scholarly articles on homeland security, executive power, and geographies of detention and confinement. Martin holds an MA and a PhD in geography from the University of Kentucky; her research has focused on U.S. noncitizen family detention policy, immigration law, borders, and homeland security. She is a postdoctoral researcher in the Mobilities, Borders, and Identities Research Group in the Department of Geography at the University of Oulu, Finland.

LAURA MCTIGHE is a faculty fellow in the Department of Religion at Columbia University. In 2000, she founded Philadelphia FIGHT's Prison Services Department, working in collaboration with formerly incarcerated leaders to create TEACH Outside, *Prison Health News*, and the Support Center for Prison Advocacy. After launching the Project UNSHACKLE national network in 2008, she returned to her Philadelphia home to co-found the Institute for Community Justice. Since 2010, she has served on the boards of Women with a Vision (New Orleans), Men & Women in Prison Ministries (Chicago), and Reconstruction Inc. (Philadelphia). McTighe received her MTS in Islamic studies from Harvard Divinity School and her BA in religion from Haverford College.

MATT MITCHELSON is an assistant professor of geography at Kennesaw State University. His research examines the economic geography of prison privatization, the urban population geographies that structure imprisonment, and the geography of controversial political representations, such as census counts, that follow from mass imprisonment.

MARIA CRISTINA MORALES received her PhD from Texas A&M University and is currently an assistant professor of sociology at the University of Texas at El Paso. Morales has published in several areas related to labor, inequality, and Latina/os, including job access and wages, ethnic resources for workers, how masculinity operates to mask discriminatory practices at immigrant job sites, wage disparities among women on the border, and gendered and sexual violence at the border.

ALISON MOUNTZ is an associate professor of geography at Wilfrid Laurier University and the Canada Research Chair in Global Migration at the Balsillie School of International Affairs. Her current research examines struggles over border enforcement, asylum, and detention, and she serves as the principal investigator of the Island Detentions Project. In 2010 Mountz published *Seeking Asylum: Human Smuggling and Bureaucracy at the Border*.

RUBEN R. MURILLO is a lecturer in the Department of Ethnic Studies at the University of California, San Diego. He worked as a Spanish-language interpreter for the Department of Justice for two years, interpreting hundreds of political asylum, suspension of deportation, and aggravated felony hearings. His publications include "Ser o no ser?: Overcoming Silence on the Border in Margarita Cota-Cardenas' Puppet," in *Transnational Resistance: Experience and Experiment in Women's Writing*. Murillo engages in social justice work along the U.S.-Mexico border that exposes the work of vigilante groups and raises awareness about U.S. immigration policies.

JOSEPH NEVINS, an associate professor of geography at Vassar College, is the author of *Dying to Live: A Story of U.S. Immigration in an Age of Global Apartheid*.

NICOLE PORTER is the state advocacy coordinator for the Sentencing Project in Washington, D.C. She is the former director of the ACLU's Prison and Jail Accountability Project, whose mission is to monitor the conditions of confinement in Texas jails and prisons. Porter graduated from the University of Texas, Austin, with a master's degree in public affairs from the LBJ School. Her BA is in international affairs from Johns Hopkins University. She also studied African politics at the University of Ghana.

JOSHUA M. PRICE directed the NAACP's Broome County Jail Health Care Project from 2004 to 2007. In 2006, he co-founded the Southern Tier Social Justice Project, composed of formerly incarcerated people and their allies, to advocate for formerly incarcerated people in the face of discrimination in housing, employment, health care, and social services and at the hands of parole officers and the police. He has been honored as Citizen of the Year by the Broome/Tioga County NAACP and received a citation from the New York State Assembly for "outstanding commitment to the civil rights of New Yorkers." Price is an associate professor in the Program in Philosophy, Interpretation, and Culture at the State University of New York at Binghamton, where he is also affiliated with the Program in Latin American and Caribbean Areas Studies.

SAID SADDIKI received his doctorate in public law from the University of Oujda, Morocco, in 2002. He is currently an associate professor of international relations at the University of Fez. He has written four books (in Arabic): *State in a Changing World: Nation-State and New Global Challenges*; *Management of Moroccan Foreign Policy*; *New Political Powers*; and *Dimensions of New Diplomacy*. He is the co-author of several other books and numerous articles on the new dynamics of international relations, including transnational immigration, foreign policies, diplomacy, Western Saharan issues, and borders.

MICOL SEIGEL is an associate professor of American studies and African American and African diaspora studies at Indiana University, Bloomington. Her research and teaching focus on prisons and policing, state discipline and surveillance, cultural politics, transnational connections, and race in the Americas, particularly in the United States and Brazil. An abolitionist scholar and activist, she teaches in the Inside-Out Prison Exchange Program; was a member of Critical Resistance, South, from 1999 to 2003 and CR, Los Angeles, from 2003 to 2007; and currently organizes in Bloomington with Decarcerate Monroe County.

RASHAD SHABAZZ is an assistant professor of geography at the University of Vermont. His work explores the linkages among race, gender, cultural production, and carceral space. He has worked with the prison abolitionist group Critical Resistance and as editor for the *Journal of Prisoners on Prisons*.

CHRISTOPHER STENKEN worked with the Florence Immigrant and Refugee Rights Project as a legal assistant in 2008–2009. FIRRP is a nonprofit organization which since 1989 has been a clearinghouse for best practices and know-your-rights materials; it continues to serve thousands of immigrants and refugees detained in central Arizona without legal representation.

MARGO TAMEZ (Ndé, Lipan Apache) is a member of the Lipan Apache Band of Texas and an assistant professor in indigenous studies and gender and women's studies at the University of British Columbia, Okanagan. She co-founded Lipan Apache Women Defense as a site to develop research and scholarship on indigenous human rights by, with, for, and alongside first peoples of the Texas-Mexico border region. Her publications include "Restoring Lipan Apache Women's Laws, Lands, and Strength in El Calaboz Ranchería at the Texas-Mexico Border" in *Signs* and "'Our Way of Life Is Our Resistance': Indigenous Women and Anti-Imperialist Challenges to Militarization along the U.S.-Mexico Border" in *Works and Days*. Tamez is the author of the critically acclaimed poetry collections *Raven Eye* and *Naked Wanting*.

ELIZABETH VARGAS joined Project WHAT! (We're Here and Talking!) in the summer of 2009 because of her experiences with an alcoholic father who has been in and out of her life and in and out of jail. The program employs young people who have experienced parental incarceration as the primary content developers and facilitators for trainings targeting service providers, policymakers, other adults, and youth. Vargas's goals in life are to become a lawyer, counselor, and teacher and help other kids in need all around the world. She is currently attending Patten University and planning on getting a master's degree in theology.

MONICA W. VARSANYI is an associate professor in political science at the John Jay College of Criminal Justice and on the doctoral faculty in geography at the Graduate Center, both at the City University of New York. Her research addresses the politics of unauthorized immigration in the United States. She edited *Taking Local Control: Immigration Policy Activism in U.S. Cities and States* and has had articles published in the *Annals of the Association of American Geographers*, the *International Journal of Urban and Regional Research*, *Law and Policy*, *Urban Geography*, *Citizenship Studies*, *Antipode*, and the *Los Angeles Times*.

MARIANA VITURRO is the deputy director of the National Domestic Workers Alliance, which organizes domestic workers for rights, recognition, and dignity for their work. Previously, as the co-director of St. Peter's Housing Committee, Viturro guided a merger with another organization, resulting in the creation of Causa Justa::Just Cause, a fierce group that brings together African American and Latino communities in San Francisco and Oakland. She has been organizing with the Latino immigrant community in the San Francisco Bay area since 1998.

HARSHA WALIA and PROMA TAGORE are members of No One Is Illegal, a grassroots, anticolonial, migrant justice group whose leaders all have migrant or racialized backgrounds. As a movement for self-determination that challenges the ideology of immigration controls, we take action to combat racial profiling, detention and deportation, the national security apparatus, law enforcement brutality, and the exploitative working conditions of migrants. We envision a world where everyone has the right to sustenance and the ability to provide it; where we are free of oppression, misery, and exploitation; and where we are able to live meaningfully in relationship to one another and with reverence for Mother Earth that sustains us.

SETH FREED WESSLER is a writer and researcher based in Brooklyn. He currently works at the Applied Research Center and Colorlines.com, where he writes on immigration, the safety net, national security, and child welfare and family policy. Wessler is the author of numerous reports, including "Shattered Families: The Perilous Intersection of Immigration Enforcement and the Child Welfare System" and "Race and Recession: How Inequality Rigged the Economy and How to Change the Rules." Wessler has received numerous awards for his reporting, and he appears regularly on broadcast media outlets.

Index

Page numbers in italics indicate photographs and illustrations.

abandonment, 3, 285
abolition: and analysis, 2–4, 8–11, 86, 317; defined 2, 10; and movement building, 2–4, 7, 9–11, 51–53, 172, 199–200, 216, 218, 226, 229, 244, 322–23; and noncompliance, 11, 202, 206n42, 235; and nonreformist reforms, 10, 250–51, 318; and practice, 171, 199, 217, 220; and strategies, 179, 217, 225. *See also* no borders, strategies or politics; No Borders movement
Abu-Jamal, Mumia, 292
Africa-Europe borderlands, 7, 28–29, 97
African Americans: and Black politics, 288–91; and civil rights movement, 339; and coalition-building, 50–53, 164, 231–32, 242–43, 251, 280–82, 342; and criminalization, 9, 123, 132, 164, 215, 267, 280, 298, 305, 317, 338; and disenfranchisement, 267–69, 272; and HIV/AIDS, 287–98, 301–11; and labor, 47–49; and liberation movements, 10, 50–51, 339; and NAACP, 242–43, 247–48, 288, 290; and war on drugs, 132, 267, 305–7
Ahmed, Leila, 301
AIDS. *See* HIV/AIDS
alien: ideology of, 62, 105–6, 109, 111, 195, 340, 343; and legal categorization, 3, 75, 107, 143, 150, 191, 338
alienation, 49, 197, 199

alien registration number, 95, 102
Allen, Jennifer, 218, 220, 223
Al'ter, Boris, 105
American Border Patrol, 182
American Civil Liberties Union (ACLU), 58, 255, 257, 259, 262; and the National Prison Project, 147
American Friends Service Committee (AFSC), 163–65, 167–68, 171, 218, 224
Amnesty International, 108, 262
Andreas, Peter, 33
Andrews, Bill, 117, 119–22
antiviolence, 3, 7–11, 58, 164–65, 167–69, 200, 278, 281–82
A-number. *See* alien registration number
Applied Research Center, 8n21
Arab Spring, 2
Arellano, Elvira, 327, 331–32
Arellano, Victoria, 325–27, 331–32
Arendt, Hannah, 24
Arizona: Davis-Monthan Air Force Base, 198; DeConcini Federal Courthouse (Tucson), 190; Department of Corrections, 211, 214; Eloy Detention Center, 212; and Florence Immigrant and Refugee Rights Project, 212; Jan Brewer, 201; Joe Arpaio, 181–83, 186–87, 202, 341, 345; migrant fatalities, 107; organizing in, 10, 99, 199, 217, 237, 341; Proposition 300, 194; SB1070, 202, 228–30, 341, 343; Tucson Sector, 191; and U.S.-Mexico borderlands, 184, 191–93, 204, 218; vigilante groups founded in, 182

357

Arizona Daily Star, 193
Arizona Prison Moratorium Coalition (APMC), 217–21
Arpaio, Joe, 181–83, 186–87, 202, 341, 344
Ashcroft, John, 340
Association of Private Correctional and Treatment Organizations, 146
asylum: and advocacy, 95, 99–100, 212–14, 256; and detention of asylum seekers, 92, 95–98, 105, 107–9, 163, 164, 253, 254; policy, 7, 75–76, 84, 107–9, 113n6, 163, 164, 253; seekers of, 75–76, 102n2, 121, 321
Auburn Correctional Facility (New York), 295
Audre Lorde Project, 316
Austin, Jim, 44
Austin, Texas, 70, 144, 254–55, 258–59

Balagoon, Kuwasi, 295
Banks, Annie, 87
Baucus, Max, 137
Bedford Hills Correctional Facility (New York), 293
Bell, John, 303–4
Berks County Family Care Shelter (Pennsylvania), 253, 264
Bernstein, Nina, 100
Binghamton, New York, 241–52
Bisbee, Arizona, 220
Black Cat Tavern uprising (Los Angeles), 330, 335
border: deaths along, 97, 193; and enforcement, 31, 34, 55, 97; fortification of, 3–8; militarization of, 3–9, 31–33, 37, 66, 123, 139, 179, 182, 190–94, 198–200, 216–26, 232, 337; movement across, 30, 38, 75, 92; and nation-state(s), 1–4, 32, 74, 82, 91, 93, 190–94, 199, 205; and no-borders politics, 80, 85, 179, 198–200; policing of, 33, 37, 84, 181–87; and prisons, 1–11, 17, 44, 55, 58, 70, 199, 215–27, 285, 311; and violence, 4, 7, 29
Border Action Network (BAN), 206, 218, 224
borderlands: and Mexico-U.S.A., 7, 21, 27–37, 44, 190–94; and Morocco-Spain, 27–37
Borderlands Autonomist Collective, 199
border sexual conquest, 17, 27, 31–33, 36–37
Braithwaite, Ronald, 294
Bratton, William, 115–23
Bratton Group, 118–20
Braz, Rose, 10
Brewer, Janice (Jan), 201
Broome County Correctional Facility (New York), 243, 251
Buchanan, Pat, 339
Burnaby Correctional Center for Women (Canada), 77

Calderón, Felipe, 34
California: and felon disenfranchisement, 267; prison system, 51–52, 291–92; and sentencing, 267
California Prison Moratorium Project (PMP), 51–52, 217–18
Cameron County, Texas, 62–64, 67
Campbell, Howard, 35
Canada: and Bill C-49, 76; and Citizenship and Immigration Canada, 80; immigration detention and deportation, 75–77, 86; migration policy, 74, 81–82, 84
Cannick, Jasmyne, 334
capitalism, 1–4, 32, 46, 53; and borders, 82; and criminalization, 79. *See also* neoliberal capitalism
Carter, John, 146
CAR-3. *See* Criminal Alien Requirement 3
Casa del Migrante, 94

INDEX • 359

Central America: deportation to, 30; migrants from, 29, 46, 222; and war, 10, 167, 185
Central California Environmental Justice Network, 51
Ceuta, Spanish enclave of, 28–31
chain gang, 181
Chávez, Juan Pablo, 345
Chertoff, Michael, 69, 144
Christmas Island, Australian territory of, 86, 92, 97
citizenship: and civil death, 8; and criminalization, 8–9, 42–43, 77–79, 108, 111–12, 186, 229–31; and exclusion, 6, 55, 112, 203; and human rights, 19–20, 24–25, 83; and ideology of "good citizen," 8–9, 78–80, 89, 231–32, 332–34, 345; and "illegality," 78–79, 88, 111–12, 343; and immigrant restriction, 5–6, 8, 77–78; and imprisonment, 6–8; and labor, 20–23, 82–84, 170, 233; and mobility, 6, 22–25, 80, 89, 233; and national discrimination, 22, 32–33; and national identity, 75, 77–80, 186, 194; and nation-state, 6–8, 24–25, 77–80, 203; and organizing across citizen/noncitizen divides, 52, 80, 111–12, 218, 237, 251, 282; and power inequalities, 10, 20–22, 24–25, 80; and punishment, 1, 3; and racism, 24–25, 182; and residence, 22, 272, 282; and rights, 20–22, 52, 266–73, 282; and voting, 228, 266–73
Ciudad Juárez, Chihuahua, 31. See also Mexico-U.S. borderlands
CiviGenics, 137
civil death, 8, 268
Civil Homeland Defense Corps, 182
civil rights movement, 233, 242, 292, 339, 340
civil society, 278, 280–81
Clinton, Bill, 161, 291–92, 333, 342

Coahuilas, 57, 59
Coalición de Derechos Humanos, 29n8, 198
coalition-building: and anti-detention organizing, 95, 98, 101, 255–263; and bridging anti-prison and immigrant justice, 3, 217–20, 224–27, 241; and indigenous, 59; and no-borders organizing, 198–201; and organizing across citizen/noncitizen divides, 6–7, 48–49, 231–32, 237, 282–84, 322–23, 345; and queer, 327, 335; and strategy, 50–53, 140, 224–27, 231–32, 243–45, 255–63, 282–84, 322–23, 327, 335, 345; and trans organizing, 315, 322–23; and voting rights, 270
Cochise County, Arizona, 192, 216–17, 219–20, 225, 227n4
coercive mobility. See under mobility
Cohen, Cathy, 289–90
colonialism: Canadian, 79–80; and capitalism, 1–2; and conquest, 17, 31, 36–37; and decolonization, 2, 8, 11, 58–61, 191, 199–200, 215–16; and dispossession, 1–5, 7, 11, 50; European, 62, 69–70; and national territorial boundaries, 57–70, 79–80, 88, 183, 191, 194, 199; neocolonialism, 17, 28, 122, 216, 245; North American, 191, 199, 201; and prisons, 86, 200; settler, 56, 58, 60; United States, 57–70, 122, 183–84, 186, 194
Comisión Nacional de los Derechos Humanos, 33
Committee on Homeland Security, 146
community: and belonging, 220; and development, 134, 221, 224–25, 227; and organizing, 48, 51, 59, 198, 220, 302–4, 310–11, 317
Concerned Citizens of Cochise County (Arizona), 227n4
condoms, 287, 293–94, 296–98

Congress of Industrial Organizations (CIO), 47
Conjunto Ceará (Brazil), 119
conquest, 17, 27–37
Conyers, John, 270
Cornell Companies, 145, 220–24
Correctional Medical Services (CMS), 243
Corrections Corporation of America (CCA), 44, 137, 143, 145–50, 211, 254, 263
Corva, Dominic, 35
Craddock, Susan, 297
Criminal Alien Requirement 3, 217–20, 224–25
criminalization: and abolitionist organizing strategies, 11, 43, 53, 226; and citizenship, 6; and class struggle, 6, 43; and coalition-building strategies, 43, 46, 226, 231–32, 322–23, 344–46; and communities of color, 81, 132, 164, 215, 277, 298, 317, 338; and dissent, 105–14, 185; and drugs, 267, 339; and education, 46; and gender-related harms, 317–21; and healing justice, 168–70; and homelessness, 229–30; and ideology, 8–10, 183; and immigration and immigrants, 4, 75, 84, 156, 186, 196–200, 229, 319; and militarization, 3, 191; and mobility, 6, 89, 196–200; and national identity, 183, 186; and national security rationales, 105–14, 191, 248; organizing strategies, 53, 226, 231–32, 278, 322–23, 337–46; and policing, 52, 229, 279; and political motivations, 80–81, 113n2, 248, 339–40; and poverty, 132–33, 139; and racialization, 6, 49–50, 187, 191, 229; and racial profiling, 81; and survival, 319; and trans, 319
criminal justice system: and HIV/AIDS, 306; and immigrants and immigration, 127, 153, 163, 185, 198, 229, 234; and organizing, 42, 163, 218, 254, 301, 315, 338, 342; and prison industrial complex, 133–34; production of, 28, 35; and racial biases, 161
criminology and criminologists, 44, 155, 231
crisis: and capitalism, 1–5, 17–18, 42–53, 169, 282–83; and HIV/AIDS, 288, 297, 306; and humanitarian crisis, 38; and imprisonment, 84, 308, 310–11; and policing, 1, 5, 8, 50; and sovereignty, 8, 55, 182; and the state, 1, 4, 8
critical race theory, 23, 32, 49–50, 59, 291
Critical Resistance (CR), 45, 51, 199, 206n35, 217–18, 225, 323, 354
Customs and Border Protection (CBP). See under United States Department of Homeland Security

Dacumos, Nico, 326
Dauvergne, Catherine, 78
Davis, Angela, 1, 7, 86
Davis, Michael (CCA chaplain and spokesman), 145
Davis, Mike, 44–45
decarceration, 250
decolonization, 2, 11, 60, 200. See also colonialism
dehumanization, 2, 20, 58, 84, 101, 105, 118
Dellums, Ron, 295
Democracy Restoration Act (U.S.), 270
Dent, Gina, 1
Department of Homeland Security (DHS). See United States Department of Homeland Security
deportation: and detention, 75, 77, 80; effects on families, 7, 159–62, 177–78, 253–65; rates, 8; and removal procedures, 30, 75–76, 195, 212, 253; and repatriation, 195, 203n1, 205n32, 328; and voluntary departure, 203n1
deregulation, 133, 254, 279
detention: and activism and advocacy,

98–102, 255–61; and concealed identities, 94–95; conditions of, 108, 110, 147–50, 242, 256–57; construction of facilities, 107, 111–12, 148, 193, 215–19, 224–26, 254, 279; detainee organizing within facilities, 99–100; and forcible confinement, 2, 7–8, 75, 127; on islands, 76, 92, 97–101, 223, 227; and legal access and representation, 92–93, 95–98, 149, 209–14, 255–61; mandatory detention, 154, 163, 168, 254, 262, 267, 341; and medical neglect, 96–97, 148–49; of Muslims and Middle Easterners, 245; remotely located facilities, 66, 87–103, 254, 258; and suicide, 76, 80, 96, 108; and telephone access, 76, 95–96, 148–49, 161, 213; transfers of detainees, 93–94, 99, 210, 244, 247, 264
Detention Watch Network (DWN), 98, 101
Detention Working Group (Texas), 254–55
deterrence, 92, 108, 192–93, 196–97
development, 45, 60, 137–39, 220; community, 220–27; prisons as development strategy, 131–35, 217; and underdevelopment, 220
diaspora, 64, 74, 332; prison-created, 301–11
differently abled, 317
direct action, 202, 317
disability. *See* differently abled
discrimination: and felons, 153, 269; and indigenous, 65; and national citizenship, 22, 55, 83, 183; and race, 105, 107, 112, 183, 269, 290; and trans, 314, 316–19
disenfranchisement, 35, 127, 266–74, 317, 339
displacement: and anti-immigrant violence, 19, 277; and colonization, 86; economic, 11, 30, 37, 79, 179, 221; ideological, 106

dispossession, 2, 7, 10–11, 20, 62, 69, 129–41, 279, 282
domestic violence. *See* violence
Dream Act, 236
drugs: trade, 30, 33, 35–36, 158–59, 185, 210, 293; war on, 28, 35, 37, 55, 78, 132, 154, 231, 248, 266–67, 292, 301–12, 339–40
Dublin Convention (I and II), 109
Du Bois, W. E. B., 50, 251
Dutch Stray Insurgent Clown Army (Clolonel), 105–6

Eisenhower, Dwight, 45, 116
El Calaboz Rancheria (Kónitsąąhįį dá'ááší Gokíyaa/Texas), 60–68
Elizabeth Detention Center (New Jersey), 148
Eloy Detention Center (Arizona), 212
emancipation, 100, 237
enemies of the state, 21, 49, 52–53, 221, 253
England: nationalism, 6, 12; policing, 6
environmental justice, 51–52, 71n7, 79, 216, 223
ethnic studies curricula, 202
European Union (EU), 22, 30, 34, 55, 108–9
exception (state of), 58, 179
expedited removal. *See* deportation: and removal procedures
extralegal enforcement, 183
extremism, 105–14, 181

Families to Amend California's Three Strikes (FACTS), 50–51
family: and effects of detention and deportation, 7, 159–62, 177–78, 253–65, 309, 337, 339, 346; and effects of imprisonment, 292, 301–4, 306, 308–9, 322, 327, 345; and reunification, 322; and separation, 7, 94, 168, 212, 254, 262, 322; and trauma of immigration raids, 279, 330

Farid, Mujahid, 295
Federal Bureau of Investigation (FBI). *See* United States Federal Bureau of Investigation
Federal Bureau of Prisons (BOP). *See* United States Federal Bureau of Prisons
Federal Housing Administration (FHA), 181
Federation for American Immigration Reform (FAIR), 228
Feingold, Russ, 270
felony, 132, 144, 150, 156, 183, 266–67, 269–70, 273n23, 305
Ferguson, John D., 145–46
FIERCE, 316
Florence Immigrant and Refugee Rights Project (FIRRP), 212; and Chris Brelje, 212
Flores v. Reno, 257, 259–60
Florida Immigrant Coalition, 345
Fortaleza project, 118–20
Fortress Europe, 28–29
Fosado, Gisela, 12n16
Foucault, Michel, 37, 39n50
Fourteenth Amendment (United States Constitution), 237, 269
freedom, 1–4, 8–11, 77, 88, 107, 111, 169, 232, 310–11, 340; and abolition, 2–4, 8–11, 89; and emancipation, 237; of movement, 1–2, 10–11, 24, 89, 113n1, 161–62, 169, 230, 232
Freire, Paolo, 47

gangs, 122, 218, 335
Garcia, Isabel, 198
Garcia-Martinez, Maria del Carmen, 149–51
gay rights movement, 238, 290, 327, 334–35
gender issues: gender-based violence, 3, 5, 7, 31–32, 36, 59, 318; harassment and policing, 32–33, 195, 315–16, 319, 322; health and mental health, 287–88, 303, 306, 321, 327; identity, 6, 60, 127, 282, 314, 319, 321; poverty, 129, 315–16; prisons, 250, 319
genocide, 2, 57–60, 67–70, 79
Geo Group, 145
geopolitics, 4, 25, 27, 203, 288
Gilbert, David, 293, 295
Gilbert, Robert, 193–94
Gilchrist, Jim, 182
Gilman, Denise, 66
Gilmore, Craig, 6
Gilmore, Ruth Wilson, 6, 42–53, 133
global apartheid, 1, 17, 19–25, 25n8, 55, 78, 82, 107, 197, 201, 203, 205n28, 338–44
Global Detention Project, 99
Global Exchange, 12n29
globalization, 36, 80, 109, 233
Gonzalez, Richard, 68
Gorz, André, 51, 250
Gottlieb, Amy, 163–72
Gramsci, Antonio, 278–79
Granger, Afuwa, *86*
Great Depression, 53
Green, Kenneth, 270
green card, 185, 337–40, 344
Grewal, Harjap, *88*
Güereca, Sergio Adrian Hernandez, 38n10

Hall, Stuart, 5, 50
Harm Reduction Coalition, 53
harms, 1–2, 5, 98, 128, 169, 171, 239, 251, 285, *320*
Hart-Cellar Act, 271
hate crimes legislation, 165, 317
Hayworth, J. D., 184, 186
healing justice, 163–65, 168, 171
health care: access to, 42, 164, 168, 205n32, 230, 283, 287, 290, 321; cutbacks, 279; HIV/AIDS, 287, 321; and immigration detention, 96, 148; and jails, 241–51, 303; and prisons, 292, 294

Health Service Corps, 148
Hernández, Esequiel, 66–67
Hininger, Damon, 143
HIV/AIDS: African American rates of, 288, 296, 312n15; and Black politics, 288–91; and homophobia, 289–90; and immigration, 289; prevention, 287, 311; and prison, 287–88, 291–96, 302–3, 306–10; and racism, 289–91; and reentry, 296–97; transmission, 296–97
Hoijer, Harry, 63–64
Homeland Security. *See* United States Department of Homeland Security
homelessness, 77, 129, 157, 160, 224, 229–30, 244, 272, 316, 321
horizontalism, 216
Horton, Myles, 47
Houston Processing Center, 143–45
Howard, John, 92, 97
Huerta, Dolores, 186
Human Rights Watch (HRW), 102n5, 108
hunger strike, 2, 77, 108
Hunter v. Underwood, 269

identity documentation, 42, 94; driver's licenses, 149, 229–30; and gender identity, 315–16, 321; and marriage documentation, 230–32; and migration status, 319; and primary and secondary education, 230; and trans people, 314–16, 321; and voting, 272
ideology: and "criminality," 3–4, 11, 43, 79, 278; and "illegality," 3–4, 11, 43, 79, 278; national, 3–4, 74, 79, 112–13, 113n2, 181–86, 203, 205n34, 285; and political organizing, 215–16; and prison expansion, 47, 129; and the state, 278–81, 285
Illegal Immigration Reform and Immigrant Responsibility Act (IIRIRA), 144, 153, 161, 185, 333
illegality, 76, 79, 195, 200

immigrant justice movement, 3, 169, 216, 226, 322–23
Immigration Act (1971), England, 6
Immigration and Customs Enforcement (ICE). *See under* United States Department of Homeland Security
immigration and immigrants: and agency, 17, 27, 223; and border enforcement, 21–22, 28–29, 34, 97, 190–95, 198–206, 337; and criminalization and national security rationales, 196–200, 248; and criminalization and racialization of 6, 84, 183; and criminalization of migration status, 4, 43, 111, 164, 169, 183, 186; and criminalization of movement, 75, 84, 89, 191, 196–200, 229; and criminalization of survival, 319; and detention and deportation, 75, 77, 80; and disenfranchisement, 266–74; exploitation of, 20, 27, 31–33, 83, 169–70, 342–43; "good immigrant" ideology, 8–9, 78–79, 88–89, 231–32, 332–34, 339, 342n4, 345; and interior enforcement, 92–94, 101, 144–46, 150, 161, 170, 213–14, 230–31, 235, 261–63, 277, 283, 337, 343nn1–2; and justice movements, 3, 216, 283–84, 322; and labor organizing and labor unions, 21, 49; legislation, 30, 80, 144, 146, 153; legislative reform, 162, 166, 203, 213, 238, 260–62, 266, 278, 281–83, 337, 341–42; policing, 3–4, 7–8, 20, 31, 33–37, 55, 81, 84, 92, 115, 139, 181, 285, 321; and pro-immigrant groups, 25; and scapegoating and xenophobia, 29–30, 139, 156, 247, 271, 280, 315, 343
Immigration and Naturalization Service (INS). *See under* United States Department of Justice
Immigration and Refugee Protection Act (IRPA), 75, 81–82

immigration policy: in Alabama, 4, 179; Aliens Act (Netherlands, 2001), 107; in Arizona, 238; Arizona Senate Bill (SB) 1070, 179, 201–2, 206n42, 228–29, 237, 341, 343, 344; Bill C-49 (Canada), 76; Chinese Exclusion Act (1882), 329; Dream Act, 236; England's Immigration Act (1971), 6; and ICE ACCESS programs, 238, 341, 343; Illegal Immigration Reform and Immigrant Responsibility Act (IIRIRA), 144, 153, 161, 185, 333; Immigration and Nationality Act (1994), 210; Immigration and Refugee Protection Act (IRPA), 75, 80–81; Immigration Reform and Control Act (IRCA), 30; Immigration Reform and Control Act (IRCA, 1986), 30; Page Act (1875), 329; and policing in England, 6, 12; Proposition 187, 185; Sensenbrenner-King bill (2005–2006), 340; and the 287(g) program, 149–50, 161, 202, 341, 343; U.S. federal, 149, 154, 201

imperialism, 4–5, 8, 20, 31, 79, 186, 241, 245, 247

imprisonment: as economic development strategy, 130, 134, 137, 139, 217, 220; and people of color, 7, 74, 86, 129, 131–35, 138–40, 154, 161, 215, 223, 225, 248, 287, 292, 305–7; and poverty, 86, 131–40, 215, 248, 287, 292; and social welfare, 131–35

innocence (paradigm of organizing), 9, 43, 256

Institute for Multicultural Development, 105

Intensive Supervision Appearance Program (ISAP), 261–62

Inter-American Court of Human Rights, 36

Inter-American Policy Exchange, 118

International Organization for Migration, 97

International Workers Day, 277

intersectionality theory and analysis, 5, 9, 27, 31–32, 69, 285–86, 317–18, 319–22, 326–28, 330–35

Isaacs, Caroline, 218–20, 223–24

James, Calvin, 152–61
Jawetz, Tom, 147–48
Johnson, Terry, 149
Johnson-Castro, Jay, 258, 265n11
Jones, Ronald T., 145, 148
Joseph, Warren, 338
Jumano Apaches, 57, 66
justice, 164–69, 171, 209–14, 284, 304, 309–10, 315–23, 327, 337
Justice for Janitors, 48

Kickapoo, 57, 59
kidnapping, 32–34, 155
King, Mackenzie, 78
King, Rodney, 2
Kingdom Care Reentry Network (KCRN) (Philadelphia), 302, 311n1
Kingston Immigration Holding Centre (Canada), 81
kinship, 57, 59–61, 67
know-your-rights (KYR) training, 209, 212, 234
Ku Klux Klan (KKK), 181, 227n4

labor: agricultural, 83, 134, 136, 138, 206n37, 254, 283, 292; and contractors, 21, 83; domestic, 67; and gender, 31–32, 84; and migration, 29, 32, 47–48; organizing, 21, 46, 48, 232, 272; and racialization, 22; and rights, 21; and slavery, 46, 83–84, 181, 278; on state's terms, 82–85; and unionization, 21, 225; and working poor, 132, 319

Larson, Rolf, 117
Latina/o people, 116, 122, 136, 149–50, 219, 223, 235, 281, 335, 344; and anti-Latino profiling and racism, 181–87, 229–31, 279–81, 340; coalition-building, 52–53, 219, 231–32, 280–82, 342; and criminalization, 132–33, 149–50, 181–82, 185–86, 229–30, 267–68; and identity, 59, 116; and Latino politics, 235, 281–84, 344
law and legal systems: administrative, 75, 97, 149–50, 154, 159, 183, 193, 195; criminal, 81, 154, 163–64, 183, 187, 254; historic, 6, 182, 206n42, 231, 237; immigration, 97, 149–50, 154, 170, 183, 193, 195; rule of law (as ideology), 1, 8, 182–87; and war on drugs, 35
Lee, Barbara, 295
legality, discourses of, 76, 79, 182, 195, 200
legal services, 209, 212, 258, 314–17, 319
lesbian and gay rights movements, 238, 290, 327, 334–35
liberation, 85, 102, 232, 273n6
Lipan Apaches, 57, 67
Los Angeles, California: county sheriff, 335; and imprisonment, 48; and labor organizing, 47; and migration raids, 328, 330–32, 335; police department, 115–23; and police violence, 121–23, 329–30
lynching, 67, 181, 184

Mahmood, Anser, 338
Malaysia, treatment of unauthorized migrants, 20
mandatory detention. *See under* detention
mandatory minimum sentences, 132, 267, 305–6
Mandela, Nelson, 19
Manhattan Institute (MI), 117–18, 120

mapping, 92–102, 287–99, 306–7
maquiladoras, 31
mass imprisonment. *See* prisons
mass incarceration. *See* prisons
Mauer, Marc, 248, 267
Mbembe, Achille, 58, 69
McMiller, Darryl, 270
media: framing and reframing, 165–66, 327–28, 334; racialized representations, 88, 181, 186, 229, 280; representations of immigrants and migration policy, 179, 186, 201, 229, 258–59, 263, 280; and strategy, 165–66, 258–59
medical aid, 195
Mediterranean Sea: dangers of crossing, 7, 97, 205n33; and drug trafficking, 29–30; and policing of migrants, 28, 38n9
Melilla, Spanish enclave, 28–31
Mescalero Apaches, 57, 59
Mexico: and *maquiladoras*, 31; migrants from, 30, 33, 193, 203n1, 221–22, 327
Mexico-U.S. borderlands, 28; and border wall, 71n7, 192; and deaths from border crossing, 29, 31, 97, 113n20; Juarez-El Paso, 35–36; and *maquiladoras*, 31; and massacre of Remolino, 67; policing, 29–30, 33–34, 62, 147, 191, 193, 201; residents of, 27, 58–66, 69, 265n11; and violence, 27–39, 67
migration: border enforcement, 55, 81, 313–37; function of migration policy, 74, 182; and global apartheid, 1, 17–25, 55, 78, 82, 107, 197, 205n28, 338–39; and interior enforcement, 84, 92; irregular, 28–29; and migrant policing, 3–4, 7–8, 20, 181, 285; policy reform, 167, 278, 281, 332; relation to crime policy, 8, 191, 241, 318–21; relation to labor 82–83, 170; and restrictionist policy, 105–14, 164, 182, 261, 271

militarization: at the border, 4, 7, 9, 139, 179, 191, 216–21, 225; and colonialism, 8, 58–61, 183; and imperialism, 20, 61–66, 79, 251, 279; and police, 4, 7, 8, 116, 119–20, 182; and U.S.-Mexico border, 29–30, 33–34, 62, 147, 191, 193, 201

military-industrial complex (MIC), 44–45, 53, 54n3

Minuteman Project, 182, 185, 187n6, 187n8, 280

miscegenation, 181

mobility: coercive mobility, 11, 148; freedom of movement, 1–2, 10–11, 24, 89, 113n1, 161–62, 169, 230, 232

Morocco: border with Spain, 27–37; garment industry, 31; and women workers, 31–32

Mothers Reclaiming Our Children (Mothers ROC), 50

multiculturalism, 74, 78, 105, 194

Nahuas, 57, 59

Napolitano, Janet, 202, 206n41, 206n43, 229, 258

nation: and identity, 270–71; and national imagination, 78, 127; and nationalism, 186; and national security, 127; and nation-state, 185; and xenophobia, 282

National Association for the Advancement of Colored People (NAACP), 241–43, 247–48, 288, 290

National Guard. *See* United States National Guard

nation-state: abolition of, 24, 191; and border regimes, 205n34; and capitalism, 82; and citizenship, 6, 8, 19–20, 35, 233; and identity, 22; Lenin's definition of, 279; and mobility, 10–11, 17, 19, 23–25, 27, 36, 75, 233; and prisons, 6; and production of vulnerability, 31, 36; and sovereignty, 1, 54, 58, 62, 66, 69, 75, 78, 89; and state-building, 55–56; and state criminality, 57–71; and state violence, 3, 18, 31–33; as victim, 79

nativism, 149, 201, 230–31, 233, 238, 251

naturalization, 83, 182, 267–68, 271

Nauru, 92, 97, 100

Ndé, 57–71; and Coahuilas, 57, 59; and Jumano Apaches, 57, 66; and Kickapoos, 57, 59; and Lipan Apaches, 57, 67; and Mescalero Apaches, 57, 59; and Nahuas, 57, 59; and Tlaxcaltecas, 57, 59

necropolitics, 58

needle exchange, 283, 293–94, 297

neoliberal capitalism: and deregulation, 133, 254, 279; and dispossession, 279; and gender, 31–32; and migrant vulnerability, 24, 31–32; and migration, 37; opposition to, 215; and poverty, 32, 109; and privatization, 279; and structural adjustment, 5, 109, 138; and subjugation of place, 32; and war on drugs, 35

neoliberalism. *See* neoliberal capitalism

Netherlands, 105–12

New York City, 152, 161; activist and advocacy groups, 269; homeless agencies, 316; human services, 160, 314, 316; police department (NYPD), 115, 117–18, 314–16; and trans refugees, 321; voting and elections in, 272

New York Times, 97, 100, 120, 169, 193, 263

Ng, Hiu Lui, 96

Nicaragua, 49, 66, 173–74, 177

Nieves, Angel, 295

Nixon, Richard, 25, 116

no borders, strategies or politics, 9–11, 179, 191, 200

No Borders movement, 80; camps, 198–99; poster, 85

No More Deaths (No Más Muertes), 97, 103n20, 198, 204n21, 205n31, 206n37

noncompliance: CCA failure to follow federal standards, 148; government failure to follow law, 149, 151n7, 257, 260; resistance to unjust laws, 11, 202, 206n42, 235
No One Is Illegal, 9–10, 80, 85–88, 89n12, 113n3
North American Free Trade Agreement (NAFTA), 64, 134, 136, 220

Oakland, California, 231, 295–96, 322
Obama, Barack: and border policy, 69, 192, 201; and deportation, 203; and Guantanamo, 97, 137; and immigration policy, 143, 149–50, 161, 170, 261, 263, 283, 342, 344
occupation, 59–60, 62, 64, 66, 79, 194, 203, 244
Occupy movement, 2
Office of Public Safety (USAID), 116, 120–21
Operation Community Shield, 279
Operation Desert Safeguard, 192
Operation Gatekeeper, 191, 196
Operation Hold the Line, 29–30, 191
Operation Streamline, 190–93, 195, 201–2, 204n10, 206n39, 262
oppression: and criminalization, 1, 7, 9, 200, 232–33, 250; and intersectional analyses, 3–9, 31–32, 82–83, 200, 232–33, 285, 328, 330; and migration policy, 82–83, 200, 232–33; and racial, 289–90; and resistance, 246, 250, 285
organizing. *See* abolition; colonialism; community; criminalization; criminal justice system; detention; immigration and immigrants; labor; no borders, strategies or politics; No Borders movement; noncompliance; prisons
Overseas Internal Security Program, 116

pateras, 29
patriarchy, 8, 31, 58–59, 221, 285, 322
Patriot Act II, 340
Patterson, Orlando, 49, 52
peace, 3, 70, 106, 167–69, 218
Peace and Justice without Borders, 36
Pearce, Russell, 229
Peña, Alfredo, 120–21
Pentagon, 45, 53
People's Party for Freedom and Democracy (VVD), 106, 109
Perez, Byron, 331–33
Perry, Philip J., 147
Personal Responsibility and Work Opportunity Reconciliation Act (PRWOA), 131, 333
Philadelphia FIGHT, 302, 311n1
police brutality, 121, 124, 283, 290, 316, 318, 330
policing: border surveillance, 34, 62, 65, 85–86, 191–92, 194, 199, 206n39, 253; effects of immigration raids, 6, 55, 93–94, 102n9, 194, 201–2, 277, 328, 337–38, 345; home raids, 93–94, 102n9, 159; local-federal collaboration, 201, 283; and racial profiling, 81, 93, 153, 161, 182, 186, 194, 283, 306, 354; raid response, 93–94, 330, 332; surveillance of daily life, 9, 77, 81, 85–86, 131, 133, 199, 261, 315; surveillance of detainees, 257; sweeps, 242; and transphobia, 320; workplace raids, 21, 74, 139, 170, 186, 241, 277, 278, 340
policing the crisis, 5, 8, 50
political organizing. *See* abolition; colonialism; community; criminalization; criminal justice system; detention; immigration and immigrants; labor; no borders, strategies or politics; No Borders movement; noncompliance; prisons
Porter, Kim, 147

Posse Comitatus Act of 1878, 34
poverty: in the American Northwest, 135–38; and deportation, 159; and documentation, 333; and HIV/AIDS, 297; and homelessness, 129, 316; and neoliberalism, 32, 109; and prisons, 86, 131–40, 168, 215, 248, 287, 292; and racialization, 130–35, 185; and restrictions on mobility in Rwanda, 23; and rural places, 130, 131–35, 315; and urban places, 130; at the U.S.-Mexico border, 28; U.S. statistics, 130–35; and welfare, 79, 130–35, 139
power: relational, 10, 224; strategies for building, 227, 239, 281, 345
Prashad, Vijay, 215–17, 227
Pratt, Anna, 77, 89n3
precariousness, 4, 20, 83–84, 94
premature death, 4
Prisoner Education Project, 295, 299n26
prisoner organizing, 50, 163, 216–17, 242, 293, 295, 297n16
prison-industrial complex: and criminalization, 43–44, 191; defined, 7; expansion of, 86, 133, 193, 220, 250, 290–91, 340; and organizing, 317, 337, 345; political economy of, 17–18, 45, 139, 282, 290–91, 317
Prison Research Education Action Project, 12n28, 13n35
prisons: abolition of, 3, 5, 7–11, 18, 51–53, 86, 139, 163, 171–72, 199, 215–18, 220, 225–26, 244, 250, 317–18, 322–23; bed space, 211, 255, 264; campaigns against, 52, 215–27, 253–65; conditions in, 76, 98, 110, 143, 148, 149, 241, 244; construction, 97, 124, 126, 136–37, 193; environmental impacts, 51–52, 216, 223; and family separation, 7, 254, 262; and felon disenfranchisement, 266–74; and HIV/AIDS, 287–88, 291–96, 302–3, 306–10; and human rights, 69, 83, 98, 101, 106, 108, 257, 262; and job creation, claims of, 101, 137–38, 221–24, 292; and prison reform, 10, 80, 151, 250, 261; and prison regime, 1–3, 9; and prison siting, 97, 111, 138, 223, 225; and private prisons, 43–44, 138, 143, 145, 191, 211, 217, 220, 254; and reentry, 302, 308–9, 311; and segregation units, 76; and telephone access, 2, 46, 76, 95–96, 148–49, 177, 213
privatization, 2, 17, 43–46, 147, 169, 254, 259, 262, 269
privilege, 3, 9, 19, 21–24, 187, 200, 326
Proposition 8, California (2008), 334–35
Proposition 187, California (1994), 185
Proposition 200, Arizona (2004), 228–29
Proposition 300, Arizona (2006), 194
prosecution, 163–64, 190–93, 195–98, 248, 305, 307
prostitution, 77, 306–7
Protect Arizona Now (PAN), 228
punishment, 37, 53, 76, 81–82, 88, 108, 132, 153, 297
Puryear, Gustavus, 147

Quaker perspective on immigration policy, 167
Queers for Economic Justice (QEJ), 316
queer theory and movement-building, 5, 9, 11, 78, 232, 316–17, 321–23, 327–28, 333–35
Quinlan, Mike, 147
qteam, 328, 330–31, 334

racism: anti-Black, 51; anti-immigrant, 6, 105, 107, 281; content of, 107; "double racism," 82; function of, 23, 107, 119; and human rights, 24; and immigration policy, 23, 106, 112; and imperialism, 31, 247; and imprisonment, 86; state racism and

violence, 107–9, 119, 186–87, 279, 281–83; structural racism, 250, 305; and 287(g), 149
raids: of homes, 93–94, 102n9, 159; immigration, effects of, 6, 55, 93–94, 102n9, 194, 201–2, 277, 328, 330, 337–38, 345; opposition to, 277, 332, 345; response, 93–94, 330, 335; of workplaces, 21, 74, 139, 170, 186, 241, 277–78, 340
Ranch Rescue, 182, 185
Reaching Out: A Support Group with Action, 303–4, 307
Reagan, Ronald, 35, 287–90, 292
redlining, 181
reentry. *See under* prisons
reforms: and immigration legislation, 30, 80, 144, 146, 153, 185; and immigration legislative reform, 161–62, 166, 203, 213, 238, 260–62, 266, 278, 281–83, 337, 341–42; and nonreformist reforms, 10, 250, 318; and prisons, 10, 80, 151, 250, 261
refugees, 31, 86, 167, 205n33; and advocacy, 99, 212, 257, 265n9; hysteria surrounding, 74–76, 78, 105–8, 185; and policy, 81, 105–8
Rehnquist, William, 269
Remolino massacre (1873), 64, 67
Repeal Coalition, 231–32
Richardson v. Ramirez, 269
Ridge, Tom, 144
rights: and citizenship, 20, 75; equal, 277, 317; human, advocacy of, 29, 33, 36, 66, 69, 98, 108, 206n37, 257, 262; human, and border policy, 33, 66, 69, 71n7; human, and criminalization, 106, 112; human, and detention, 83, 98, 101, 108, 257, 262; human, and militarization, 120; human, for migrants, 20, 23–24, 83, 98, 108, 112, 169; labor rights, 79, 84; legal, 317; migrant, 218; and mobility, 10, 22–25; political, 22, 25,

282; prisoner, 218; and residence, 20–24; statutory, 212; and voting, 270–72, 273n23
Rita's Clowns Promotion Team, 105–6, 110
Robillard, T. C., 145
Rockefeller, Nelson, 116–7
Rogers, Hal, 146
Romero, Daniel Castro, Jr., 65, 67, *68*
Rural Australians for Refugees, 100
Rwanda, 23

safety, government promise of, 3, 78, 106, 112–13, 127, 138, 177, 221, 278
sanctuary movement, 9–10, 330
San Diego, California, 38n9, 191
San Diego Correctional Facility, 147–48
Sandinista government, 49
San Francisco, California, 176, 272, 277–79, 282, 287
Sans Papiers movement, 236
Santibanez, Luisanna, 144
Santibanez, Sergia, 143–45, 151
scale, geographic, 4, 91, 133
Schengen Agreement, 34, 199
Schiphol-East fire, 110–11
School of the Americas and the Latin American Ground School, 116
SCOMM, 150
Seasonal Agricultural Workers Program (SAWP), 83
Secure Border Initiative (SBI), 144, 192, 253
Secure Communities program. *See under* United States Department of Homeland Security
security: and ideology, 3; private security companies, 118; security-industrial complex, 190–206
Security and Prosperity Partnership (U.S. and Canada), 74
segregation, 22, 78, 181, 218, 221, 223, 225, 227n4, 267

self-determination, 5, 11, 59, 69, 75, 80, 88, 199
self-governance, 59–60, 216
Sentencing Project, 269
settler colonialism, 56, 58, 60
sexuality: and gender-based violence, 3, 5, 7, 31–32, 36, 59, 318; and harassment and policing, 32–33, 195, 315–16, 319, 322; and health and mental health, 287–88, 303, 306, 321, 327; and identity, 6, 60, 127, 282, 314, 319, 321; and poverty, 129, 315–16; and prisons, 250, 319
sex work, 77, 306–7
Sharma, Nandita, 75, 79
Simcox, Chris, 182
Simonovis, Ivan, 121
slavery, 2, 4, 8–10, 21–22; and abolition, 10; contemporary, 32; and emancipation, 237; and imprisonment, 49–50; and Orlando Patterson's analyses, 49–50, 52
Smith, Lamar, 169–70
social safety nets. *See* welfare
solidarity, 6, 25, 69, 200, 247, 281–82; and coalition-building, 69, 111, 139, 200, 284
South Africa: 19–25, 327; and anti-immigrant pogroms, 19; and apartheid, 17, 19, 22, 24–25
Southern California Library, 117, 121
Spade, Dean, 314
Spain, 27–39, 97; and Ceuta and Melilla, 28–31; and Morocco-Spain borderlands, 27–37
state: and colonization, 57–73, 79, 179, 194–95; and construction of criminality, 3–4, 11, 42–43, 191, 194–95, 199–202, 231–32, 278–79, 283; and construction of illegality, 3–4, 79, 84, 181, 195, 200; and marriage, 230–32; and migration policy and policing, 7–8, 20, 81, 84, 92, 321; and militarization, 3–4, 33–37, 115; and nationalism, 4, 55, 84, 185; and national security claims, 3, 29, 33–36, 55, 74, 78, 80–82, 91, 109, 112, 159, 162, 182–83, 194–98, 204n25, 239, 315; and production of vulnerability, 31, 33–37, 285; and sovereignty, 1, 54, 58, 62, 66, 69, 75, 78, 89; state violence, 3, 18, 31–33, 60, 67, 285; and territorial sovereignty and boundary enforcement, 20, 22–25, 33, 55, 58, 97–98, 179, 190, 194–95, 199, 201, 205n34, 233; and territorial sovereignty and international inequality, 17, 20, 22–25
St. Peter's Housing Committee, 282
structural violence, 4, 171, 186–87
Student Nonviolent Coordinating Committee (SNCC), 233
students: and immigration status, 214, 236; and political organizing, 36, 202, 216, 219, 225, 231, 236, 241, 243–44, 249, 277
Sudbury, Julia, 84
Support Center for Prison Advocacy (SCPA), 301–12
surveillance: of borders, 34, 62, 65, 85–86, 191–92, 194, 199, 206n39, 253; of daily life, 9, 77, 81, 85–86, 131, 133, 199, 261, 315; of detainees, 257; technology of, 38n9, 85–86, 100, 192, 253
Sylvia Rivera Law Project (SRLP), 314–23
Syracuse, New York, 93–95

Tamez, Eloisa Garcia, 60–61, 68–71
Tamil refugees, 76
T. Don Hutto Family Residential Facility (Taylor, Texas), 146, 253–65
TEACH Outside, 303–4, 307
territory: indigenous, 60, 67–69, 83, 136, 194; sovereign, and boundary

enforcement, 20, 22–25, 33, 55, 58, 97–98, 179, 190, 194–95, 199, 201, 203, 205n34, 233; sovereignty of, and international inequality, 17, 20, 22–25
terrorism, 33, 35, 55, 62, 78, 80–81, 84, 106, 112–13, 233, 279–80
Texans United for Families (TUFF), 256–65; and grassroots organizing, 258; and legislative advocacy, 260–61; and litigation, 256–57; and media advocacy, 258–60
Texas Rangers, 184, 188n15
Thomas, Jim, 296
three-strikes laws, 35, 50, 132, 267, 305
Timoney, John, 119
Tlaxcaltecas, 57, 59
Tohono O'odham nation, 192, 194
Toronto, Canada, 76
trafficking: drug, 27, 29, 30, 33–37, 267; human, 28, 32, 33, 37
transformative justice, 163–65, 168, 171
Transforming Justice conference, 322–23
transgender issues: and political organizing, 250, 282, 314–23; and transphobia, 317, 321–22, 333; and trans-related violence, 316–19
transnational, 4, 9–10, 25, 32, 55, 62, 127, 220, 233, 246, 279, 335
Tucson, Arizona, 190–93, 195–96, 198–201, 204, 217–19, 223–24, 235–36
Tucson Samaritans (Los Samaritanos), 198, 205n31
287(g) program, 149–50, 161, 202, 341, 343

unions, labor, 21, 225
United Arab Emirates, 20
United Nations, 24, 262; human rights resolutions, 38n5; worker rights resolutions, 38n5; Working Group on Arbitrary Detention, 89
United States Department of Homeland Security, 70, 144, 147, 190, 192–94, 196, 202, 204, 206–7, 253–54, 261; and Corrections Corporation of America, 148; Customs and Border Protection (CBP), 8, 201, 283; Health Service Corps, 148; Immigration and Customs Enforcement (ICE), 8, 44, 152, 169–70, 186, 206n41, 210, 242, 253, 263, 330, 338; Intensive Supervision Appearance Program (ISAP), 261–62; Secure Communities Program (SCOMM), 150; 287(g) program, 149–50, 161, 202, 341, 343
United States Department of Justice, 148, 183, 249; and Immigration and Naturalization Services (INS), 147, 192, 242, 257
United States Federal Bureau of Investigation (FBI), 117–18, 150, 201, 338; and Special Intelligence Service, 117
United States Federal Bureau of Prisons (BOP), 147, 150, 217, 221, 224–25
United States Federal Housing Administration (FHA), 181
United States Marshals Service, 44, 147–48, 150, 190, 255
United States National Guard, 33–34, 194, 201–2, 206n39
University of Texas School of Law, 66
Urban League, 288, 290
U.S.-Mexico border. *See* Mexico-U.S. borderlands

Vancouver, Canada, 76, 79, 85, 89
Venturella, David, 150
Vera Institute, 260
Verdonk, Rita, 105–6, 110
Verryn, Paul, 19
vigilantes: American Border Patrol, 182; Gilchrist, Jim, 182; Minuteman Civil Defense Corps, 182, 187n8; Minuteman Project, 182, 185, 187n6, 280; Ranch Rescue, 182, 185; Simcox, Chris, 182

vigilantism, 181–84, 186–87, 227n4, 280
Villawood Immigration Detention Centre (Sydney, Australia), 96
violence: gender-based, 3, 5, 7, 31–32, 36, 59, 318; institutional, 186; racial, 107–9, 119, 186, 279, 281–83; state, 3, 18, 31–33; structural, 4, 171, 186–87; vigilante, 181–87
voting, 112, 266–74, 311n3; and myth of voter fraud, 228–29
vulnerability, 17, 21, 24, 82, 93, 151, 288–89, 301–11

Wackenhut, 44, 145
war: in Central America, 10, 185; defined, 1–2; U.S.-Mexican War, 184; war-making, 3–5
War Measures Act (Canada), 78
war on drugs, 28, 35, 78, 132, 221, 248, 266–67, 292, 301–11, 339–40
war on poverty, 132
war on terror, 55, 78, 80, 106, 198, 253, 279–80, 315, 339
Washington, D.C., 45, 70, 103n28, 146, 214, 221, 259–60, 263, 269, 281, 296
Webb County Detention Center, Texas, 148
Weissman, Deborah, 149
welfare, 131–35; and Aid to Families with Dependent Children, 131; and Personal Responsibility and Work Opportunity Reconciliation Act (PRWOA), 131, 333
wetback (racial/ethnic epithet), 29
White, Ryan, 291

white supremacy, 8, 50, 62, 78, 181–82, 185–86, 203, 228–29, 233, 237, 269, 280–82
Willard, Tania, 85
Willcox, Arizona, 217, 219–24
Williamson County, Texas, 254, 258, 263
Wilson, Pete, 185
Wilson, Phil, 291
women: and agency, 31; of color, 3, 84, 333; criminalization of, 151; and gender, 319, 321, 333; and HIV/AIDS, 288–89, 293, 296, 299n29, 303, 305; indigenous, 59–71, 79, 84; and labor, 31–32, 84, 86; rates of imprisonment, 7, 84, 305; violence against, 19, 32, 33, 37, 184, 319; and voting, 271
Women's Refugee Commission, 257, 265n9
Woomera, Australia, 97
workers. *See* labor
Workers' Center of Central New York, (1994) (1994) 93
working poor, 132, 319

xenophobia, 19, 30, 107, 109, 247, 271, 280, 315, 343

youth, 36, 61–62, 77, 87, 206n37, 216, 219, 314, 328

Zapatistas, 2
zero tolerance, 192
zones of exclusion, 75
Zuazua, Augustina, 63, 71n12

GEOGRAPHIES OF JUSTICE AND SOCIAL TRANSFORMATION

1. *Social Justice and the City*, rev. ed.
   by David Harvey

2. *Begging as a Path to Progress: Indigenous Women and Children and the Struggle for Ecuador's Urban Spaces*
   by Kate Swanson

3. *Making the San Fernando Valley: Rural Landscapes, Western Heritage, and White Privilege*
   by Laura R. Barraclough

4. *Company Towns in the Americas: Landscape, Power, and Working-Class Communities*
   edited by Oliver J. Dinius and Angela Vergara

5. *Tremé: Race and Place in a New Orleans Neighborhood*
   by Michael E. Crutcher Jr.

6. *Bloomberg's New York: Class and Governance in the Luxury City*
   by Julian Brash

7. *Roppongi Crossing: The Demise of a Tokyo Nightclub District and the Reshaping of a Global City*
   by Roman Adrian Cybriwsky

8. *Fitzgerald: Geography of a Revolution*
   by William Bunge

9. *Accumulating Insecurity: Violence and Dispossession in the Making of Everyday Life*
   edited by Shelley Feldman, Charles Geisler, and Gayatri A. Menon

10. *They Saved the Crops: Labor, Landscape, and the Struggle over Industrial Farming in Bracero-Era California*
    by Don Mitchell

11. *Faith Based: Religious Neoliberalism and the Politics of Welfare in the United States*
    by Jason Hackworth

12. *Fields and Streams: Stream Restoration, Neoliberalism, and the Future of Environmental Science*
    by Rebecca Lave

13. *Black, White, and Green: Farmers Markets, Race, and the Green Economy*
    by Alison Hope Alkon

14. *Beyond Walls and Cages: Prisons, Borders, and Global Crisis*
    edited by Jenna M. Loyd, Matt Mitchelson, and Andrew Burridge

15. *Silent Violence: Food, Famine, and Peasantry in Northern Nigeria*
    by Michael J. Watts

Lightning Source UK Ltd.
Milton Keynes UK
UKHW041918120219
337198UK00001B/36/P